Understanding
the
Invisible Shakespeare

Understanding the Invisible Shakespeare

Brenda James

Cranesmere Press

Copyright © Brenda James 2011

All rights reserved. No part of this book may be reproduced or transmitted in any form, electronic or otherwise, without written permission from the publishers.

Published by CRANESMERE PRESS
9 Hambledon Place, Bognor Regis, West Sussex, United Kingdom, PO21 2NE
Email orders and enquiries: nevillejournal@yahoo.co.uk

Cover design by Kaspars Vilnitis (kvilnitis@gmail.com)

ISBN: 978-0-9569495-0-9

Sir Henry Neville, c. 1597.
From an engraving by WN Gardiner

CONTENTS

CONTENTS	6
INTRODUCTION	10
AUTHOR'S PREFACE	12
ACKNOWLEDGEMENTS	14
PART ONE	**15**
SHAKESPEARE, NEVILLE AND THE STATE	**15**
Chapter One	*16*

THE POLITICS OF SECRECY: A DANGEROUS TREATISE 16
    Shakespeare, Neville and Syncretism   19
AN ANONYMOUS DECLARATION TO PARLIAMENT: The first idea of Constitutional Monarchy?   21

AN ADVICE [BY SIR HENRY NEVILLE] TOUCHING THE HOLDING OF A PARLIAMENT. 23

TABLE OF HENDIADYS 30
    Neville and Kingship: a linguistic and literary perspective concerning some overlapping points in the Treatise and the Plays   38
    Neville's Proposed changes to some Laws   44
    Neville's Political Theatricality   47

Chapter Two   **52**

THE SHAKESPEARE-NEVILLE REFORMATION 52
    The Politics of Secrecy   58
    Politics, myths, and the Shakespeare Plays   59
    Reflections on Neville's Political Thesis   60
    Neville's secret and the Politics of Ancient Greece   68
    Pericles (c.495 – 429 BC) and Thucydides (c. 460 B.C. – c.395 BC)   69
    Neville's practical realisation of Pericles' ideas 70
    Neville's political treatise, and *Plato Redivivus* 72

Neville's complete disguise: revisiting some
previous evidence and mingling it with the new   76
    Revisiting the Worsley Collection   79

Chapter Three   82

MONARCHY v. REPUBLICANISM, AND
HOLINSHED v. *LEICESTER'S COMMONWEALTH* 82
    Medieval politics and the portrayal of Lucrece
                                                    88
    Dangerous moonlighting   96
    Neville, Republicanism, the Succession and
Leicester's Commonwealth   101
    Reviewing some of Neville's annotations   106
    Leicester's Commonwealth as one source of the
early History plays   107

PART TWO   115

THE SHAKESPEARE–NEVILLE IDENTITY   115

Chapter Four   116

THE SIGNS OF A WRITER CALLED 'FALSTAFF' . 116
    'Francis' (Bacon) in the tavern   123
    Joseph Hall and his Shakespearean Accusations
                                                   129
    Sir Henry Neville and Sir Francis Bacon – links of
kinship and profession   137
    Henry Neville and the Vintner   140
    Later echoes of other pretenders?   142
    More double-meanings   143
    Pint-pot   144
    Falstaff, Neville and John Colville   150

Chapter Five   158

THE WRITER WHO CAN ONLY BE 'NE-VILE' ... 158
    The compelling evidence of Sonnet 121   158
    The Implied Syllogism   162
    The Just Pleasure   165
    Falstaff in the Sonnets: the linguistic physicality of
Neville   167
    'Not Veal' in *Love's Labour's Lost*   169

The Turning Point: *Henry IV, part 2,* and Nevillian circumstances ... 174

Chapter Six   179

THE RULE OF CHIVALRY: THE TEMPLARS, HOSPITALLERS, AND THE ORDER OF SION ... 179

How Medieval and Tudor politics affected the Nevilles ... 182
Shakespeare and Chivalry ... 183

Chapter Seven   203

THE KNIGHTS' LEGACY: SECRET SYMBOLISM AND SECRET SOCIETIES? ... 203

Esotericism within the Shakespeare plays? ... 212
Neville and *Macbeth* ... 226
How King René and the Knights bring signs of Neville's authorship ... 232

Chapter Eight   237

RELIGION, HENRY VI, AND THE GREEK CONNECTION ... 237

Some Greek Influences ... 237
Religion and some of its personal and political implications in the Shakespeare plays ... 239
Connections between Religion and Politics in the *Henry VI* trilogy ... 242
Plot summary of Henry VI, part 1. ... 243
Reading between the lines ... 246

Chapter Nine   252

SUPERSTITION AND IMAGERY IN *HENRY VI, PART ONE* ... 252

Shakespeare's characterisation of Joan of Arc ... 257

Chapter Ten   278

NEVILLE'S GRANDFATHER IN THE WIDE SEA OF WAX – A TRANSGENERATIONAL WARNING ... 278

The Love/Hate relationship between the Nevilles and the Tudors ... 282

Edward Neville and the King's Wardrobe   286
Edward Neville's break with the King   287
Edward Neville and Some Forgotten Sources of *Richard III* and *Henry VIII*   291

Chapter Eleven   295

SIR HENRY NEVILLE AND THE SONNETS IN THE TOWER 295

Addendum 1   312

WILLIAM SHAKESPEARE – THE SCRIBE? 312

CHRONOLOGICAL TABLE OF PLAYS, WITH DETAILS REGARDING THEIR AUTHORIAL ATTRIBUTION. 323

Addendum 2   329

IS THE CHARACTER OF MARGARET OF ANJOU in the *HENRY VI* PLAYS, BASED ON MARGUERITE DE VALOIS? 329

Addendum 3   334

THE LANGUAGE OF NEVILLE'S TREATISE   334

An advice [by Sir Henry Neville] touching the holding of a Parliament. 334

ANALYSIS OF THE LANGUAGE USED IN SIR HENRY NEVILLE'S TREATISE 342

ENDNOTES   351

INTRODUCTION

by

Nicholas Prosser, Screen and Media Advisor

Some years ago, a neighbour (who was not Brenda James) thrust a book at me, knowing "I was in television." She could write the script and I could make a programme on the discovery that William Shakespeare had not written the plays and sonnets, but "her man" had. Intrigued though I was, I was not totally convinced. However, the mystery of the authorship teased my inquisitive senses, only to be truly satisfied when, years later, I read a book which instantly dispelled all previous theories and beliefs on the subject.

In THE TRUTH WILL OUT, Brenda James revealed for the first time her astonishing discovery that Shakespeare's plays and sonnets were not written by the Stratford man, or indeed any of the other contenders, including the one promoted by my neighbour, but by a well-travelled ambassador, MP and knight of the realm who hitherto had been missed from all the microscopic studies – Sir Henry Neville. In her second book HENRY NEVILLE AND THE SHAKESPEARE CODE, Brenda James followed up her introduction to this, the most convincing candidate, by telling her compelling personal story of discovery and introducing the reader to the code she had cracked which revealed his name. This also showed how all the jigsaw pieces of Neville's life fitted so well together with those of the writer of the plays and sonnets.

In her latest book, UNDERSTANDING THE INVISIBLE SHAKESPEARE, Brenda James digs deep into both the detailed life of Henry Neville and the texts of the 'Shakespeare' plays and sonnets to extinguish all possible doubt on the authorship of the greatest collection of writing in the English language.

Forget Poirot, Marple or Morse; this who dunnit is by far the most exciting. This is not some airy fairy theory. The author has really done her homework and uncovered such a wide range of clues to reveal the man behind the pseudonym. Through profiling Neville's life in such detail, she demonstrates the inner thinking, fears, personality and ambition of this 16th century genius. After reading this book, not only should you be convinced that Neville wrote the plays and sonnets attributed to Shakespeare, but you will have a true understanding of the author and why it was so dangerous for him to take quill to parchment.

AUTHOR'S PREFACE

The case for Sir Henry Neville is strengthening by the day. I had hoped to complete some of my writing on other subjects before bringing out this book, but my continuing research into Sir Henry as Shakespeare refused to wait its turn! It was as if a whole avalanche of new information, and parallels between Neville and the Shakespeare works, pushed me down the Authorship hill and enveloped me, so that my only way out was to hack at it, piece by piece in the hope of attaining some sort of orderly exit.

Yet my first way out – writing everything down as I came across it – resulted in such an overwhelming mass of disparate yet interconnected material that I finally had to split my work into two more books, and then split this one down into two sections.

Those who have read either *Sir Henry Neville and the Shakespeare Code* and/or *The Truth Will Out* will already be aware of the first points of evidence which I discovered after unexpectedly uncovering Sir Henry's name. This book therefore assumes that readers are aware of those points and so expect only the occasional reference to them rather than a complete and tedious re-working. Chapter 1 of this book launches into an analysis of a whole political treatise, which Neville wrote three years before he died, and then revised one year before his death, in order for someone to present it **anonymously** in Parliament. This is such an important and momentous work that it prompted me to examine further some aspects of the political side of the Shakespeare works.

I finally decided, therefore, to call Part One of my book 'Shakespeare, Neville and the State'. However, for those who would initially prefer the excitement of new analyses of the Shakespeare texts, alongside new information pointing out remarkable parallels in Sir Henry's life and ideas, it might be better to begin with Part Two, 'The Shakespeare–Neville identity'. I leave the choice entirely up to the personal preference of each individual reader. Above all, I'd like to stress that Professor Neal Platt – who is a practising lawyer to boot – has contributed a wonderful commentary on Sonnet 121, applying analytical principles commonly used by lawyers for analysing legal texts. This is presented in Chapter 5. With eloquence, insight, and supreme reasoning, Professor Platt brings forward incontrovertible evidence that the writer of 'Shakespeare' Sonnet 121 can only be a man named Neville.

Before writing the last chapter of this book, I considered I had already finished my 'Part Two' theme. Once again, however, some new evidence rolled my way. Letters from and to Sir Henry while he was imprisoned in the Tower of London proved a most meaningful addition, explaining some of the most perplexing sonnets. This new information is poignant and exciting; it really deserves first chapter status. But one can never predict the order in which new discoveries may present themselves – so here it is, presented as more of a sunset than a dawn. Being the lowest point of Sir Henry's life and hopes, perhaps it found its rightful place after all.

My fourth book on Sir Henry will, hopefully, be published in a few months' time; this too contains new discoveries and unique insights, some of which have been provided by readers, according to their individual special studies and experience. Knowing about Neville, his life, interests and style of writing illuminates the Shakespeare works beautifully, and most movingly. I do hope you enjoy the journey of discovery.

Brenda James,
West Sussex, September, 2011.

ACKNOWLEDGEMENTS

As always, my first thanks go to my long-suffering family. They have not only helped in practical terms – assisting in the tedious business of household chores, advising, etc. – but also suffered my 'Neville talk' to intrude upon their thoughts during the past eleven years.

Secondly, I'd like to acknowledge warmly the kindness and support of my patient literary agent, Robin Wade. Also that of my many kind emailers. Their words of support, wisdom and consolation have greatly eased many ordeals during the past two years. Next, but with no thought of any order of priority, I would like to express my thanks to the actor, Martin Bishop, for his enthusiasm and for commissioning and advising on my first play about Sir Henry Neville.

Then comes my heartfelt gratitude to Neal Platt, special Professor of Law, for his brilliant court-room analysis of Sonnet 121.

Next, a huge round of thanks to those writers whose work I have consulted, as acknowledged in my text and endnotes. Without their painstaking research and exposition, many of the points of evidence I have been able to produce in favour of Sir Henry Neville's authorship would not have been possible.

Finally, I'd like to thank the staff at the Lincolnshire Archives, without whose ever-friendly and efficient services I would not have had first-hand access to Neville's secret works.

PART ONE

SHAKESPEARE, NEVILLE AND THE STATE

Chapter One

THE POLITICS OF SECRECY: A DANGEROUS TREATISE

Sir Henry Neville was an invisible writer. He clearly wished to remain that way for some time. The encrypted Greek inscription on his portrait in Audley End House reads *"Everywhere, without visible signs,"* leaving us in no doubt as to his intentions. Yet Sir Henry chose a pseudonym – William Shakespeare – which is so challenging in so many different ways that its very sound ensured the authorship question would be asked down the ages. William was certainly shaking a spear at authority, and also at those who really believed he could be the true author, for what little we know about William of Stratford is generally at odds with the knowledge and erudition displayed in the Shakespeare canon. On the contrary, however, there is an overwhelming corpus of details concerning the *invisible* but real Shakespeare – Sir Henry Neville – that emerges quite naturally in the plays. I have already presented some of the very powerful evidence for Neville's authorship in my previous books. Now my further research and textual examination have uncovered additional information, plus wide-ranging, carefully-structured clues which are presented here for the first time.

In writing this book, it was tempting to go over yet again the story of how I discovered Sir Henry's name. However, the amount of *new* material and research I amassed precluded the possibility of repeating that part of the case for Neville's candidature. [This can be accessed in detail in *The Truth Will Out*, and in *Henry Neville and the Shakespeare Code*, and in brief on my website, www.henryneville.com] As my title suggests, therefore, the present book helps with understanding Neville and the way he approached his writing, both within the texts of the Shakespeare Works, and in extraneous documents associated with him. Moreover, as one learns more about the times and Neville's connections, the references within the Works become more meaningful. Neville certainly left pointers to his authorship for posterity; but he made sure the clues would not be easy to find or interpret. (Had they been so, then he might as well have proclaimed his name from the rooftops, instead of using a pseudonym.)

For example, Sir Henry was an M.P. most of his adult life, which explains why the Shakespeare works themselves are often political, and always display a *trained* politician's expertise in rhetoric. It is therefore not surprising to find that the plays sometimes contain references drawn directly from political arguments of the day, and even from written works of the occasional specific politician too. Indeed, the only surprise comes if we consider Shakespeare of Stratford as their author. Shakespeare was never a politician, neither had he any training in rhetoric. As prelude to the introduction of a whole political treatise by Neville, therefore, my first new piece of evidence is drawn from a connection between *Othello,* Sir Henry Neville and a contemporary political writer. That writer was a certain Lewis Lewkenor.

The observation that Shakespeare knew a book by Lewkenor was first put forward by Kenneth Muir in 1956, and has been repeated by scholars ever since.[1] *Othello* is set in Venice, as was the earlier, *The Merchant of Venice.* An ongoing interest in that city, therefore, may well betray an interest in a Republican form of government. That aside, however, there are *direct* connections between Lewkenor and Henry Neville, but none with Shakespeare of Stratford. Lewkenor translated an Italian political treatise, which is echoed in both 'Venetian' plays. The original Latin text of Lewkenor's work – *De magistratibus et republica venetorum* by Gasparo Contarini (1483-1542) – was available only on the continent. There were Italian and French translations (also available only on the continent), and it was Lewkenor who first brought those translations to the attention of Sir Philip Sidney. However, he had to acquire a copy of it in *Italy* in 1573. Lewkenor's translation into English appeared in 1599, whereas *The Merchant of Venice* was registered in 1598. There is no known connection between Sir Philip Sidney, Lewis Lewkenor and William Shakespeare; but the Nevilles and the Sidneys were best friends. Sir Henry actually toured the continent with Sir Philip's younger brother during the years 1578–83, which means it is highly likely that he saw Latin and Italian versions of Contarini's work at an early date. Moreover, Lewkenor's *The Commonwealth and Government of Venice* (1599) was "the *first* English book entirely devoted to Venice,"[2] but was published one year *after The Merchant* was completed. Young Shakespeare could not have known the book.

Contarini's book was solely concerned with Venice's form of government and was in no way a guide to the city itself. Thus, even if Shakespeare found Lewkenor's translation before writing *Othello* in 1604, it would not explain either plays' references to the city itself. The first actual travel book in English about Venice was only published in 1611[3]. (Neville, however, was in Venice in 1581.)

As the Shakespeare scholar Kenneth Muir said, *Othello* echoes very specific references to Lewkenor's work. It is therefore interesting that Neville's daughter Mary married a Lewkenor in 1610! Interesting too that Lewis Lewkenor himself was an M.P. when Neville was an M.P., that Lewkenor once sat for a Cornish constituency – just like Neville – and that Lewkenor had argued (in writing) for a separation between religion and politics.[4] This separation of religion and politics was espoused by both 'Shakespeare' and Neville, as we shall soon see.

Lewkenor's translation was commissioned by the Countess of Warwick. It has therefore been argued that Shakespeare 'could' have had contact with her when he purchased a leasehold house of which she was the freeholder. Now, as a Warwickshire lass born and bred I can tell you that this is so improbable as to be counted impossible. I was born into a family who had bought a house where a local aristocrat owned the freehold, and to whom we paid annual ground rent. When the 99 year lease ran out, a purchase of the freehold was arranged. That arrangement was made through solicitors; neither side would have dreamt of contacting each other in person. Even in the more enlightened days of my own youth, therefore, it would have been extremely extraordinary for a purchaser of a lease to have had any contact with the freeholder. Houses were and are purchased through lawyers, and the local aristocrat would no more stoop to meeting one of his prospective purchasers/leaseholders than flying to the moon! This being true of the 20th century, it beggars belief that aristocrats in the sixteenth and seventeenth centuries would have concerned themselves with such mundane matters as meeting with one of their prospective leaseholders of lowly origin.

When we look at *Neville's* connections with the then Warwickshire Earls, however, the circumstances are changed utterly and a terrible beauty is born, as W.B. Yeats might have put it. The then Countess of Warwick – commissioner of Lewkenor's translation of this Shakespeare source – was none other than Penelope Rich, née Devereux, sister of Robert Devereux, Earl of Essex. Moreover, Penelope Devereux had been the love of Sir Philip Sidney's life, with Sidney writing many sonnets to her, even though she turned down his marriage proposal. Thus, the lady who commissioned Lewkenor's translation that was used by 'Shakespeare' in his plays was well and truly inside the Essex–Sidney–Neville circle. It was involvement in this circle which ultimately led to Neville's and Southampton's dual downfall and imprisonment, as I have detailed in previous works. It is even possible, therefore, that Neville, who had spent almost a year in Venice during his early European tour, actually helped Lewkenor with his translation. (Neville had a habit of helping people with their writing and translating yet never taking credit for it, as has been evidenced in my previous books.) This possibility becomes even more likely when one considers too that Lewkenor and Neville both had an interest in metals and mining: Lewkenor became involved with a scheme for extracting silver from a lead mine in Wales.[5] He later became master of ceremonies at the Court of King James I (1603), where he would definitely have met up with Sir Henry Neville once again, both being present at the Court Christmas celebrations of 1604.

Lewis Lewkenor and his Nevillian connections clearly deserve further research and documentation. However, I am keen to concentrate on a tract by Neville that is all his own. As far as I know, this treatise has never before been studied against the background of the politics expressed in Shakespeare's plays. Yet it bears the same hallmarks as those plays, and even the same terminology. Above all, Sir Henry Neville's Treatise aims at political Syncretism in an attempt to avoid a worsening political situation which he considered might well end in Civil War. This is precisely the direction in which the Shakespeare History Plays are attempting to steer their audience and readership.

Shakespeare, Neville and Syncretism
'Syncretism' is a term that deserves to be better known. It stems from a Greek expression which referred to the Cretans' pride at having overcome differences sufficiently to form a working State. Syncretism has therefore come to suggest a union of disparate, even opposite, religious, political and philosophical points of view. The quest for syncretism in every area of human

existence shines through the works of Shakespeare. Where better to forge such a union of ideas than in the theatre? The exposition of disparate points of view is as important on the 'Shakespeare' stage as the unfolding of the narrative, especially in the political/historical dramas. Yet it is impossible to envisage the essential formulation of advanced political ideas, and the very persuasive syncretic messages which shine through the History Plays, emerging from the pen of an under-educated, politically-inexperienced young actor, like Shakespeare. Sir Henry, however, the 'invisible' (and therefore necessarily secretive) political philosopher, securely displays his conscious awareness of the syncretism he personally was trying to achieve in the works appearing under Shakespeare's name.

King James I and others had observed Neville's propensity to set all to rights in any argument. Not only did he probably know about Neville's secret writing, but he had certainly witnessed Sir Henry taking "great pains to reconcile and set all in tune"[6] between 'officers' of the court and Parliament during the "secret Wheels and Windings"[7] following the death of Robert Cecil, Secretary of State, in 1612. Neville had just become the leader of the Popular Party in Parliament. The King therefore turned to him for advice on many occasions.[8] So, in 1612, when Parliament was refusing to vote through the King's request for an increase in his personal finance, James asked Neville to advise him on any possible way forward. The result was that Neville sent him private advice, suggesting firstly that he approach Parliament in friendly terms, as a partner rather than opposer in governing the country. He went on to suggest how a new trust between King and Parliament would not only help the country but also be likely to result in more finances for the King, together with the love, support and trust of Parliament.

The King rejected this advice, and there is even a cryptic letter in one of Neville's 'secret' notebooks implying that Sir Henry had received threats as a result of this. However, he was not the man to be permanently intimidated when he felt the country was in sore need of Syncretism. Neville therefore revised this advice and set it into the form of a Political Treatise.

Naturally enough, however, he decided that this Treatise must be presented anonymously, and also read out in the House by someone other than himself. By the time his treatise was presented in open Parliament, in 1614, Neville's new, *extended* reticence about putting his name to any of his writing was understandable, especially if he had indeed written many plays under a pseudonym. Thus, he was even afraid to declare the Treatise as his work, until absolutely forced to do so by Parliamentarians, following the kafuffle which ensued after its reading. Those who have read my previous two books on Sir Henry will know how lucky he and the Earl of Southampton were to have survived their imprisonment, following the Essex Rebellion. Neither of them wished to try Lady Luck any farther! After he was freed from gaol, Wriothesley, Earl of Southampton, pursued an international trading career, spending much of his time abroad and keeping a low profile whenever he was back in England. His support for Neville's candidacy for the post of Secretary of State (following the death of his wife's cousin, Robert Cecil) was well-known, yet conducted discreetly. Neville, however, had no wish to be anywhere else but inside the English Parliament, where he kept up *vocal* pressure for Parliamentary rights, while at the same time doing anything morally possible to please the new monarch, James I. Neville was by nature more outspoken than Wriothesley, which eventually brought him into the occasional open, *vocal* argument with the King. Through this and other honest exchanges and investigations, he gained much respect from many of his fellow Parliamentarians, which is why he was voted Leader of the Popular Party.

Yet his political outspokenness gained him powerful enemies too. (One of them even poisoned Sir Henry's friend and also possibly arranged for a murderous attack on his son.) Sir Henry therefore considered this *vocal* opposition was a step far enough. He had also already been cold-shouldered by the King, firstly, by the King's refusal to bow to popular pressure and appoint him secretary of state, and secondly by having his private political advice effectively thrown back in his face. To have followed this up by producing any public, *written* oppositional document under his own name might well put him in danger of imprisonment, or worse, once again.

AN ANONYMOUS DECLARATION TO PARLIAMENT:
The first idea of Constitutional Monarchy?
On the morning of the 14th May, 1614, Parliament had discussed a number of private bills. Yet what really obsessed M.P.s at this time was an issue which they perceived as a threat to Parliament's very existence. King James I was increasingly autocratic: he wanted Parliament to grant him extra funds, and

had strongly hinted that he might close Parliament down, if those funds were not forthcoming. On this particular day, then, M.P.s looked forward to the reading of a Paper which was rumoured to consist of some personal advice on how both the King and Parliament ought to be conducting themselves. No one knew who its author was.

The Paper/treatise was far-reaching and daring. It advised the King that he should try and consider the Commons as a partner in Government, rather than a rival. As gently as it could, yet firmly too, it also told him that he would have little hope of raising extra funds from the country and its people unless he was prepared to live in a "loving relationship" with Parliament. Any alternative projects the King had in mind for raising his own funds, it said, were most likely doomed to failure. And it did not stint to state that, in any case, the King could not bring any of those projects to fruition on his own but would need the support and assistance of experts, many of whom were either in Parliament or had connections with Parliamentarians.

The treatise cleverly rounded up by putting the *King's own* fears into words too. The writer understood that the King might think that if Parliament held all the cards in the partnership, then Parliament would use this fact to play on the King's weaknesses and push through Members' own designs. The author therefore assures the King that this would not be the case, since there was truly no such ill will in the minds of the M.P.s. They wanted to love the King, and they wanted the people to love the King, said the writer, full knowing that this would create the strongest impression abroad. In fact, (it advised), the King really ought to have a care when entering into such public arguments with Parliament, because this inevitably caused rejoicing among England's enemies and despair among her supporters.

Finally, Neville compiled a list of necessary reforms which he said he had gleaned through consulting the wishes of his Parliamentary colleagues. He therefore averred that he spoke not just for himself but for his very able colleagues, and for the welfare of the whole country.

Then comes another aspect of the Paper: it is very Shakespearean in style. The use of multiple instances of hendiadys, coupled with a literary/historical parable which includes personal names used in the Shakespeare plays, tend to give the game away. This was doubtless one more reason why

Neville decided not to read it out himself and not to put his name to it.

So here is the Treatise in its entirety. Its language and style may be daunting on first sight, but it repays close reading – in exactly the same way as we approach a Shakespeare text. After the text, there is a discussion concerning its timely relevance, and its relevance within the context of some of the Shakespeare plays. (I have revised the spelling of the Treatise so that it is easier to compare with the present spelling found in most editions of the Shakespeare plays. I have occasionally updated some of the punctuation too, which was employed differently in the 17th century. Instances of Hendiadys – the doubling up of substantives, joined by a conjunction, which is such a typical and specific devise of Shakespeare's[9] – are listed in a separate table following the transcription. [For my charted linguistic analysis of the Treatise, please see Addendum 3])

AN ADVICE [BY SIR HENRY NEVILLE] TOUCHING THE HOLDING OF A PARLIAMENT.[10]

THERE is a question grown and much debated amongst us, whether the King should relieve himself in his great want (whereof the world taketh knowledge both at home and abroad),[11] by a Parliament, or by some projects and devices to raise money, which may be set on foot to that purpose.

For my part, I will not examine what these projects may be, although by the experience of such as have been put in use since the dissolution of the last Parliament, I am induced to believe that either they will fail or fall short in the practice, howsoever they may appear likely in the theory; or that they will prove like some medicines, which do rather take away the sense of pain for the present than cure the grief for which they were applied.

But admit there may be other ways devised to relieve the King, yet am I clearly of opinion that there is none so fit, so honourable, and so necessary as by a Parliament. My reason is this: I consider on what terms the King and the last Parliament parted at the dissolution, full of distaste and acrimony[12] on His Majesty's part, and not without some discontentment on theirs. I consider also that from the Parliament, the apprehensions that are taken there are spread and dispersed over the whole realm. And further that the knowledge of these misunderstandings between His Majesty and the Parliament is not confined within this kingdom only but is flown abroad into all foreign parts that have any commerce or dealing with us.

Now what disadvantage this opinion may breed us, and what hopes it is like to raise both in our enemies abroad and our discontented persons at home, may easily be gathered. For, as there is nothing that more upholds the reputation of any Prince than the opinion of his strength at home, which consisteth principally in the love and concord between him and his people, from whence there followeth naturally a sequence of all other duties on their part to make him strong and able to help and hurt his neighbours, so there is nothing that emboldens more an enemy, either open or secret, to attempt the disturbance of the peace of any State than the imagination that the Prince and people stand not in kind and loving terms together.

And to this purpose I remember a story of Antigonus, one of the immediate and mightiest successors of Alexander, who, being solemnly set in great state to give audience to some other prince's ambassador, as he was in that solemnity, his son Demetrius came in from hunting, and being arrayed in his hunting attire, with his darts in his hand, presented himself so unto his father, and, after a salutation given according to the manner of that people, sat down by him.

The audience being ended, and the ambassadors retiring themselves, Antigonus called them again and willed them to report one thing more to their masters, namely, in what fashion they had seen his son and him converse together, intending that it would be taken for a great argument of his strength and a great assurance of his safety that his son and he lived in that confidence and concord.

If this were true in that case between the father and the son, how much more is it verified between the Prince and the people. And hereupon I conclude that the world being possessed with a conceit that the last Parliament ended with some sourness and distaste on the King's part, and not with the best satisfaction on theirs, there is nothing more necessary for the King's Majesty, either in regard of honour or safety, than to deface that opinion, and to make it apparent to the world that as he was received into the kingdom at his first entry, with the greatest demonstrations of the love and joy of his people that ever Prince was, so he is still rooted and established in their hearts. And that whatsoever cloud or mist might seem to have darkened or overshadowed the kind respects between them at that time, it was no other but that which happens often by some distemper between a tender father and dutiful children, which quickly vanish when the distemper of either side is removed.

For the effecting of this I can think of no other way but by another Parliament, for there this error grew, and there and no-where else it must be repaired. The harsh conclusion of the former Parliament bred that ill conceit, and the sweet close of another must beget a better. And by this means two notable effects will be wrought together if matters be well handled: the removing of that erroneous and dangerous conceit of a misunderstanding between the King and his people, and the relieving of the King's present necessities in a sure, speedy and plentiful manner; whereas that other cause of projects may happily prove slow and fail in the most, and in very few succeed according to the first design.

And for rectifying the misconceit between the King and his people there is no hope at all that way. It is rather to be feared it will do hurt, and rather aggravate than cure that malady if there be not great judgement used in the choice of the projects, and much dexterity in the managing of them.

Against this opinion there are two objections: the one that the Parliament may still continue adverse and unwilling to relieve the King at all, and so no hope of making up the breach; the other that as long as it is conceived the King cannot help himself without them, they will play upon the advantage of his necessities and extort some unreasonable demands from him before they yield to do anything for him. Both these objections are grounded upon the same false foundation, namely, that whatsoever the last Parliament did in that kind, they did it out of evil affection, which I do know, and do confidently avow to be otherwise, and have before in speech delivered the true reasons of that averseness, as one that lived and conversed inwardly with the chief of them, that were noted to be most backward and know their inwardest thoughts on that business, so as I dare undertake for the most of them that the King's Majesty proceeding in a gracious course toward his people, shall find those gentlemen exceeding willing to do him service, and to give him such contentment, as may sweeten all the former distastes, and leave both His Majesty and the world fully satisfied of their good intentions, and of the general affection of his subjects.

It is true (as I lately delivered unto His Majesty), that some things will be desired and expected of him by way of grace, which may both give some contentment to them that shall pay what is given, and justify the care and honest regard of them that shall give it. And without this I dare promise nothing. For it is most certain that as in private families and all other societies where the straitest bonds of nature or election do concur to unite affections, there is almost a continual necessity of mutual offices of kindness to nourish and maintain that love, so in kingdoms, besides that great bond of protection and allegiance between the sovereign and the subject, there is a like necessary use of the frequent change of mutual effects of grace and love to cherish and foster that tender affection that daily is to be renewed between them.

But what be the things that will be demanded or expected by the Parliament on behalf of the people will be hard for any one man to set down. Yet what I have collected out of the desires of sundry of the principal and most understanding gentlemen that were of the last Parliament, (and are like to be of this) I will be bold to deliver in a Memorial hereunto adjoined, whereby it shall appear that they aim not at anything unjust or unreasonable, or that may derogate from His Majesty in point of sovereignty further than His Majesty hath already been pleased to offer in writing to the last Parliament (which no doubt will be remembered), nor in point of profit to any matter of certain and considerable value, but only at such things as being now of small moment and loss to His Majesty to depart with, because they have been sifted and ransacked to tire bottom, may yet be valued to the subjects, both in opinion and truth, at a high rate, because they shall thereby enjoy a great repose and security from vexation which any of them may otherwise be subject unto.

THE POLITICS OF SECRECY: A DANGEROUS TREATISE

These things being taken into His Majesty's consideration, and receiving His gracious approbation as matters not unfit to be yielded of grace unto his subjects, the next points to be thought of are the time of holding the Parliament, the things preceding to be done by way of preparation, and the manner of proceeding with the House of Commons when the Parliament is assembled. For the first, I see no cause why it should be deferred longer than Michaelmas, for after the session there must be a time proportionable for the Commissioners to sit, and for the money to be levied and brought into the Exchequer, which the sooner it is done, the sooner will the King be eased of his debts for which he payeth interest, and the sooner will his reputation be recovered and settled, which is the thing that most deserves to be respected. If the Parliament begin at Michaelmas, the Term may be adjourned to Hallowtide or, if not, yet till that time there is little business done, so as the lawyers may well attend the Parliament, whose absence will otherwise breed delay. And I do not see but in a month or five weeks this point of supplying the King, and of his retribution, will be easily determined if it be proposed betimes and followed close afterwards.

For the second, which concerns matter of preparation, these be the things that I would humbly offer to His Majesty's gracious consideration:

to forbear to use any speech to the Parliament that may irritate, and to seem rather confident than diffident of their affections, casting the fault of any former error upon evil offices done on both sides, and want of true understanding rather than want of good affection.

To speak graciously and benignly to the people that shall flock to see His Majesty this progress. And especially to take notice of the principal gentlemen, and let them kiss his hand, and do them some other grace.

To give order to the Archbishop to prohibit all books and invective sermons against the Parliament, so as notice may be taken of His Majesty's commandment before the meeting.

To peruse the grievances exhibited the last Parliament, and if His Majesty would please to be gracious in any of them, to do it of himself before he be pressed, for a small thing in that manner will give more contentment than much more obtained with importunity.

And especially to call to mind if His Majesty promised anything to the last Parliament which is not yet performed; for upon the performance of that men will be like to ground their trust and hopes in those things which shall be offered now.

For the last point concerning the manner of proceeding, I wish that His Majesty will be pleased to make his propositions unto the Commons by himself or by his ministers and servants that are of their own body, and not by mediation of the Lords. For the Commons will be rather willing to make oblation of their affections themselves unto His Majesty than that any others should do it, and intercept both the merit and thanks from them.

I wish also that the King should forbear to nominate any particular men to be sent unto him from the Commons to treat upon any point or occasion, but after His Majesty hath declared his own desires and made likewise known his gracious inclination to gratify his subjects with any favours and graces that with reason and moderation they can desire for them, His Majesty may be pleased to require the House to nominate a competent number of thirty or forty or fewer which may repair unto him with their demands, and be authorized both to ask and answer such questions as the debate about them shall beget, without concluding or binding the House in any point but only to clear things and report all back to the House. This course, I conceive, will much expedite the business, avoid jealousies, and give good satisfaction to the most, when they shall see that the King shall understand their desire immediately from themselves without any interposition, or danger of misinterpretation, and that upon any point of doubt they shall be admitted to clear their own intentions and not to be subject to the construction of others. Matters being thus prepared beforehand, and thus managed at the time, and His Majesty being pleased to be gracious to his people in the points proposed or any other of the like nature which may be thought of by the House, when they meet (for beforehand no man can precisely say these things will be demanded and no other) I have no doubt, but am very confident that His Majesty shall receive as much contentment of this next Parliament as he received distaste of the former, and that all things will end in that sweet accord that will be both honourable and comfortable for His Majesty and happy for the whole realm. And when His Majesty hath made use of his people's affection to put him out of want, any fit projects that shall be offered may be the boldlier entertained to fill his coffers. For whatsoever shall be done in that kind will be the less subject to offence when there is a perfect renewing and reunion of affections gone before; whereas otherwise whiles dislikes continue seu bene, se male facta premunt.

Endorsed:
"Sir H[enry] Neville of Billingbar his opinion which he presented to His Majesty between the end of the last session of the first Parliament, in the eight year of King James, and for the calling of the Parliament following, in the twelfth year of his Majesty's reign, in anno 1614"

In the above Treatise, Neville uses all the words used by Shakespeare – and more. (A table charting a vocabulary concordance between the Treatise and the Shakespeare works can be found in Addendum 3) This is important: the real author of the stage works would obviously possess a greater vocabulary than he would use in writing meant for the general public. He might very well fear that some of his newer or more learned vocabulary might not be understood by his audience. One general and very telling observation is, however, that (overwhelmingly) when a significant word is used more than once in the political treatise, then that word is also a favourite of Shakespeare's and used repeatedly by him. I say 'overwhelmingly' because it is also noticeable that some of the words which Neville uses here in the treatise – written late in his life – are found only in the *later* works of Shakespeare. This is exactly what one would expect if we are indeed looking at the true writer. However, experts in linguistic analyses also find it important to compare passages with the same **function** behind them, because their vocabulary would then be more likely to be overlapping. But with Shakespeare and Neville we are forced to compare extracts which are not designed to perform the same function: 'Shakespearean' verse was designed for the stage whereas Neville was a politician and diplomat, writing for State organisers. Yet, even so, we still find overlapping vocabulary, even when it comes to some less common words and phrases. This makes the parallel analysis altogether more convincing. Yet Neville's political treatise is much more flowery and more sown with hendiadys and parables than one would expect in a *political* exposition, so again, this is what one would expect if the political writer is also a poet and playwright. It is interesting that Ben Jonson famously accused Shakespeare of being too philosophical for the stage, thus underlining the fact that we are dealing with a writer who leads a dual life as far as his writing is concerned!

According to some scholars (e.g. Ted Hughes) it was a concern with being correctly understood that resulted in Shakespeare's favourite grammatical usage of hendiadys in his plays. (For example, not just 'grounds' but 'grounds and reason'.) But as Frank Kermode was later to say[13], there is no real evidence to substantiate Hughes' opinion, because even well-known words are often doubled. No, it seems that Shakespeare had a love of hendiadys, just like Neville. I examined Shakespeare's and Neville's generally frequent use of this device in my previous book. The analysis of Neville's political treatise reveals even more such doublings, as will be seen from the table which follows:

TABLE OF HENDIADYS

EXAMPLES FROM NEVILLE'S TREATISE	INSTANCES IN SHAKESPEARE
projects and devises	13 instances of 'project' and 73 of 'devise'
fail or fall short	'fail' and 'fall' – over 100 uses
distaste and acrimony	'distaste' used 4 times, 'acrimony' 0
spread and dispersed	'spread' 32, 'disperse[d]' 25
love and concord	'love' 2,298 'concord' 9
help and hurt [a doubling of opposites: . alliteration as well as hendiadys. But alliteration is a *literary* device]	Each of these words used over 100 times
kind and loving	Each of these words used over 100 times. 'kind love' used twice.
confidence and concord [alliteration again]	'confidence' 16

THE POLITICS OF SECRECY: A DANGEROUS TREATISE

sourness and distaste	'sourness' 0, (but 'sour' 76)
love and joy	
rooted and established	'rooted' 11, 'established' 7
cloud or mist	'cloud' 123, 'mist' 828
darkened or overshadowed	'darkened' 2 (both in late plays - *M for M,* and *Coriolanus.*) 'overshadowed' 0
erroneous and dangerous	'erroneous' 2, 'dangerous' 108
speedy and plentiful	'speedy' 21, 'plentiful' 7
adverse and unwilling	'adverse' 13, 'unwilling' 19
nourish and maintain	'nourish' 26 'maintain' 59
protection and allegiance	'protection' 15, 'allegiance' 26
grace and love	'grace and love', the complete phrase is used **twice**, whereas the other way round, 'love and grace' is **never** used!
cherish and foster	'cherish' 33 and 'foster' 10
principal and most understanding	'principal' 9 times,
unjust or unreasonable	'unjust' 24 'unreasonable' 4
sifted and ransacked	'sift[ed]' 5 'ransack[ed]' 6
repose and security	'repose' 31 'security' 18
graciously and benignly	'graciously' 6 , 'benignly' 0, 'benign' 1
favours and graces	'grace and favour' used 3 times

Looking at the above table, I too would once again argue that not all the doublings on Shakespeare-Neville's part can be dismissed as simply a means of helping the audience/readers towards a better understanding of the writer's meaning. For instance, the word 'judgement' was widely understood at the time, so there was no need to add the word 'reason' to make it more comprehensible. Yet analyses of the Shakespeare plays, Neville's letters, and the above treatise, uncover a virtual obsession with hendiadys. I therefore strongly suggest one of the main reasons for this obsession stems from the Greek origins of the hendiadys, so that whoever the writer was, he was certainly learned in Greek, which was not taught at the village grammar schools. 'Hendiadys' was a common device in ancient Greek literature and in virtually none other. This and other pointers in the plays strongly suggest that 'Shakespeare' had to be someone conversant with Greek literature on an everyday basis. Moreover, its *frequent use* attests the kind of careful concern for words and subtle nuances, such as one might expect of a *writer*; but it is device even more commonly used by a *politician*, who would have studied the art of rhetoric. This art itself springs from Greek learning, and the *effect* of the hendiadys, when spoken, is almost like that of the anaphora in rhetoric, where the beginning of a phrase is used repeatedly, in succession. Indeed, Winston Churchill often used both devices together, e.g. 'We shall not flag or fail. ... We shall fight on the seas and the oceans', etc. The more one examines the Shakespeare plays, the more one sees a politician's rhetoric at work.

The Oxford English Dictionary states that the term 'Hendiadys' was first noted by an English writer in 1586. Then, in 1589, Puttenham says that hendiadys is "Another manner of speach when ye will seeme to make two of one, which therefore we call the figure of Twynnes, the Greekes Endiadis."[14] Neville, like all the Essex circle, was always studying Greek. But Henry Neville had especial need to do so because he was helping Savile with his research and writing on 'Chrysostom' for most of his boyhood and adult life. (John Chrysostom is a saint of the Greek Orthodox church.) Thus it is impossible for Neville ultimately to conceal his authorship from those who are determined to analyse his language, try as he might; he simply cannot avoid using his favourite Greek device of Hendiadys in his political rhetoric and in his secret stage works, and even in his personal letters.[15]

If the presence of multiple hendiadys on their own were not enough to prove a strong background of Greek learning, there are also direct references to Greek characters and Greek literature too throughout the writings of both Shakespeare and Neville. Many of these references will be uncovered during the course of this book; but to begin with, there are the allusions to Alexander, Demetrius, etc. in Neville's political declaration. To use what is a virtual parable here in order to illustrate his point immediately suggests Neville as a writer of more than diplomatic letters and political theories. To use a *Greek* parable furnishes us with even more clues to his authorial identity. It is also significant that the names of the protagonists mentioned in the political parable are the very same as those used by Shakespeare in his various plays. Altogether, therefore, this parallel analysis of Neville's treatise and Shakespeare's works results in the discovery of linguistic overlapping which can now be added to my analysis of parallel extracts from the writer/s, which I presented in *Henry Neville and the Shakespeare Code.*

So why has Neville chosen a Greek parable when it comes to illustrating his political meaning, and why does his chosen illustration involve a model family? As the father of eleven surviving children, the image of the family is easily explained. But Neville was a Christian, so why did he not choose a *Biblical* parable? To begin with, Neville had friends on both sides of the Christian division between Catholic and Protestant, so definitely seems to have agreed with his fellow politician Lewis Lewkenor's opinion that religious faith should not be associated with political leanings. And Lewkenor was by now his relative by marriage. Secondly, there is a paucity in the Christian gospels of the New Testament when it comes to giving precedents from family harmony. Additionally, if Neville did indeed write the Shakespeare plays, then his choice of the Greek analogy is in line with those plays' marked distrust of characters who wear their Christianity on their sleeves or use Christian imagery to support their own ideas.[16] Besides, according to the gospels accepted by the established Churches of Western Europe, Christ never married or had a family. Moreover, his disciples were seen as leaving their own families to follow Christ. On the other hand, the classical pre-Christian manuscripts deal with family relationships – and with war and government – in detail. No wonder Sir Henry has been forced to seek *outside* Christianity for his imagery and for governmental precedents. Again, this becomes a recognisable trait in the plays too.

There may also have been yet another important element dictating Neville's choice of non-Christian imagery when trying to persuade King James I to rule in partnership with Parliament. It was, after all, St. Paul who gave Christian Princes the idea that they were ruling by divine right! In his epistle to the Romans he says:

> Let every soul be subject unto the higher powers: For there is no power but of God. The powers that be are ordained of God. Whosoever therefore resisteth the power, resisteth the ordinance of God: and they that resist, shall receive to themselves damnation.

So who were the historical characters Neville mentioned in the classical, *non–Christian*, illustration of his point? Alexander, Demetrius and Antigonus were successive Kings of Macedonia who lived just about 60 years after Pericles. One of the main sources of knowledge concerning them in Neville's time was Plutarch's *Lives*. This work has always been considered a major source for Shakespeare's Roman plays though, once again, one cannot account for Shakespeare's possession or viewing of it, whereas it is easy to account for Neville's knowledge of the work. All these books, now counted as sources for Shakespeare, were expensive works, available mainly to the rich and highly-educated. Like Holinshed's *Chronicles*, they were large tomes and cost the equivalent of hundreds of pounds in today's currency

Neville, however, knew that King James would have possessed a copy of Plutarch, and that he would have known the story of Antigonus and Demetrius. This was carefully chosen, because Demetrius ultimately took control of Macedon in 294 BC and Antigonus' descendants managed to hold on to it for most of the time right up until its conquest by the Romans in 168 BC. (As in his Shakespeare works, therefore, Neville was sowing implicit, almost subliminal, messages through his cleverly-chosen political similes.) In this case, Neville was saying that if the King showed the same partnership with Parliament as Antigonus had done with Demetrius, then James' descendants might rule England for a very long time. (The disastrous converse was of course meant to be understood by the King too; and how prophetic Neville's fears turned out to be, with later Stuarts being continually ousted.)

So, in the final analysis it was even possible, thought Neville, that if Parliament and King became used to acting separately and refusing to negotiate with each other then there could be civil war.[17] It was in an attempt to avert such a terrible outcome that Neville actually communicated his private advice to

THE POLITICS OF SECRECY: A DANGEROUS TREATISE

the King in writing, in or before 1612. But, given the Parliamentarians' mood, this was a somewhat dangerous thing to have done. Many Parliamentarians had for some time been suspecting that their discussions were being reported to the King by ambitious members of their own House, with a view to currying the monarch's favour. When they heard (Neville's) anonymous treatise read out, then, some M.P.s were ready to shout that the Paper must have been written by some 'undertaker' traitorously telling the King their secrets.

An 'Undertaker' was the term Parliamentarians gave to Members they suspected of 'undertaking' to manage Parliament for the Monarch. Shakespeare even mentions them in passing in *Twelfth Night:*

> **Sir Toby** You, sir? - why, what are you?
> **Antonio** [Drawing] One, sir, that for his love dares yet do more
> Than you have heard him brag to you he will.
> **Sir Toby** [Drawing] Nay, if you be an undertaker, I am for you. *Act III, Sc.iv*

This means that either the business of 'undertaking' (and thus working out a partnership between King and Parliament) had been mooted for a long time, or the play had been revised after James I succeeded to the throne, the only other possibility being that it referred to the English who were 'undertaking' to manage the poor Irish at the time, which again was not heard of much outside of Parliamentary circles. Either way, as all these 'undertakings' were quite secret, the inclusion of this reference in the play strongly suggests that it was written by someone involved in these secretive enterprises, not by Shakespeare. As we shall see in the next chapter, however, there were only three men involved in 'undertaking' in the sense of taking new ideas of political management to the King. One of these men was Sir Henry Neville.

It is interesting to look at some of the immediate Parliamentary responses to Neville's paper on the day it was presented, but first of all it is also interesting to see a list of some Parliamentary committee members with whom Neville had been working in 1614. They included:

> Sir Dudley Digges [brother of Leonard Digges, the contributor of a Commendatory Verse in the First Folio of Shakespeare's works.]

35

Mr. Christopher Brooke [a best friend of John Donne and a frequenter of the Mitre Tavern, along with Sir Henry Neville and Inigo Jones]

Sir Thomas Roe, diplomat; also a friend of John Donne and Ben Jonson.

Sir Roger Owen [M.P. for Shropshire]

Francis Moore [M.P. for Reading, a Catholic]

William Hakewill [a lawyer, Cornish M.P. and opposer of the King's insistence on an autonomous right to raise import and export duties]

Sir Edwin Sandys [prominent Parliamentarian, friend of the Earl of Southampton, and a foremost member of the Virginia Company. Neville once complained that some things Sandys said and did were put down to him!]

John Hoskins [a Parliamentary 'rebel' and member of the Mitre Club - sitting next to Neville in this Parliament. He also wrote a verse about Neville's presence at the Mitre.]

James Whitelock [a judge, Neville's friend; fond of playacting. His son, Bulstrode Whitelock, read William Davenant's works through for him]

John Dunn [doubtless John Donne, the poet, who was by 1614 M.P. for Taunton. He too was a member of the Mitre Tavern club and gave after-dinner talks there, alongside Neville. Donne was also studying Greek at this time so may very well have called on help from Neville, whom he was seated near to in many Parliamentary committees[18].]

Thomas Wentworth [lawyer and politician, son of Elizabeth Walsingham (d. 1596), who was the sister of Sir Francis Walsingham, secretary of state. Strong anti-catholic and anti King James I's attempts to seek absolute power. Outspoken, and a friend of Sir Henry Neville.]

Some of these men are reported as having spoken in support, after the reading of Neville's treatise. However, the general immediate reaction of M.P.s was to ask that the author of the paper declare himself and be examined. After much prevarication, the parliamentary reporter wrote that "Sir Henry Neville ... did avow it to come from him and said his Majesty, about some 2 years past, being at Windsor, sent for him and propounded 2 things unto him: for the first, he said he had no warrant to disclose it unto us; the 2nd was about the parliament;..." (So Neville obviously explained that this was therefore the origin of his letter of advice to the King, eventually[19.]) When questioned as to why he had not put his name to his resultant treatise, and not

THE POLITICS OF SECRECY: A DANGEROUS TREATISE

admitted his authorship straight away, he replied that he had had no idea into whose hands his writing might fall and, besides, he had also no idea that it was going to be read publicly in the House.

Instead of pursuing the question of how it came to be read in the Commons, however, M.P.s continued to worry that Neville might be one of the 'undertakers' who had revealed Parliamentary discussions to the King and therefore offered to 'manage' Parliament. Neville's rhetorical skills must have been considerable, because he was able to calm the ensuing outcry and persuade them all that he was no sort of traitor to the Parliamentary cause.[20]

The man who supported Neville's ideas most strongly that day was Dudley Digges. While others present were still debating the rights and wrongs of Sir Henry's action in dealing with the King privately before putting his ideas before Parliament, Digges declared that he thought "a private man might go and move the King for the good of the country, uncalled..." He recalled how his own father had "projected divers things to Queen Elizabeth and yet was a parliament man after, without being excepted against." It is therefore interesting that this supporter of Neville was also the brother of a man who wrote in praise of 'Shakespeare' [in verses which preceded the First Folio]. After all, it did indeed look as if Sir Henry was trying to manage Parliament - even if it was in the interests of preventing Civil War. So was Dudley Digges – a keen Parliamentarian – giving Neville more leeway because he knew another side of him, and therefore knew about his writing for the theatre? Probably.

Certainly, other parliamentarians were not so tolerant of Sir Henry's lack of proper procedure. Not even those who had been privy to some of Neville's ideas *before* the formal reading of his treatise liked the 'hole in the corner' manner in which it had been presented. We may gather from Sir Edwin Sandys' remarks, for instance, that he was a friend of Neville but much more in favour of Parliament's freedom to make its own decisions, rather than totally agreeing with Neville's idea of a partnership between King and Parliament. However, Sandys soon changed his mind in favour of Neville's solution when, less than a fortnight later, some M.P.s began to foment a direct confrontation with the King. Had Neville had a quiet word with Sandys in the interim? Very probably. He seems to have been a persuasive person. Indeed, he must have been, as had been demonstrated by his ability to save his skin, after being so deeply involved with the Earl of Essex.

But Neville's treatise was, after all, presented at a rather tense time. A member of the House of Lords had angered the Commons by a speech he gave, and many M.P.s wished to demand that the King should intervene to prevent the Lords saying anything inflammatory against the Commons. But on this occasion Sandys was the first to point out that if M.P.s did that, then there would be nothing to stop the King also agreeing with the Lords to proscribe certain debates in the Lower House. Sandys had therefore implicitly admitted that Neville's idea of a partnership between King and Parliament was the only way forward, even though he initially opposed it. Ultimately, indeed, the wisdom of Neville's policy was underlined when the King, hearing of the Parliamentarians' projected protest, threatened to close the House of Commons forthwith.

Neville and Kingship: a linguistic and literary perspective concerning some overlapping points in the Treatise and the Plays

The function of Neville's treatise is obviously one of political persuasion. He did not write this with the intention of it becoming entertainment. Nevertheless, if we step aside from its function for a moment and look at the treatise for its linguistic beauty and eternal truths we cannot help but be struck by its similarity to Shakespeare in those respects. How homely is his tale of Alexander, and how moving his description of the way to live harmoniously within a family: "... there is almost a continual necessity of mutual offices of kindness to nourish and maintain that love,". Then he goes on – in such a Shakespearean manner – to use a simile to emphasise how this homely love can be made universal, " so in kingdoms, besides that great bond of protection and allegiance between the sovereign and the subject, there is a like necessary use of the frequent change of mutual effects of grace and love to cherish and foster that tender affection that daily is to be renewed between them." When read aloud, it is indeed as if we are hearing a passage from one of the great plays, perhaps its greatest echoes occurring in *Henry V*. In that play, Shakespeare chooses to depict a king who is loved, just as he wishes King James to be loved. It is therefore legitimate to look at the attitude to kingship as expressed in both the Treatise and in the plays.

Neville urges James to show grace when dealing with Parliament, and in *Henry V* Shakespeare has Canterbury proclaim,

THE POLITICS OF SECRECY: A DANGEROUS TREATISE

"The king is full of grace and fair regard." In fact, 'grace' seems Shakespeare's most desired quality in a King, and Henry V himself is aware that he must possess it:

King Henry We are no tyrant, but a Christian king,
Unto whose grace our passion is as subject
As are our wretches fettered in our prisons.

This was clearly how Neville thought a King should control himself, and one criticism he voiced elsewhere concerning King James was that he was a man against whose 'humour' it was dangerous to strive[21], which is the very opposite of Shakespeare's *ideal* king, as well as Neville's. In Addendum 3 I have numbered the lines of Neville's Treatise; line 118 emphasises yet again the need for the King to show grace. Then he goes on to repeat the need for this same quality another three times in the remainder of his treatise. Emphasising this quality of grace therefore certainly picks out Neville as being the writer of Shakespeare's plays concerning kingship. In total, the word 'grace' is used 5 times in this short treatise. It is used 600 times in the Shakespeare works: Neville's obsessions are clearly Shakespeare's obsessions. The word 'confident' however is used only 3 times in the treatise, and 19 times throughout the Shakespeare works. 'Diffident' is used only once in the treatise, and never in the plays, with only two occurrences of its associated noun, 'diffidence' throughout the works. Search as we will, therefore, we find a correlation between Neville's word frequency and that of Shakespeare when it comes to defining a human quality. This is what we would expect to find if Shakespeare is Neville, because the words used to describe human qualities can be justifiably separated from the vocabulary necessary to fulfil the otherwise different *functions* of Shakespeare's works and Neville's treatise.

I find the following passage from the Treatise also very Shakespearean in sound. Again, it echoes the kind of sentiment found in some of Henry V's speeches:

> For, as there is nothing that more upholds the reputation of any Prince than the opinion of his strength at home, which consisteth principally in the love and concord between him and his people, from whence there followeth naturally a sequence of all other duties on their part to make him strong and able to help and hurt his neighbours, so there is

> nothing that emboldens more an enemy, either open or secret, to attempt the disturbance of the peace of any State than the imagination that the Prince and people stand not in kind and loving terms together.

'Loving terms' is actually found in *Romeo and Juliet*, Act 1, Sc.i, but the whole tenor of this passage reminds me strongly of the prose speech King Henry makes when talking to a discontented soldier. (Note how Henry uses the analogy of family relationships to illustrate his point about the relationship between the King and his subject. Neville chooses the same analogy in his Treatise.):

> **King Henry** So, if a son that is by his father sent about merchandise do sinfully miscarry upon the sea, the imputation of his wickedness, by your rule, should be imposed upon his father that sent him. Or if a servant, under his master's command transporting a sum of money, be assailed by robbers, and die in many irreconciled iniquities, you may call the business of the master the author of the servant's damnation. But this is not so. The king is not bound to answer the particular endings of his soldiers, the father of his son, nor the master of his servant; for they purpose not their death when they purpose their services. ...

Similarly, the feeling and expression within one of the passages in the Treatise by Neville reminds me greatly of Portia's speech on Mercy from *The Merchant of Venice*:

> The quality of mercy is not strained;
> It droppeth as the gentle rain from heaven
> Upon the place beneath. It is twice blest:
> It blesseth him that gives, and him that takes.
> 'Tis mightiest in the mightiest, it becomes
> The throned monarch better than his crown.
> His sceptre shows the force of temporal power,
> The attribute to awe and majesty,
> Wherein doth sit the dread and fear of kings;
> But mercy is above this sceptred sway,
> It is enthroned in the hearts of kings,

Replacing 'mercy' in Portia's speech with 'grace' from Neville's Treatise gives us the same sentiment – 'grace' is twice blest: likewise, in the Treatise, 'contentment' is the reward "to

THE POLITICS OF SECRECY: A DANGEROUS TREATISE

them that shall pay what is given," and this 'justifies' "the care and honest regard of them that shall give it.":

> It is true (as I lately delivered unto His Majesty), that some things will be desired and expected of him by way of grace, which may both give some contentment to them that shall pay what is given, and justify the care and honest regard of them that shall give it. And without this I dare promise nothing.

But there are also *thematic* concordances between Neville's and Shakespeare's attitude to kingship. To begin with, both Neville and Shakespeare are exceptionally concerned with the role of the King. This is remarkable enough, in an age when it was safer to accept kingship – unquestioningly – than discuss it. It is therefore further worthy of remark that Neville's and Shakespeare's patterns for the ideal king are completely concordant. Neville urges the king to trust Parliament, listen to Members and be gracious with them, which is exactly how Shakespeare's one and only ideal king,, Henry V, behaves with his advisers, and even with his soldiers. Similarly, whenever there is an argument between a king and his barons in the history plays, Shakespeare often puts much of the blame on the king. In the same way, Neville uses vocabulary which, when analysed, suggests the king is more blameworthy than Parliament in the present situation. At the dissolution of Parliament, for instance, the king departs full of "distaste and acrimony" while Parliament only shows "some discontentment".

Altogether, there are many signs of Shakespeare in this speech by Neville. That speech contained imagery drawn from Greek references, so it will eventually be helpful to examine some Shakespeare texts for signs the true writer was indeed familiar with Greek culture. Indeed, this is a subject which will be touched upon in further chapters of the book, where it will be found to link in with something quite unexpected too.

Finally, reading this Treatise makes me wonder whether Neville had written one of the Shakespeare plays as an early warning regarding the King's arrogant dealings with any 'underlings' and especially with Parliament. That play is *Coriolanus*. The play begins with protest from the Plebeians, which is unique among plays of the time. They are demonstrating because they need more food and are sure the senate is holding

41

grain to which they have privileged access. But it is the attitude of Marcius (later Coriolanus) that is interesting. Instead of treating the underlings with kindness and understanding, he approaches them with insults:

> **MARCIUS**... What's the matter, you dissentious rogues
> That, rubbing the poor itch of your opinion,
> Make yourselves scabs?

Later, in just the same way as King James is reluctant to approach Parliament and ask for funds with the customary politeness, Marcius Coriolanus does not wish to 'beg' the commons for their votes when he wishes to become a consul. He certainly does not like to be told that the 'price' he must pay is to 'ask it kindly', just as King James rejected Neville's advice to do so.

> Re-enter three of the CITIZENS.
> **Coriolanus** Bid them wash their faces
> And keep their teeth clean. So, here comes a brace.
> You know the cause, sir, of my standing here?
> **3rd Citizen** We do, sir. Tell us what hath brought you to't.
> **Coriolanus** Mine own desert.
> **2nd Citizen** Your own desert?
> **Coriolanus** Ay, but not mine own desire.
> **3rd Citizen** How not your own desire?
> **Coriolanus** No, sir, 'twas never my desire yet to trouble the poor with begging.
> **3rd Citizen** You must think, if we give you anything, we hope to gain by you.
> **Coriolanus** Well then, I pray, your price o'th' consulship?
> **1st Citizen** The price is to ask it kindly.

By the time this play was completed (c.1610) Sir Henry Neville had written several letters to friends saying how disappointed he was concerning Parliamentary proceedings in general and how the king could be 'sudden and violent'. This kind of demeanour might well have made Neville think of the king as a somewhat military type of leader. Throughout the play, Coriolanus (a military leader, initially) wishes to issue orders rather than conferring with others, and this was patently King James' attitude too. With this attitude, Coriolanus, though a successful leader in battle, cannot hold his place in civil society.

THE POLITICS OF SECRECY: A DANGEROUS TREATISE

He even turns away his supporters and friends because he cannot be 'civil' with them. In the end, Coriolanus is murdered. A warning indeed, and just the kind of character and narrative which would have suggested itself to Neville, given his relationship with the King. Moreover, Coriolanus actually declares that he acts 'alone':

CORIOLANUS ...'tis there
That like an eagle in a dovecot I
Fluttered your Volscians in Corioles.
Alone I did it.

And:

CORIOLANUS ...though I go alone,
Like to a lonely dragon that his fen
Makes feared and talked of more than seen - ...

In fact, the word 'alone' is used 14 times throughout the play, as if Neville is wanting to echo the King's would-be 'divine', autocratic state.

The dating of this play is said to be between 1608 and 1610, which therefore fits in with the King's attitude at the time, and Neville's feelings. It also calls (possibly) on the circumstances of the time: there were corn riots during the early years of King James' reign, and the theme of the poor's protests for corn is repeated throughout the play. Plays must always catch something of the mood of the times, otherwise they are less likely to be taken notice of. It is also very unlikely that any writer would remain unaffected by his or her cultural surroundings, which obviously included just such a 'moment.' Someone – like the Earl of Oxford, who died only one year after King James I came to the throne – would neither have seen these riots nor lived long enough to experience the autocratic leanings of the new King, and therefore would hardly have chosen a subject like *Coriolanus*. This is yet another in a long line of factors against Oxford being the author, and is of course in addition to the insuperable fact that he died eleven years before twelve more plays came out under the name of 'Shakespeare'. To keep so many literary creations locked away in a drawer is unprecedented as well as inexplicable; and the Oxfordian argument that topical themes were added later is ridiculous. As noted, the theme of the poor and their corn opens and runs through the whole of *Coriolanus* so could not have been an afterthought. Besides, 'Zeitgeist' is a necessary ingredient in any political play, and Coriolanus is, par excellence, political. This is surely why it is one of the most topical, and therefore least performed, plays in the Shakespeare canon. Only when we look at a true political writer of the moment – an elected representative – can we account for its composition.

Neither do the concerns within *Coriolanus* run parallel with the background attributed to Shakespeare of Stratford. Besides not being a politician, the lowly-born Shakespeare would surely have shown deep concern for the poor and their reasons for rioting over their lack of corn. Indeed, Plutarch stresses that they had several causes for discontent, including the fact that they had low wages, and were therefore forced to borrow, then hounded by their usurious 'creditors'; yet the playwright leaves out any such extra vindications for their actions. This of course implies that the true playwright was a politician from a very different walk of life from the Stratford man: the true author's interests did not entirely lie with the poor. This is the same politician who clearly wrote the *Henry VI* trilogy, with its disapproval of too rooted a popular uprising, like that illustrated by Cade's rebellion.

North's translation of Plutarch is certainly the major source of *Coriolanus*. It is therefore noteworthy that passages concerning religion and a belief in God are included in North's translation of Plutarch's life of Coriolanus, but that these religious mumblings play no part in the Shakespeare dramatisation. This shows precisely the same attitude to religion as Neville's and Lewkenor's, i.e. that religion and politics should be kept apart. As already noted, Neville uses no religious imagery in his political Treatise.

Neville's Proposed changes to some Laws
Copies of Neville's *Memorial* proposing amendments to the law are included in various collections,[22] and were seen by Parliament at the same time as his declaration was read.

The laws Neville wanted to amend illuminate some of his *personal* thinking, even though they were presented as a consensus of the opinions of various Lords and Commons of the time. Though never given to corruption, Neville could not help promoting his own and his family's interests alongside the laws he knew others wanted too. Most noted in this respect is the fact that the Memorial requested old debts arising from Queen Elizabeth's fines to be 'stemmed' by the levying of a single yearly payment.

THE POLITICS OF SECRECY: A DANGEROUS TREATISE

Neville had of course been paying back a large fine levied by the Queen after his involvement in the Essex affair. This trait of family interest is also found in the Shakespeare-Neville plays, where the Neville family was portrayed in the best light possible, even if it meant falsifying history! Examples of just such falsifications will appear throughout the book. My point is that only a Neville – and a Neville just like Sir Henry – would have written these Neville-specific glorifications and fabrications for the public stage. But the plays nevertheless always point in the direction of a moral outcome and the good of society. In exactly the same way, in his *known* profession, Neville was prepared to promote changes in the law which would benefit him personally, but he would not have asked for any of these changes if they clashed with the public good or were going to cause disadvantages for others.

Even the first of the laws which Neville mentions 'several' men desire should be amended is highly relevant to his own interests too. It concerns the law of treason, and we cannot help noting that Neville himself almost fell foul of this. He wishes:

> A law to be made for the declaration of all treasons. [*The word 'treason' is itself used 125 times in the Shakespeare plays.*] Hereby is not meant to alter the law or to make anything not to be treason that now is, but only to declare what is treason that every man may know it and avoid it; and not to fall upon a hidden work before he be aware that it may not be in the power of a judge by an inference or a super-induced[23] interpretation to ruin a man and his posterity.

Neville may justifiably have thought that the Essex trouble was only going to result in a demonstration, so his recommended amendment really opens the way for defining the difference between a demonstration and a treasonable action, and was obviously a prelude to the task of making a general index of treasonable actions so that everyone would know what to avoid. It is perhaps also significant that Neville talks about falling upon 'a hidden work.' Ambiguity abounds, but Neville was always the man to choose his words carefully and be aware of their double meanings, despite what Ben Jonson thought![24]

Following hard on the heels of this came Neville's recommendation that a man's property and/or liberty should not be intruded upon merely because of an accusation of wrongdoing, but only on proof of the accuser's case. The next point is partially obliterated and torn, so it is difficult to see Neville's precise argument. Then comes a measure recommended to help those who fall into debt because of service to the King or state. (This had of course happened to Neville, who claimed that he had had to pay £4,000 of his own money towards his expenses while Ambassador in France. The sum would amount to several millions in today's terms, and Neville knew others had had similar experiences.)

Neville even mentions an unjust amendment to the gathering of alienated rents – a rule which he says was instituted by, and for the benefit of, the Earl of Leicester (the Queen's favourite.) He wishes this right to be cancelled. But in mentioning the Earl of Leicester in this unfavourable light we may also allow ourselves to become suspicious of Neville's and his friends' role in that banned manuscript, *Leicester's Commonwealth*. This will be followed up briefly in the present book.

An amendment to the law of trespass is also requested in this list of 'boons' asked of the King which would, says Neville, 'happily breed peace and contentment to the poorer sort, which must not be altogether neglected.' He says this is an idea which he personally has inserted because it only concerns landed, wealthy men (like himself) who could easily afford to give up some of their rights. Neville's writing that the 'poorer sort ... must not be altogether neglected' may well be an understatement of his true feeling for the poor, because he left some of his own money to the poor of four Berkshire parishes in his will.[25] The wording in this, his Memorial to the King, may therefore perhaps also be an ironic echo of something the King had said about the poor and of which Neville disapproved.

Neville, however, puts the whole background to his case in as eloquent and conciliatory fashion as possible, and one cannot help noticing a similarity of style between this statement and Shakespeare's dedications of *Lucrece* and *Venus and Adonis* to the Earl of Southampton:

> These points I have collected from the desires of several men, some gentlemen, some lawyers, who if they have miscarried[26] my judgment in any point out of the

compass[27] of my profession I hope I shall be pardoned. But for the trial of it, I humbly desire his Majesty will be pleased to call his learned counsel upon a sudden[28] and examine them what loss or damage certain or what prejudice they conceive it will be to his Majesty to depart with those things and at what value they do esteem them. For surely we aim not to take from his Majesty any matter of value but only some small things which may be abundantly[29] recompensed in the gift he may expect from his people. And if it fall out otherwise in these particulars, we are mistaken in them.

After this, Neville adds some points which he says he has gathered from the Lords. The second of these might perhaps contain the grain of an idea which might help give security of tenure in our own troubled times: "That no lease of the King's land should be voided for non payment of rent at the just day, but the penalty for default to be double the rent."

Then comes "No impositions upon commodities exported or imported to be henceforth raised without the consent of parliament." (One could justifiably comment that many Parliamentarians by this time had therefore diversified their own sources of income by becoming involved in international trade, just as Neville had, and just as is a major concern in the plays.) They also wanted 'obsolete and unprofitable laws' to be repealed.

Neville's Political Theatricality

Finally, I think we should look at the very contrived, theatrical way in which Sir Henry's treatise was presented. To begin with, Sir Henry himself eventually admitted that he had already sent his paper as a private letter to the King. (He was probably wanting to give Parliamentarians the impression that he was being brave in telling the King to treat Parliament with more respect, rather than offering to 'manage' Parliament for the King.) True, he had discussed some of the points with Sir Edwin Sandys, but it looks as if he had never told him that he had actually written down his ideas, otherwise Sandys would immediately have known that the paper read out in the Commons was by Neville.

Put yourself in Neville's position. The King has approached you for advice, but when it comes he dislikes it, and also therefore begins to dislike you. You would feel very vulnerable. So did Neville. Less than two years after Neville sent that letter, and one month before its political contents were read out in Parliament, the King had passed over Neville's strong and popular candidacy for the post of Secretary of State. Neville now needed some support for his ideas in quarters other than the King's. Sir Henry always considered himself a capable politician who had never managed – or wished – to be promoted merely because he was someone's favourite. He wished to rise by the merit of his ideas alone, yet with all the surrounding favouritism and corruption, he had been unable to do so. He found this doubly frustrating, because he knew his ideas would benefit the whole kingdom – and that was his current point of motivation. True, he enjoyed the drama which parliamentary power could bring, but his main concern was to get his ideas accepted and to win the support of influential people so that these ideas could be implemented. But if he had openly presented Parliament with a whole treatise of his own – based on private advice he had already sent to the King – then he knew the King would have been furious. Not only would the King's anger then rebound on Neville personally; it would also make him oppose the *ideas* more hotly than ever, simply because they had come from Neville! Neville therefore tried to bring out his ideas surreptitiously and – as with the plays – began by pretending they were not by him at all. One of the M.P.s immediately questioned why the paper had not been read before a *full* house, so Neville must have chosen his time carefully. What reason could he have had for this, other than that, characteristically, he had not wanted himself but his *ideas* to be known? He knew that the few, though influential, men then present would discuss the ideas with every M.P. who had not been present. Besides, the men then assembled in the Commons were his allies, for the most part, so this too must have been a situation designed by Neville. These men knew him and his ideas well enough to work out that he was the author – eventually. But Neville had at least given himself the chance of saying that he had no idea his treatise was going to be read out at all, so why should he have put his name to it? After all, as he said, the incident just proved that you never know into whose hands your writing might fall.

What a piece of theatre! No one but Neville could have instigated the paper's complete presentation in Parliament, but he knew from his secret writing of the plays that something which is mysterious always creates more interest. The MPs had been discussing the possibility of Parliamentary spies and 'undertakers' for days prior to the reading of Neville's paper, so they did not spend their time enquiring into the background of the paper's presentation but instead concentrated on the question of whether or not Neville himself should now be named as an 'undertaker.' This was a serious allegation, and one which could have seen him cast out of the House. However, when Neville gave a résumé of the circumstances under which the paper had first been written – *two years previously* – he successfully deflected their accusations of his being an undertaker (which was the equivalent of a double agent.) Besides, they agreed that the *ideas* in the paper were of no harm to Parliament at all.

Altogether, then, Neville scored a theatrical success. He gained the support and approval of a small but influential group of Parliamentarians. They could therefore do the work of spreading these ideas to others. Neville himself knew there was a lot of 'kicking' against him in Parliament[30], so would have been happy to have his ideas mediated by others, without direct reference to himself personally. (This was exactly his position concerning the plays and their political content, too.) For Sir Henry, politics and stagecraft were obviously part and parcel of the same thing. To see yet a further example of the man's theatrical tendencies we have only to think back to Neville's casual admittance to Sir Robert Cecil that he had gone in disguise to the King of Spain's Memorial Service in Notre Dame.[31] I think we might best move towards an understanding of Sir Henry's complex character by likening him to the kind of professional actor who wants recognition while he's on the stage – demonstrating his professional skill – but hopes he won't be recognised when he steps out of character and into private life. During James I's reign he 'performed' well on the Parliamentary stage, being known as a great Parliamentarian, but when he did not gain the role for which he had rehearsed – that of Secretary of State – he decided to drop out of the limelight, wherever and whenever possible. What *is* known is that he took on a backstage role. He advised and supported his friend and one-time secretary, Sir Ralph Winwood, who in fact did finally gain the role which Neville had sought. Dudley Carleton and John Chamberlain write about this happening, wishing 'accomplishment' to the one (Ralph Winwood), and 'continuance' to the other (viz. Sir Henry Neville.)[32] One cannot avoid the feeling that this backstage role was one for which Neville was well prepared, after a lifetime of writing in secret.

Altogether, Neville manages to balance two otherwise conflicting concerns: in his Treatise I could not help seeing a *factional* as well as a *popular* interest, intertwined with the global aim of improving things. But it is *the same* factional interest which also presents itself in the plays – a leaning towards the rights of the 'barons' and educated commons, rather than promoting the interests of an overbearing king on the one side, or those of the ignorant masses at the other end of the pole. Yet, as in his will,[33] Neville looked kindly on those masses and wished to improve their lot. This is, however, a different matter from *empowering* the under-educated by giving them a political voice. It is precisely *this same* fear of 'uneducated' rule we find enacted in an episode in the *Henry VI* plays, where Shakespeare-Neville portrays a disastrous situation engendered by an incompetent king, leading to the ignorant Jack Cade's rebellion with its murderous consequences.

Nevertheless, Sir Henry Neville did his best in his treatise to widen the monarch's whole perception of social rights, despite the terrible pressures and threats which politicians were heir to in his day. This was something of a dangerous path to tread under James I's rule. In the end, therefore, one must admire the brave ideals Neville presented in his thesis, despite the fact that they may seem somewhat tame by modern standards. In the same way, seeing the Shakespeare plays as works of eternal truths has tended to blinker us from appreciating just how daring, political and topical these were too, in their day. As the times were cruel, the plays' suggestions for a change in general outlook, and a consequent change in the way things are run, were necessarily expressed in a more subtle, symbolic fashion than that employed by oppositional playwrights of the 1970s and '80s. Thus does Neville's political viewpoint, as expressed in his treatise, become inevitably entwined with the Shakespeare plays, written by his same, invisible hand. As Professor Neal Platt remarked on seeing a draft of my first chapter, "Over and above the word count/comparison, I can hear the playwright's voice in the Treatise. I can even detect his 'best behaviour' demeanour, taming his wild and fanciful phrases to suit the present task."

To the Reader.

Hough I haue been euer readier to wonder at the effect of things extraordinarily strange; then wel prouided of iudgement to examine their causes, subiecting sundrie times mine eares to the report of rare and vnusuall accidentes, with a greater bent of attention, then perchaunce to a well tempered stayednes will seem conuenient, yet mee thinketh that this humor of mine, howsoeuer faulty, is much more excusable then that contemptuous derision of Theyras, who presentlie doe condemne for false fryuolous & impossible whatsoeuer is not within the narrow lymits of their own capacitie included, therein to excuse their owne ignorance by the disgrace of a better experience, for mine own part therefore, though no mans conceipt weaker or vnapter to apprehend then mine, yet I euer held it decent to yeeld a respectiue gesture, and due reputation to him, that vpon his owne knowledge taketh vpon him to deliuer vnto the hearers matter mouing them to maruell, and such as common experience sometimes fayleth to approue, of which sort vnlesse the partialitie of my affection deceiue mee, there is not any that doth more beautifie the speaker or delight the hearer, then the description of forreine regions, the manners & customes of farre distant

Wise and discrete speech beautifieth the hearer and delighteth the speaker.

Opening page of Lewkenor's *The Commonwealth and Government of Venice* (1599) – a book which finds echoes in *The Merchant of Venice* and *Othello*.

Chapter Two

THE SHAKESPEARE-NEVILLE REFORMATION

During the 16th and 17th centuries in England, it was not at all uncommon for authors to write anonymously or to choose a pseudonym. Various levels of disguise and secrecy were necessary ingredients for certain key players of the time, especially those involved in politics and the diplomatic service. Such men were necessarily drawn from established, high-profile families too, with the Neville family being one of the greatest. As descendants of the old Plantagenet dynasty they were also one of the most vulnerable. If 16th and 17th century Nevilles wanted to survive, they had better try to remain as necessary yet as invisible as possible, and especially so if they wished to criticise or reform established beliefs. It should therefore come as no surprise that the real Shakespeare was a Neville politician and diplomat in disguise. However, after he was imprisoned in the Tower, Neville felt it necessary to disguise authorship of his *political* writing too. As he was eventually to declare, he did not like to put his name to his writing because one never knew into whose hands it might fall.

Sir Henry was a man of many parts. Above all, however, he considered his efforts in the field of politics could make a difference to the development of English society and culture. To this extent even his secret, *literary* writing contains a large element of 'a man on a mission'. This is one reason, surely, that the Neville-Shakespeare plays have endured. No one comes away from the performance of any one of them without feeling one's outlook has been transformed, no matter how many times one has read and re-read the texts. Neville must therefore have realised that imparting a new outlook and new insight through his plays was at least as important in his overall mission as was his input within the much smaller audience of Parliament. Confirming this conclusion, we have the fact that Neville was reading a symbolically political play by Beaumont and Fletcher – *A King and no King* – during the time he was writing his political treatise.[34]

Until Henry Neville's identity was placed firmly within the Shakespeare framework, however, it was not easy to tease out the precise political messages contained in the plays. By 'political' I mean themes and dialogues in the works which inevitably initiate thought and discussion about the organisation of society. Everyone throughout Europe at the time knew how dangerous it was to present one's opinions openly on such matters, so no wonder the political outlook within the Shakespeare plays has seemed more ambiguous than it truly is. In her book *The French Academies,* Frances Yates pointed out that it was standard practice in France to teach budding poets how to use imagery and mythological reference to *infer* a quite *precise* meaning.[35] Ronsard, the French Renaissance poet, for instance, was taught in that manner, (and there are one or two passing quotations from Ronsard [in English translation] in the Shakespeare *Sonnets.*)[36] I shall therefore be examining the imagery and mythological references in the *Henry VI* trilogy during the course of this book, which does indeed result in *precise* meanings within those plays being laid bare.

I suggest that the main reason such political 'truths hidden in symbols and images'[37] within the Shakespeare works have not been fully explored is because in doing so one inevitably concludes that a man who had studied French and studied generally on the continent would be seen as the inevitable author, instead of Shakespeare. (Sir Henry Neville actually visited France and Italy as a student in the 1570s to 80s, and later became our French Ambassador.)

There is also the point that young men from the wealthier classes were increasingly taught the art of rhetoric at University or with private tutors. One of the features of this study was learning to argue for both sides of a question. However, rhetoric was not on the curriculum of the grammar schools attended by lucky boys from the lower classes. It is therefore easy to see how Neville's background suited him to a seemingly ambiguous form of writing. Only the educated members of the then audiences, however, would have understood that the arts of rhetoric and symbolism were involved in the plays' *seeming* ambiguity. Shakespeare of Stratford learnt neither rhetoric nor the use of precise inferential imagery. Some scholars (including Professor Jonathan Bate) endeavour to persuade us that Shakespeare showed his experience of the local grammar schools when he included in his plays a very fleeting reference to a Latin lesson, and the unwillingness with which pupils crept 'like snails' to school. However, every man who had endowed or initiated these schools would know very well what went on there. Our Sir Henry himself set up some of these schools on his own lands. Nevertheless, it is – as always – impossible for these same scholars to explain how William Shakespeare gained his knowledge of politics, rhetoric or the then very secret skill of ironworking – and yet the echoes of these skills are far stronger and more frequent in the works than the occasional references to the schoolroom!

Moreover, books on these and most subjects were rare commodities in these poor, one-roomed, village institutions. Their main owners were those with manor houses and private libraries, or advanced educational institutions, where there would be space enough to lay the books out and candle or oil light enough to read them by. As the famous Elizabethan educationalist, Roger Ascham, said:

> I remember, whan I was yong, in the North, they went to the Grammer schole, litle children: they came from thence great lubbers: alwayes learning, and litle profiting: learning without booke, euery thing; vnderstandyng within the booke, litle or nothing: Their whole knowledge, by learning without the booke, was tied onely to their tong & lips, and neuer ascended vp to the braine & head, ...
> ...for all your constructions in Grammer scholes, be nothing els but translations: but because they be not *double* translations, (as I do require), they bring forth but simple and single commoditie; and ... also they lacke the daily vse of writing, which is the onely thing that breedeth deepe roote ... for good vnderstanding, and in ye memorie, for sure keeping of all that is learned. [38]...

How Shakespeare gained access to the books' mere physical presence, therefore, has never been explained. It is a historical fact that rich men's sons (and a very few, selected promising scholars like Ascham) entered the universities at what we would now think of as middle-school age. It was only at the universities that poorer, sponsored scholars had access to books and learned any foreign languages. Such books as there were at the village Grammar Schools must have been in short supply, otherwise the children would not have had to spend all their time at rote learning, *without books*. As seen from Ascham's own words, the so-called 'Latin' learnt at the grammar schools consisted of nothing more than translations of a few extracts, probably made and circulated by the schoolmaster. I was born and brought up within a mile of one of these little old schools. It consisted of one room and had only one master. I know how difficult it was for me in the 1960s to work at my studies, as a girl from a poor family who could not afford the necessary text books, nor a warm, separate room in which to study, so I can fully assert that it would have been impossible for poor children who attended the one-roomed grammar schools of 16th century England to learn much at all. It seems to me that myths about the old English grammar schools of the time have been invented to substantiate the Shakespeare myth itself, and secondly the myth of 'merry, enlightened, Elizabethan England.' Both these images are very wide of the mark.

There is one advantage of rote learning, however. I remember being taught folk songs and passages from plays by teachers writing these texts on the board, or simply saying or singing them, and getting us to repeat them. I therefore learned quite a lot of Shakespeare, even as a junior, and am still able to remember a huge repertoire of folk songs, and classical arias, which I learned initially from 78 rpm records! This kind of aural training therefore fits one to become a performer. I had to work extraordinarily hard and often in adverse conditions, however, to gain any *academic* learning. Yet Shakespeare never had any access to academic training at all. Perhaps, therefore, Shakespeare had a good enough aural memory to learn his lines. If he ever attended the Stratford school, then it is quite feasible that he could have become an actor. But he lacked even my own initially poor opportunities when it came to further and higher education, and I do not pretend to have had nearly enough background knowledge and talent to write like 'Shakespeare.' The Stratford boy would not have been trained in academic study, research, politics and literary writing. Neither would he have possessed, or had access to, the necessary books to teach himself these skills. I could at least turn on an electric light or torch to see my books, but how would Shakespeare even have afforded enough candles? Again, the myth exceeds all logical and historical explanation.

The discovery of Neville's political treatise is therefore extra 'good news' for his Shakespeare authorship, helping us along the trail of increasing, admissible evidence. The discovery of any document which can be definitely verified as coming from Neville's hand is exciting, because if Shakespeare was indeed Neville, then we should find parallels between the political ideas expressed in Neville's known writing and those expressed in the plays. We did indeed find these parallels and were also lucky enough to find overlapping linguistic evidence too.

But it must inevitably be the case that what stands as **admissible** evidence in *favour* of Sir Henry also stands as evidence *against* the authorship of William Shakespeare. I am aware that blowing away a myth always carries with it a certain trauma. Yet in this case the reality which replaces the myth brings with it a thrill too, as always happens in genuine research. It is also poignant to realise that justice is at last being performed for the true writer.

The emotional impact of the Stratford myth has been beguiling, even though unfounded on any hard evidence. He is a 'rags to riches' hero whose history is virtually invisible. It is almost as if his very invisibility has given him a mystical, magical status! We have nothing directly from the hand of the Stratford man, and no external evidence for him being either educated or a writer. His name does not even appear on the rolls of the Stratford Grammar School. The little documentation ever found about him, together with what his contemporaries wrote of William Shakespeare, the actor, as a man, conflicts strongly with the sensitivity and humanism expressed in the plays and poems. The *content* of the works proclaims a highly-educated, politically-experienced author. William Shakespeare was neither highly educated nor a politician. If he had been so, then it would have been documented and commented upon repeatedly during his lifetime. It is therefore a syllogistic argument that he was not the author and, consequently, that the name 'Shakespeare' was used by another, as a pseudonym. If one turns one's back on this fundamental kind of evidence, then one is in great danger of seeing the three-dimensional plays in two dimensions only: you undergo the experience but miss some important points regarding their meaning. How much better than studying the plays on their own is the enlightening experience of studying them against the background of the only man who has encrypted his name, connections and knowledge within the plays and poems, and whose life events help to clarify the works and the times in which they were written. We simply *have to* follow up such a unique, unpredicted, unprejudiced and exciting lead.

With Sir Henry, we find we do not need to fabricate his life and works beyond the grave, as is the case with Marlowe and the Earl of Oxford. Nor do we need to inject the author with a different style and different political opinions from those evidenced in the works, such as needs to be done if we try to insist that either the Earl of Oxford or Sir Francis Bacon was Shakespeare. In any case, looking for a chance sighting of the real Shakespeare among authors who had already published or written works under their own name was almost bound to lead up blind alleys. If the real Shakespeare had ever published anything under his own name, then he would have been more easily discovered. Only invisibility to the masses, accompanied by the obscure, complex cover of encoding and laying of 'in-house clues' for his friends, could have protected a politician and diplomat, while at the same time ensuring that his authorship might not be completely and permanently overlooked. Yet his known occupations meant that his words would be scrutinised for signs of disaffection or symbolic criticism of the state, had his true name been *openly* proclaimed. Only a pseudonym and a code could protect him from such over-zealous scrutiny by the government spies of the day. "On my frailties, why are frailer spies?" the author askes in sonnet 121. He was obviously a man who knew he was under surveillance, and such a man was therefore inevitably in a position of some importance to the state. Sir Henry Neville fits this description precisely, so it is not merely a flight of fancy which names him in the Dedication Code, and in that very sonnet, 121.[39]

In the last chapter of her book, *Ungentle Shakespeare*[40], Katherine Duncan-Jones advises us not to read any more books about William Shakespeare, the man, because nothing ties up. This logical train of thought carries a corollary, however. The initial discovery and consequent evidence for Henry Neville's authorship is so strong that we can sensibly follow his life and connections with the works, because *everything* ties up. Only if I had broken the code correctly, and only if the decryption had named the *true* writer, would everything interconnect so completely.

For example, besides encoding his name occasionally, the Shakespeare Sonnets also proclaim Neville's life and experiences.

For instance, we find repeated assertions that, because of some overwhelming yet hitherto uncharted shame, he fully accepts that his name can never be known. With Sir Henry Neville we know precisely what that 'shame' was: he was involved in the Earl of Essex's uprising and then imprisoned in the Tower of London alongside his friend, the Earl of Southampton, to whom all his poetry was dedicated. All this is explained in some detail in my previous books. Suffice it to repeat here that at the very moment of Sir Henry's imprisonment, the plays change in tone from historical chronicles and light comedies to some of the darkest tragedies ever written. The chronology of Neville's life experiences go hand in hand with the emergence of the plays. The combined weight of practical and textual evidence is truly irresistible. The reasons for his completely covert writing – and his 'shame' – are now investigated and understandable. The rest of this chapter will therefore consist of a voyage around the secrecy and politics of Shakespeare-Neville, fuelled by the Political document of his examined in Chapter 1.

The Politics of Secrecy
The political concerns of Neville's day were different from our own, and politics was at least as tricky and pragmatically-dictated a profession as it is now. It therefore helps to examine the circumstances prevailing in Elizabethan and Jacobean politics in order to appreciate further the impact and importance of Neville's Treatise.

Neville was a politician and the Shakespeare plays are highly political. Politics was a dangerous profession in Neville's day, so it was obviously important that he should not proclaim his identity too openly in any of his written output. Besides, he knew very well that some of the ideas in his plays would then be seen purely as political propaganda. (This has happened to the plays of Bertolt Brecht. Knowledge of their political connection is apt to prevent us from seeing the full humanism and humour in those plays.) Added to this, if Neville's authorship of the plays had been known during his lifetime, then his more controversial political metaphors within those plays stood a chance of being exaggerated or misconstrued by his enemies, especially by his *political* opponents. As we have seen, he finally expressed this fear of misconstruction, in Parliament itself.

Politics, myths, and the Shakespeare Plays

Discussion of political issues dominates the Shakespeare History Plays, and even the plays touching on less overtly political issues contain political messages. Nevertheless, the plethora of books purporting to be biographies of Shakespeare which emerged at the end of the twentieth century and in the beginning of the new millennium hardly carried any real analysis of the author's political outlook. This is largely explained by the fact that Shakespeare of Stratford had no known acquaintance with politics, so that discussion of the political issues within the plays could easily have undermined the raison d'etre behind the many fanciful 'lives' of the Bard. One or two excellent academic books have appeared, linking Shakespeare with Republicanism, and these are analyses of the politics of the era, quite rightly linking the content of the plays with their cultural circumstances.[41] Problems and contrivance emerge, however, if these otherwise excellent analysts try to link their cultural investigations with the *supposed* writer. Neville is indeed the only authorship contender absolutely *evidenced* to have possessed the type of political knowledge and opinions discovered by a cultural analysis of the plays.

Yet still the romantic, personalised myth of Shakespeare persists, and is unfortunately supported by some ungrounded statements. The curriculum and supposed standard of education within the poor little village grammar schools in Elizabethan England, for instance, are puffed up beyond their capabilities and beyond all historical evidence; the possibility that Shakespeare *might* have overheard politicians in discussion; that he *might* have been singled out to become friendly with aristocrats and to have used theirs and printers' libraries are ideas endlessly and unrealistically proposed in order to perpetuate the myth. Of course, there is an added unreality: in those days, none of these elevated and/or busy individuals would have stooped to impart their ideas and experiences to an actor, and would certainly have been careful not to let their utterances be accidentally overheard by such a man. Only someone with direct experience of all these restricted circles – and especially someone within the cut and thrust of political debate – would have dared to attempt to write about the noble families, the knights, barons, and the total political experience encapsulated in the history plays. Moreover, many of these plays must have been planned and written before Shakespeare ever left Stratford and began to seek his fortune.

His chances of coming to the notice of aristocrats and printers *before* he had written his first works were nil, and yet he would have needed the books contained exclusively in their libraries in order merely to begin thinking about his playwrighting enterprises! His whole situation was therefore a classic of the 'catch 22' variety. Such is the length and depth of knowledge within the very earliest plays that even a political 'insider' – with a background income to buy himself time away from everyday chores, and with all his libraries on tap – would have taken several years researching and planning the great *Henry VI* trilogy alone. This trilogy appears to have been written alongside poems too, together with early comedies and the great tragedy of *Titus Andronicus*. Additionally, it is probable that *King John* was also composed early in the writer's career, before the 1588 armada[42]. Altogether, then, the case for Shakespeare falls at the first hurdle: there is no explanation of his necessarily *early* personal wealth and access to this specialised knowledge; ergo his candidature to be anything other than a convenient pseudonym defies historical evidence and logical conclusion.

With Sir Henry, however, more evidence of interconnections between his life and the plays appears in every aspect of the Bard's work. I have now put one extra piece of evidence forward, in the form of his Political Declaration, which therefore deserves to be reflected upon again to see how it connects with strongly foregrounded issues in the plays.

Reflections on Neville's Political Thesis
Sir Henry's core concern in his political thesis is the relationship between King and Parliament, and he is advising the King and Parliament to work together.

Enmity between King and Parliament began mainly as a result of James I's wish to be an absolutist monarch, and Neville views both the King's point of view and the enmity itself as highly dangerous. As with many political concerns, however, there was also an *economic* element in the quarrel between James and Parliament. The King wished Parliament to grant him more money, and Parliament was resisting. There was good reason for their reticence. James gave lavish presents to his favourites – paid for out of the money granted him by Parliament – yet he tended to ignore some obvious needs of the country, and also to disregard those in Court and Parliament towards whom he felt less friendly. He also overlooked the situation of the poor, which clearly marks out Neville's comment that their needs "cannot be entirely ignored" as being bravely targeted at the King himself.

Neville had carried out private research and was able to quote precise figures to James, who, Neville declared, was the English King who had received more money from Parliament than any other monarch in history. (A notebook containing this precise financial research is to be found among the Worsley Manuscripts.) So, though wanting to promote harmony, Neville (under the disguise of anonymity) does not entirely pull his punches. He blames mainly the King for the growing enmity. But his wording is so careful that it directs the listener's attention beyond attributing personal blame and focuses it primarily on the dangers inherent in the situation itself. Then it issues advice as to how these dangers might be averted.

All this was therefore a brave attempt on Sir Henry's part to bring about peace at a time when relationships had broken down to such an extent that *other* MPs felt it necessary to side with either the King or Parliament, defending their decided stance vigorously instead of attempting to resolve the situation. They probably felt this was the only *safe* way of going about things. By being polarised, they would gain protection: either from the King, or from Parliament. To stand in the middle was to leave oneself vulnerable to attack from both sides. Even the cautious Robert Cecil had continued to shower public and private money on the King, in the hope that he would remain favourably disposed to him. Yet Sir Henry was brave enough and incorruptible enough to place himself right in the middle, attempting to bolster both sides of the argument, all the while knowing the possible consequences. He clearly felt it necessary to do so – not in his own interests but in the interests of the country as a whole. No wonder he only allowed his treatise to be read to Parliament **anonymously**. Yet this position of syncretism and reconciliation is precisely what is being advocated throughout the Shakespeare History plays and, par excellence, in *Romeo and Juliet,* **pseudonymously**. In hiding behind the pseudonym of William Shakespeare when writing his plays, Neville is showing the same caution as he did when producing his political thesis behind the cloak of anonymity.

Thus, the real Shakespeare was a selfless politician, first and foremost. So how do we move away from the Shakespeare myths and attempt to enter the authorship debates and politics of the 16th century, as if we were actually there at the time? It is always easier to understand a historical point if we pose a possible contemporary example. What if, for instance, our own lifetimes had been as dangerous for political insiders as it was in the 16th and 17th centuries? Well, then surely that excellent political series of books and television dramas, *House of Cards,* would have been presented under a pseudonym too. If, however, *House of Cards* had claimed to be written by a known actor – moreover, an actor known not to have come through any academic training or to have been even vaguely involved with politics – would we not all be unwilling to trust such a pretence? We might very well indulge in a guessing game, trying to imagine who the true author might be. We might easily come to all the wrong conclusions before perhaps discovering that the author had actually encoded his own name somehow, somewhere, more than once, and that that name really linked up with the specialist knowledge encapsulated in the series. The reason we do *not* question the authorship of *House of Cards* is because the named author is *known* to have been a political 'aide'. We find it obvious that a huge amount of *inside* knowledge is essential if a writer embarks on a play set at the top of English State politics, even in this technological age, when information is so much easier to come by. In the age of Shakespeare, then – an age with no such easy access to information – how was an unknown, politically-inexperienced youngster ever going to be able to embark on a set of political plays?

It can therefore be readily understood just why no *informed* contemporary of Shakespeare would really have believed in the Shakespeare pseudonym. In those class-ridden, private, socially-exclusive days, perhaps few would have commented on these authorship problems in print; the whole thing would have been so obvious that many educated people would have smiled, chatted about it – just taken it for granted that everyone who was anyone knew some amusing deception was going on. Most of them would probably have been afraid of the consequences of guessing wrongly too. To offend a powerful man in those times carried even more risks than it does today.

Moreover, one must explain the *standpoint* from which these 16th and 17th century political opinions given in the plays emanates. When we look at the works of Shakespeare in their political context we note that they were written at a time when England was emerging from the Medieval notion of the total dominance of Kings and Barons into a political world in which a new class of governmental ministers and administrators was taking shape. These administrators were usually drawn from within the feudal structure, but they also called on intelligent personnel from the merchant classes to join and assist them. Even the dictatorial King Henry VIII often had to battle with the red tape which this rising system produced. Any monarch was consequently having to adapt his or her own ideas to fit in with the newly-emerging governmental structure. If he did not adapt, then he faced the possibility of civil war breaking out again. It was a structure of reform which had come about primarily as a reaction to the slaughter, social unrest and economic disasters caused by the dynastic struggles at the core of the Wars of the Roses.

It is therefore significant that even the earliest of Shakespeare's plays – *Titus Andronicus* – has a guarded political message at its heart which inevitably leads the audience to conclude that the new, corporate ministerial government is better than the overwhelming power wielded by squabbling individual monarchs and dynasties. It is this new corporate administration which laid the foundation of 'the State.' The most likely person behind the Shakespeare authorship was therefore bound to have been someone supporting the new politics of the day – and also someone actually working in that field.

Promotion of the new, administrative order fits in with the very *genre* of the Revenge Plays. The horrendous cruelty depicted in these plays, as in Shakespeare's *Titus,* is, at root, a warning of what can happen if powerful individuals are left without the overarching power of the State to check their actions. In this sense, Titus Andronicus and his rivals are dynastic strugglers on the same level as those in the Wars of the Roses. This early play therefore uses the displacement of place and time to mask its main message: that all should now accept and welcome the new ministerial government of State rather than resorting to personal vengeance and violence as a way of sorting out arguments, at either the political or personal level. The true writer of *Titus* is fully aware that as soon as one accepts the dominance of the State with its lawmaking machinery, one devolves personal arguments and group injustices onto the State, leaving the State to sort things out. This necessitates *recognising* the State as an arbitrator in all disputes.

The concerns of *Titus Andronicus* are therefore the concerns of a politician. Only a few aristocrats of the time, however – mainly the Earls of Essex, Southampton and Pembroke – were willing to accept this new kind of law whole-heartedly, and only they were willing to negotiate with the House of Commons in order to support it. The Earl of Oxford, for instance – besides dying eleven years before many of the Shakespeare plays were written – was not politically progressive. Nor was he sympathetic in his attitude to women. On these scores alone, therefore, it is extremely unlikely that he wrote the plays. (A concern for women was another *basic* theme of the Shakespeare plays, right from *Titus Andronicus* onwards.)

At the time, a sympathetic attitude to women and a respect for their intelligence and potential was almost a political point in itself, and this was expressed in all the early plays. The Earl of Oxford treated his wife badly, and Shakespeare of Stratford never saw to it that his daughters were even taught to read and write. Neville, on the other hand, was a loving, understanding husband and father. His wife was the daughter of one of the Cooke ladies – reputedly the five most educated women in England – and he himself expressed his wish to do the best for his own daughters.[43] Eventually, he even allowed one of his daughters to marry his manservant, which clearly expresses a sympathy towards women's wishes, even when they went against his own financial advantage. Daughters were usually seen as possible 'currency' at the time, to be married off to rich husbands, and the Neville girls were all eligible, in every respect. Many families wished to be connected with the Nevilles, yet even these considerations did not persuade Sir Henry to wed his daughter to a man for whom she had no liking. Once again, Neville is just the then rare kind of man who can feasibly and reasonably be seen as the author of those 'Shakespeare' plays in which women in love almost invariably get their way, or else (like Juliet) die in the attempt.

The general and immediately-recognisable political standpoint of Shakespeare's plays stems from a view of kingship and personal power *moderated* by the new politics of Parliament and the State administrators. Neville was a firm supporter of this developing ministerial, reformed government, and he thoroughly understood its implications too. Yet in supporting the new politics Neville never lost his respect for the monarch, nor for pageantry, nor for any *positive, cohesive* achievements of feudalism. He was therefore the man with the precise yet syncretic opinions expressed (however covertly) even in the *early* plays.

Having established these logical conclusions, one can focus in on the political opinions implied in the plays, without being hampered by an unwieldy authorial image. One problem when analysing any plays for their political opinion, however, is that the writer is necessarily speaking in character. Thus, if he writes speeches for a character who has one particular point of view, he must express that outlook, even if it is different from his own. True, there are ways in which the author can signal whether he approves of any particular outlook or not, but this is not always easy to tease out of the seemingly-ambivalent plays of Shakespeare. The writer is skilled enough to lead us down several garden paths before he brings out his real conclusions, and I think *Troilus and Cressida* is a brilliantly experimental play which poses seemingly logical political opinions, set against *events* which undermine those very standpoints. We are therefore forced to admit that the true writer had enough experience of politics to understand and present the arguments on both sides of any political question he raised. The writer's skill in finally letting events speak for themselves, with the echoes of various opinions still ringing in listeners' ears, also betrays the skill of a politician who wishes to initiate further discussion.

The History Plays place the Nevilles in a good light, even when the chronicles sometimes position them negatively. The Nevilles are often also identified with a 'good' cause, or even given an actual physical presence in the plays, when, in reality, they were not associated with the issue in hand, and never chronicled as having been so. Neville's pseudonymous writing consequently becomes palpable and even amusing, when one knows the truth. The author of the Treatise and the plays wanted the works to be judged solely on their merits, with no reference to the real person behind them. Neville clearly wanted his plays and his political policies to appear as if they were part of a natural and inevitable development, not expressions of a merely *Nevillian* standpoint. Neither did he wish them to be perceived as stemming from *any* factional interest whatsoever. Placing his name on either his Treatise or his plays, therefore, would have destroyed this overall aim. In 'Shakespeare,' we have a virtually unknown quantity who never even wrote letters and appeared only very occasionally on stage. Because William's background would accord neither with the image of a playwright, nor with the knowledge encapsulated within the plays, Neville could be pretty sure no one – during his own lifetime – would connect them with the name at their head. Even the educated section of the audience would therefore have no prejudices associated with their authorial image. Sir Henry and the Nevilles were, on the contrary, well known, and either loved or hated. No wonder he did not wish his name be associated with any writing he produced. The very fact that he was so well known also makes it reasonable to infer that he may have been afraid that both the writing style and opinions within his Treatise might be discovered as uncannily parallel to those of the 'unknown' Shakespeare, had it been read out under his name.

Neville's declared answer to M.P.s who questioned his policy of anonymity also reveals a further and constant worry of his: he did not know into whose hands his writing might fall.[44] This was undoubtedly a true statement of one of Neville's main, additional concerns: his intentions could be purposely warped by others. This had indeed happened, as evidenced on at least one previous occasion. Following the Gunpowder Plot, Neville had offered some advice on subsequent precautions which might help prevent another such terrorist action. However, Robert Cecil misconstrued some of Neville's recommendations, yet still proceeded to present these recommendations to Parliament, as stemming from Sir Henry. "Thus are my good intentions clean perverted," complained Neville in a private letter.[45] This must have been one incident which confirmed his decision to attempt 'invisibility' in his political writing, just as he had in his writing of the plays, even though it was not the only reason for his pseudonymity.[46]. One of the consequences of his possible illegitimacy, for instance, should it be discovered, was that his family might have been disinherited. Had the spotlight been turned too strongly in his direction then the secret may have surfaced.

As evidence that Neville was technically illegitimate, we have the following circumstance. Neville's parents were married 'in settlement' at St. Margaret's, Lothbury, in 1568. Now, not only had our Neville been born in 1562, but the word 'settlement' then had a specific legal meaning. Until the married woman's property Act of 1870, a woman had to pass on all her property to her husband when she married – *unless,* that is, there had been a marriage 'in settlement.'[47] Under this arrangement, the woman's property and inheritances passed to her children, not to her husband, though he could hold her property in trust if she died while the children were under the age of majority. This happened in the case of Henry Neville senior. There is no possibility of Elizabeth Gresham and he having married sooner, because the 'settlement' agreement had to be in place before the wedding could happen.

From correspondence held in the archives of Longleat House, however, it seems that Henry Neville senior and Elizabeth Gresham had been expecting this settlement to happen for some time before 1562.[48] Yet they could not actually get married until everything had been agreed, which did not happen until 1568. However faithful to each other Henry and Elizabeth may have been, therefore, any children born prior to 1568 were not legitimate and could not be truly legitimated under the then laws. This explains why our Henry Neville was born at Blackfriars not Billingbear, (where his father was a well known Lord of the Manor) and also why young Henry was baptised at St. Annes Blackfriars. This church was served only by the occasional itinerant vicar, because there was an ongoing dispute about whether the Church or the Office of the Revels owned it. Itinerant vicars were less likely to demand complete documentary evidence, as they clearly only had a short stay in which to perform all their necessary duties. (See also *Henry Neville and the Shakespeare Code*.)

Yet however confused the Gresham–Neville marriage 'settlement' may have been, it was obviously legally binding: Lady Gresham (mother of Neville's deceased wife, Elizabeth,) wrote and complained when Neville senior announced his intention to marry Elizabeth Bacon-Doyly four years after her own daughter's death. Lady Frances, then, wrote to Sir J. Thynne "on the desire of 'Mr. Nevell'" [Henry Neville, of Billingbeare, her son in law] to marry "Lady Doyle my Lord keppers dafter," thus breaking the promise he made to her and her deceased daughter in order to provide a jointure.[49] This suggests that Neville senior may have proposed to give Lady Doyly some of Elizabeth Gresham's property which, in law, he held as a trustee only. This was to cause friction between our Henry and his step mother following his father's death.

Added to this enormous reason for our Henry Neville's reluctance to enter the spotlight with anything he wrote, the times were demonstrably harsh. John Stubbe – a contemporary writer – had his right hand chopped off in public as a punishment in 1579 for daring to write down his opinions concerning the possible marriage of Queen Elizabeth to a French Catholic prince. Neville's own grandfather had been executed for supposed involvement in a political plot, and this man's open nature and voiced opinions were factors that contributed to his downfall. I have now found the grandfather's real-life acquaintances and experiences to be curiously echoed and characterised in one or two of the early History Plays of Shakespeare, as will be detailed later in this book. This definitely shows that Sir Henry Neville studied the whole background to his grandfather's execution. And the story of Neville's grandfather begins with his acting, singing and composing of (often comic) poetry, so one immediately begins to see how even the *young* Henry Neville absorbed lessons from his own family history. There is therefore a sense in which Sir Henry Neville's habitual secrecy – through multiple causes – was so deeply grounded that it became second nature to him. When mentioning him in correspondence, friends sometimes said that he would finish his statements by saying 'but that's a secret.'[50]

Neville's secret and the Politics of Ancient Greece
Even without its original context being immediately displayed, the inscription on his portrait – 'everywhere without visible signs' – tells us that Neville intended part of his life to remain beyond public view. But to know the context of this quotation is to begin to understand the conflict that must have existed between Neville's need for invisibility and the necessity of creating a recognisably-educated provenance for his works. The words on the portrait are from the Greek historian, Thucydides: "The whole earth is the tomb of heroic men, and their story is not graven only on stone over their clay, but abides **everywhere; without visible signs**, woven into the stuff of other men's lives." Thucydides reports these words as being part of a funeral oration given by Pericles. This quotation and its writer were chosen carefully by Neville, because Pericles was both a politician *and* a promoter of arts and literature. The passage from Pericles alluded to on Neville's portrait is therefore just as relevant to a playwright as to a politician. A playwright leaves us with images of 'heroic men' whose story is thereby not merely 'graven on stone'. Knowledge of these heroes – mediated by playwrights and enacted by the players – inevitably becomes "woven into the stuff of other men's lives." It is therefore reasonable to conclude that one 'invisible' side of Neville's life was his writing of the plays, since everyone *knew* he was a politician.

Neville was known by his friends as being able to disguise, to act a part, to produce work anonymously, to hold private 'readings' and discussions and, ultimately, to be involved in secret plotting with the Earls of Essex and Southampton. But as he was also a 'straight' politician, it must have been difficult for anyone to say that they truly knew him. Thucydides' rendering of Pericles' cryptic and encrypted words are therefore aptly quoted on Neville's portrait, and if we examine both Pericles and Thucydides, his chronicler, we are led along a path of parallels between their ideas and those of Sir Henry Neville. The inscription on his portrait was anything but *randomly* chosen. In his political Treatise, Neville cites examples from ancient Greek politics, so it is certainly fitting to investigate some of the elements in ancient-world affairs of state that clearly influenced Neville. The portrait's inscription affords us our strongest clue and our starting point. The strong yet sometimes lightly-concealed influence of Greek ideas on the Shakespeare plays will be referenced frequently within this book.

Pericles (c.495 – 429 BC) and Thucydides (c. 460 B.C. – c.395 BC)

Thucydides named Pericles as the 'first citizen of Athens', and his assessment was based on Pericles' leadership in both peace and war. Both men's political philosophy was influential, their lives well documented; and their works would have been known to Renaissance, University-educated Elizabethans. Henry Neville and his tutor, Henry Savile, had been in Venice in 1581, selecting works among the shiploads of ancient Greek documents which were then being distributed in that city. Thus, Neville would have encountered the works of Thucydides.

In war, Pericles was unrelenting in defence of Athens, his ideal city-state, and in peace time he promoted the arts so resolutely that, through his efforts, Athens became the cultural centre of the ancient Greek world. He was the instigator of the building of the Parthenon, whose construction provided work for the people and became an inspirational foundation piece of the beautiful city, which in turn stimulated further artistic creativity. During his own lifetime, Pericles was indeed called a populist for promoting the welfare and aesthetic aspirations of the people. Similarly, Neville himself became leader of the popular party during King James I's reign. Neither can it be purely coincidental that Neville took yet another lesson from Pericles: Sir Henry became a main shareholder in, and promoter of, the New River project. This brought a much needed water supply to the citizens of North London, and also – as with the building of the Parthenon – provided civic work for men thrown off the rapidly-declining aristocratic estates. (Incidentally, a poem was recited publicly by the workmen at a celebration for the completion of the project. One wonders who wrote it!)

Pericles saw to it that the great funeral oration (reported by Thucydides and proclaiming Pericles' political philosophy) was given in the Theatre of Dionysus. This was the place in which all the people of Athens would assemble for theatrical presentations. In just the same way, Shakespeare/Neville intermingled aesthetic and political feeling by having his plays presented in the new London theatres, which men and women of all classes could attend. (For those who felt themselves above such venues, or were afraid of the dirt and disease there, the plays were still performed in private venues too, so their appeal and influence was certainly universal.) The Shakespeare plays synthesised Neville's examination of monarchical and political motivation, as well as promoting social cohesion. The parallels between Neville and Pericles therefore become so meaningful that one can begin to understand the import of the clues left by the painter of Neville's portrait.

Neville's practical realisation of Pericles' ideas
In his *History of the Peloponnesian War, Book 2* Thucydides records Pericles' speech and political philosophy. Fourteen years after his portrait was painted, Sir Henry Neville also wrote a political treatise, which bears many similarities to the ideas Pericles put forward, through Thucydides, his chronicler. Thucydides recognised that absolute power corrupts absolutely, which parallels Neville's attempt to stem King James I's progress towards absolute monarchy. Even before his Treatise was presented to Parliament, Neville was already privately asking the King to give an ear to the Commons, thus bringing ancient Greek theories to bear on his own times. The history plays of Shakespeare are imbued with the same circumstances as those addressed in Neville's Treatise: kingship in crisis; King at loggerheads with the country's representatives. Through all this, the Nevilles in the plays are trying to steer the King through, just as Sir Henry Neville was trying to steer King James I. Pericles, Prince of Tyre, was not the same Pericles quoted in the portrait inscription, but one wonders if the coincidence of naming was toyed with by Shakespeare-Neville when he wrote his famous, esoterically-symbolistic play.

As Neville encountered Thucydides' and Pericles' ideas *before* writing his own political treatise, I shall quote some of

Pericles' speech. [The extract is taken from *History of the Peloponnesian War, Book 2*, by Thucydides, translated by Richard Crawley]:

> Our constitution does not copy the laws of neighbouring states; we are rather a pattern to others than imitators ourselves. Its administration favours the many instead of the few; this is why it is called a democracy. If we look to the laws, they afford equal justice to all in their private differences; ... class considerations not being allowed to interfere with merit. Nor again does poverty bar the way – if a man is able to serve the state, he is not hindered by the obscurity of his condition. The freedom which we enjoy in our government extends also to our ordinary life. ...

(As seen in the Memorandum attached to his Treatise, Neville too expressed concern about laws and a man's access to them.)

My next chosen extract illustrates how Pericles, like Shakespeare/Neville, saw entertainment as playing an important role in civic life:

> Further, we provide plenty of means for the mind to refresh itself from business. We celebrate games and sacrifices all the year round, and the elegance of our private establishments forms a daily source of pleasure and helps to banish the spleen; while the magnitude of our city draws the produce of the world into our harbour, so that to the Athenian the fruits of other countries are as familiar a luxury as those of his own.

No wonder Neville had a pointer from this speech encoded on his portrait! Not only does Pericles' perfect city state interweave politics and entertainment; it also brings in mention of international trading, in which Neville himself had been involved up to the very moment the portrait was painted.

Just like Thucydides, however, Neville did not confuse Grecian-style democracy with mob rule. Fear of mob rule is decidedly conveyed in the portrayal of Jack Cade's rebellion in *Henry VI, part 2*. In the same way, Thucydides always felt democracy should be 'administered' in the hands of a good leader.[51] For both Thucydides and Neville, a good leader was not an absolutist monarch.

Neville's political treatise, and *Plato Redivivus*

Unlike the plays, Neville's political treatise did not have a pseudonymous cover. It was produced anonymously, the consequence of which was that all the MPs present at its reading began to discuss its possible authorship. An actor's name on the *plays*, however, ensured there would be fewer questions about their true authorship, at least as far as the wider, uneducated public was concerned. There was no way of pinning down the Shakespeare pseudonym, with any certainty, unless you were the privileged member of a very small circle. Neville himself was firmly located within a very tight political net. His wife was a favourite cousin of Robert Cecil, Secretary of State, and his father had been one of Lord Burghley's best friends. This meant that if these 'top men' wished a secret to be kept, then there was very little hope of anyone except this small, privileged group ever daring to talk about it, except in whispers or in writing cloaked with artistic symbolism.

Then, later, history repeated itself. The propensity for secret writing within the Neville family continued, for Henry Neville's grandson – also called Henry Neville – was an 'invisible' writer too. Again, the necessity for secrecy was thrust upon him by the dangerous times, and by the fact that he was from this same, high-profile, erstwhile royal, family of Neville.

Despite this noble background, Henry Neville, the grandson, was a republican who had fought on the Parliamentary side during the Civil War. He wrote (anonymously) many political treatises, satires and poems, but the political tract in which he actually mentions his grandfather also has Greek overtones: it is entitled *Plato Redivivus*. The whole work is a fascinating read, delving into the history of political and social structures, and – like *Leicester's Commonwealth* – is written in the form of a dialogue. It was sent to the publisher anonymously, because its ideas must have been so challenging for the times The author obviously speaks with some true knowledge of what really happened to his grandfather, for our Neville is revealed as being secretly involved in 'undertaking' for many years. Here is the passage in which the grandson tells of his grandfather's impeachment [prosecution], which was never recorded in the Parliamentary journal. [A GENTLEMAN is speaking to a VENETIAN representative; I have italicised the points which greatly echo Henry Neville's, grandfather's 'Political Treatise']:

GENT ... but now that many of the lords, (like the bishops which the popes make at Rome in heathen lands,) are merely grown titular; and purchased for nothing but to get their wives' place; it cannot be wondered at if the king slight their addresses, and the court-parasites deride their honourable undertakings for the safety of their country. Now the commons succeeding ... have inherited likewise, according to the course of nature, their power: but being kept from it by the established government, (which not being changed by any lawful acts of state, remains still in being formally, whereas virtually it is abolished) so that for want of outward orders and provisions, the people are kept from the exercise of that power, which is fallen to them by the law of nature: ... but however, are altogether unquiet and restless in the intervals of parliament; and when the king pleases to assemble one, spend all their time in complaints of the inexecution of the law; of the multiplication of an infinity of grievances; of misspending the public monies; of the danger our religion is in by practices to undermine it and the state, by endeavours to bring in arbitrary power; and in questioning great officers of state, as the causes and promoters of all these abuses: *in so much, that every parliament seems a perfect state of war;* ... So that the court sends them packing; and governs still worse and worse in the vacancies, being necessitated thereunto by their despair of doing any good in parliament; and therefore are forced to use horrid shifts to subsist without it, and to keep it off: *without ever considering, that if these counsellors understood their trade, they might bring the prince and people to such an agreement in parliament, as might repair the broken and shipwrecked government of England; and in this secure the peace, quiet and prosperity of the people, the greatness and happiness of the king, and be themselves not only out of present danger, (which no other course can exempt them from,) but be renowned to all posterity.*

NOBLE VEN. I beseech you, sir, how comes it to pass, that neither the king, nor any of his counsellors could ever come to find out the truth of what you discourse? for I am fully convinced it is as you say.

ENG. GENT. I cannot resolve you that; but this is certain, they have never endeavoured a cure, though possibly they might know the disease: ... possibly, such a reformation might not consist with the merchandize they make of the prince's favour; nor with such bribes, gratuities and fees as they usually take for the dispatch of all matters before them. *And therefore our counsellors have been* *so far from suggesting any such thing [*i.e. the King ruling in partnership with Parliament*] to their master, that they have opposed and quashed all attempts of that kind: as they did the worthy proposals made by certain members of that parliament in the beginning of king James's reign, which is yet called the undertaking parliament. These gentlemen considering what we have been discoursing of, viz. that our old government is at an end; had framed certain heads [*suggestions for discussion*], which, if they had been proposed by that parliament to the king, and by him consented to, would, in their opinion, have healed the breach [between King and Parliament]: and that if the king would perform his part, that house of commons would undertake for the obedience of the people. They did believe that if this should have been moved in parliament before the king was acquainted with it, it would prove abortive; and therefore sent three of their number to his majesty: sir James Croft, grandfather or father to the present bishop of Hereford; Thomas Harley, who was ancestor to the honourable family of that name in Herefordshire; and sir Henry Neville, who had been ambassador from queen Elizabeth to the French king. These were to open the matter at large to the king, and to procure his leave that it might be proposed in parliament: which, after a very long audience and debate, that wise prince consented to; with a promise of secrecy in the meantime, which they humbly begged of his majesty. However, this took vent; and the earl of Northampton, of the house of Howard, (who ruled the roost in that time) having knowledge of it, engaged sir R. Weston, afterwards lord treasurer and earl of Portland, to impeach these undertakers in parliament, before they could move their matters: which he did the very same day; accompanying his charge (which was endeavouring to alter the established government of England) with so eloquent an invective, that if one of them had not risen, and made the house acquainted with the whole series of the affair, they must have been in danger of being impeached by the commons, but however it broke their design, which was all that Northampton and Weston desired; and prevented posterity from knowing any of the particulars of this reformation: for nothing being moved, nothing could remain upon the journal.*

So here we are intriguingly presented with a somewhat new scenario regarding the background to our Sir Henry's attempts at reforming Parliament: his grandson says the initial negotiations took place at the *beginning* of James' reign. This means that Neville might well have been (secretly) impeached before the publication of the Shakespeare *Sonnets*. This, in turn, means that we have yet another explanation for Neville not wishing to name openly his dedicatee of those Sonnets. It also explains a number of the *angry* sonnets, and especially sonnet 125, which actually mentions being impeached:

> Were't aught to me I bore the canopy,
> With my extern the outward honouring,
> Or laid great bases for eternity,
> Which proves more short than waste or ruining?
> Have I not seen dwellers on form and favour
> Lose all, and more, by paying too much rent,
> For compound sweet forgoing simple savour,
> Pitiful thrivers in their gazing spent?
> No, let me be obsequious in thy heart,
> And take thou my oblation, poor but free,
> Which is not mixed with seconds, knows no art
> But mutual render, only me for thee.
> Hence, thou suborned informer! A true soul
> When most impeached stands least in thy control.

Thus there are multiple reasons for our particular Neville wishing to keep his political treatise secret. But on this occasion, he failed to do so, both in the short, and the long, term. After all, by 1613 Robert Cecil was dead, and Neville had few such powerful friends in the new Jacobean regime to protect his 'secretive' interests. True, Sir Ralph Winwood, Neville's firm friend, was now Secretary of State, but he did not possess the power of the Cecils nor the towering intellect of Sir Henry. Indeed, King James I probably chose Winwood as his Secretary of State instead of the popular choice – Sir Henry Neville himself – because he was able to manipulate him to a certain extent. Neville, however, structured much of Secretary Winwood's work himself (as some of his closer political allies knew well.[52]) When it came to the relationship between James I and Sir Henry Neville, therefore, it was never quite clear from one moment to the next who was manipulating whom. James went to Neville for private advice on his own writing, and for a straightforward, honest opinion on most matters, so in these respects he was reluctant to lose Neville from his everyday world. Besides, James' son and heir, Prince Henry, formed a close relationship with Neville. After all, the poor boy did not find much of a role model in his own vain, sometimes violent, always sexually-confused father. Young Prince Henry even called for Neville when he was on his tragically-early deathbed. He confided to him that he thought he might be dying young because he had allowed himself to be persuaded to consider marrying a Catholic![53] Thus we know that, in real life, Neville was as able to approach the heir apparent as was his joking alter-ego, Falstaff. Although the Falstaff plays were written before Prince Henry came to England, it was nevertheless as if the true writer was saying "I am someone who *knows* that it is possible for knights from certain families to be able to contact the King." When it comes to the relationship between Falstaff and Prince Hal, we are left hanging for a while before we discover that Prince Hal is in control. But it is nevertheless in the Falstaff plays that Neville revealed his identity to his own private circle. He (Neville), the true author, was jokingly manipulating Falstaff in the plays just as assuredly as Prince Hal was manipulating him too. The linguistic means by which he revealed his authorship during this clever, double manipulation will be revealed in chapter four. This involves an intricate set of circumstances, which Neville clearly delighted in creating, both in his concealed works and in his own life.

Neville's complete disguise: revisiting some previous evidence and mingling it with the new
When viewed through the historical perspective of the times, the Shakespeare works were at least controversial, always reformatory, and sometimes even revolutionary in their inferences. The assumption that the author wished to disguise himself is therefore logical. In *Henry VIII*, for instance, does the playwright guide us to sympathise with the establishment figures of the King and Wolsey, or with Buckingham, the rebel? In *Richard II*, are we led to favour that king, or to cheer for Henry Bolingbroke, the usurper? The evidence is there – the true writer certainly had an anti-establishment streak in him. As I shall show later, most historians of the time had narrated some *favourable* points concerning all these historical figures implicitly disparaged by Shakespeare. This clearly demonstrates that the true author was making a personal choice. Firstly, he was choosing less available references which favoured his own point of view; and secondly, he was slanting history and references towards his personal opinions. At the time, the point of view he chose could be seen as threatening the status quo. To have declared his true identity, therefore, would have meant a swift end to *all* Sir Henry Neville's activities! No reforming politician, and especially one stemming from an establishment

family viewed as rival dynasts, could afford to reveal his authorship.

Speculation and wishful thinking have often branded 'Shakespeare' as an *establishment* man, bolstering the old feudal order. But this assessment is rather sweepingly romantic: it only partially accords with the Shakespeare texts. Richard II is deposed on stage, and the usurper is validated, for instance. Over and over again this one message is repeated in the History Plays: the feudal framework should remain intact but change and reform within that framework becomes inevitable and essential. The idea that reform, and even rebellion, can therefore be justified (albeit *only* when conducted by educated men) was a dangerous one. It is not an opinion which a politician from the Neville family would like to have circulated under his own name. Yet in Sir Henry Neville we have a politician who was involved in a rebellion in real life, even though reluctantly and passively. Couple this with the fact that Neville was so unexpectedly and unpredictably named when I decrypted the code contained in the Dedication to Shakespeare's *Sonnets*, and we at last have *concrete* evidence on which to base further investigation of the Authorship Question. As Conan-Doyle said, "Circumstantial evidence is occasionally very convincing, as when you find a trout in the milk, to quote Thoreau's example ..."[54], and my decipherment certainly bears analogy to that 'trout'. Thoreau used it as an example because it was definitely not what one would expect to find there. However, there had been suspicion that some dairymen were watering down milk, so Thoreau always suspected he might find some kind of evidence for this one day. The only way the trout could have got into the milk was if the dairyman was not only actually watering it down, but also using *unclean* water! The evidence was unexpected, yet at the same time convincing. In the same way, the Code's revelation of Neville's name is *doubly* convincing in that even though it was unexpected, it is at the same time concordant with many Shakespearean phenomenae which had never been linked together before in peoples' minds and yet were always interlocked in reality.

Neville was always afraid of his authorship being widely uncovered during his lifetime: his greatest defence when he was accused of involvement with the Essex rebellion was that he had been innocently drawn into something he never knew was an actual plot. Had his authorship of the History Plays (and especially of *Richard II*) been known then this defence would have been completely blown away. He must indeed have been glad that he had decided to remain an 'invisible' author, though the total weight of evidence for his authorship certainly adds up within the clues and investigative information which appeared during my initial research, (as detailed in my previous two books.) Yet one has to dig for all this evidence, and the digging isn't easy.

One must now inevitably ask and answer the question, "How is it that such a great man could lie for centuries almost forgotten by history?" I think the best way of understanding this is to consider the recent sad death of the American diplomat, Richard Holbrooke. Holbrooke had worked in the background for years in the diplomatic service, rectifying injustices and instituting humanitarian solutions. He was seen as 'second rank' among those involved in politics, but his life nevertheless demonstrates how such seeming second rankers can become prime movers, just as was the case with Neville. Richard Holbrooke, for instance was the man whose humanism initiated and pushed through the settlement of many of the Vietnam Boat People in America. In the same way, Henry Neville was 'second rank' when it came to political office, but it was nevertheless he – not the hierarchy – who initiated the re-integration of wrongly-ousted men, such as Paget, into English society. It was Henry Neville too who kept alive 'on the ground' negotiations with the Scots, prior to the death of Queen Elizabeth, for he used his time in France to make contacts, even friends, amongst them. Without his good offices, therefore, it is entirely possible that the Succession Question (a subject the living, childless Elizabeth forbade to be mentioned) may not have been settled in such a smooth manner. It was Henry Neville who kept the Scots sympathetic to his own humanistic, political, social and Protestant way of thinking, suspecting that it would be a Scottish ruler who took over the key position as monarch, once Queen Elizabeth was dead. In just the same way as Richard Holbrooke, therefore, Henry Neville became a 'prime mover' in global terms; yet he was not celebrated, or put into the front rank of famous men by later English historians, because he personally never held high office.

Looking for the humanistic philosophy of Shakespeare among the ranks of those already famed was therefore probably always doomed to failure. These leading, titled men were often ruthless and bound by their office, or by their known works, or their front-line positions. It should surely then come as no surprise that the Dedication Code led to a man who was not famed and –

from the point of view of many mainstream, 'great man' theorists – 'second rank.' It is in this 'second rank' that we find our humanists. Moreover, the Henry Neville solution to the Code ties in with the fact that the writer of the Shakespeare *Sonnets* claimed more than once that he knew his name would die with him and not be remembered. Neville certainly knew the ways of the world and the tendencies of mainstream historians!

More, solid, evidence of many types has now emerged for Sir Henry. Various unique circumstances may have dictated that no other pseudonym has been so persistent as Shakespeare's, yet mere *persistence* and popular mediation of a belief are no signposts of its truth, especially when they are clung to in the face of all evidence to the contrary.

Only the brashest and bravest contemporaries of 'Shakespeare'– like the extraverts, Robert Greene and the vituperative Joseph Hall – dared put their ideas concerning the Shakespeare Authorship into print; though whispering behind hands there must surely have been a-plenty. Some extant evidence for such whispering will indeed be presented in chapter four.

Such whisperers knew too that the true writer would leave just one or two pointers behind him, so they were always on the lookout for these buried signs. It was a kind of Elizabethan and Jacobean game. The detective story had not yet been invented, but mankind has always had a basic love of mysteries and investigations. My book will therefore go on to chart more **new** investigations and also uncover more clues from the 16th and 17th centuries in the form of contextual and documentary evidence. The weight of evidence then speaks for itself, and the light that Sir Henry Neville's presence sheds on Shakespeare's works helps to explain areas of the texts previously glossed over, and even sometimes omitted from the supposedly 'complete' BBC recordings of the plays. Part Two of my book therefore also examines some of the most obscure, puzzling and hitherto unexplained passages in the Shakespeare canon and shows how knowledge of Neville's authorship explains them at last.

Revisiting the Worsley Collection
The Nevilles had always possessed a boisterous, playful side, and Sir Henry was no exception. Keeping a great secret yet leaving clues and a difficult conundrum was typical of him. Some of the new documentary evidence I discovered has been so wide-

ranging and/or fragmentary that I have had to visit and revisit it again and again, which was a situation surely intended by this man of mystery.

In tracing part of the Worsley Collection back to Sir Henry's possession, I had the help of two different kinds of clues. Firstly, I found that his second daughter married Richard Worsley of Appledurcombe House, Isle of Wight. Richard had a large library which his heirs kept intact and added to until the direct male line died out at the beginning of the 19th century. The house was then inherited by a great niece. She married the Earl of Yarborough and took some of the contents of Appledurcombe library up to the Yorkshire/Lincolnshire border, where her husband lived at Brocklesby Park.

The 16th to 17th century Worsley documents were presented to the Lincolnshire Archives in the 1950s, with no note of their origins. However, my second clue towards the identity of the first owner of this part of the Worsley collection came in a letter now in the Berkshire Record Office. This letter was from one Richard Brooke, the husband of Neville's oldest daughter, stating that Neville had produced a 'Book of Knights' Fees', which was compiled and edited by a 'Mr. Downes'. Lo and behold, I found this very book in the Worsley collection at the Lincolnshire Archives, with its note from 'Downes' still present. In this same collection there was also a book on the Royal Mint, written by Richard Martin, a friend of Neville's. The scribe who had copied this book also signed it: it was none other than Neville's personal scribe, John Packer.

These books were placed together with copies of *Leicester's Commonwealth,* in which there were pertinent annotations about the Wars of the Roses, and which included a very telling feature: the name 'Neville' was emboldened every time it appeared in the text. Alongside all this was 'The Tower Notebook', containing annotations relevant to the Shakespeare plays. [Once again, a fuller account of my discovery is given in *Henry Neville and the Shakespeare Code,* and in *The Truth Will Out,* while I also make further reference to a number of these documents during the course of this book.]

However, it is in the nature of ongoing research that one discovers more about the clues themselves as time goes on. I had at first thought that the 'Mr. D[o]wnes' who compiled and edited Neville's 'Book of Knights' Fees' might have been John Donne, with whom Neville spoke at after-dinner events in the Mitre Club.

Donne did indeed take on such work to help earn his bread and butter, before he gained the post of Dean of St. Paul's. However, I have now discovered that Neville's compiler was much more likely to have been Andrew Downes – a Cambridge man who assisted Sir Henry Savile in his research and supervision of background work for the King James Bible. Neville and Savile were life-long friends and fellow workers, so this now introduces the probability that Neville himself had a hand in the King James Bible project. Indeed, the Shakespeare-Neville phrase 'I am that I am' in sonnet 121 is the exact phrase found in this 1611 version of the Bible. (This is what God tells Moses he wishes to call himself, viz. 'I am'.) I shall be returning to this subject briefly in a later chapter. Meanwhile, it is important to note that the Bible containing this exact phrase was published *two years later* than the Shakespeare-Neville *Sonnets*. Previous English translations of the Bible (such as Coverdale's) used a different phrase: 'I wyl be what I wyl be' which is literally closer to the Hebrew but perhaps not so musical as the Shakespeare-Neville version. I shall be revisiting this Worsley collection and pointing out more of its connections in the following chapter.

Chapter Three

MONARCHY v. REPUBLICANISM, AND HOLINSHED v. *LEICESTER'S COMMONWEALTH*

It is Neville's thoughts and Neville's alone which account for the totality of theme, ideas and references within the very political Shakespeare History Plays. Only Neville possessed the ability to fuse – in dramatic form – political ideas which had formerly polarised main-stream Medieval politics. The multi-faceted nature of Sir Henry Neville's life experience accounts for the diverse yet precise imagery in those plays. This imagery and political outlook becomes so entwined with the identity of the playwright that it will be examined continually in the next section of this book, alongside other layers of new textual and documentary evidence.

To round off this section dealing wholly with politics, however, it is important to see if we can further explore Shakespeare's and Neville's notions of Kingship and Republicanism. Ideas of Kingship have to do with government of a country. For the writer of the plays and poems, both kingship and republicanism were viable methods of government; whoever he was, he had certainly encountered both political systems when he studied the background to his plays and poetry based on Roman history and mythology. However, it is the *imperfection* inherent in the office of a monarch which concerns the majority of his History plays. These plays therefore imply that another, better, reformed, governmental system might be needed; so why did 'Shakespeare' never portray an *ideal* republic, to set against his portrayal of imperfect monarchies?

One answer to this question surely lies in the fact that a politician is writing the plays, and a *good* politician must combine idealism with realism. A good politician also knows about history, and therefore would know that there had been just as many abuses and failures under Republican rule across the world as under Monarchies. As an incorruptible politician,[55] and one who understood the lessons of history, Henry Neville realised too that history could neither be denied nor easily forgiven and forgotten. He was therefore concerned to bring about a solution that pragmatically included features of a system of government to which people had become accustomed, instead of overturning previous systems so completely that a witch hunt might ensue against the 'old guard.' The Earls involved with the Essex conspiracy were part of the 'old guard' aristocracy, so Neville's involement in this projected change shows that he recognised the need for continuity. Perhaps the conspirators planned an interim republic, but all their backgrounds were such that they would eventually have chosen a (probably elected) monarch from within their ranks. But these conspirators were precisely the forward-looking earls who respected Parliament too, so it is probable that whichever monarch they chose would rule in partnership with Parliament, just as later suggested by Neville.

Neville was the politician who openly tried to promote a halfway house between rule by kings and rule by elected parliamentarians. Neville, therefore, was just the man to have written the seemingly politically-ambivalent Shakespeare plays. The other candidates for the Shakespeare authorship held no such mixture of progressive ideas interwoven with a knowledge of, and lingering love for, some of the best traditions of the past. (Neither were they the men whose name rests in the Dedication Code)

Orthodox scholarship has tended to promote Shakespeare as an upholder of the feudal system, and therefore of the monarchy too. But this all-too-simplistic assessment of the complex works has been challenged, occasionally, and the *textual* evidence is certainly in favour of the challengers. One of the first to analyse the politics in the texts was Richard Simpson (1820 – 1876):

> ... There was a political current in Shakespeare's mind, which in the days of Elizabeth led him into opposition. If he welcomed the accession of James, he was soon undeceived, and when he set his hand to the history of Rome, the winter of his discontent had become gloomier than before. His tragedies point to the same conclusion, and show that the sentiments of the 66th Sonnet, and of Hamlet's 'To be or not to be.' were his real ones.[56]

Charles Mills Gayley followed this same line, claiming in his *Shakespeare and the Founding Fathers of America* that Shakespeare must have belonged to the 'rebel thinkers' at the Mitre Club. How prophetic, and how right he was! Much more recently, however, came the work of Professor Andrew Hadfield of Sussex University.[57]

Professor Hadfield has shown how the English Renaissance became fascinated with republican theories. This fascination was to spread over a couple of generations of the Neville family, with his grandson and namesake openly declaring for Parliament and Republicanism. I hope now to relate how the Neville interest in either reforming monarchy or encouraging republicanism is reflected in some of the Shakespeare works. When I say 'encouraging republicanism', however, I do not mean that the true writer of the works was doing this under any conditions and any monarch. No, a republican solution was a last resort, if an individual monarch proved unwilling to put the interests of the country and the people first, and/or unwilling to take notice of wise councillors. By the time Neville's grandson was writing, he had experienced civil war and a number of impossible, silly and autocratic monarchs, so it is not so surprising that he personally eventually came down firmly on the side of a republic.

In the 'Argument' preceding the very first work bearing his name, *The Rape of Lucrece,* Shakespeare takes up the question of Kingship and Republicanism. With such a political argument being chosen for the entrance of the Shakespeare name onto the literary stage, we are straight away warned that a politician is the true writer of the works. The story is also doubtless chosen because of its question of chivalrous and unchivalrous behaviour towards women, so it neatly combines Neville's concerns. (Neville wrote to the Earl of Southampton that he wanted to provide a good education for his sons "at the least, so that I may do the better for my daughters.") But the poem, and indeed the whole story of Lucrece, has only rarely been examined in the light of the *political* side to its argument. I'd therefore like to begin by looking at why Shakespeare-Neville chose it, and what had already made the history of Lucretia a political theme, even during Medieval times.

After telling the terrible story of the bad emperor, Tarquin, raping the chaste Lucretia, the writer ends his 'Argument' with the line, "...Brutus acquainted the people with the doer and manner of the vile deed, with a bitter invective against the tyranny of the King; wherewith the people were so moved that with one consent and a general acclamation the Tarquins were all exiled, and the state government changed from kings to consuls." Shakespeare therefore accepts that if a monarch behaves so badly, then there is bound to be a change in the form of government. There is no plotted treason in such a case: republicanism is a *natural* consequence. The author of the poem therefore followed in a line of writers who reviewed – and presented – this story as justification for a change in the nature of government. The great Chaucer had written a version of the same story in around 1370, and a disguised political intention was necessarily present in that too. Moreover, Chaucer figured among the Neville ancestry and counted a Sir William Neville[58] as one of his supporters. [Chaucer married Katherine Swynford's sister, and Katherine Swynford was first the mistress, then later the wife, of John of Gaunt – Neville's ancestor.]

But at the same time as the political thread running through the early works, no one can fail to notice a concentration on cruelty to women in the early Shakespeare plays. It somehow seems as if there may have been more than just a political motive behind what could be termed Shakespeare's early obsession with rape. We find it in *Lucrece* and also in *Titus Andronicus*. No such tragedies, however, are recorded as happening in the Shakespeare family. Could one of Henry Neville's sisters have been maltreated? We shall probably never know. However, one piece of evidence I have come across tends to suggest that it was something that happened much further back in the history of the Neville family that would inevitably have caused monarchy and cruelty to women to be forever bound together in his mind. For Neville, history was part and parcel of himself and his times, so what he discovered must have come as a shock to him when he first read of it.

I first heard of this particular historical scandal when reading the Dedicatory Epistle to Bulwer-Lytton's *The Last of the Barons*. (This book is a novel about Richard Neville, Earl of Warwick.) Bulwer-Lytton found an incident recorded in *Halle's Chronicles,* and we know that many of the earlier history plays are based as much on that work as on Holinshed. Lytton is discussing the various reasons why Richard Neville changed sides from supporting King Edward, the Yorkist, to supporting Henry VI and his redoubtable wife, Margaret of Anjou. In doing so, he recounts a reason which was never widely publicised, largely at the Nevilles' behest, because they felt it was so scandalous. It may also have been dangerous to speak of it, and thereby be seen to be criticising a king, because the 'scandal' involves a King's misdeeds. Lytton says:

> We find it broadly and strongly stated by Halle and others, that Edward [King Edward IV] had coarsely

attempted the virtue of one of the earl's female relations. "And farther it erreth not from the truth," says Halle, "that the king did attempt a thing once in the earl's house, which was much against the earl's honesty; but whether it was the daughter or the niece," adds the chronicler, "was not, for both their honours, openly known; but surely such a thing WAS attempted by King Edward," ...

Bulwer-Lytton continues:

Any one at all familiar with Halle (and, indeed, with all our principal chroniclers, except Fabyan), will not expect any accurate precision as to the date he assigns for the outrage. He awards to it, therefore, the same date he erroneously gives to Warwick's other grudges (namely, a period brought some years lower by all judicious historians) a date at which Warwick was still Edward's fastest friend.

Once grant the probability of this insult to the earl (the probability is conceded at once by the more recent historians, and received without scruple as a fact by Rapia, Habington, and Carte), and the whole obscurity which involves this memorable quarrel vanishes at once. Here was, indeed, a wrong never to be forgiven, and yet never to be proclaimed. As Halle implies, the honour of the earl was implicated in hushing the scandal, and the honour of Edward in concealing the offence. That if ever the insult were attempted, it must have been just previous to the earl's declared hostility is clear.[59]

And indeed, this outrage is never 'proclaimed' in the *Henry VI* trilogy. However, yet again, who but a Neville would have been at pains to conceal it, especially when it was an incident partially charted by Halle? Also, we may recall (from my previous book) that Neville's father in law, Sir Henry Killigrew, was officially entrusted with the job of revising Holinshed's *Chronicles*. As Neville and his wife were living in Killigrew's house at the time (and for many years) it beggars belief that Neville would not have helped his father in law with the revisions. In order to do this, he and his father in law would have looked at all the primary sources of history they could lay their hands on, so they would definitely have known about this particular scandal. We also know from Neville's *Tower Notebook* that he had been reading Halle too. Lytton stresses that *all* the principle chroniclers except Fabyan carried the above story, so there is no doubt that Neville would have read it, exactly at the time he was writing the early Shakespeare-Neville works.

This, to my mind, is another of the great Shakespeare – and historical – mysteries solved, but solved only when Sir Henry Neville is viewed as the writer. The question of what prompted Richard Neville to change sides so completely and so suddenly is nowhere else answered so completely and convincingly. 'Shakespeare' had groomed Richard Neville for stardom in the plays, and yet still did not write lines for him declaring this scandalous reason for changing sides, even though it would have been such a strong excuse for switching his loyalty. It is unthinkable that anyone but a Neville descendant would have omitted this incident from the plot of his play and thereby missed gaining the **maximum** sympathy for his hero. It must be remembered too that Shakespeare-Neville was writing of a time which was only as far distant to him as events of the nineteenth century are to us. The emotional impact of what had happened to one of his female kin would therefore have been felt all the more keenly by Henry Neville, the true writer, and especially by his older relatives. It is consequently not at all surprising that this young Neville writer should have looked to family precedents for linking dictatorial monarchy with cruelty to women.

When seen in this context, it is also less surprising that a Neville writer could write a play so totally condemning King Edward's brother, Richard III. It is as if our Henry Neville had to suppress his knowledge of King Edward's attempted (or even actual) rape, simply because he was a Neville himself. This suppression would have resulted in this Neville-writer releasing a barrage of hate against Edward's brother, Richard III. Richard III had, after all, married the widowed Anne Neville, daughter of the Earl of Warwick. This must have been judged a treble wrong, in Henry Neville's eyes. Firstly, Richard III had actually killed Anne Neville's first husband in battle; secondly, he then married the teenage widow, Anne, just for political purposes, rather than for love, or so it seemed. Thirdly, this same Richard III may even have known that his brother had raped Anne, so his crime in marrying her would have been unforgivable in Henry Neville's eyes.

Then there was the political aspect of the play itself: it was expedient for Henry Neville, the true writer, to focus all his anger onto this one man, for Richard III was the king defeated by the first of the new Tudor dynasts, which same family was still ruling when Shakespeare-Neville was writing this play. (As I mentioned in *The Truth Will Out,* The Earl of Southampton was later to address a treatise to Sir Henry Neville – a treatise based on evidence that Richard III was not so bad as he had been painted.[60] Why would Southampton have done this, unless he thought that it was indeed he – Henry Neville – whom Southampton considered to have been blinded by more rage and expediency than evidence when he wrote this play?)

In the case of Lucretia, however, Neville had to look no further than manuscripts of Chaucer for his conjoined themes of rape and tyrannical monarchy. Chaucer's documents were known to have been collected by his own family. Like our Henry Neville, Chaucer was a courtier and a diplomat, and served with influential persons, so it was necessary that he, like Neville, should present his political messages *subtly*. In the end, it was left to Chaucer's contemporary John Gower to spell out *openly* the link between the legend of Lucrece and the emergence of the Roman Republic, relating it to the supposed incompetence of the then king, Richard II.

Medieval politics and the portrayal of Lucrece
Chaucer (c.1340–1400), wrote of Lucrece in his *Legend of Good Women*. The fact that he wrote such a book immediately classifies Chaucer as a liberal thinker in an age when the majority of men were happy to consider women as inferior beings. Anyone who knew the story also knew that the Lucrece incident was a prelude to the Roman Republic, but to have talked too openly of this would have caused problems for both Chaucer and 'Shakespeare', considering the climate of the times in which each author lived. As Peter Brown[61] says, therefore, Chaucer uses a device to help disguise his political intentions: the writer declares he must truncate the story because Cupid has ordered him to do so! Chaucer is therefore clearly under some serious political *constraints*, whereas John Gower, in writing of the same incident, seeks to *stress* the political side of events. Chaucer – a government employee – became used to *hinting* at the **political** ramifications of love and desire rather than stating them too openly. Neville was also employed in governmental services and therefore would have felt the same constraints as Chaucer, whereas Shakespeare of Stratford would have had less to worry about.

I think we might therefore examine the reasons for the political openness of John Gower's presentation, comparing them with both Shakespeare's and Chaucer's. But before doing so, it is essential not to omit mention of another Medieval English writer who dealt with the story of Lucretia, and whose work one or two previous scholars have tentatively suspected of influencing Shakespeare. (I say 'tentatively' because these scholars then find it difficult to see how the Stratford man could have gained access to this particular author's work, especially so early in his career, when Shakespeare was impoverished and lacking patronage.) This writer was John Lydgate, who was Chaucer's contemporary and a friend of his son. Moreover, Lydgate openly entitled his long poem *Fall of Princes,* and in it he wrote of Lucretia and others. Lydgate's work was based on Boccaccio's *De casibus virorum illustrium* (1355-60). As such, *Fall of Princes* is a daring English rendition of Boccacio's tragedy, which was itself an encyclopaedic collection of the misgovernance of various monarchs. But Lydgate's version, unlike Chaucer's, also offers political advice, in that it includes *positive* as well as negative examples of 'princely' politics.[62] As a result, Lydgate's work exudes a political syncretism which pre-echoes that expressed in the works of Shakespeare and in the Treatise of Neville. After all, one ideal king is painted by Shakespeare–Neville, and that King is Henry V.

Just as in Shakespeare's *Lucrece,* Lydgate hides the starkness of a potentially revolutionary objective beneath a warning message which can only be described as cleverly-constructed, entertaining, conciliatory, yet subtly-discernible. But there is one great difference between Lydgate and Shakespeare's work. Shakespeare is presenting plays which lead to discussion about *worldly* rights and wrongs. He does not seem to mind if he leaves his audience with dualities, because he recognises that this is how the world is constructed. Implicitly, therefore, Shakespeare's message is that it is up to men to tussle with these ambiguities, in the hope that their collective search after what is good, just and right will ultimately advance mankind. Lydgate, on the other hand, was a monk, and so unsurprisingly leaves us with a sense of hopelessness as far as Earthly politics are concerned, suggesting that it is only in an afterworld that things can improve.

This did not, however, excuse princes from at least *attempting* to improve their behaviour, said Lydgate. He urges them to do everything in their power to prevent the horrors which can proceed from discord and strife between kinsfolk – once again a theme taken up by Shakespeare. Yet, as with all such *religiously-based* messages, the suggestion is that princes can only be encouraged to behave well by making them afraid of the hereafter. The distinction between Lydgate's and Shakespeare's rendering of Lucretia's story is therefore clear: in *Fall of Princes* by Lydgate, a man of the Church was writing of Lucretia, as well as of kingship, whereas a *politician* was writing Shakespeare's *Rape of Lucrece*, and all the other Shakespeare works. Like Brutus, the **true** Shakespeare was concerned with 'general honest thought and common good to all' on Earth. He was not concerned with Heaven, which is one reason, surely, why neither Shakespeare nor Neville used Christian imagery in the overtly political works 'they' produced, such as Shakespeare's History Plays and Neville's political Treatise.

However, it is interesting to realise that an English politician was **behind** Lydgate's translation of his *Fall of Princes*. This politician was none other than Humphrey, Duke of Gloucester[63] – the 'good Duke Humphrey' of the *Henry VI* plays. John Julius Norwich, in his book, *Shakespeare's Kings*, mentions that the *chroniclers* do not portray Humphrey as overwhelmingly good, even though Shakespeare always portrays him as such. But Lydgate (who was not a chronicler) certainly praised his patron's goodness, and Humphrey was indeed Lydgate's patron. In his prologue to his English translation of *The Fall*, Lydgate describes Humphrey as "prynce ful myhti of puissaunce", and goes on to laud the Duke's political insight. It is difficult to find any other source of Shakespeare's good opinion of Duke Humphrey, ergo Shakespeare-Neville surely must have been reading Lydgate's work.

Then Lydgate and Boccaccio also both say that *popular* rebellion must be put down. This of course parallels Shakespeare's rendition of Jack Cade's rebellion in *Henry VI, part 2*. Altogether, therefore, we are getting a picture of the young 'Shakespeare' having probably read Boccacio, and definitely read Lydgate's *Fall of Princes*. Indeed, he has taken this work and its unique praise of Duke Humphrey as a major starting point for his early literary output.

But if 'Shakespeare' knew Lydgate's work this produces yet another problem for the Stratford man having been the author. In his 'New Variorum' edition of Shakespeare's *Troilus and Cressida* (1953) Harold N. Hillebrand argues that it was rather difficult for the general public to access Lydgate's works in Shakespeare's time, even though (as Hillebrand confirms) Shakespeare's play of that name seems to have been informed by Lydgate's *Siege of Troy*. *Troilus and Cressida* is considered to be a late play, yet Hillebrand suggests that even then Lydgate's work was hard to get hold of. How much more difficult would it have been, therefore, for the young, penniless Shakespeare to have accessed Lydgate and used it for his early work, viz. *Lucrece*. When Shakespeare's *Lucrece* was published in 1594, there had been only one work attributed previously to that author's name. This was his *Venus and Adonis*, which has a letter of dedication to the Earl of Southampton. But it is never recorded that Shakespeare actually gained Southampton's patronage, and he was certainly not known to be a wealthy writer at this stage in his career, so it is difficult to see how he could have accessed Lydgate's works at this time. The nearest date I have found to Shakespeare's time for the publication of *Fall of Princes* is 1527 and it was never reprinted during Shakespeare's lifetime, which meant it was already becoming rare by the 1580s and 90s. And yet Lydgate's opinions definitely informed this, one of Shakespeare's earliest works. The *Henry VI* trilogy was likewise researched and written before 'Shakespeare' was even thought to have possibly gained *any* patronage, and if the character of Duke Humphrey in these plays is attributable to Lydgate's assessment, then there is absolutely no known way in which Shakespeare of Stratford could have come across such a rare publication.

Since writing the above paragraphs on Shakespeare's knowledge of Lydgate, I have discovered that Sir Henry Neville's family actually possessed a manuscript of *Fall of Princes*. The known provenance of this manuscript (from the third quarter of the fifteenth century) begins with its being owned by James Baker, John Dowman and John Salisbriensis in the early sixteenth century. Next comes the name 'Mary Sidney', who was the daughter of the Duke of Northumberland and mother of Sir Philip Sidney. She owned the book in 1552, which was one year after her marriage to Sir Henry Sidney, Neville's father's best friend. Indeed, Henry Neville's father made history by being the first English person to mention his falcon in his will, and he left this bird to his great friend, Sir Henry Sidney, because, he said, the bird loved him and if he did not go to him it would die.

Mary Sidney obviously treasured Lydgate's book, because she wrote on the flyleaf:

> This bouk is mine Mary Sidney
> If it [be] fonde before it be lost
> Lett them that finde it of it make no bost
> For of souch gayn is lek to come mouche payne.

  But next, on the same page, comes the name 'Elizabeth Nevell'. This can be none other than our Sir Henry's mother. As Sir Henry Sidney was such a good friend of her husband, it is likely Mary lent it or gave it to Elizabeth Neville. An Italian inscription following Elizabeth's name carries the sense that it was acquired from one of her lady friends. Then comes the name Thomas Myddleton. This is unlikely to be the playwright; more probably it is the father of Hugh Myddleton, with whom Neville began the New River project. (However, the possibility that Thomas Middleton, the playwright, may have been related to the Myddletons cannot be ruled out, since the playwright's birth and ancestry are not known for certain.) The Myddletons therefore seem to have been family friends of the Nevilles, so this Lydgate manuscript would probably have been passed on from one to another of them. Certainly, if the Myddletons finally took over the manuscript this would explain why it is the *early* works of 'Shakespeare' that were the ones mainly influenced by Lydgate's assessment of monarchy and, most especially, of 'good' Duke Humphrey.

  Lydgate's *Fall of Princes* was even harder to obtain in Shakespeare's time than his work on Troilus, viz. *The Siege of Troy*. It would have been a simple matter for Neville to have obtained Lydgate's work, however, but not for many other people. As can be seen, Mary Sidney was afraid that others might be tempted to take the book, which would not have been the case if it were readily available. The fact that even her rich circle could have been thus tempted makes it virtually impossible that a poor boy from Stratford could have gained access to it. However, Neville's interest in Lydgate would have begun early with seeing the book in his mother's possession, and would then have been re-inforced later when he learned that Lydgate studied at Oxford University.[64] (As I explained in my last book, I do not think Shakespeare ever knew who was writing the plays which were coming out under his name; there is no evidence that Neville and Shakespeare ever met and, indeed, it would have been dangerous for Neville to have informed a poor actor about his identity. The opportunities for blackmail would have been immense, had he done so. Moreover, Shakespeare the actor clearly did not know anything about their true authorship when he was questioned by Queen Elizabeth, following the Essex rebellion.)

Returning to Chaucer's presentation of Lucretia, we are immediately struck by the fact that, whether he considers he has truncated the story or not, its opening lines refer directly to the political consequences of Tarquin's barbarism:

Now moot I seyn the exiling of kinges
Of Rome, for hir [their] horrible doinges ,
And of the laste king Tarquinius,
As saith Ovyde and Titus Livius.[65]

Nevertheless, the lines which follow straight away seem to undermine the political message:

But for that cause telle I nat this storie,
But for to preise and drawen to memorie
The verray wyf, the verray trewe Lucresse,

Thus we see pre-echoes of Shakespearean ambivalence. So why bother to mention the *political* side of Lucretia's rape at all, if what you, as a writer, are truly concerned about is her personality, virtue and integrity? One obvious answer is that the story of Lucrece was then being *generally* perceived in its political as well as its personal dimension, but that some authors, especially those employed in governmental work, were afraid to state this too blandly.

It is interesting, therefore, to discover signs of the authors' times in these Medieval versions of the tale. Chaucer was writing at a time when Richard II was being greatly criticised for 'misgovernance' – a word which Neville uses in regard to that same King in his Tower Notebook.[66] It was a time too when Henry Bolingbroke was making moves towards the King's overthrow. It was through his ambivalent writing that Chaucer managed to survive the situation – for a while, at least. Later, Shakespeare was writing on the same subject at a time when he knew the Tudor dynasty was coming to a finite close. But, like Chaucer, the true Shakespeare writer was working in a governmental capacity, and therefore in a sensitive, possibly dangerous, situation. If the real writer were not a politician, therefore, he would just have ignored the political implications of the story. The fact that he did not do so but, instead, pointed out in his 'Argument' that this bad emperor begat the coming of a republic certainly argues against the writer being anyone other than a man directly involved in government service.

I am not suggesting that merely personal considerations underlay the hovering ambivalence sometimes present in the writing of either Chaucer or Shakespeare-Neville. Both were honest men with a larger amount of selflessness in their political viewpoints than was average for either of their eras. It is quite possible, therefore, that Chaucer, like Neville, had a deep enough understanding of politics to know that neither side – monarch nor republic – could rule in peace without at least tacit support from the other. I am also still aware of a) the influence the study of rhetoric had on persuading educated writers to present their cases with a degree of ambivalence, and b) the influence of the French school of thought – i.e. that, by using the right imagery, it was possible to hide quite precise meanings within a seeming ambivalence. All these factors – literary and political alike – therefore dictated that surface ambivalence was probably the safest and most interesting form for literary expression which touched on political discussions.

John Gower, nevertheless, was not so cautious. He prefaced the whole work in which he dealt with Lucretia, (i.e. Book VII of *Confessio Amantis,*) with an openly political preamble, even though he was a friend of Chaucer and therefore lived under the same broad cultural and political influences:

> Practique enformeth ek the reule,
> Hou that a worthi king schal reule
> His Realme bothe in werre and pes.

Gower then outlines first the perfect state, following this by telling of the division that has grown in his own times. Gower dares to do this, whereas Chaucer is much more subtle. Yet I do not think Chaucer and Gower actually differed that much in their opinions. No, their great difference was the **level of government at which they were working.** (This is a most important and telling point.) Chaucer worked directly with John of Gaunt, father of Henry Bolingbroke, – the future King Henry IV. He was therefore always close to the highest courtiers, and he also worked in the diplomatic service. Yet Chaucer was a good friend of King Richard II too and agreed with many of his policies. John Gower's political offices, however, remain obscure. It is likely that he was some sort of lawyer, but never seems to have served in the higher realms of government, nor to have been close enough to the centre of power to have shared Chaucer's close acquaintance with courtiers, rulers and politicians. To be sure, Bolingbroke, when king, gave Gower a gift of a collar of SSs and a stipend, but this appears to have been in gratitude for changing his dedication of *Confessio Amantis* from Richard II to himself, after he became King Henry IV. No known official governmental service on Gower's behalf is recorded, which is in great contrast to Chaucer's known career.

It is thus clear that Gower was safer in writing openly of his political opinions than was Chaucer. Gower, it seems, was allowed a poet's licence. But Chaucer, even though he seemed to steer a much more careful course in the political side of his poetry, may very well have been assassinated.[67] This certainly illustrates the different levels of danger to writers, depending on their differing levels of government service. No one knows for sure when or how Chaucer died.

Was this unfortunate ancestral example one very big warning for Neville? It is likely that Neville, being family, could have known what truly happened to Chaucer. So this, together with his illegitimacy, plus the execution of his grandfather, would have been yet another highly persuasive reason for Neville's decision to write under a pseudonym. After all, Neville, like Chaucer, dealt directly with the monarchs of the day, was a well-known politician, and also a diplomat and ambassador. He lived near the centre of power, both literally and metaphorically. Little wonder Neville might have decided that discretion was the better part of valour. And as an extra insurance, the subtle, symbolic manner in which he expressed his political opinions in the Shakespeare works would have helped. Should he ever be finally exposed as the true writer, it would have been difficult for any lawyer to make a good case for either pure monarchy or pure republicanism, from examining the texts of the plays. Thus are Neville's inner political convictions of harmony and gradual transition, rather than polarisation and revolution, displayed clearly in the early Shakespeare plays. (It was only the intransigence, and dangerous gagging order, of Queen Elizabeth that pushed Neville to any open action against a monarch. He would have done anything he morally could to have prevented civil war.) Yet, as a politician, he also knew how to place just enough political emphasis in his works to insure that if experienced *politicians* read or saw his plays, then they would start to think about things in a new way. He was having his cake and eating it – to the best of his ability!

Dangerous moonlighting
If Chaucer's days were dangerous ones in which to write, then Shakespeare's were even more hazardous. When Chaucer *began* to write, the state seemed much more at peace with itself and with its neighbours. Even though the extant Chronicles do not record Richard's reign as being such a good one, it has to be remembered that Henry IV – the usurping King – destroyed the existing annals and initiated new ones, slanted in his own favour. The French, for instance, record that Richard lived in peace with France, and sought to extend that peace when it came to dealing with other countries. His peaceful, liberal outlook also extended to allowing writers, such as Chaucer, to write almost anything, even if they were employed in the then civil service. It is scarcely surprising, therefore, that Chaucer felt no compunction about using his own name when he *began* his writing career. But things changed. Powerful opponents challenged King Richard, and Chaucer had perforce to work with them too. He must also have had it in mind that a revolution could be on the cards. Henry IV was much more repressive, so it seems that Chaucer, despite trying to be subtle, may well have fallen short of writing what that new King, or the powerful Churchmen, wanted to hear. There were and are rumours that Chaucer was murdered. If only he'd started out by writing under a pseudonym!

Chaucer therefore became a lesson from history, as far as some later writers were concerned. Even if you thought you were safe, things could change, drastically. And when it came to Shakespeare's time, everyone *knew* that things would indeed change radically during their lifetime, because Elizabeth seemed less and less likely to produce an heir, meaning that a new dynasty would have to be inaugurated, eventually. Even though writers of openly challenging political treatises were usually writing under Parliamentary privilege, not all such writers could access such protection. If they wanted to write a literary work with progressive overtones, then they usually wrote anonymously or under a pseudonym (unless they were either incredibly brave or incredibly short-sighted.) Even under the more liberal King James I, Ben Jonson was imprisoned for what he wrote, and threatened with having his ears and nose cut off. Elizabeth's days were especially harsh, though. Unlike King James, she didn't just issue empty threats. Neville would have felt himself to be in clear and present danger, had he written *published* political advice (e.g. in the form of dramas) under his own name. John Stubbe was a secretary of the great William Cecil, Lord Burghley, but it was nevertheless pointed out to him that his position did not give him the privilege of offering advice.[68] Despite this warning, Stubbe wrote a book – under his own name – with the plain intention of advising the Queen not to marry Anjou. His right hand was cut off, in public.

Sir Henry Neville was abroad at the time this happened, but would have been kept informed by Camden, who actually witnessed this bloody punishment, because Camden was the best friend of Henry Savile, with whom Neville was travelling. In that same group was Robert Sidney, younger brother of Sir Philip Sidney, who was also against Queen Elizabeth's proposed marriage. Philip Sidney, however, did not publish his ideas openly but, instead, addressed them in a personal letter to Elizabeth in 1580 (Sidney Papers, pp. 287-292.) Even though Sidney hedged his opinions round with some careful compliments to the Queen, and even though he asserted that "those whom he was bound to obey" had told him he should write the letter, the Queen forced Sidney to retire from Court.

The news of Sidney's letter and all its consequences would definitely have reached the Savile-Neville travelling group, since Robert Sidney was travelling with them. It seems it may have had a lasting effect on Henry Neville, because mention of Philip Sidney's letter is scribbled on the Northumberland Manuscript, which belonged to Sir Henry.[69] In later years, Neville was to become even more closely tied in with the Walsingham circle. Not only was Walsingham's daughter married into the Sidney family – the Nevilles' closest friends – but Neville's father in law (Sir Henry Killigrew) was also a close associate of Walsingham. Revealingly too, Walsingham's second wife was none other than the widow of Sir Richard Worsley – father and namesake of the man who was later to marry one of Sir Henry Neville's daughters. The Worsleys also therefore became the secret custodians of our Sir Henry's notebooks and annotated manuscripts. The Worsleys were always the chief family on the Isle of Wight. Also, during Henry's later life, the governor of the

Isle of Wight was none other than his friend, political supporter and Tower companion, Henry Wriothesley, Earl of Southampton. Walsingham's relatives included the Lewknors too, one of whom married yet another daughter of Sir Henry Neville.

Thus, one begins to see Neville's extremely close ties with the Elizabethan spy service, and also to understand the dangers of Neville ever revealing himself outside this group of international intelligencers which he inhabited. It must have felt as if his private and public life was entirely encompassed by this secret circle. The document known as the Northumberland Manuscript becomes an illustration of the mental pressure Neville was suffering when surrounded by all these powerful forces. In this Manuscript, Neville is listing some of the works in his possession, musing on his background, and also practising a 'Shakespeare' signature. (A longer description of the document can be found in my first book on Sir Henry Neville, *The Truth Will Out.*[70]) Few people could have found it so vitally necessary never to write under their own name as the 'secret' Sir Henry.

The Northumberland 'Manuscript' was actually a rough paper cover which once held some of the works haphazardly listed on it. Neville's name and family motto head this paper cover, while repeated practising of Shakespeare's 'signature' are to be seen at the foot of the document. The words 'Philip against Monsieur' are scribbled there too. 'Monsieur' stood for Anjou, meaning that this paper cover contained Philip Sidney's letter about Anjou. The fact that Neville only called Anjou 'Monsieur' on this cover immediately suggests that he had been scared of naming the Duc d'Anjou openly, after what had happened to both Stubbe and Sidney. 'Richard II' and 'Richard III' are also mentioned there, and these titles of the plays herald the scribbling of various forms of 'Shakespeare'. But this is not the only place 'Shakespeare' is scribbled; it appears repeatedly at the bottom of the page. There is also a version of lines from *The Rape of Lucrece* scribbled on the cover, and those very lines speak of the writer's fear of discovery: "Revealing day through every cranny peepes, and see Shak, Shak, Shakespeare". These words appear on the left hand side of the page – the same side as that on which Neville has written his own name and family motto. On the right hand half of the page, Francis Bacon's name is written, with a list of some of his essays bracketed together beneath his name. (These essays contain philosophical, uncontroversial stuff.) Below the list of these essays, however – and merging with the poem written under Neville's name – there is a list of *controversial* material, including *The Isle of Dogs* by Thomas Nashe; Sidney's letter to the Queen, the banned book 'Leicester's Commonwealth' (which vilifies the Earl of Leicester, the Queen's 'boyfriend') plus *Richard II* and *Richard III*.

The whole impression given by this document is that the writer of the scribble page – Sir Henry Neville – is working out in his own mind that he must continue to write under a pseudonym because he wishes to side with people and works which are controversial. But his step-mother's younger step-brother – Francis Bacon – has no need to worry, because *his* works cannot offend. Indeed, right below Francis Bacon's name we read 'Of tribute, or giving what is due', as if the writer is telling us that that is how all of Bacon's essays can be classified – no hidden dangers in announcing those on the page. And those Bacon works are listed in a clear italic script, as if the writer had no fear of listing and owning them, while the more 'dangerous' works are in a scribbled Secretary Hand which, incidentally, only men were usually taught to read and write, while girls were taught the italic hand.

Even into King James I's reign we find Bacon giving the sort of advice to the King that he knew the King wanted to hear, which is in direct contrast with Neville's advice. However, the fact that Neville and his family were related to the Bacons in so many ways makes it easy to understand that Neville would have been given a number of copies of Francis Bacon's works. Neville also seems to have been on friendly terms with Francis' older brother, Anthony[71]. (The name 'Anthony' is said to appear on the 19th century *transcription* of the Northumberland Manuscript, though personally I think the word – in its original Elizabethan Secretary Script – reads 'Anthem', not Anthony: it is extremely strange that anyone could suppose they are reading 'Anthony' in a word which clearly does not end with a 'y'! Are the Baconians blinded by mere hope here, I wonder?) 'Anthem' also makes more sense of the words which follow, viz. 'Anthem: All Comfort and Consol[ation]'. These words appear in many religious texts,[72] and it is quite feasible that they would have been turned into a church 'anthem'. We are dealing with a cover which held written and printed works, so this anthem was likely to have been among these works, originally.

If Neville ever needed any proof that he was right to continue being careful, he received it while he was Ambassador in

France. That proof was contained in a letter from Sir Robert Cecil. Cecil was warning him that the Queen thought he was "too much like one now in heaven to carry coals at the hand of any Frenchman". That 'one now in heaven' was none other than Sir Philip Sidney, who had offended her eighteen years earlier, and had died following a battle in 1584, after offering his water bottle to a dying soldier. He was also a known writer, so Elizabeth may well have been suggesting that she thought Neville might be a writer too. She had in fact just initiated an economy drive on the amount of paper supplied to her diplomatic corps, and was questioning Cecil about how much Sir Henry seemed to use!

Queen Elizabeth liked neither Sidney's outspokenness nor his love of the people. Neither did she like the French King Henri IV's consulting too much with his 'underlings' – an attitude which led Henri to say Neville "we shall see which shall speed better, she with her Gloriousness, or I with that she calls Baseness."[73]

The see-saw changing from one religion to another during the Tudor period must have been another cause of upset for many a writer. If you hinted at religion in your works, it was always open to some potential enemy to interpret them in an anti-establishment way, and so put the writer in danger. Moreover, the Nevilles inevitably had many rivals at Court. Much safer, then, never to put one's name to anything at all – as Sir Henry Neville so rightly said[74]. Also, if a new, Catholic, monarch were suddenly to take the throne, there would be much less danger to any Protestant writer who had written under a pseudonym than to one who had expressed his religious ideas in his works, even symbolically. (We have to remember that there had been no Reformation – no split in the Christian Church – by Chaucer's time. This too would have been a reason why Chaucer initially felt more secure in writing under his own name.)

'Shakespeare' was, however, able to show his broadmindedness, just in case a Catholic monarch ever did suspect and challenge him. In *Henry VIII*, Catherine of Aragon is portrayed sympathetically, even though she is a Catholic. Had a Catholic monarch ever come to the throne, and Shakespeare have been revealed as being Sir Henry Neville, then the true writer could have pointed at this fact, which may well have stood him in good stead. However, it must also be said that she was the Catholic about whom Sir Henry would have found it easiest to write favourably. To begin with, she was betrayed by the same King who had executed Neville's grandfather. Secondly, she was indeed a virtuous and wronged lady. Thirdly she was related to the Nevilles. Neville had always pointed out that the Catholic *Priests* were the 'fountain and head of all the trouble' and had wanted to see *them* – not innocent Catholic laymen – hunted down. This is precisely the impression given in the Shakespeare plays, where it is the Catholic clergy who are portrayed as villains, not the individual laymen. When discussing Republicanism v. Monarchy in respect of those times, one therefore has to be aware of *all* the surrounding situation.

Neville, Republicanism, the Succession and *Leicester's Commonwealth*

With the kind of political background that was persisting towards the end of the reign of Elizabeth I, and with the possible problems associated with any future monarch, Neville had to proceed with great caution. There is no doubt he took an interest in republicanism, as did many in ministerial office at the time, though none of them dared to voice their ideas too openly. But the signs that Neville was concerned about the state of affairs surrounding the succession question date right back to at least 1584, when he would have been about 22 years old. (1584 was the year in which a book called *Leicester's Commonwealth* was published abroad, though it remained illegal to publish it in England. Nevertheless, I was to discover that Henry Neville owned copies of this document and annotated them too.) Neville was already an MP at this time, so was of course concerned about what would happen when Elizabeth died. She was childless, and appeared likely to remain so, which meant that there could be trouble when the Tudor dynasty disappeared.

I traced Neville's copy of *Leicester's Commonwealth* after I discovered his name in the Dedication Code. It was not an easy journey of discovery. Neville had eleven surviving children, so I followed up a lot of dead ends before I discovered where Neville had stowed some of his documents away. The fuller story of how I eventually traced the manuscripts' movements – over the space of three hundred years – from Berkshire to the Isle of Wight and then to Yorkshire, is told in my previous two books. By the time the manuscripts reached Yorkshire, however, the origins of Neville's bundle of papers had been totally forgotten.

After tracing the whereabouts of these documents, I went through Neville's letters in the Berkshire Record Office once more and eventually found a cross reference to one specific manuscript in the 16th / 17th century bundle among the Worsley papers. These Worsley Papers had been inherited by the Yorkshire Earls of Yarborough and eventually placed by them in the Lincolnshire Archives. The husband of another of Neville's daughters, Richard Brooke, had made reference to a *Book of Knights of Lancaster* compiled by one 'Mr. Dwne' for Neville. Richard Brooke's letter was in the Berkshire Record Office. But the subject of his reference, *Book of Knights of Lancaster,* was actually among the Worsley Papers I had discovered in the Lincolnshire Archives – with its still extant inscription by 'Mr. Dwne'. Brooke's reference could be to none other than this document. Brooke actually writes to Neville that his own father is reluctantly to let **'your** book' go. (In chapter 2, I have explained more of the connections between Neville and this section of the Worsley Collection, and also in *Henry Neville and the Shakespeare Code*. There can be no doubt, then, that these Lincolnshire papers were *originally* owned by Neville.)

When the documents were taken up north after a Worsley lady married the Earl of Yarborough, the family used a certain Allason to bind the documents, and Allason's assistant, Stewart, was the man who compiled the catalogue for a Miss Richardson-Curer's famous Yorkshire library. That library also contained two copies of *Halle's Chronicles,* and it seems likely that one of those copies was the one which was later bought by Alan Keen at an auction in York. Keen subsequently wrote his famous book, *The Annotator*. This states how his edition of *Halle's Chronicles* seems to have been annotated by none other than the man who wrote the early history plays of Shakespeare. But Keen failed to trace the Chronicle's movements correctly, so he came to many wrong conclusions about which branch of the Worsley family had owned it.

Keen's copy of the *Chronicles* had been trimmed to fit Stewart's and Allason's covers, and just the same vandalism had been done to the copies of *Leicester's Commonwealth* and the *Tower Notebook,* which I found among the Worsley papers. The covers were the same too. It seems Miss Richardson Curer, the lady with the Yorkshire library, probably purchased one of the copies of *Halle's Chronicles* from the Worsleys' great niece, for there is a copy of that book listed in her library catalogue. (The Worsley's great niece had married the Earl of Yarborough and was living in Yorkshire.)

Suffice it to say here that *Leicester's Commonwealth* is a document obliquely warning of succession troubles ahead. The warnings had necessarily to be oblique because Elizabeth was openly enraged when anyone discussed the succession problem, and eventually even pronounced it treasonable to do so. It was therefore presented as a book which dealt with the failings of Robert Dudley, Earl of Leicester – hence its title. But it went on to pronounce that the Earl would be one of the main contenders for monarchical position, if Elizabeth were to die soon. Some even feared that Leicester would present one of his illegitimate children as being the child of the Queen herself. (By the time *Leicester's Commonwealth* was written, the Queen was already nearly fifty years old, so it was indeed unlikely she would have children, and her age itself was already an advanced one for the times.) Moreover, the book claimed that it was none other than Sir Henry Neville senior who was involved in hinting at the danger of Leicester's monarchical ambition! No wonder our Sir Henry Neville was reading and annotating this book, even though its *printing* was banned in England and even though the Queen did not allow ownership of it.

Leicester's Commonwealth, on the surface, appears as if it could have been written by a discontented Catholic, because the Catholics hated Dudley, partly because he had led English forces against the Catholic dictatorship in the Netherlands. However, Protestant ministers in the English government also disliked and distrusted Leicester, especially Robert Cecil and Francis Walsingham. Elizabeth needed the expertise and intellects of the likes of Walsingham and Robert Cecil, though she probably did not actually like them, and especially disliked both the Cecils' – father's and son's – attempted interference in her relationship with the Earl of Leicester. It therefore appears more likely that the book was an underground work commissioned by Walsingham, perhaps with the collusion of the supposed Catholic (but really double agent) Charles Paget, who was at one time payrolled by Walsingham. After all, over half its contents are not related directly to Leicester but to a summary of the problems caused by the Wars of the Roses, which were nothing but wars of dynastic succession. The question of succession was therefore clearly at the top of the author's mind. The Catholics might have stood to gain if civil warring were to happen after Elizabeth's death, because the battle this time would surely be between Protestants and Catholics, and the Catholics could summon up a number of powerful nobles to support their side. But, on the contrary, the *lack* of any civil strife following the death of Elizabeth would probably mean a continuation of the status quo, with Catholics therefore continuing in their position of subordination. The only logical conclusion, therefore, is that the book was commissioned and partly written by Protestants concerned at the prospect of a change for the worse – from their point of view – which could be the outcome unless the question of the Protestant succession could be settled prior to Elizabeth's death.

The dangerous *Commonwealth* was therefore published anonymously because whichever way one looked at it, it presented material Elizabeth was not going to like. Nevertheless, our Henry Neville owned two copies of it, and I maintain that they are the very copies of *Leicester's Commonwealth* mentioned on the Northumberland Manuscript. These two copies are now part of the Worsley collection, housed in the Lincolnshire Archives. Neville annotated these manuscript copies. The annotations demonstrate his worries for the future of the state, as well as pointing to material he was to use in the 'Shakespeare' History plays. This makes it certain that a main concern of the History plays was indeed political. They pointed out lessons from history, showing again and again what might happen if the Tudors were to die out without a clear successor. They also portray kingship in crisis, making it obvious through their imagery, etc. that the only solution (in the absence of a clear monarchical successor) would be the declaration of a (perhaps temporary) republic. But this is indeed also the point made in *The Rape of Lucrece* too – better a good republic than a bad monarch.

The *Commonwealth* also contains references to Richard Neville, Earl of Warwick, and even compares him with the Earl of Leicester:

> In the stories both sacred and profane, foreign and domestical, of all nations, kingdoms, countries, and states, you shall read that such as meant to mount above other and to govern all at their own discretion [i.e. like the Earl of Leicester]... getteth secretly into his hands or at his devotion all the towns, villages, castles, fortresses, bulwarks, rampires [ramparts], waters, ways, ports, and passages about the same, and so without drawing any sword against the said city he bringeth the same into bondage to abide his will and pleasure.

...This did all these in the Roman Empire who rose from subjects to be great princes and to put down emperors. This did all those in France and other kingdoms who at sundry times have tyrannized their princes. And in our own country the examples are manifest of Vortiger[n], Harold, Henry of Lancaster, **Richard of Warwick,** Richard of Gloucester, John of Northumberland, and divers others who by this mean specially have pulled down their lawful sovereigns[75]

So this *Commonwealth* was portraying a Neville kinsman as showing similar ambitions to a Roman emperor. No wonder Sir Henry wanted to scrutinise its text.

Henry Neville's attitude to the Earl of Leicester must have initially been somewhat ambivalent, however, during the 1580s and 90s, when he would have got hold of this manuscript. On the one hand, Leicester had been a great Protestant battle leader, much admired by Neville's father and father in law. But on the other, our Neville would have known him to be dynastically ambitious. A great soldier, from a noble family, and a believer in dynastic inheritance were three key points Leicester held in common with Richard Neville, Earl of Warwick. It would certainly have been easy, therefore, to have based the Earl of Warwick's character partly on that of Leicester. It would also have been an ideal opportunity for the writer to warn his audiences – both commoner and courtier – of the potential danger Leicester and his ilk posed, by making a few well-known points of his character coincide with that of Richard Neville, on stage.

But there were one or two problems: the true writer was himself a Neville, so he would not have wanted to show *all* of his ancestor's faults. Neither would he have wished to portray Warwick as a Queen's paramour, like Leicester! So what better way to overcome the problematic mis-matched points between Leicester and Warwick than to put the 'sexual' aspect of Leicester's misdeeds onto another character in the play, viz. the Earl of Suffolk? From a Protestant, knightly and/or anti-clerical point of view, this would have been fine, because William Pole, Earl of Suffolk, was known to have sided with the Church on most issues, not to have been a man of war. Moreover, if Queen Elizabeth even had the tiniest suspicion that in referring to the relationship between Suffolk and Queen Margaret the playwright was aping her relationship with Leicester, then this thought would soon be quietened by her advisors, because Leicester was a soldier, like the Earl of Warwick, not at all like the Earl of Suffolk. However, anyone who made a connection between the Earl of Suffolk in the play and the Earl of Leicester in real life would soon see the overwhelming ambition of both men to rule through romantic attachment to the Queen. Suffolk declares this at the end of *Henry VI, part 1,* whereas Leicester never openly declared this thought. No, it was left to the 'seditious' *Leicester's Commonwealth* to suggest it, and men such as the Cecils and Walsingham to whisper it. (The historical dramas of the 16th and 17th centuries subtly and symbolically pointed out parallels with their own day, just as does good science fiction of our present day society.)

The writer is therefore purposely leading his audience to make a distinction between the Nevilles and the Poles/Dudleys. (The Earl of Leicester was Robert Dudley, whose brother Ambrose, by the way, was the then Earl of Warwick and also head of the office of the ordnance – the very man who had crossed swords with Henry Neville over his cannon-making in Sussex.)

Within his broader portrayal of Warwick, the writer is therefore implying that the Nevilles work in the interest of the State, while other lords may be impelled by nothing short of personal ambition. He is also saying that *anyone* who is blindly dynastic in his attitude to government has the potential to cause great danger to the State. He certainly does not let Richard, Earl of Warwick entirely off the hook. A republic therefore begins to look much more attractive than this endless dynastic bloodshed – a situation which is not solved in the History plays until the arrival of King Henry VII, who is left unquestioned. Through the omission of a biographical play on the first Tudor king, the unavoidable subtext is that Henry VII has more in common with a deus ex machina than a human being. With no new deus ex machina on the horizon to follow Queen Elizabeth's death, however, the implication is that everyone who has the wit and education to help the State must now actively seek a solution, even if Elizabeth, 'the mortal moon,' has officially banned such activities.

Reviewing some of Neville's annotations
The first annotation in Neville's copy of Leicester's Commonwealth [Worsley MS 47] is '2 sortes of dealings against the State - Directlie', which immediately shows the annotator's political concern too. The next annotation is 'Indirectlie', and it

stands alongside mention of the 'Roman Religion', so we have evidence that the annotator is a Protestant, and that he was concerned about the possible outbreak of strife in the state, based on religious causes. The annotator therefore sees two sources of 'Dealings against the State':

1. The *direct* dealings of conspirators, who basically seem infected more by personal ambition than by truly political or altruistic considerations; and
2. The *indirect* power of Catholicism and the banding together of Catholics as a combined force, which can also eventually undermine the new Protestant state,

Both these concerns reflect our Neville's own fears. The fact that the annotator of this banned book is a Neville is indeed graphically pointed out by the emboldening of the name '**Neville**' every time it appears in the text of the document. No other family name is emboldened consistently throughout the text. [76] There are also the occasional marginal scribblings which could be a kind of Henry Neville signature. There were probably even more indications of the ownership of these manuscripts, but the 19th century binder of the books has actually cropped off the edges of the 16th century manuscript, as well as hiding some recto annotations in the binding itself, so some of the annotations have fallen victim to his processing. [The binder obviously had covers in stock which he wished the manuscript to fit. This was all done by one 'Allason' (or his assistant) of New Bond Street in 1833, who was commissioned to preserve these books by the inheritors of the Worsley's Appuldurcombe House and its library.]

Leicester's Commonwealth as one source of the early History plays

I wish now primarily to look at some of the direct evidence for *Leicester's Commonwealth* being a source of the first anti-civil war plays – the *Henry VI* trilogy. This had – most surprisingly – never been mentioned before my discovery of Henry Neville and his documents.[77]

First and foremost, *Leicester's Commonwealth* seems to be the only source portraying the Earl of Suffolk exactly as he was painted in those plays. As many scholars have pointed out, none of the history chronicles of Shakespeare's time had made the point that he was having a love affair with Queen Margaret. But in

Leicester's Commonwealth we find the following lines: [I have kept the original spelling of Worsley Ms. 47 in this extract]

> ...Queen Margarett ye wiefe of K: Hen:6 had favored ... many yeares to geather Wm. D: of Suffolk ... whereby he committed many outrages and afflicted the Realme manye waies yet she being a woeman of great prudence when she sawe the whole comunaltie demaund iustice of him for demerits, albeit she liked and loved the man still yet for satisfaceon of ye people upon so general accompte she was content first to commit him to prison and afterwards to banish him the Realme. But the providence of God would not permit him soe to escape, he was behedded in ye ship & soe received some pte [part] of condigne punishment for his most wicked, loose and licentious life ....

So here, for the first time, we have an actual source for the character of the Earl of Suffolk, as portrayed in the Shakespeare plays. What's more, the annotator – Henry Neville – points out this whole passage with his marginal annotation, 'The punishmte of Wm Earl of Suffolk Ao 30 Hen: 6./'[78]

In future chapters I shall, moreover, show that to be against William Earl of Suffolk was to align oneself with a faction which was against the (then Catholic) church, because William had encouraged the young Henry VI to be on the side of the clergy. The very fact that the author of *Leicester's Commonwealth* therefore mentions the perfidy of the Earl of Suffolk also provides extra evidence against the supposition that this book was written by a Catholic. The theory that it was therefore likely to have been an 'inside job' on the part of Walsingham et al looks increasingly likely.

We also have the annotation: "The Kinges of England overthrowne by too much favouringe of some pticular persons"; then 'Ed:2' R:2' and 'Henr: 6' are the kings chosen out as examples of such Kings.

Richard II is of course famously portrayed as choosing the wrong friends in Shakespeare's play, and Henry VI's favouring of the Earl of Suffolk and the Cardinal Beaufort is portrayed in the plays as completely misguided. References to the 'Red rose and the White' are also words which appear in the annotations of these copies of the book.[79] Thus, altogether, there can be little doubt of their importance, and little doubt that Sir Henry used the book as one source of his plays.

Then there are points of contemporary interest within the *Commonwealth*. For example, Anjou is referred to as 'Monsieur' throughout the document – just as he is referred to on the Northumberland Manuscript.

It was pretty certain that no child would ensue from any marriage, given the age of the Queen, so if she had named her **successor** as a Protestant, then even some of the Protestants might have seen her marriage to Anjou as a good solution. Is this part of the thinking behind the following extract from the text of this banned book?

> ...Our differences in religion at home had been either less or no greater than now they are, for that Monsieur, being but a moderate Papist and nothing vehement in his opinions, was content with very reasonable conditions for himself and his strangers only in use of their conscience, not unlikely (truly) but that in time he might by God's grace and by the great wisdom and virtue of her Majesty have been brought also to embrace the gospel, as King Ethelbert, an heathen, was by noble Queen Bertha his wife, the first Christian of our English princes.[80]

The above section certainly does not make it look like a Catholic is writing the book. But *Leicester's Commonwealth* also made the point that the Earl of Leicester had consistently thwarted the Queen's proposed marriages, which makes him seem just as ambitious as Suffolk is portrayed in the *Henry VI* plays.

The *Commonwealth* further affirms that the Earl of Leicester himself is ambitious to become king:

> The words also of Sir Thomas Leighton to **Sir Henry Neville**, walking upon the terrace at Windsor, are known, who

> told him, after long discourse of their happy conceived kingdom, that he doubted not but to see him one day hold the same office in Windsor of my Lord of Leicester which now my Lord did hold of the Queen. ... Which was plainly to signify that he doubted not but to see my Lord of Leicester one day king, or else his other hope could never possibly take effect or come to pass.

Sir Henry Neville senior is the man referred to here, and he strenuously denied that he had ever had such a conversation with Leighton or anyone else. However, most importantly, **Sir Thomas Leighton was the overseer of Richard Newport's grandfather's will, and Richard Newport was the man who owned the copy of** *Halle's Chronicles* **which was annotated in a similar way to the Worsley copies of** *Leicester's Commonwealth***.** This reference therefore makes it quite obvious that Sir Henry Neville senior was a friend of Thomas Leighton, grandson, as well as being related to the Newports on his mother's side. Leighton's descendants are mentioned in Richard Newport's own will. The Leightons also married in with the Devereuxs and became ancestors of Robert Devereux, Earl of Essex. Again and again, the evidence builds up for Sir Henry Neville being the annotator of Keen's *Halle's Chronicles*.

Here is yet another extract comparing Leicester with the 'ambitious' Nevilles in the Wars of the Roses:

> In like sort, when the two Nevilles [father and son] took upon them to join with Richard of York to put down their most benign prince King Henry VI, and after again in the other side to put down King Edward IV, it was not upon want of advancement, they being Earls both of Salisbury and Warwick and lords of many notable places besides. But it was upon a vain imagination of future fortune, whereby such men are commonly led, and yet had not they any smell in their nostrils of getting the kingdom for themselves as this man hath to prick him forward.[81]

It is indeed amazing that the playwright decides to omit such common criticism of the Nevilles, yet not half so amazing if the playwright is himself a Neville!

'Ingratitude' also figures among the Nevilles' supposedly bad qualities:

> If you say that these men hated their sovereign and that thereby they were led to procure his destruction, the same I may answer of my Lord living [i.e. the Earl of Leicester], though of all men he hath least cause so to do. But yet such is the nature of wicked **ingratitude** that where it oweth most and disdaineth to be bound, there upon every little discontentment it turneth double obligation into triple hatred.

[Did this word 'ingratitude', associated here with the Nevilles, play upon Henry Neville's mind? Charles Paget – the spy and double agent – was with Neville while he was Ambassador in France. Paget is a suspected writer of the *Commonwealth*. Did Neville conceive his idea for the song, 'Blow, blow thou winter wind, Thou art not so unkind as man's ingratitude', while talking with him?]

My next extract can surely be said to underpin the Wars of the Roses plays; the single, and highly significant, difference being that the Nevilles are portrayed as less self-seeking in the plays than they are in *Leicester's Commonwealth*:

> Neither is this art of aspiring new or strange unto any man that is experienced in affairs of former time, for that it hath been from the beginning of all government a trodden path of all aspirers. In the stories both sacred and profane, foreign and domestical, of all nations, kingdoms, countries, and states, you shall read that such as meant to mount above other and to govern all at their own discretion did lay this for the first ground and principle of their purpose, to

possess themselves of all such as were in place about the principal; even as he who intending to hold a great city at his own disposition nor dareth make open war against the same, getteth secretly into his hands or at his devotion all the towns, villages, castles, fortresses, bulwarks, rampires, waters, ways, ports, and passages about the same, and so without drawing any sword against the said city he bringeth the same into bondage to abide his will and pleasure.

This did all these in the Roman Empire who rose from subjects to be great princes and to put down emperors. This did all those in France and other kingdoms who at sundry times have tyrannized their princes. And in our own country the examples are manifest of Vortiger[n], Harold, Henry of Lancaster, Richard of Warwick, Richard of Gloucester, John of Northumberland, and divers others who by this mean specially have pulled down their lawful sovereigns.

[Mention of the Roman Empire reminds us of the predominantly pre-Christian imagery used in the *Henry VI* plays, which will be examined in Chapters 8 & 9.]

There is no mention of Duke Humphrey's death being by anything but natural causes, in the Chronicles of the time, yet it *is* presented as murder in *Henry VI, part 2*. This is how it is presented in *Leicester's Commonwealth*, which certainly suggests the writer had been reading this forbidden script:

Henry VI (being a simple and holy man), albeit no great exorbitant affection was seen towards any, yet his wife Queen Margaret's too much favor and credit (by him not controlled) towards the Marquess of Suffolk that after was made Duke, by whose instinct and wicked counsel she made away first the noble Duke of Gloucester and afterward committed other things in great prejudice of the realm and suffered the said most impious and sinful Duke to range and make havoc of all sort of subjects at his pleasure (much after the fashion of the Earl of Leicester now, though yet not in so high and extreme a degree) – this I say was the principal and original cause, both before God and man (as Polydore well noteth), of all the calamity and extreme desolation which after ensued both to the king, queen, and their only child, with the utter extirpation of their family.

Did Neville (alias Shakespeare) find his inspiration for the garden scene in *Richard II* from *Leicester's Commonwealth* too?

Consider the fruit of the garden, and thereby you may judge of the gardener's diligence. Look upon the bishoprics, pastorships, and pulpits of England and see whence principally they have received their furniture for advancement of the gospel. And on the contrary side, look upon the seminaries of Papistry at Rome and Rheims, upon the colleges of Jesuits and other companies of Papists beyond the seas, and see wherehence they are especially fraught.

It is not my intention here to carry out a full analysis of *Leicester's Commonwealth* and its echoes in the Shakespeare plays. But I'm sure readers by now will understand what a valuable source it was for the plays nevertheless, and that it should surely at last take its place beside Holinshed's and Halle's *Chronicles* as an important influence on the History dramas. It also points to Sir Henry Neville as being the author of these plays, and especially so since his annotations are present alongside the scribe's manuscript copies of the text. Of course it would not have been an openly-acknowledged source; nor yet a source available to the Stratford man: it was a banned book, and as such could only be safely owned by those who were placed somewhere within the Walsingham secret circle.

When reading the whole of this banned book, however, one simply cannot avoid the feeling that it may be something of a disguised republican tract too. It denigrates Kings as subject to the whims of their favourites and leaves 'gentlemen and scholars' as the only people who can sort things out for the good of the state. (The whole work is presented in the framework of a conversation between a gentleman and a scholar.) However, during Henry Neville's lifetime it was pretty clear that it was probably going to be an impossible task to get rid of monarchy altogether. Indeed, only the most extreme of circumstances, brought on by Elizabeth's strange attitude to the succession, forced the thought of forming a republic to the top of his mind. Moreover, the Shakespearean Roman plays describe the shortcomings of Republicanism too. Altogether, it is only Neville's 'partnership' solution that can solve the problems which the Shakespeare plays present when viewed as a totality.

PART TWO

THE SHAKESPEARE– NEVILLE IDENTITY

Chapter Four

THE SIGNS OF A WRITER CALLED 'FALSTAFF'

My first two chapters demonstrated that placing the Shakespeare texts alongside documents verified as being written by Neville himself produces an ever-increasing weight of evidence in favour of Sir Henry as Shakespeare. However, it is also possible for *extraneous* documents of the time to be traced as confirmatory information. A few letters written during Neville's lifetime allude to someone nicknamed 'Falstaff', and one of the letters says that this person was a writer. Henry Neville was a man of Falstaffian proportions, which is an important pointer, as nicknames are often based on physical appearance. It is therefore as if the true writer (who stemmed from a 'knightly' background) stepped aside and took time out to laugh at himself, when he created Falstaff, the fat, less-than-perfect, knight.

'Falstaff' is of course a name that puns on 'Shakespeare', but the original version of that name (as a character in the plays) was Sir John 'Oldcastle'. 'Oldcastle' is in turn an antonymic pun on 'Neville'. The origins of the Neville surname spring from the French for 'New Town' or, when viewed in a more anglicised way, 'New Villa.' 'Falstaff' was, however, the name which ultimately stuck to the character in the plays, and it was this name which appeared in the **printed** version of *Henry IV, part 1* in 1598. It is therefore a highly feasible theory that the Countess of Southampton alluded to Neville when she cited 'Falstaff' and his son in a letter to her husband:

> All the news I can send you that I thinke will make you merry is that I reade in a letter from London that Sir John Falstaffe is by his mrs. dame pintpot made father of a godly millers thumb, a boye thats all heade and a litel body – but this is a secret.[82]

(Evidence for Neville being identified as Falstaff in that letter has appeared in my previous two books.) The writers of two letters discussed in this chapter were certainly in the 'Neville circle'. It is therefore interesting to review Lady Southampton's letter again in the light of another contemporary 'Falstaff' reference, which was brought to my attention by the actor, Martin Bishop. This 'new' letter was written sometime after 1597 by a certain Tobie Matthew, who clearly says an *author* bore the Falstaff nickname:

> As that excellent author Sir John Falstaff sais, what for your bysiness news, device, foolerie and libertie, I never dealt better since I was a man.[83]

Tobie Matthew wrote this to Sir Francis Bacon. Referring to a writer known as 'Falstaff' within a letter to Francis Bacon probably discounts Sir Francis as the 'Shakespeare-writer'. Yet at the same time it confirms that the true writer was *known* to Bacon. But who was Tobie Mathew, and why would he refer to Shakespeare as 'Falstaff?' How did Tobie enter the Neville circle?

Tobie Matthew, like Neville, was a son of a father who bore the same name as he. Born in 1577, he was some fifteen years younger than Neville, but Neville would definitely either have known, or known of, his father. I can say 'definitely' because Tobie Matthew senior was the Dean who travelled up to Durham with one of Neville's fellow students at Oxford. This erstwhile student friend was Richard Ede, who wrote *Iter Boreale*[84] – the long poem in Latin celebrating Dean Matthew's journey from Oxford to Durham in 1583. On his way up to Durham, Ede encountered our Henry Neville, who was accompanying Walsingham and the young Earl of Essex on their journey back from visiting King James VI of Scotland.

Neville would also have encountered Tobie Matthew senior through his greatest friend and mentor, Sir Henry Savile. At Oxford, Tobie Matthew senior had become associated with Christ Church, Oxford. In 1573 he became reader in Greek, and this is what brought him into contact with Henry Savile. Savile was at that time already researching John Chrysostom, the Greek orthodox saint, and searching avidly through Greek documents. 1573 was the year in which Neville's mother died, and in which he himself entered Oxford University. In 1579, while Neville and Savile were together on the continent, an Italian protestant lawyer, Albericus Gentilis, fled from Italy. On coming to England, he found a friend in Tobie Matthew senior and, most significantly, Matthew defended Gentilis' views on the legitimacy of the theatre.[85] (It was probably because of Christ Church's affinity with the theatre, and through his acquaintances in that college, that Neville recommended his own son in law, Sir Richard Brooke, to Christ Church rather than his own old college of Merton.) Tobie Matthew senior would also have known Neville's father in law, Henry Killigrew, because in 1597 Matthew was concerned in the Anglo-Scottish settlement, during which time Killigrew had been the Scottish Ambassador. Moreover, Matthew's closest companion at one time was Sir Thomas Posthumous Hoby – Neville's wife's cousin. Hoby resided at Bisham Abbey, Berkshire, Richard Neville's home and burial place. With all these connections, therefore, our Henry Neville would have known Tobie Matthew senior for certain, and thereby his son too.

Sir Tobie Matthew junior, then, – the letter writer – was born in 1577. Although closely connected with many Protestant churchmen, and despite the strong opposition of his companion, Francis Bacon, he eventually became a Catholic. Nevertheless, he remained Bacon's life-long friend, after being involved with him in 1595 in a Court entertainment. In 1598 he went to France to visit one of the Throckmortons, who were nominally Catholic, but to one of whom Neville's aunt was married. As can be seen through all this, Neville and Bacon had at least one thing in common: although they opposed the Catholic church as a power base, they were still tolerant of moderate, devotional Catholics. And Neville must have met Tobie Matthew junior through politics too, because he became an MP for a constituency in Cornwall – the county from which Neville's father in law haled, and in which our Neville himself became an MP after the death of one of his wife's relatives there.

Tobie Matthew was also friendly with Neville's friend and supporter, Dudley Carleton, whom he went to visit in the Hague in 1605. It was after this that Tobie went to Rome and even became involved with Robert Parsons (or Persons) an English Jesuit opposed by Neville, and even opposed by some less strict English Catholics. This must surely have marked an end to any *open* friendship Tobie might have had with Neville. But Tobie would nevertheless have been in the Neville circle long enough to have discovered Sir Henry's secret authorship. Young Matthew also became something of a poet, although this did not redeem him in his father's Protestant eyes.

We also have to remember however that Neville, like Falstaff, was able to make friends with all manner of men. Though it was politic for Neville to abjure all Catholicism while in Protestant England, he (like the Earl of Essex) nevertheless counted moderate Catholics among his friends. There is therefore no guarantee that he did not maintain some sort of covert contact with Tobie Matthew and his new Catholic group. This is precisely the attitude of toleration we glean from the plays. But toleration is not to be confused with 'liking' or even with 'sympathy.' All the signs in the plays are totally against their author emanating from a Catholic persuasion.

So, returning to the Tobie Matthew letter, it is surely significant that he calls the author 'Falstaff' when corresponding with Sir Francis Bacon. The logical conclusion is that both knew who was meant by that epithet. It is also worth noting here that Matthew *never* mentions the name 'Shakespeare' in connection with writing – a feature which was echoed within the answer to a petition sent to Philip Herbert, Earl of Pembroke, in 1635. (Philip was one of the patrons of the First Folio.) Some petitioners had asked Philip if he would approve of them having a greater share in the takings from the Globe and Blackfriars theatres, but they were opposed by Cuthbert and William Burbage (sons of James Burbage, the actor, and the original owner of Blackfriars.) They sent their answer to Philip Herbert, opposing the petitioners. In that answer, the Burbages described William Shakespeare as a 'player', **not as a writer**:

> We then ... at like expense built the Globe, with more sums of money taken up at interest, which lay heavy on us many years;... Now for the Blackfriars, that is our inheritance. Our father purchased it at extreme rates, and made it into a playhouse with great charge and trouble; ... it was considered that house would be as fit for ourselves, and so purchased the lease remaining from Evans with our money, **and placed men players, which were Heminges, Condell, Shakespeare, &c.**[86]

Now, the Burbages were not writing to someone who knew nothing about Shakespeare – far from it, indeed. They were writing to the patron of the First Folio. Yet they describe Shakespeare as a 'player' and are therefore satisfied that Philip Herbert – a famous patron of the Folio – will be content to see him thus described. Similarly, Dudley Carleton (a friend of Neville's, and the cousin of his widow's second husband) simply said "our author" whenever he quoted anything from a Shakespeare play. It is thus surely clear that those who knew the truth never mentioned the author's true name, and always referred to Shakespeare as a 'player', not an author, even years after the First Folio bearing the Shakespeare name had been published.

The Countess of Southampton would have known the true identity of the author too, but she never mentioned 'Shakespeare.' Neither was she a friend of Sir Francis Bacon, nor did Sir Francis ever have any children! Yet her letter, like Tobie Matthew's, refers to a man nicknamed 'Falstaff'. This letter seems to have been written while Neville was in France – about two years after Matthew's letter. From the evidence within both letters – as analysed below – it is probable that she too was now using the name 'Falstaff' to signify an author. Yet this 'Falstaff' has recently become the father of a son, so cannot be Sir Francis Bacon.

Her letter is dated 'June' but no year is given. Tobie Matthew's letter is completely undated, but both letters can be roughly dated. Both letters must have been written after the composition of *Henry IV, part 1,* (completed around 1597) because they both quote from this play. The letter writers had therefore either seen that play and/or read it. If they had both seen *and* read it, then this would date the letters as some time during or after 1598 – the year of the first printing of the play. Tobie Matthew's extended quotation argues that he was probably copying from the printed version, so the letters were most likely written in 1598/9. By writing "I never dealt better since I was a man" etc. Tobie Matthew is quoting directly from Act 2, Sc.iv.; and in this same scene Falstaff calls Mistress Quickly, 'pint-pot', which is the term the Countess uses for 'Falstaff's' wife. Something in that very play, act and scene must therefore have seemed significant to *both* letter writers; and that significance also suggested the same real person and the same nickname – Falstaff – to each of them.

This remarkable coincidence is certainly worthy of careful investigation. Even if both letter-writers knew the Shakespeare-Neville-Falstaff-Oldcastle secret, they could have chosen to allude

THE SIGNS OF A WRITER CALLED 'FALSTAFF'

to *any* play, act or scene in which Falstaff appeared. Could it be possible, then, to discern *why* each letter writer chose the *very same* play, act and scene from which to quote? I think so. There is a Latin line spoken by Falstaff in that scene which may give the clue to the letter-writers' conscious or subconscious trains of thought: in the same speech as the one in which Falstaff says "I never dealt better since I was a man," he also says "ecce signum" [behold the sign.] If both letter-writers knew that Neville was the real Shakespeare, then "ecce signum" was surely enough to make them listen attentively. Both letter-writers must therefore have examined this scene for **signs** of Neville. They would not have been disappointed.

To start with, they didn't have to look any further than the Falstaff figure to see Neville's physique appearing on stage. (Note that this was *not* the physique of Sir Francis Bacon.) Moreover, as both letter writers knew Neville, they would know about his and his family's love of disguising and bravado. Prince Hal – Neville's other namesake, (as 'Hal' is a form of 'Henry') – shows this same bravado at the beginning of the scene; so the Countess and Tobie Matthew would have listened carefully to what Prince Hal had to say about his wandering among the public houses of the town as a common man and getting on first name terms with some of the publicans. They knew too that, in the same way, Neville – for all his loftiness – frequented that melting pot of society, the Mitre tavern. While the Mitre tavern was rather more philosophical and elevated than the kind of inns which Prince Hal hinted he was frequenting, Neville's friends knew that Sir Henry (like his grandfather before him) would disguise at the drop of a hat, and might therefore well have frequented even such lowly taverns as Prince Hal did, under the protection of fancy dress. In the Mitre tavern Neville associated with Ben Jonson, Inigo Jones, Hugh Holland, Thomas Coryate, Richard Martin and John Hoskins, as well as with John Donne and his circle. All these men were in some respect artists and/or thinkers of a non-establishment turn of mind. During the early 1590s, Neville's friend the courtier Thomas Edmondes (who became Neville's steward in France) was a member of the Mermaid club, so Neville clearly always had access to a lot of 'drinking friends' as well as literary and philosophical debaters.

But at the same time, Prince Hal curiously makes the point that 'Jack' Falstaff is somewhat loftier than he in his actual manner towards the underclass:

Prince: I am no proud Jack like Falstaff, but a Corinthian, a lad of mettle, a good boy - by the Lord, so they call me! - and when I am king of England I shall command all the good lads in Eastcheap. They call drinking deep 'dyeing scarlet', and when you breathe in your watering they cry 'hem!' and bid you 'Play it off'. To conclude, I am so good a proficient in one quarter of an hour that I can drink with any tinker in his own language during my life.

A 'Corinthian' meant a man who enjoyed a good time and was easy in company, and Hal is saying that this side of his own behaviour contrasts with that of Falstaff.

Yet, curiously, Falstaff does not seem quite so proud and lofty in company when it comes to his dealings with the underclass of the pub world as Prince Hal is painting him. Falstaff is not above bantering with Mistress Quickly, and in *Henry IV, part 2* he takes sufficient ease in the presence of his tavern friends to cavort openly with Doll Tearsheet. Could it be that Hal is describing some of *Henry Neville's* outwardly lofty manner more than that of Falstaff? [Only those who knew of Neville's authorship would have truly understood whom Prince Hal was aiming at.] After all, Henry V (as Prince Hal became) was the son of a usurper, and therefore could have felt a little less lofty than previous princes. There was a sense, therefore, in which Falstaff (if he is supposed to be Neville) is bound to be loftier than a usurper's son. Besides, everyone knew Sir Henry Neville was lofty in manner – at least, when he was not in disguise. They thought of him as a man of 'quality' whom one did not approach unless one had serious business to discuss.[87] No one ever named him in any formal writing without also calling him a 'noble knight'. Dudley Carleton was amazed when John Hoskins actually wrote a poem – in Latin – in which he mentioned Sir Henry coming to the Mitre club, alongside those 'great fools' (like Ben Jonson!)[88] (Carleton's amazement at Hoskins' outspoken poem suggests that those who knew of such associations were supposed to keep quiet about it all.)

One certainly therefore gets the impression that Neville's public face whenever he frequented such clubs as the Mitre was generally one of lofty observance rather than boisterous revelry. It is therefore surely Neville's – rather than wholly Falstaff's – stance that Prince Hal is thinking of. But perhaps Prince Hal is affording us one 'visible' sign that Neville might have picked up his own ability to use 'street talk' in the plays when wandering in disguise. Prince Hal, however, attributes these experiences not to the lofty Sir John, but to himself:

> They call drinking deep 'dyeing scarlet', and when you breathe in your watering they cry 'hem!' and bid you 'Play it off'. To conclude, I am so good a proficient in one quarter of an hour that I can drink with any tinker in his own language during my life.

Neville, who was at least as intelligent as Prince Hal, would certainly have become just as proficient in the tinkers' language in just such a short time.

'Francis' (Bacon) in the tavern
If we continue analysing the text of this tavern scene in *Henry IV, part 1*, we note that it also contains a character named 'Francis'. Prince Hal says he now knows tapsters by their Christian names, so he demonstrates this fact by referring to them as 'Tom, Dick and Francis'. Of course, after 'Tom' and 'Dick' everyone in the audience would have been expecting to hear 'Harry'; but perhaps that would have been one sign too many for Harry Neville – the writer leaves the audience to interpolate the usual name! By introducing the unexpected 'Francis', the image of Francis Bacon would have come to mind among Neville's and Bacon's mutual friends in the audience. Francis Bacon himself would also have been alerted – early on in this scene – to the fact that his friend and relative, Harry Neville, might be about to add something of significance concerning him.

In this scene, then, Prince Hal asks Poins to keep calling out 'Francis', so the name is actually mentioned 33 times in the play! How better could the author give a 'sign' that he intended that name to be noticed, and that he wanted the cognoscenti to pay particular attention to what he was saying about 'Francis'? Yet those who would now like to interpret this as meaning that 'Francis' was the playwright are proven wrong: the 'Francis' in this scene is presented as an incompetent underling, which hardly fits with him being a master writer.

Only if both Francis Bacon and Tobie Matthew understood the *true meaning* of the allusion to that particular scene in that play would Matthew have quoted from it in his letter; and only if they both knew the true author of Shakespeare's plays would Matthew have called that *author* 'Falstaff', not 'Shakespeare'. Falstaff, as both Bacon and Matthew would have known, was an epithet for the large Harry Neville, fond of food and drink, like Falstaff. It was not an epithet for the slimmer, sterner Francis Bacon. Indeed, the 'Francis' scene in the play makes it certain that 'Francis' was *not* the author, as will be demonstrated.

As far as I am aware, no one has really attempted before to give any detailed explanation of what is going on in the Prince Hal/Francis episode in this scene. Only when it is viewed in the context of the 'Neville circle' can we make any sense of it at all. On the surface, its meaning seems so impenetrable for modern audiences that it is usually omitted from modern productions. We have to understand the context of the times and the *true* writer's circle in order to appreciate its blatant satire.

So what precisely happens in this scene? Prince Hal insists that his friend, Ned Poins, should repeatedly call the name of an apprentice wine-server (Francis) while he (Hal) taunts Francis and does his best to keep him from being able to answer Ned's call. Furthermore, Hal asks Ned to listen out for the fact that Francis is unable to invent any witty speech and can only repeat – parrot fashion – phrases he has already heard. In fact, Hal taunts Francis throughout the scene, accusing him of wishing to take over his master's job and not keep to his 'station'.

So the *cognoscenti* would first work their minds on the fact that the scene foregrounds a *Prince* Hal (Henry) and a *subservient* Francis, which for Nevillians becomes highly significant! Yet these names seem so superfluous (unless you know the true background) and the whole incident so curious that even the Arden edition of the play tends to brush it all aside. Its notes simply repeat what Kittredge wrote about the scene in 1946[89] – which actually tells us nothing at all: "The Prince is talking incoherent nonsense to mystify Francis. One is tempted to make sense of it, and perhaps Hal has some thought or other in the back of his mind: "You'd better stick to your trade and learn to serve wine. If you rob your master you'll become a fugitive. A white doublet like that you are wearing will not keep clean long". Moreover (the Arden edition continues) an 18th century commentator had simply labelled the episode 'humbug'.

Nevertheless, I think I have an explanation which has the virtue of explaining both the reference in Matthew's letter *and* the privileged information encapsulated in that whole scene of the play.

THE SIGNS OF A WRITER CALLED 'FALSTAFF'

Prince Hal [who bears the same name as **Henry** Neville] is telling Francis, the wine-waiter [who bears the same name as **Francis** Bacon] not to respond to Ned's calls, and also not to be tempted to pretend to be something greater than he really is. In other words, and in real life, Henry Neville (the true 'Shakespeare') is telling Francis Bacon not to respond to someone who is annoyingly calling him 'Shakespeare', nor to be tempted to pretend that he is the writer of the plays. This is of course a complex situation, so, before going into more detail, here is the curious episode in question:

> **Prince Henry** ...but, Ned, to drive away the time till Falstaff come, I prithee do thou stand in some byroom, while I question my puny drawer to what end he gave me the sugar, and do thou never leave calling 'Francis!', that his tale to me may be nothing but 'Anon'. Step aside, and I'll show thee a precedent.
> [*Ned POINS stands aside*]
> **Poins** [*Within*] Francis!
> **Prince Henry** Thou art perfect.
> **Poins** [*Within*] Francis!
> *Enter FRANCIS, a Drawer.*
> **Francis** Anon, anon, sir. [*Calling*] Look down into the Pomgarnet, Ralph.
> **Prince Henry** Come hither, Francis.
> **Francis** My lord?
> **Prince Henry** How long hast thou to serve, Francis? *[i.e. serve his apprenticeship]*
> **Francis** Forsooth, five years, and as much as to -
> **Poins** [*Within*] Francis!
> **Francis** Anon, anon, sir.
> **Prince Henry** Five year? Byrlady, a long lease for the clinking of pewter. But, Francis, darest thou be so valiant as to play the coward with thy indenture, and show it a fair pair of heels and run from it?
> **Francis** O Lord, sir, I'll be sworn upon all the books in England I could find in my heart -
> **Poins** [*Within*] Francis!
> **Francis** Anon, sir.
> **Prince Henry** How old art thou, Francis?
> **Francis** Let me see - about Michaelmas next I shall be -
> **Poins** [*Within*] Francis!
> **Francis** Anon, sir. Pray, stay a little, my lord.

Prince Henry Nay, but hark you, Francis. For the sugar thou gavest me, 'twas a pennyworth, was't not?

Francis O Lord, I would it had been two!

Prince Henry I will give thee for it a thousand pound. Ask me when thou wilt, and thou shalt have it.

Poins [*Within*] Francis!

Francis Anon, anon.

Prince Henry Anon, Francis? No, Francis; but tomorrow, Francis; or, Francis, a Thursday; or indeed, Francis, when thou wilt. But, Francis -

Francis My lord?

Prince Henry Wilt thou rob this leathern-jerkin, crystal-button, knot-pated, agate-ring, pukestocking, caddis-garter, smooth-tongue, Spanish pouch?

Francis O Lord, sir, who do you mean?

Prince Henry Why then, your brown bastard is your only drink; for look you, Francis, your white canvas doublet will sully. In Barbary, sir, it cannot come to so much.

Francis What, sir?

Poins [*Within*] Francis!

Prince Henry Away, you rogue! Dost thou not hear them call?

[*Here they both call him; he stands amazed, not knowing which way to go*]

Enter VINTNER.

Vintner What, stand'st thou still and hear'st such a calling? Look to the guests within.

Exit FRANCIS.

Vintner My lord, old Sir John with half a dozen more are at the door. Shall I let them in?

Prince Henry Let them alone awhile, and then open the door.

Exit VINTNER.

Poins!

Re-enter POINS.

Poins. Anon, anon, sir.

Prince Henry Sirrah, Falstaff and the rest of the thieves are at the door. Shall we be merry?

Poins As merry as crickets, my lad. But hark ye, what cunning match have you made with this jest of the drawer? Come, what's the issue?

Prince Henry I am now of all humours that have showed themselves humours since the old days of goodman Adam to the pupil age of this present twelve o'clock at midnight.

Re-enter FRANCIS.

THE SIGNS OF A WRITER CALLED 'FALSTAFF'

> What's o'clock, Francis?
> **Francis** Anon, anon, sir.
> *Exit*
> **Prince Henry** That ever this fellow should have fewer words than a parrot, and yet the son of a woman! His industry is upstairs and downstairs, his eloquence the parcel of a reckoning. ....
> *Enter FALSTAFF, GADSHILL, BARDOLPH, and PETO; followed by FRANCIS, with wine*

To begin with, I think Shakespeare-Neville is name-punning on several levels. The two main characters in the whole scene – outside of the above episode – are Prince Hal and Falstaff-Oldcastle. Falstaff-Oldcastle is equivalent to 'Shakespeare-Neville', while Prince **Hal**'s name (besides being the same as Henry Neville's) also happens to be similar to that of a writer of the time who had a few unflattering things to say about Shakespeare; and that writer was one Joseph **Hall**.

By the time this play was written, Hall had virtually accused Francis Bacon of being the real author behind the Shakespeare name. But it was an absolute gift for the *true* writer that Hall's name resembled that of Prince Hal. Falstaff addresses Prince Henry as 'Hal' throughout the play. Moreover, in the First Folio of Shakespeare's plays, at the very beginning of the scene in question, Poins addresses the Prince as **Hall**, (spelt with double 'l', therefore echoing Joseph Hall's name.) Additionally of course, Sir Henry Neville's name is also 'Hal', and Hal is the man directing everyone else's actions in the scene. (In other words, someone called 'Hal' (Henry) is the main director of affairs, i.e. the true writer,)

On top of this, bearing in mind that the name 'Francis' is intoned so many times in the scene, it must also be worthy of note that this same Francis appears again in *Henry IV,* part 2, and once again in Act 2, Sc.iv – the same act and scene numbers as those which are the significant ones in *Henry IV,* part 1. Clearly, Shakespeare-Neville did not wish his friends to miss the complex layers of joking and the intricate parallels he was employing. 'Francis', I think, can be none other than 'Francis Bacon'. His constant calling of 'anon' perhaps even slightly suggests 'Bacon'. Moreover, even the title of the play '*Henry IV, part 1*', and the 'Act 2, sc. iv' instances of 'Francis' are echoed in Joseph Hall's poetic commentary on Shakespeare, which appears in Hall's

second volume of Satires, [thus echoing Act 2 of Shakespeare's plays] ref. IV, i. [which echoes the very title of this play itself.]

Yet the *Francis* character (in the play) is portrayed as anything but the director of affairs. He is merely a minor wine-waiter, ergo, he cannot be a representation of the true writer. This scene in *Henry IV, part 1* therefore appears to be the *true* writer's answer to Hall's erroneous conclusion.

Also, Just as Prince Hal is rebuking 'Francis' the wine-waiter and advising him to stick to his trade, so had Joseph Hall rebuked Francis Bacon, because Hall not only suspected Bacon of writing the plays, but also considered playwriting to be something in which Bacon, as a prominent lawyer, should not be involved. As if to underline the fact that Prince Hal is indeed talking about a real-life *lawyer* but not a *writer* when he refers to 'Francis' in the play, we may note that both his opening and final words on the subject of 'Francis' use a legalistic vocabulary. Right at the beginning of the scene, Hal talks about a 'precedent'. The word is, however, strangely employed in the *dramatic* context, so can be assumed to carry its *legal* meaning, as too may Hal's reference to a 'puny' drawer:

> **Prince Henry** ...but, Ned, to drive away the time till Falstaff come, I prithee do thou stand in some byroom, while I question my **puny** drawer to what end he gave me the sugar, and do thou never leave calling 'Francis!', that his tale to me may be nothing but 'Anon'. Step aside, and I'll show thee a **precedent**.

Was Prince Hal obliquely referring to the position of a 'puisne' – the *junior* member of a court, not the chief justice? Probably, especially as Bacon had been passed over for promotion to that position. A legal 'precedent' is created when a judge sets forth the essence of the reasoning behind his judgement in a case. In effect, this 'precedent' then becomes a principle of law which should be quoted in courts of equal or lower status as support for a future judge's findings, when dealing with a case which bears some essential similarity to the previous judge's case.

Then, at the very end of the scene, Hal adds the word 'reckoning' which also carries the meaning of calling to [a legal] account:

> **Prince Henry** That ever this fellow should have fewer words than a parrot, and yet the son of a woman! His industry is

upstairs and downstairs, his eloquence the parcel of a **reckoning**.

'Francis' the wine-waiter works "upstairs and downstairs" – i.e. with high and low society – just as a lawyer must do. But according to this scene in the play, all the "eloquence" he has is "the parcel of a reckoning". With reference to Francis the wine waiter, the 'reckoning' is the bill, or 'account'. But with Francis Bacon, the *lawyer*, the 'reckoning' means 'a calling to account', as in a legal case. Shakespeare sometimes did indeed use 'reckoning' in this sense, e.g. in *Much Ado About Nothing,* Act V, Sc. iv:

Friar Did I not tell you she was innocent?
Leonato So are the prince and Claudio, who accused her
Upon the error that you heard debated.
But Margaret was in some fault for this,
Although against her will, as it appears
In the true course of all the question.
Antonio Well, I am glad that all things sort so well.
Benedick And so am I, being else by faith enforced
To call young Claudio to a **reckoning** for it.

(Benedick had challenged Claudio to a duel for his wrongful accusations, which he was then 'legally' entitled to do. The proposed duel was therefore a 'legal' reckoning.)

Joseph Hall and his Shakespearean Accusations
When Joseph Hall printed guarded accusations of Francis Bacon being the author of the Shakespeare works, he clearly took the risk that he might be wrong. In the scene quoted above, we have the true author assuring everyone that Francis was not the author. Indeed, as we shall see, Hall's accusatorial suggestions were later banned, thereby implying that he had certainly come to some wrong conclusions. But who was Joseph Hall, and what interest did he have in castigating 'Shakespeare'?

Joseph Hall (1574 – 1656) was primarily a clergyman, and eventually became Bishop of Norwich. He always inclined towards Puritanism, which at that time was prejudiced against the new-fangled popular entertainment called the Theatre. Not born into a rich family, Hall's education was delayed and interrupted through lack of funds. Nevertheless, he attended Cambridge University and ultimately gained an M.A. Hall subsequently carried a little chip on his shoulder, especially in the early part of his career, and this attitude seems to have prompted a somewhat ruthless ambition in the man. He was just the kind of person to stick his neck out, and blow the consequences, if things went wrong.

One of the first things Hall actually wrote were castigating satires. In 1597 he published *Virgidemiarum,* which meant 'a bundle of rods', signifying that he was hoping to whip certain authors into shape. Besides being personally ambitious, therefore, he was young, energetic, and clearly on a mission to reform. This meant that even some courtiers and writers whom he otherwise admired were thrown into his satirical melting pot, because Hall believed that they might be straying from the puritanical track. One of his once admired courtiers/writers was Francis Bacon, who had also been a Cambridge graduate; but Hall began to turn the whip in his direction.

When he suspected that Bacon might be Shakespeare, Joseph Hall therefore appears to have castigated him in the *Virgidemiarum* satires, calling him 'Labeo'. This name recalled a certain Roman lawyer. Francis Bacon was a lawyer whose ability was noted by Ben Jonson and by the Earl of Essex, among other prominent men of the time. However, despite his fame and despite Essex's support, Bacon was passed over when it came to all possible high office in the legal profession between 1594 and 1598. This became the subject of comment, particularly as the Earl of Essex was such a favourite of Queen Elizabeth during those years. Hall therefore seems to be suggesting that Bacon was probably passed over because he was secretly writing popular entertainments – something which the Puritanical Hall would have considered a good enough reason for such a gifted lawyer as Bacon to be left out in the cold. This has been one of the pieces of *circumstantial* evidence linking Joseph Hall's 'Labeo' with Bacon. There is indeed also the strong possibility that the word 'Labeo' was the nearest Hall dared to come to punning on Bacon's name ('**La Becon**').

There were actually many parallels between the personalities and careers of Labeo and Bacon. In fact, there were two 'Labeos' in ancient Rome, each bearing some similarities to Bacon.

Marcus Antistius Labeo , who died around 11 AD, made his name as a jurist. As a man from a distinguished family, he soon rose in politics. This was also true of Francis Bacon. But Bacon and Labeo also had other traits in common: their manner was sometimes off-putting and they could be somewhat inconsiderate. Consequently, despite his abilities, it was Labeo's rival who was appointed to the consulate, even though Labeo had proven himself to be of greater ability. Bacon had been similarly passed over when it came to promotion.

Again and again, Bacon is presented as a difficult, though able, man. Sir Ralph Winwood (Neville's secretary and friend) was attacked by Bacon's dog, and Bacon showed no sympathy. John More, the politician and relative of John Donne, records that Bacon's vocal answers to King James I were long-winded.[90] But Joseph Hall was not inside these circles at the time and was not in Parliament. He would therefore probably not have been aware of the nature of the man. Hall would, however, have read Bacon's learned works, could have seen his brilliance in a Court of Law, and would therefore have concluded that there was a very *secret* reason for his lack of success. Was Hall therefore putting two and two together and making five, simply because he was not aware of the whole picture? He could scarcely have known about Bacon's personal propensity to annoy fellow politicians. Nor would Hall have then been aware of Francis Bacon's additional character flaws: not only did Bacon later turn on his greatest patron, the Earl of Essex, but he was eventually also found guilty of bribery and corruption and consequently banned from Court. Those who were in closer contact with the man may well already have seen or experienced Bacon's earlier attempts at bribery and corruption; but Hall would not have known about this. Little wonder he suspected a *different* cause for Bacon's lack of promotion! Knowing the man only through his writing, therefore, Hall came to the conclusion that Bacon must be involved in some secret writing of which many in Parliament and Court did not approve. After his own lack of promotion, the Roman Labeo devoted his whole time to the law, which is just what Hall thought Bacon should do.

Yet, ironically, Sir Henry Neville's own future career was to turn out a little like Labeo's too. Neville was later also passed over for promotion to the office of Secretary of State, even though he was clearly the fittest man for the job. Like Labeo too, Neville also had more than a passing interest in Republicanism (with which, incidentally, Bacon had no sympathy.) Also like Labeo, Neville was a great linguist and interested in society and culture in general, as witnessed by the sort of committees with which he was involved in Parliament – reform of recruiting methods and military discipline, problems of abandoned children, institutions set up for continuing remembrance of great men, etc. Then, finally just like Labeo, Neville turned down an office he was offered because he had wanted a different one.

So is it just possible that Hall had Neville in mind too when he wrote his accusations against men who might be 'Shakespeare'? The other Roman Labeo bore the forename 'Claudius' and flourished in the first century AD. Strangely enough, he was involved in a rebellion, just as Neville was later to be. But Hall was writing before all this had happened to Neville, so there can be little doubt that he was trying to signal that he *mainly* suspected Bacon of being Shakespeare. However, the 'Francis' scene in *Henry IV,1* seems to have given him pause for thought: after this play was performed, Hall gave a hint that he suspected Bacon was working with someone else! So perhaps Hall hoped that even Neville, as a serious politician and respected intellectual, might take notice of his advice, if the cap fitted him too.

Nevertheless, Joseph Hall was fixed mainly on Bacon. In the first volume of his satires, he had criticised 'Labeo' for his early love-poetry published under the name of Shakespeare, and clearly others (such as Marston) had seen that Hall was using 'Labeo' to mean 'Bacon'. So it must have come as quite a slap in the face when the true writer wrote his 'Francis' scene in *Henry IV, part 1,* making it pretty clear that Bacon was **not** the man!

Hall, however, did not *initially* back down when he wrote his next 'Labeo' criticism, after witnessing this play and this scene. He only shifted his ground a little, at first declaring that he thought the 'Francis-denial' scene to be just another element in Bacon's disguise:

> *Labeo* is whip't, and laughs me in the face:
> Why? for I smite and hide the galled place,
> ...Long as the crafty cuttle lieth sure
> In the black cloud of his thick vomiture
> Who list complain of wronged faith or fame
> When he may shift it to another's name?

But at least Hall was therefore sure 'Shakespeare' was just a pseudonym – "another's name", in fact. (The 'cuttle' [cuttle fish] produces a black ink to cloud the vision of his predators. Hall is saying that he believes this is precisely what Bacon is doing, the cloudy ink being the name 'Shakespeare.')

Hall wrote this in the second volume of his satires (IV, i). [Again, notice how the volume of Hall's work bears the same number as the play of *Henry IV, part I* and how the very Act and scene numbers in which Francis appears echo the sequence of Hall's attacks. This was the **second** attack Hall had made, and the 'Francis' episodes appear in **Act 2** of both the Henry IV plays. Surely both Hall *and* the *real* Shakespeare were trying to make certain no one should mistake their meanings: this was the play in which he (Hall) was being metaphorically slapped in the face.] Precisely in that 'Francis' scene in *Henry IV, part 1,* 'Shakespeare' says, in effect: "How could you ever imagine that such a drone as 'Francis' would be capable of writing poetry and plays?" Francis, the wine-waiter in the play, is called a man who lacks 'eloquence' and skill in anything but his own profession. By implication, therefore, Joseph Hall is being made to look stupid in imagining that 'Francis' (i.e. Francis Bacon) could be 'Shakespeare'. But, disregarding this slap in the face, here we have Hall hitting back – he thinks that this scene in the play is merely the true author – Francis Bacon – putting up yet another smoke-screen.

However, the slapped-down Joseph Hall must eventually have taken some note of the Francis scene and of the rest of the rhetoric, after all, for he next begins to accuse the real Shakespeare (whom he still supposes to be mainly Francis Bacon) of writing with *another*, worse spirit, whom Hall consequently presumes to be a man who is misleading Bacon, the main writer:

> For shame, write better, Labeo, or write none:
> Or Better write, or, Labeo, **write alone**,
> Nay, call the Cynick but a wittie foole,
> Thence to abjure his handsome drinking bole:
> Because the thirstie swaine with hollow hand,
> Convey'd the streame to wet his drie weasand,
> Write they that can, tho' those that cannot, doe:
> But who knowes that, but they that do not know?

Nothing short of the satirist's understanding of the message contained in the 'Francis-denial scene' could account for what amounts to a substantial change in Hall's position: Hall is no longer accusing Bacon of being the *sole* author of these scandalous works.

The Hall quotation given above is difficult to understand, especially the last line. But surely that last line represents the last link in the chain of pride which allows Hall to reckon he might still be right about Bacon, and that it may be that Bacon himself is still trying to pull the wool over everyone's eyes. Remember that

Hall has been "laughed" in the face for hinting at the wrong man being the author of the plays. So here he still attempts to hang onto his own supposition that he (Hall), who is accused of not knowing the true writer, is the only one who really *does* know. (Arrogance indeed!) The arrogant Hall simply refuses to step down completely and admit he was wrong, even though the *true* Shakespeare is making it plain that he should do so. Thus Hall's intended meaning and implications in the extract quoted above can be interpreted as follows: "Write better things, Labeo, or write nothing at all. Either that, or write alone (because – after seeing your last play – I now begin to think you may be writing with someone else.) I, Joseph Hall, am accused of being the man that really does *not* know who the true writer is. Yet here I can hint that I am indeed privy to information about you. For instance, I now know that you write with someone else, and that that 'someone else' is known for his drinking."

The "Cynick" referred to by Hall was Diogenes, who lived in a tub and whose only possession was a drinking bowl, which he later did without, using only his hand to hold his drinking water. So Hall is probably being sarcastic, suggesting that the person with whom Bacon supposedly writes is not at all like this self-denying Diogenes.

A fellow-writer, John Marston (1575 – 1634), however, also called Shakespeare 'Labeo' (following Hall's lead), though Marston *praised* the writer rather than castigating him:

> So Labeo did complaine his loue was stone,
> Obdurate, flinty, so relentless none;
> Yet Lynceus knows, that in the end of this
> He wrought as strange a metamorphosis.
> John Marston, *The Metamorphosis of Pygmalion's Image* (1598), p. 25.

This passage by Marston refers to the main theme in Shakespeare's *Venus and Adonis*, that of unreciprocated love. Also, in his *Certain Satires, Book 1,* Marston identifies Labeo as Bacon most positively, by referring to the motto of the Bacon family, 'mediocria firma': "What, not mediocria firma from thy spite?" (line 77.) Thus Marston leaves us with little doubt that both he and Joseph Hall were naming Bacon as Labeo/Shakespeare.

It is interesting that Marston was willing to follow Hall's lead. Clearly, Francis Bacon was a greater self-publicist than Neville. That is probably why both Marston and Hall focused in on Bacon rather than Neville. Yet it is hardly to be expected that a writer wishing to remain pseudonymous would publish so much other work under his own name, which is what Bacon did. No, a purposeful pseudonymous writer would surely remain quietly persuasive, in the background, an astounding intellectual who nevertheless published nothing under his own name – just like Neville, in fact.

So now let's put forward a theory of the whole scenario, in the light of the hindsight which this long length of time and research has afforded us. If Bacon had been the true author, why would he ever have bothered to go to such lengths as to a) conceal his authorship of the plays, or b) portray himself on stage as being as stupid as Francis the wine-waiter is made to appear?

Portraying oneself as a shallow-thinking parrot would provoke the mockery of callous courtiers, and would also be highly unlikely to advance one's career in either Politics or the Law. Only if the true Shakespeare was truly **not** Francis Bacon would such a passage have been inserted in the play. After all, public figures such as courtiers and politicians accepted that they were satirised by other writers – just as they do now. Their fellow professionals accept that this is done, and do not take it too seriously. But who has ever heard of a politician or lawyer castigating *himself* in such a manner, in public entertainment? To do so would inevitably make the audience read this as a self-assessment, or a kind of confession. They would therefore take such an utterance as a substantially authentic statement, to be taken more seriously than a satirist's jest!

My contention has been that the 'Francis' scene in *Henry IV, part 1,* is the one in which Joseph Hall is lampooned because of this persistent, erroneous belief, and that this lampooning comes from the very same scene that Tobie Matthew quotes when writing to Francis Bacon. It seems that everyone in the Neville/Bacon circle was having a good laugh at Joseph Hall's misconception. But Tobie has an advantage over Joseph Hall: Tobie *knows* that it is a man like Falstaff who is the true author, not like Francis Bacon: "As that excellent author Sir John Falstaff sais, what for your bysiness news, device, foolerie and libertie, I never dealt better since I was a man." Indeed, Joseph Hall's book was later banned because of its libellous allegations, which is as good as saying that his supposition about Bacon was untrue. Certainly, Hall had begun his satire by disregarding all Shakespeare's 'signs' against Bacon's authorship, laid so purposefully in this scene. Yet it is a case of 'Ecce signum' indeed, for we even have Hall's name for Bacon (Labeo) being used as a hint *against* Francis' authorship: 'Labeo' means 'lips', and this same act and scene now under scrutiny is the only one in the whole of the play which mentions lips – and note that the lips belong to Falstaff, *not* Francis -

> **Falstaff** ... Give me a cup of sack: I am a rogue if I drunk today.
> **Prince Henry** O villain, thy lips are scarce wiped since thou drunk'st last.
> **Falstaff** All is one for that.
> [*He drinketh*]

Is Shakespeare-Neville here taking the chance to echo (and extend) Joseph Hall's image of 'Labeo'? He may indeed well be doing so. 'Labeo' in its sense of 'lips' is just as capable of producing the image of a drinker as it is capable of referring to the name of a lawyer who existed in Ancient Rome. Is Falstaff (Neville) also perchance hinting that he and 'Labeo' (Lips) sometimes wrote together, when he says '**All is one** for that.'? 'All is one' could mean that the two writers are one. But the term 'All is one' also suggests that their phase of joint writing – if it ever occurred – is over, because 'All is one' also means 'All is past and done now.'

Indeed, analysis of the rhetoric in this scene supports the proposition that any joint writing which took place between Bacon and Neville is now over. As if to signal the fact that 'Francis' had played only a minor part, Prince Hal calls him a 'puny', and also makes the point that Francis (the wine-waiter) has given him only a pennyworth of sugar. (For 'sugar' read 'sweetening of the text.') This passage therefore continues the complex layers of doubling and punning going on throughout the scene. For instance, Prince Hal's character seems to be made up of *two* people, when he addresses Francis. Firstly, he is 'Hal Neville' – the true writer – showing up Francis' puny position; secondly, Hal is Hall (Joseph Hall, the satirist), advising Francis, the wine-waiter, or 'drawer' [figuratively Francis Bacon, the lawyer] to stick to his trade.

But in his persona of Hal Neville, the Prince is also advising Francis not to rob *someone else* of the credit for doing something quite different. This 'someone else' is well-dressed, in the then style of a vintner, says Hal:

Prince Henry Wilt thou rob this leathern-jerkin, crystal-button, knot-pated, agate-ring, pukestocking, caddis-garter, smooth-tongue, Spanish pouch?
Francis O Lord, sir, who do you mean?

Francis pretends not to know to whom Hal is referring. This could well mean that in real life Francis Bacon has been told to keep secret the identity of the true writer.

But why should the real writer of the play conjure up this image of a well-dressed vintner at all? Again, we will find the answer in Joseph Hall's further satires, because Hall (after thinking about all the signs in the play) at last begins to suspect that Bacon may be writing with 'another' man, and that 'other', (hints Hall), must be known for his love of drinking. As the whole of this scene of the play takes place in a tavern, Hall was simply forced to come to this conclusion – a conclusion ensured by the skill, and rhetorical signs, constructed by the dramatist himself, the overweight food and drink lover, Sir Henry Neville.

Sir Henry Neville and Sir Francis Bacon – links of kinship and profession

Was Joseph Hall merely guessing (on the basis of the content of the relevant scene in *Henry IV, part 1*) that Francis' writing companion was fond of drinking? Or had it come to Hall's puritanical attention that Francis Bacon might have been seen in the company of that 'noble knight' Sir Henry Neville, who had grown fat with wetting his lips with drinking, and with eating venison? Well, Hall might have discovered that Bacon's half-sister was Neville's step mother, so it is possible that he might have been watching out to see if the two men were ever seen together. Bacon and Neville, besides being related, were the same age and were both Members of Parliament, so it is most likely that they were often overtly in each other's company.

Their kinship was created by intermarriage between their two families. Moreover, their shared interests in science and the law must have led to many conversations between them, even though they did not agree on politics. Neville was the progressive, the humanitarian, nevertheless the man from a great feudal family who knew about and loved pageantry, while Bacon was a strict, personally-ambitious politician who sided with Absolute Monarchy. But this need not have divided the two men completely, there being so much shared interest, kinship, and shared experience to bring them together. Kinship there was in plenty. Besides Neville's stepmother being Elizabeth Bacon, there were yet more relationships between the two families. The illegitimate daughter of Sir Thomas Gresham (who was Neville's great uncle and benefactor) was educated alongside Anthony and Francis Bacon, within their home.[91] This lady eventually married Nathaniel Bacon, Francis' half brother. There would surely have been many childhood meetings between the Bacons, Nevilles and Greshams. These facts also point out the strong regard these three families must have had for educating women, which was by no means a universally-accepted idea at the time. That on its own would have provided a strong tie between them all, especially with Neville's stepmother, Elizabeth Bacon, being so strongly in favour of girls' education. Indeed, she outlived Francis and Anthony, and Henry Neville, so she must have been a life-long influence on all of them. Later in life, Henry Neville and Francis Bacon frequented the same MPs' debates, their names often being listed one after the other in Parliamentary records, meaning they probably sat next to each other.

Neville and Bacon had homes in London, attended Court, etc. so they could speak to each other in person, without needing to exchange letters. Also, whenever their separate business took them apart, they would probably both think it expedient not to write to each other, as they might very well only end up quarrelling about politics, which was then a dangerous thing to do in writing. (As we have seen, Neville declared he was always reluctant to own up to anything he wrote "because one never knows into whose hands it might fall.")

Anthony Bacon – Francis' brother – was a known friend of Neville's. Not only had Neville visited him in France, but Sir Ralph Winwood never failed to send Neville news of Sir Anthony in his letters.[92] So altogether, Hall might indeed have suspected Neville of being "the thirsty swaine" (in a different sense from Diogenes' thirst) who worked with Francis Bacon. What Hall then saw in Shakespeare's play was a thirsty John Falstaff who so closely resembled Harry Neville that he (Joseph Hall) continued to put two and two together. Hence, therefore, Shakespeare-

THE SIGNS OF A WRITER CALLED 'FALSTAFF'

Neville's decision to correct Joseph Hall's perception of the situation by demonstrating, in the play, that Francis was certainly never the *senior* member of any writing partnership.

In the play, Prince Hal even suggests that Francis would like to 'rob' the vintner/writer, which may well mean that Neville suspected Francis Bacon was reluctant to confess that he was *not* the Shakespeare writer. Perhaps Bacon thought he might one day profit by the allegation, however untrue it may have been! Francis Bacon eventually showed himself to go along with some nefarious schemes that would earn him money. Indeed, King James ultimately banned him from Court because of the charges which were proven against Bacon. The signs must have been there, even when Bacon was younger. This is surely why Prince Hal finally calls Francis a rogue (in the play), especially after Francis says that he does not understand who the person is to whom Hal refers: "O Lord, Sir, who do you mean?" says the feigning Francis. In real life, this would certainly mean that Francis Bacon was pretending not to know who the true writer of the plays really was, even though it is clear from what Tobie Matthew says that they were both aware of the identity of the writer they call 'Falstaff'. Perhaps Francis Bacon was keeping quiet because Neville had given him the thousand pounds which Hal offers Francis in the play:

Prince Henry Nay, but hark you, Francis. For the sugar thou gavest me, 'twas a pennyworth, was't not?
Francis O Lord, I would it had been two!
Prince Henry I will give thee for it a thousand pound. Ask me when thou wilt, and thou shalt have it.

There are many reasons, therefore, why any joint writing was now 'all one' – over and done with.

Altogether, therefore, from what Prince Hal says, Joseph Hall had guessed incorrectly when it came to one important detail. Hall was presuming that Bacon was the senior writer, not Neville. Joseph Hall and others were bound to think this, (if they ever suspected Neville at all) because Neville studiedly never published anything under his own name, as we have seen, whereas Francis Bacon was not so shy. He had already published many works under his own name.

Thus it would have been difficult for Hall to see the truth of the matter, which seems to be that the two men once tried working together but that 'Francis' had little to contribute. At least, this is certainly the sense conveyed by Prince Hal. Francis is a 'parrot' – he can therefore remember, and quote, what he has heard (or read), but he cannot invent his own lines for something so imaginative as a play. It will be remembered that Bacon once called Neville an impossible dreamer, and also said that he thought an early idea of electricity would come to nothing. Francis was an analyst at best, and not a visionary. He surely must have realised this for himself, eventually. He always said he could not write poetry, and there is no 'c' in the Dedication Code preceding the Shakespeare Sonnets, so it is indeed impossible for his name, Francis Bacon, to be encoded there. Additionally, Bacon never visited Italy, so he would have been unlikely to set any of his writing there, or to display the local Venetian terminology and knowledge demonstrated in *The Merchant of Venice,* nor have talked of Venice, and hinted strongly at its prostitutes, as the playwright did openly in *Love's Labour's Lost* and *Much Ado About Nothing.*

Joseph Hall probably learnt about his own error at some future date, because both Francis Bacon's father, and his kinsman, Edmund Bacon, became supporters of Hall's later works. They would hardly have done this, had Hall not finally realised, and privately admitted, that his satires had missed the mark. Then – and only then – would Hall know, and admit, that his unkind remarks were not to be worn by Francis Bacon but by 'another.' Nevertheless, Hall's (ultimately banned) remarks were published in 1597 and 1598, so they would not have escaped the notice of either Bacon or Neville at that time.

Henry Neville and the Vintner
If Joseph Hall had examined the 'Francis' episode in the play a little more closely he might well have read what is perhaps the greatest sign of all in this scene leading to the assertion that 'Falstaff' was the true writer, not 'Francis'. The Vintner is the man whom 'Francis' envies, and near the end of the episode, the Vintner suddenly materialises. It is a short appearance, and one wonders why the writer bothered to introduce a new character at this point. He must have had a hitherto unfathomed purpose. As will be seen, there was no *dramatic* reason for bringing in a vintner: Mistress Quickly could well have performed the part:

THE SIGNS OF A WRITER CALLED 'FALSTAFF'

Enter VINTNER.
Vintner What, stand'st thou still and hear'st such a calling? Look to the guests within.
Exit FRANCIS.
Vintner My lord, old Sir John with half a dozen more are at the door. Shall I let them in?
Prince Henry Let them alone awhile, and then open the door.
Exit VINTNER.

The Vintner adds nothing to the scene or the plot. But he says, "... old Sir John with half a dozen more are at the door." For the initiated, (which included the Countess of Southampton and Tobie Matthew), this could well have had a double meaning: "Falstaff [i.e. Neville, the true writer] is standing at the door with half a dozen more plays." So the true writer, (nicknamed Falstaff) does not appear on stage at the same time as the Vintner, who is therefore standing in for the writer at this point. The situation is perhaps parallel with the Fool/Cordelia situation in *King Lear*. When Cordelia is absent, in comes the fool. He is given the role of telling Lear the kind of home truths which Cordelia had begun to utter before she was banished. Once Cordelia returns, the Fool disappears. Now the Vintner has disappeared, there is a break before Falstaff enters, together with his half a dozen more companions which are likely to stand as metaphors for his plays.

'Shakespeare' had indeed written upwards of half a dozen plays by 1598 – and while we (and the true writer) are on the subject of punning names, why choose an unnamed VINTNER for this character of the writer in absentia? Surely because VINTNER contains the word 'riten' [written] with the letters NV left over. (We may recall Ben Jonson's later poem to 'My beloved, the author, Mr. William Shakespeare...' which begins: "To call no envie (NV), Shakespeare, on thy name..." – both instances suggest the name NEVILLE.) But Hall was a young man; he was not yet initiated into the upper echelons of society and their conundrums, and, besides, he had attended Cambridge not Oxford University. At Cambridge he would have heard much about Francis Bacon, who studied there, but much less about Henry Neville, who had studied at Oxford, and abroad.

But what of Prince Hal's assertion that Falstaff and his friends be "let alone *awhile*" before the door is opened? Perhaps this even means that Neville was planning to reveal his authorship eventually, had all gone well enough in his political career to make him fireproof. Perhaps those plans included the Earl of Essex's seizing power, in the absence of the Queen naming a successor. After all, Neville was chosen by Essex to become his first minister, if all had gone according to plan. (By the time this play was written, Essex was a friend of both Neville and Bacon. Anthony Bacon also supported Essex, and, strangely. disappeared after Essex's capture.) When Essex's plans came to naught, everything turned around. Francis Bacon treacherously changed sides and bore witness against Essex, his former benefactor. Neville was imprisoned in the Tower, alongside the Earl of Southampton. The door was opened to the plays, but Falstaff, their writer, was firmly shut away. But when *Henry IV, parts one and two* were written, and when the Countess and Tobie Matthew wrote their letters, all these staged conundrums presented a pastime full of endless fun for the Neville circle.

Later echoes of other pretenders?
The passage quoted from the play also reminds me of the scene with 'Will' in *As You Like It,* Act V, Sc.i. There too, the metaphor is one of drinking. Touchstone is reminding 'Will of the Forest' (most probably therefore William Shakespeare) that he (Touchstone) is the one who pours the liquid from the cup into the glass, meaning that *Touchstone* is 'he' (the writer, the owner of the liquid) not Will, because Will merely *receives* the drink (i.e. the Text of the plays). Touchstone was an appropriate name for Neville. This time, it was not based on a series of puns on the name 'Shakespeare-Neville' itself but on Neville's profession. Neville had inherited Sir Thomas Gresham's ironworks, and a touchstone was a piece of basalt which was used for testing whether a metal was gold or not. But the naming of *Francis,* in one play and *Will,* in the other, was of course done to emphasise precisely whom the true playwright was talking about – i.e. the false candidates for the role of having written the plays: Francis Bacon and William Shakespeare.

The question and answer form of each of the scenes is also parallel. The true writer even uses one of the same questions in the scene from *As You Like it* as in *Henry IV, part 1.* ("How old are you, friend?", asks Touchstone; "How old art thou, Francis?" says Prince Hal.) Why, I wonder, is this question so important? Perhaps because both Bacon and Shakespeare were born very near the same time as Henry himself. This, therefore, made it easier for the three men to become confused, and even fused, into the identity of the author. But 'Touchstone' is a feasible name for

THE SIGNS OF A WRITER CALLED 'FALSTAFF'

Henry Neville, and so is 'Hal', being yet another form of 'Henry'. (A touchstone was a piece of basalt used to scrape off a sample of gold from an object or an ore. The sample 'gold' was then tested by being placed in acid. If it dissolved, then it was not gold. Neville was a metal worker and therefore would have known this test.) We have the clever, informed characters (Prince **Hal** and Touchstone, i.e. **Henry** Neville) questioning those who are clearly not up to the job (Francis and Will.) In both cases, the dominant character tells the other to be gone. All Ned's shouting of 'Francis' has not convinced Hal or anyone else that he (Francis) is in control of the situation. As such, Francis can do nothing but stay out of the way.

More double-meanings
Returning to the word 'puny' being applied to Francis in the *Henry IV* scene, we can see that such vocabulary automatically puts Francis into an inferior position. But it is also a term used for junior justices, and for freshmen at Oxford University and at Gray's Inn. Neville attended Oxford and Francis Bacon attended Gray's Inn, along with Anthony Bacon, his older brother. *The Comedy of Errors* was produced at Gray's Inn as part of the 1594 Christmas celebrations. Francis Bacon played a large part in these general entertainments, and there was famously a riot during the production of the Shakespeare play. However, the riot itself was 'staged' and a lot of fun was had by all. It is entirely possible that Francis collaborated with Shakespeare-Neville in producing that play, and that the idea of double twins may even have sprung from the fact that Anthony and Francis were born within eighteen months of each other and that Henry Neville and his sister, Elizabeth, may well have been twins, or at most only one year apart. But eventually two writers became one in the persona of Henry Neville alone: everything finished; it was 'all one now.' *Henry IV part 1* was completed in about 1597, so if Shakespeare-Neville is meaning Prince Hal to suggest that Falstaff (Neville) had only recently 'wiped his lips' after his one-time collaboration with Francis Bacon (in 1594), then this could be relatively true. But it does not negate the fact that Francis is nevertheless here depicted as only having had a very small input; and there was even a contemporary suggestion that Anthony Bacon had had one of his speeches written for him by Henry Neville.[93]

The fact that Tobie Matthew was able to write to Francis Bacon and proclaim Falstaff as the author of Shakespeare's plays, however, suggests strongly that things were ultimately put right between Bacon and Neville. Bacon must have known more about Neville's involvement with Essex than he ultimately brought to public notice during the trial of that Earl. Moreover, it was Francis Bacon's intervention which finally put an end to allegations of Neville's son being involved in piracy in 1610.[94] Neville and his step-mother, Elizabeth Bacon, also reached an agreement about the land which they had jointly inherited, so it appears that the Bacons and Nevilles ultimately lived in peace and harmony, even though their politics never merged and Francis and Henry never sought to write together again.

Pint-pot

Turning to the letter written by the Countess of Southampton, it is this same 'Francis' scene of the same play which contains Falstaff's name for Mistress Quickly, 'Pint-pot'. The man the Countess calls Falstaff is therefore immediately associated with Shakespeare, and so most probably denotes the same person as the one to whom Tobie Matthew was referring. She was also surely referring to someone whom both she and her husband privately called 'Falstaff', and that person had obviously just had a baby by a lady who was much smaller than himself. In the light of all the other evidence, therefore, it can surely be no coincidence that Neville's wife, Anne, had several baby boys, and that she was the child of a father whose small stature is recorded.

Now, whereas there are a number of references to the popular character of 'Falstaff' at the time, the two letters above are especially noteworthy because they both call to mind definite literary allusions, whereas an oft-quoted reference to Falstaff by the Earl of Essex, for example, is not set in a literary context at all. So I'll turn to the Earl of Essex's reference later.

In the case of the Countess of Southampton, we know that the writer who went under the name of Shakespeare was definitely in her circle. But the fact that the letter bears no year in its dating could cause some ambiguity. It is often thought that she wrote the letter in 1599, when Neville was Ambassador in France, while the Earl of Southampton went to Ireland and the Countess was staying in Penelope Rich's house. When I first researched Neville, I leapt to that conclusion too, and I still think it is a highly likely one. However, after further research, I see that there are other possible datings for the Countess' letter. Lady Southampton's mother was a Devereux, and Penelope Rich (née Devereux) was her cousin, so she was always visiting her. (Indeed, Countess Southampton was also the cousin of Robert Devereux, Earl of Essex, who was a patron of Francis Bacon, so the circle around Neville is quite narrow and inter-related.) Penelope Devereux-Rich died in July 1607, so it is perfectly possible that the Countess went to see her cousin in June of that year, because she was ill. If so, then the baby boy mentioned in the letter could easily be Charles Neville, who was born in 1607 and died in 1626. The "very litel body" and large head could have denoted a deformity, which would then account for poor Charles' death at such a young age. However, my first thought was that the baby mentioned might have been the one born to Neville and his (little) wife in 1599 – a baby who died in September of that same year. Yet there might be a problem with this dating: it seems that Robert Cecil (Anne Neville's cousin) was expecting the Neville baby to be born in August or September, not in June (the month of the Countess' letter) and it was on the 26th September that Neville apologised to Cecil for writing a shorter dispatch than usual "by reason of some domesticall Misfortune in the Losse of my Son lately born."[95] However, it is still possible that the baby may have been born as early as June and kept secret. Any baby born abroad in those days was automatically deemed a citizen of that country, which would not have been something the Nevilles would have wished to happen. Perhaps it was therefore only when he died that Neville admitted to anyone but his close – and secretive – friends that the baby had been born at all.

But whatever the case may be, it is difficult to see that the Countess' letter can be referring to anyone else but Neville and one or other of his sons. Neville had known the Earl of Southampton since he was a boy at old Lord Burghley's house, and he was to join with that Earl (passively) in the Essex uprising, only just over a year after the birth of his baby in France, and then to be imprisoned with Southampton in the Tower of London. Yet there is also little doubt that the Earl and Neville became even closer *after* these shared catastrophes, so it is highly likely that they had nicknames for each other by then. Seeing Falstaff and Quickly on the stage would therefore have immediately suggested the Nevilles to their friends, the Southamptons. Added to this, Falstaff was acting the part of Prince Hal's father – King **Henry** - at the very moment he addressed Mistress Quickly as 'Pintpot', so this appropriate naming would have re-inforced the connections with Sir **Henry** Neville in the minds of those who already knew him to be the author.

I am not of course suggesting that everything about the character of Falstaff is parallel with the personality of Henry Neville. It is in the nature of nicknames that they are affixed to a person for perhaps just one single reason. But there are three principle reasons for *choosing* a nickname; the first is often based on appearance, the second on the name of a person, and the third is based on his profession. (That is how surnames such as 'Cooper' – barrel maker – came about, and also why Neville may be seen in the character of Touchstone.) With Neville, all these reasons were pertinent. Falstaff had originally been called Oldcastle, so the antonymic punning on the name is obvious. Even when the name was changed to Falstaff, the only switch was from a pun on the *real* author's name to one on that of the pseudonym. But Neville's physical appearance did not change, so his new nickname was still appropriate. For the most part, that was as far as the observable overlapping between the fictional Falstaff and the real Neville went; that was enough for the nickname to persist. But Neville's eventual realisation of the persistence of his Falstaff nickname must have tempted him to throw in the occasional, purposely-ambiguous lines for the character. Those who were privileged to know the secret would therefore go on recognising signs – in the form of double meanings – behind what he was saying.

Bearing in mind that a major source of a nickname can be the real name of a person, are there any other contemporary references to the nickname 'Falstaff' which seem to denote someone other than Henry Neville? Well, the allusion to Falstaff by the Earl of Essex in one of his letters in 1598 does not seem to have been aimed at Neville but at someone who actually bore Falstaff's previous name - Oldcastle. Essex wrote to Cecil in that year, saying "I pray you commend me to Alex. Ratcliff and tell him for newes his sister is maryed to Sir Jo. Falstaff." Alex Ratcliff had served with Essex in Ireland, and his sister Margaret was a maid of honour to the Queen. She and another maid of honour – one Mistress Kildare – were reputedly vying for the attention of one Lord Brooke.[96] Lord Brooke's family bore the name 'Oldcastle'. There is no suggestion in Essex's letter that he was referring to any association between Falstaff and authorship.

THE SIGNS OF A WRITER CALLED 'FALSTAFF'

The only suggestion is that Essex knew about the change of name from Oldcastle in the plays to 'Falstaff'; that seems to be the only reason why Essex refers to Lord Brooke as 'Falstaff.'

Brooke seems finally to have rejected Margaret Ratcliff, but her brother Alex must have been worrying terribly about her, because by then Margaret had lost three other brothers. Perhaps Essex was trying to comfort Alex in what he suspected might have been his last days, because Alex too died very soon afterwards. Poor Margaret was so overcome with grief that she stopped eating and died one year later. Ben Jonson wrote an epigram about her.

Very few men were really big and fat in those grim days, so only one or two courtiers would have fitted the Falstaff nickname based on their size and weight. Lord Brooke [whom Essex called 'Falstaff'] was not known to be fat, so there can be no connection other than the name change in the plays. The name was changed to Falstaff before the actual registration of *Henry IV, part 1* in 1598. It may even have been Brooke, 8th Lord Cobham and an enemy of Essex, therefore, who objected to this naming and persuaded the Shakespeare-writer to change it. But it may also have been the fact that the name Oldcastle was beginning to raise the suspicions of an increasing number of courtiers perhaps cottoning on to the Oldcastle–New–Villa–Neville connection. This is especially likely when the *physical* clues to Neville's identity in the *Henry* plays are taken into account. The Mitre dinners were well known for their expense and size,[97] and Neville was known as a prominent member. Indeed, I suspect that the so-called 'Shakespeare rhyme' at the Mitre was really by Neville. (Shakespeare had never been known to frequent the Mitre, despite the title of the piece.) The rhyme is only short, but one can imagine a merry Neville saying it: "Bring me a cup of good canary wine/ Once the Mitre's [drinks it] now it's mine." It is surely to Neville and the 'Shakespeare rhyme' that Jonson is referring in *Bartholomew Fair* when Littlewit says, "A pox to these pretenders to wit! your Three Cranes, Mitre and Mermaid men! not a corn of true salt, not a grain of right mustard amongst them all. They may stand for places, or so, again the next wit-fall, and pay two pence in a quart more for their canary than other men... ." It was *Neville*, not Shakespeare, who 'may stand for places', because he was an M.P. Likewise, it was Neville, not Shakespeare who was at the Mitre club where the so-called 'Shakespeare rhyme' originated. Jonson was obviously joking, because he too was a member of the Mitre Club; but he may indeed have been throwing in some hints as to the authorial identity of some writers who emanated from there. (As detailed in the final chapter of my previous book, Jonson peppered at least one of his plays with references to Neville being Shakespeare; and it was Jonson who edited the First Folio and was subsequently given a post at Gresham College – the college founded by Neville's great uncle, from whom Neville received the lion's share of legacies, since Gresham died with no child except an illegitimate daughter.) Falstaff is witty, and so was Neville when in company he knew well. His wife was the cousin of Robert Cecil, and Robert Cecil remarked what a merry crew he and his family were; and even Robert Cecil knew that Neville disguised from time to time. Neville was therefore quite accustomed to 'acting' in real life!

However, there were even more reasons for Neville choosing Oldcastle for his roguish knight – reasons other than the name, that is. The historical Oldcastle had been associated with the notorious Cheyne family, who had been well-known brigands in Medieval days. True, some of them had been Lollards too, but even this early Protestant stance would not have wiped out their roguery, as far as our very decent Neville was concerned! Indeed, Neville was just the man to have made the point that an outwardly religious stance could be – and actually was – used by some families to put an acceptable gloss on their illegal activities. Such men were dangerous: they could besmirch the reputation of the new, progressive Protestantism which Neville espoused. This Cheyne family and their friends had been promoted by Henry VIII largely because of their support for his dissolution of the monasteries. Roguish go-getters had profited from the dissolution, alongside true-hearted social reformers. There were thus many aspects to Neville's choice of naming and characterisation when it came to the original Sir John Oldcastle in the plays, which definitely included the joke on his family name. Yet changing it to 'Falstaff' gave a chance for his friends and supporters to use the new name without giving the game away.

One feels that, in real life, however, Neville kept his Falstaffian side under control for the most part, and certainly did not let it appear at Court. He knew it was there, all the same, so gave it full rein on the stage. The cavorting with Doll Tearsheet in *Henry IV, part 2,* however, was much more Falstaff than Neville. (Neville had written letters expressing his disgust at King Henri IV's womanising.) But *fictional* womanising obviously did no harm, and, in any case, this was neither the play nor the scene to which Matthew's and Lady Southampton's letters refer.

The Countess' reference to 'secrecy' also marks the reference to Falstaff as meaning Neville. Neville regularly used ciphers in his letters and was most meticulous about keeping private information private. In fact, he often judged men's worth by observing whether they were able to keep a confidentiality or not, and promptly dropped acquaintances who proved themselves untrustworthy in this respect. (This aspect of his personality will be further illustrated by the connections with another Falstaff incident.) There is certainly extant *documentary* evidence for Neville's insistence on secrecy:

Sep 15 1612   Sir Robert Naunton to Winwood from Holeborne:

The same day, hearing that his Majesty was determined for Windesore, I went thither, and the next morning delivered your enclosed to Sir. H. Nevil at Sir H. Savill's in Eton, where I was by him resolved of a steady purpose in your honourable friends towards you and myself, *but was at no hand to give suspicion of any such intention at all there, much less of any privity of his, in respect of their feeling sympathy with the Ambassador at Venice.* [i.e. Sir D.. Carleton]. So I held it fitting not to trouble my Lord of Rochester, lest an inexpe[   ] visitation should seem a faint kind of importunity, but saluted Sir Thomas Overbury en passant, which was sufficient to continue me in both their remembrance ... volunt, valde velint.[98]

1613? [no other date] Winwood to Neville:

Has received his letter of the 10th enjoining secrecy, ending "There is great reason you should again and again recommend this cause to my secresy; for if there come forth but the least vent of it, I know actum est de me." Refers to his servant Moore. [Sends a cipher too.][99]

Altogether, Neville's love of secrecy was (unsurprisingly) paralleled by evidence within the Shakespeare canon. The word 'secret' and 'secrecy' is used 130 times in his plays and poems. And Shakespeare, just like Neville, insists that the ability to keep an oath of secrecy is the safest sign by which to judge the basic honesty of a person:

> **Brutus** ...What need we any spur but our own cause
> To prick us to redress? What other bond
> Than secret Romans that have spoke the word
> And will not palter? And what other oath
> Than honesty to honesty engaged
> That this shall be, or we will fall for it?
> *Julius Caesar: Act 2/Sc.1*

Falstaff, Neville and John Colville

There is yet another episode in one of the plays which links Neville with Falstaff. This occurs in *Henry IV, part 2*. Neville, as I suspected, did indeed use the chance of constructing the occasional scene relevant to himself when writing more than one episode for Falstaff. By the time he wrote this play, Neville must have heard about Falstaff's effect on his circle of friends and how he himself was beginning to wear that nickname.

In Act 4, Sc. iii Falstaff is seen capturing one John Colville during a battle. Strangely, John Colville gives himself up quite readily. However, Colville's quick surrender turns out to be understandable only when the links with Neville's life are known. Colville was a very minor character in the rebellion against Henry IV, so why did the writer of the play choose him? Well, Neville, and only Neville, had reason to choose him. Neville included this minor character because he had already picked over a few bones with a real-life character he knew personally, who was also called John Colville. Neville used Colville for a time as an intelligence agent in France, but he learned to distrust him. He may even have had Colville in mind *before* going over to France, because by then Colville was already known to him, Walsingham and Sir Robert Cecil. However, the dates of letters in which Neville writes about his distrust of Colville overlap with the date, in 1600, when *Henry IV, part 2* was actually placed on the Stationers Register. It is therefore possible that Neville added this odd scene during his time in France.

THE SIGNS OF A WRITER CALLED 'FALSTAFF'

First of all, however, here is the incident in *Henry IV, part 2*, Act 4, Sc.3:

Scene 3. Another Part of the Forest. (Falstaff is fighting off men who are rebelling against King Henry IV.)
Alarum. Excursions.
Enter FALSTAFF and COLEVILLE, meeting.
Falstaff What's your name, sir? Of what condition are you, and of what place?
Coleville I am a knight, sir, and my name is Coleville of the Dale.
Falstaff Well then, Coleville is your name, a knight is your degree, and your place the Dale. Coleville shall be still your name, a traitor your degree, and the dungeon your place - a place deep enough; so shall you be still Coleville of the Dale.
Coleville Are not you Sir John Falstaff?
Falstaff As good a man as he, sir, whoe'er I am. Do ye yield, sir, or shall I sweat for you?
If I do sweat, they are the drops of thy lovers, and they weep for thy death; therefore rouse up fear and trembling, and do observance to my mercy.
Coleville I think you are Sir John Falstaff, and in that thought yield me.
[Kneels]
Falstaff I have a whole school of tongues in this belly of mine, and not a tongue of them all speaks any other word but my name. And I had but a belly of any indifferency, I were simply the most active fellow in Europe - my womb, my womb, my womb undoes me. Here comes our general.
Retreat sounded.
Enter Prince John of LANCASTER, WESTMORELAND, BLUNT, and OTHERS.
Lancaster The heat is past; follow no further now.
Call in the powers, good cousin Westmoreland.
Exit WESTMORELAND.
Now, Falstaff, where have you been all this while?
When everything is ended, then you come.
These tardy tricks of yours will, on my life,
One time or other break some gallows' back.
Falstaff I would be sorry, my lord, but it should be thus. I never knew yet but rebuke and check was the reward of valour. Do you think me a swallow, an arrow, or a bullet? Have I in my poor and old motion the expedition of

thought? I have speeded hither with the very extremest inch of possibility; I have foundered ninescore and odd posts; and here, travel-tainted as I am, have in my pure and immaculate valour taken Sir John Coleville of the Dale, a most furious knight and valorous enemy. But what of that? He saw me, and yielded, that I may justly say, with the hook-nosed fellow of Rome, "I came, saw, and overcame".
Lancaster It was more of his courtesy than your deserving.
Falstaff I know not. Here he is, and here I yield him; and I beseech your grace, let it be booked with the rest of this day's deeds; or, by the Lord, I will have it in a particular ballad else, with mine own picture on the top on't, Coleville kissing my foot;...
Lancaster Is thy name Coleville?
Coleville It is, my lord.
Lancaster A famous rebel art thou, Coleville.
Falstaff And a famous true subject took him.
Coleville I am, my lord, but as my betters are
That led me hither. Had they been ruled by me,
You should have won them dearer than you have.
Falstaff I know not how they sold themselves; but thou, like a kind fellow, gav'st thyself
away gratis, and I thank thee for thee.
Re-enter WESTMORELAND.
Lancaster Now, have you left pursuit?
Westmoreland Retreat is made and execution stayed.
Lancaster Send Coleville with his confederates
To York, to present execution.
Blunt, lead him hence, and see you guard him sure.
Exit BLUNT with COLEVILLE.

Once again, this is a curious incident – almost as strange as the one with 'Francis'. It is worth noting too that the supposedly complete BBC films of the two plays omit the Francis episode altogether from their performance of *Henry IV, part 1*, and that the scene with John Coleville is curtailed – indeed, some of Falstaff's lines are omitted. It looks very much, therefore, as if the BBC's academic advisors could offer no explanation for either of these sets of lines. Only with Sir Henry Neville's presence can there be a complete solution of the puzzle which these lines present.

The real 'Coleville' who lived during the time of Henry IV was not at all prominent among the rebels, so the true writer must have had another reason for hitting on his name, and here it is.

THE SIGNS OF A WRITER CALLED 'FALSTAFF'

The John Colville who lived during *Neville's* time was born in 1540. He was a Scotsman and had been employed by Walsingham as a spy. Sir Francis Walsingham was a friend of Neville and his father in law, and Walsingham's daughter was married to the Earl of Essex. (Once again, the Neville circle contains all these relevant connections.) Colville was ostensibly a Presbyterian minister, but while on the continent, being paid by the English Secret Service to spy, he had allegedly been won over to Catholicism. By the time Neville used his services in Paris, Colville was already under suspicion of being a double agent, though no one was really sure. Neither Neville nor Sir Ralph Winwood – Neville's secretary – really trusted him.

Colville, as a Catholic, was most probably getting frightened of Neville's close watch on King James VI, whereby Neville was making sure James was sticking to the Protestant faith. It is therefore feasible that Colville would indeed be putting around rumours to discredit Neville. Sir Henry Neville wrote to Winwood: "I distrust Colvel every day more and more; I will quit my self of him."[100] But Neville's next letter included more specific information about Colville/Colvel. (His name was, like Neville's own name, spelt variously at the time. 'Poverty', by the way, was Colville's code name):

Sir Henry Neville To Ralph Winwood, London, 28th August, 1600
I received yesterday letters from Poverty [Colvel] by his owne boy that came to Bulloigne. ... I would have him knowe that I am weary of promises without effect, and will be drawn into no further charge till I see some particulars that may deserve it; for I have been hitherto intertayned with generalities, of no great importance. But if he perform any real service, it shall be really acknowledged; in the mean time I suspend both my judgment and my purse.[101]

Now, *Henry IV, part 2* was entered into the stationer's register on 23rd August, 1600 – five days before Neville's letter to Ralph Winwood. (The play had been performed before this date.) Neville was by then back in London. Prior to Neville's return, Winwood had been desperately addressing letters to him at Boulogne, but had heard nothing from him for nearly a month. During this time, Neville had been writing to Robert Cecil and begging him for the Queen's permission to return home. He famously threatened to go and "live hermit" in Ashridge or the

153

Forest and "contemplate my time as a bad Ambassador" if the Queen's permission was not forthcoming.

From his letter of 28th August, therefore, we can see that something must have happened. He had obviously been home – officially – in London for some time when he wrote the above letter to Winwood. The coincidence of John Colville's name appearing in both the Neville letter and the registered edition of the play now add up. The play was not printed until 1600, i.e. *after* Neville returned from France. It looks very much as if Neville added the scene sometime after experiencing John Colville for himself in France. He may also have heard how successful the play had been in London during his absence, and found out too that he was beginning to be nicknamed 'Falstaff' in some quarters. What he wrote in this scene explains his reactions, both to Colville and to the fact that his fictional character might be starting to cause comment – and even amusement – in certain circles. As we shall see, it was as if Neville was giving his friends yet more to smile about by including this scene.

Colville/Colvel had in fact been caught giving away confidences and secrets for some time – one of the very worst betrayals of trust in Shakespeare-Neville's estimation. Robert Cecil wrote to him and reprimanded him. Colville's replies show him to have been quite naïve. He actually admitted that secrecy was not his strong point! As he was a spy by profession, this was of course ridiculous. The funny side of it could not have been missed by Neville, hence why he would have included the Scottish spy in a *comic* scene:

Colville To Cecyl, Aug 26, 1599
> By your answer doth appear that your Honour is sumwhat greved with my insecrecy and hant with the French Ambassadour, and that I can not remane heir [here] without the Kingis offens [offence]; for answer wharof, God and my conscience beareth me record, I never did, or shalldo, any thing that may justly offend your Honour. As for Secrecy, I must confes I am neither indewit [endowed] with that nor no other good qualite, bot with much imperfection....¹⁰²

In other words, John Colville the spy admitted his fatal flaw and gave in! In the play, John Colville shows a similar stupidity in simply yielding to Falstaff when he could have run away. It is clear that Neville is having fun at the real-life spy's expense. This would obviously have made a laughing stock of the man whenever the scene was viewed by those who knew about him and Colville, the failed spy.

But Neville also takes the chance to give Falstaff some very meaningful lines which impinge on his own situation. Indeed, the whole incident may even hint that Neville had some extra pressure – put upon him by the senior branch of his family – not to admit that he was a playwright.

To begin with, Falstaff makes a point about Colville being 'of the dale.' The Scottish Colville had connections with just about every Scottish place ending in 'dale' – Clydesdale, Niffidale, etc., so the writer is definitely hinting at the John Colville of his own acquaintance. Falstaff then hints that the only sorrow he feels in doing away with him is for his "lovers". Now, through a curious set of circumstances, Neville was actually sent some intercepted letters from Colville to his wife, and this may well have made him feel sorrow for *her* when he informed Cecil of his mistrust of Colville.[103] Then Falstaff says something rather strange:

> **Falstaff** I have a whole school of tongues in this belly of mine, and not a tongue of them all speaks any other word but my name.

It looks very much as if Neville – the true writer – is beginning to tell us something of himself. Neville knows he has been nicknamed Falstaff mainly because he looks as fat as Falstaff, so it is his "belly" that speaks his name. And his meaning would surely have been even *more* obvious when the character was still called 'Oldcastle' [the antonymic pun on 'Neville.'] Perhaps it was while at the Treaty of Boulogne, and in very bad spirits, that Neville heard he was achieving the nickname Falstaff around the Royal Court. Moreover, the title page of this newly-registered edition made a specific point about Falstaff: "... With the humours of sir John Falstaffe and swaggering Pistoll. ..." Neville obviously needed to make the point that the character's name had changed from a pun on 'Neville' to a pun on 'Shakespeare', once and for all.

Then we must ask why Neville was *so* desperate not to be revealed as 'Shakespeare' at that time. Surely it was because of *Richard II*, with its scene depicting the deposition of a monarch. This was the play performed on the eve of the Essex rebellion in order to whip up feeling against the Queen, and its performance was specifically ordered by the Earl of Essex. This then of course begs the question of whether the Essex group had been planning their rebellion for a much longer time than has previously been discovered. Certainly, their use of the *Richard II* play must have been planned well in advance. All that eye wash about actors being able to rustle up their parts from memory at a moment's notice was surely nothing more than an attempt to hoodwink the Queen into believing that everything happened merely because of a sudden, hot-headed whim. When one really thinks about it, how could so many sets of actors have been so suddenly prepared to perform the play forty times in one night up and down London, in the inns as well as in the Globe theatre? No, this co-ordinated showing of the play with its deadly simultaneity must have been planned over a longer time. Neville was involved in that rebellion, despite all his pleading to the contrary. If he had been proven to be the true author, then he would have been executed along with his friend, the Earl of Essex. Yet Neville's placement of those lines of Falstaff-Oldcastle's, subliminally suggesting there is a connection with his own 'Neville' name, shows that there must always have been a terrible conflict in poor Neville's mind. While living, and being involved, with the Earl of Essex's plans, he knew he could not name himself. But he must have constantly lamented the fact that his name might be lost forever. At the same time, there was the possibility of his being discovered as the author, and then being executed for his involvement with Essex. If this had happened, then he would no longer be in any position to add pointers to his true identity in the plays. It is also quite probable that the Queen would have suppressed knowledge about his authorship after having executed the best playwright in England. No wonder he was anxious to leave such great pointers to his identity, then, in this play.

Falstaff's words "I have a whole school of tongues in this belly of mine, and not a tongue of them all speaks any other word but my name," (quoted above,) also remind me of Sonnet 76:

> Why is my verse so barren of new pride,
> So far from variation or quick change?
> Why with the time do I not glance aside
> To new-found methods and to compounds strange?
> Why write I st*ill* all one, ever the same,
> And keep in*ven*tion in a noted weed,
> **That every word doth almost tell my name,**
> Showing their birth and where they did proceed?

THE SIGNS OF A WRITER CALLED 'FALSTAFF'

The name 'Nevill' is clearly encoded in that sonnet. And was the "noted weed" meant to suggest clothes worn in the play by the character who resembled him, or did Neville perhaps also mean that merely his outward appearance was giving him away as Oldcastle-Neville, (alias Falstaff) the true writer? His "weed" had indeed been "noted"; and here he is in this sonnet, echoing the words he already put into the mouth of the character after whom he was being called: **every word doth almost tell my name.** Certainly, when one knows the true writer, one begins to examine his look-alike's *words* more closely too.

Then comes the thrice-repeated word 'womb' in the Colville scene:

And I had but a belly of any indifferency,
I were simply the most active fellow in Europe - my womb,
    my womb, my womb undoes me.

Though the 'womb' is ostensibly used here to mean 'belly', it surely has a deeper meaning too. It suggests that Neville means he cannot help writing about the family – the "womb" from which he stems – and he certainly does pepper his History Plays with Nevilles. This, he thinks, may "undo" him – give him away. The word 'womb' also seems a precursor of how Ben Jonson was later to finish his epigram on Neville: "Thy deeds unto thy name will prove new wombs, Whilst others toil for titles to their tombs."

Perhaps mentioning the "womb" so many times just before yet another historical Neville comes into the scene (in the shape of the Earl of Westmoreland) is meant to convey yet another sense too. The Earl of Westmoreland represents the senior branch of the Nevilles, so I wonder if some sort of pressure to remain pseudonymous was put on Neville, ab initio, by some senior member of his family? It is possible. If so, then he must have been grateful for it, when he decided on diplomacy and political intrigue as a career. Certainly, while his father had been alive, using his real name could have been misleading: his father had been known as a Court entertainer, so he, rather than the son, would probably have been blamed for writing the politically sensitive *Richard II*. His father had died in 1593, but there was still another Henry Neville in the family – his cousin, who was the son of the Earl of Abergavenny. So once more, our Henry would have felt the pressure and needs of his wider family when considering whether to use his own name.

Chapter Five

THE WRITER WHO CAN ONLY BE 'NE-VILE'

The compelling evidence of Sonnet 121
The most significant naming of the true 'Shakespeare writer' certainly comes in sonnet 121, reinforcing the discovery of Neville's name in the Dedication code prefacing the whole sequence of sonnets. After the publication of my last book, *Henry Neville and the Shakespeare Code,* in which I wrote a chapter on this sonnet, Neal Platt, Special Professor of Law in New York, contacted me and pointed out that the linguistic evidence on its own in this sonnet make it difficult to argue that anyone other than Sir Henry Neville could have written it. Applying the techniques commonly used in the interpretation of legal texts, such as statutes, contracts, and wills, Professor Platt's learned analysis demonstrates that the sonnet is a highly probative item of evidence, contributing greatly to the overwhelming weight of evidence supporting Neville's authorship of the whole Shakespeare canon.

The crux of Special-Professor Platt's argument is that Neville names himself as the author quite unmistakably in this sonnet, using clever linguistic stratagems in order to do so. Yet the manner in which he sets out his identity is primarily recognisable only by anyone who was already privy to the secret. Before constructing the encryption of his name in the Dedication to the sonnets, the poet must therefore have relied on two assumptions to effect his disguise: firstly, that only his close circle of friends and family knew him to be a writer, and secondly, that only those who knew his family name would be able to understand *completely* the true meaning of his text:

> 'Tis better to be vile than vile esteemed,
> When not to be receives reproach of being,
> And the just pleasure lost, which is so deemed
> Not by our feeling but by others' seeing.
> For why should others' false adulterate eyes
> Give salutation to my sportive blood?
> Or on my frailties why are frailer spies,

THE WRITER WHO CAN ONLY BE 'NE-VILE'

Which in their will count bad what I think good?
No, I am that I am, and they that level
At my abuses reckon up their own;
I may be straight though they themselves be bevel;
By their rank thoughts my deeds must not be shown,
Unless this general evil they maintain:
All men are bad and in their badness reign.

As Professor Platt goes on to say, "The 'mechanics' of the sonnet's text are striking, and strikingly Nevillian. This sonnet is toying with a barely concealed logical syllogism. Second, its word-play seems deliberately designed to tease the reader into an uneasy equipoise between the copular and non-copular senses of that all-powerful Shakespearean verb 'to be.'" [The term 'copular' refers to the verb's ability to include an extra word – such as an adjective – to complete its meaning. For instance, the statement 'I am' consists of a subject followed by a verb, so it can stand on its own. But if we add the adjective 'tired' then 'tired' becomes the complement of the verb 'to be' - as in the phrase 'I am tired.' In this case, 'I am' then takes on its copular sense.]
"So now we must examine the first two lines of the sonnet to see if the verb 'to be' stands on its own or is meant to be linked with the adjective, 'vile'.
It is these first two lines of the sonnet which actually suggest the syllogism. The lines are:

Line 1: 'Tis better to be vile than vile esteemed,
Line 2: When not to be, receives reproach of being.

"It is line 2 which therefore forces us to ask a question. Do the words 'when not to be' carry the meaning of simply, 'When *not to be* receives reproach of being,' or do they mean "When not to be *vile* receives reproach of being"? The poet *forces* us into asking this question by the very way in which he constructs the first line. In line 1, the poet posits a dismaying rhetorical universe in which one must either 'be vile' or be 'esteemed' vile, invoking the theme of 'being' as distinguished from 'seeming' addressed in so many of the plays, and perfected in *Hamlet*.
Line 2 has always been something of a puzzle. Any reader of the Bard would recognize its first clause as being characteristically poly-sematographic. *'When not to be...'* could mean simply, 'when not to exist.' Or does it mean, 'when not to be *vile*'? In this second, alternative reading, 'to be' is afforded its

copular (complementary) sense, and its complement ('vile') is carried over from the immediately previous line.

The reader, naturally confused, looks to the latter clause of line 2 to attempt to resolve the ambiguity, and determine the poet's intended meaning of 'to be.' But the poet frustrates any such attempt at resolution, as — even in light of the second clause — the appearance of 'to be' in the first clause can *still* sensibly be interpreted as either copular or non-copular. In other words, is the writer saying:

It's better to be vile than simply not to exist at all; or

It's better to be vile than not to be vile if one is nevertheless going to be blamed for being so;

"Read in conjunction with the second clause, the first clause could *still* have either of the following meanings:

When not to be ['vile'] receives reproach of being, that is,
   "even if one *is not* vile, one receives reproach of being so"
or
When not be ['to exist'] receives reproach of being, that is,
   "when not to exist still (nevertheless) receives reproach of *being* (i.e. existing).

"To the reader's dismay, the second clause not only obstinately refuses to aid the reader in confidently resolving whether the first clause's 'to be' is copular or non-copular, but it *compounds* the reader's confusion by means of an *additional* ambiguous (copular/non-copular) invocation of "to be"! The reader wonders: Does the poet intend the *second* clause to be interpreted

receives reproach of being vile (notwithstanding that, by the poet's dichotomy, he evidently believes he is *not* vile); or
receives reproach of existing (that is, "is faulted on grounds that he does not *exist*")?

"Where the first clause and second clause each has at least two possible meanings, then by simple arithmetic, line 2 as a whole must have at least *four* possible meanings. Knowing Shakespeare as we do, of course, we can expect that each of the four possible meanings may shed some light on the poem's topic.

Nevertheless, the mind tends to narrow the alternative interpretations of line 2 down to **two**, as follows:

<u>Interpretation 1:</u>
It is better to be vile (than to be not vile) when someone (such as the poet) who is not vile winds up being falsely reproached for being vile nevertheless. And some, who *are* indeed vile, escape reproach by not *seeming* vile.

This seems a more universal and poetic complaint than the following alternative interpretation.

<u>Interpretation 2:</u>
It is better to be vile (than to be not vile) when someone (such as the poet) is regarded as *non-existent* on grounds that he is not vile (**ne-vile**).

Under either interpretation, it is almost impossible to argue that the writer is anyone other than a 'Neville'!"

To round off this section by Neal Platt I'd like to incorporate a few notes of my own concerning the predominating sense in which the word 'reproach' was used in the 17th century: the noun 'reproach' then meant 'a source of dishonour'.

Extended meanings of line 2, "When not to be [in its *copular* sense of 'not to be vile', i.e. to be called 'Neville'] receives reproach of being", therefore include the following:

To be 'not vile' (ne-vile) has become dishonourable, or to be called 'Neville' carries with it a 'reproach' (i.e. a dishonour.) Neville receives the reproach simply because he is called 'Neville', so it would be better to be vile than to receive the reproach which this particular Neville is receiving, just because he is a 'Neville', and not because he carries the quality of 'vileness'.

I justify my assumption that the poet is referring to a *particular* Neville at the beginning of the sonnet, because at the end of it he refers explicitly to a *general* 'evil'. The writer therefore distinguishes this 'general evil' from the particular '[ne]vile' person he was talking about at the beginning, because the final two lines state: "Unless this general evil they maintain: All men are bad, and in their badness reign."

The incipient Stuart dynasty might well perceive Nevilles as having been *generally* bad throughout history, because they were part and parcel of the once *reigning* Plantagenet dynasty, who were often failures as kings, and who still remained potential rivals at the Stuart court, and even in Parliament. [Hence another meaning of the final "...and in their badness *reign*."]

The *particular* Neville who is writing this sonnet, however, is at pains to distinguish himself from those *general* Nevilles past. The particular Neville who was receiving opprobrium during James I's reign, and being passed over by the King for appropriate promotion, regardless of his intrinsic worth, was Sir Henry Neville. This is surely the Neville who is described in the sonnets' Dedication code as being 'of the Sein[e]' – i.e. the one-time English Ambassador to France/ a descendant of the Nevilles whose family originated from the area round the Seine/ the man who was at the 'sein' [i.e. the womb] of the mystery surrounding the true poet's identity. It is indeed remarkable that one translation of the French 'sein' is 'womb' – the very word, (as we may recall from the previous chapter), which Falstaff uses to denote the source of his identification in *Henry IV, part 2*, Act 4, Sc.3:

> **Falstaff** I have a whole school of tongues in this belly of mine, and not a tongue of them all speaks any other word but my name. ... - my womb, my womb, my womb undoes me.

The Implied Syllogism

As Professor Platt then says, "The reader who does not know that the poet is named "ne vile" tends *to discount* Interpretation 2, i.e.:
> It is better to be vile (than to be not vile) when someone (such as the poet) is regarded as *non-existent* on grounds that he is not vile (**ne-vile**).

"It seems to make no sense to posit that someone could be deemed not *to exist* simply because he is not vile. But, in true Elizabethan fashion, the true writer knows that some of his readers – i.e. those who are already in his close circle, or those who have decoded the Sonnets' Dedication – will gain delight in reading his true name and realising the mind-boggling extent of his linguistic playfulness.

THE WRITER WHO CAN ONLY BE 'NE-VILE'

Indeed, even if the reader has not already been admitted to the secret, it is surely impossible not to notice how many times 'ne-vile', 'nevel', etc. are inescapably suggested throughout this sonnet. Unless the reader therefore considers that the great 'Shakespeare' wrote superfluously, or chose his wording unconsciously, then this second interpretation can surely not be merely *conjectural*: it is patently real and actual. The poet is not vile (ne-vile = Neville.)

By family custom, Neville's very name *means* he is not vile: 'ne vile velis'. The formerly discounted Interpretation 2 was clearly intended *not* to be discounted, indeed may rather be a *preferred* or, at least equally worthy, interpretation. Stated syllogistically, the argument of the sonnet is:

Some misanthropic people believe:
In order to exist, one must be vile.
The poet is not vile (that is, he is by definition *and name* "**ne vile**").
Therefore (in the estimation of such people) the poet does not exist.

"Far from being conjectural, therefore, the above interpretation is surely the *only* meaning to be reinforced (or concluded) by the plain meaning of the heretofore mysterious final two lines of the sonnet:

Unless this general evil they maintain,
All men are bad and in their badness reign.

"By discovering that the poet is named "Neville," we can see that the "general evil" posited in the final line is merely a one-line expression of the above syllogism, which is suggested by the sonnet's first two lines. This is no doubt another intended reward for the one who deciphers the Dedication Code.

In addition, the syllogism appears to aid in interpreting the meaning of the rather foreboding use of the word "reign" in the last line. Going beyond poetical mechanics for a moment, it seems that Sir Henry believed his refusal to be a scoundrel like the Bevilles[104] in his pursuit of high office, made him "non-existent" (or, as we might say today, "invisible") to the king. Sir Henry appears to suggest: *If the king regards me as non-existent simply because I am held in low esteem by vile people, such as the Bevilles, then the king himself (who "reigns") must be one of those misanthropic people who fails to acknowledge the existence of anyone who is not vile.* This is more than the mere attribution of guilt by association; it borders on sedition. Evidently, this former Essex 'rebel' disliked James at least as much as he did Elizabeth.

Thus, as always with the bard, we have a multiplicity of meanings inherent in the very wording of this sonnet; but the *specific* meanings become clear only when we take into account the true 'Neville' name of the poet. Then, and only then, can the poet display the full extent of his consummate skill, for we become aware of his *preferred,* more readily understandable meanings only when we know that his name is Neville."

In view of Professor Platt's excellent analysis, I would also ask "Is it perhaps additionally possible that the non-existence of 'Ne-vile' suggested in this sonnet could viably refer to the true writer's name not being known?" The few contemporary reports we have of William Shakespeare, i.e the man who had the *known* name, proclaim him to have been a mean man, yet many of the sonnets openly despise meanness and use the term 'usurer' as one of abuse, condemning the practice of meanness and usury in general:

> The statute of thy beauty thou wilt take,
> Thou usurer that putt'st forth all to use,
> And sue a friend came debtor for my sake;
> *Sonnet 134*
> Profitless usurer, why dost thou use
> So great a sum of sums, yet canst not live?
> *Sonnet 4*
> That use is not forbidden usury
> Which happies those that pay the willing loan -
> *Sonnet 6*

Altogether, Henry Neville was quite differently reported from Shakespeare. Sir Henry was a man who defended Parliament's, his own, and other people's rights – a man who (in his own letters) bemoaned the weight of his debts – he was clearly a *debtor*, not a usurer. So because he is 'Ne-vile', (*not* vile) he is *not* the **vile** Shakespeare! (In his own estimation, joining with the Earl of Essex was not vile; it was done in the interests of the country – an attempt to avoid the civil war many feared would ensue if Elizabeth did not name her successor.)

As Professor Platt concludes, "In sum, sonnet 121 appears to be the poet's copular/non-copular exploration of 'to be.' His rather more famous non-copular exploration of the same verb begins, of course: 'To be or not to be'. But he *is* most assuredly 'not vile = Neville'."

The Just Pleasure
Line 3 of the sonnet suggests that the writer loses his "just pleasure"; but looking at the copular/non copular meanings of the first two lines, are we to assume that
- The writer obtains his pleasure from simply 'being', or
- The writer obtains his pleasure from being 'Ne-vile', i.e. 'not vile'?

As the first assumption seems far too broad, we must assume that the second, copular meaning is the more likely. If so, then the writer's 'pleasure' at being 'Ne-vile' is lost; and it is lost "not by our feeling but by others' seeing." Once again, the poet is confusing our senses, by playing with the copular/non copular implications of 'to be'. When we know the true writer is called 'Neville' we might then be led to think that he is losing pleasure because others are not recognising him as such.

But are we right to assume that this might be the case? 'Ne-vile' confuses us yet again by confusing the *connections* of lines 3 and 4 with the rest of the sonnet. This confusion is engineered by the way he uses the conjunction 'And'. This appears at the beginning of line 3. At first, it makes the reader or hearer want to connect lines 3 and 4 with lines 1 and 2, so that we may take in the *two* senses given above, i.e.:

- that the writer would obtain pleasure from being recognized as *being* (existing), or
- that he would obtain pleasure from being recognized as *being not vile* ('Ne-vile').

The second of these interpretations may also imply that he would obtain pleasure from the public recognising that the author of the works attributed to Shakespeare is in fact Neville, and thus not the 'vile' Shakespeare.

But lines 5 and 6 somewhat undermine that reading by making lines 3 and 4 look as if they refer *forwards* to those very lines, 5 and 6:

3 And the just pleasure lost, which is so deemed
4 Not by our feeling but by others' seeing.
5 For why should others' false adulterate eyes
6 Give salutation to my sportive blood?

This reading then either *changes* the writer's meaning or (more likely) *adds* a further one. So now let's examine that further meaning which occurs when we make "And the just pleasure lost which is so deemed/Not by our feeling but by others seeing" refer *forwards* to "For why should others' false adulterate eyes/Give salutation to my sportive blood?" The whole, consummate meaning of lines 3 – 6 then becomes, "When others' false, adulterate eyes give salutation to my sportive blood, then my just pleasure at feeling good about my 'sportive blood' [works of entertainment] is lost." This of course would mean that Neville does *not* want people to know his identity as the writer, because they might give a false interpretation to what he means and what he is. Altogether, therefore, these lines become very close in meaning to what Neville said in Parliament about the anonymity of his political treatise, i.e. that he did not like to acknowledge his writing because one never knew into whose hands it might fall.[105]

It might therefore seem on the one hand that Neville is *regretting* his anonymity. Yet, as demonstrated, surely the next two/three lines undermine that fleeting feeling:

For why should others' false, adulterate eyes
Give salutation to my sportive blood?
Or on my frailties why are frailer spies... ?

The writer therefore further extends the dichotomy and irresolution of the whole theme of the sonnet – 'To be or not to be' or 'To be vile or not to be vile', with its extended meaning (for those who know his name) "is it better to be 'Ne-vile' or not to be Neville?"

This reading of the raison d'etre behind the whole sonnet is further substantiated by his use of the term 'sportive blood', for 'sportive' (says the Oxford English Dictionary) was the term used at the time to indicate 'a playfulness of expression.' But who other than someone called 'Neville' could be playing with language in this precise way, and on so many Neville/Ne–vile levels?

Neal Platt has also actually pointed out some additional potentially important ingredients in the remainder of the sonnet that are not referred to in my Chapter 10 of *Henry Neville and the Shakespeare Code:*

> 1. "I am that I am" is the King James translation of God's name, as spoken by God to Moses out of the burning bush. (This may be a subtle clue to the reader that this sonnet is all about names);
> 2. "They that level / at my abuses, reckon up their own" could be a modern English translation of the motto of the Order of the Garter, "Honi soit qui mal y pense." Both Neville and Beville were knights (although not necessarily of that Order.)

Regarding Professor Platt's first point, I think it is viable to add a historical fact: Sir Henry Savile was the man who oversaw the King James translation of the Bible. Besides being kinsmen, Savile and Neville were life-long friends and associates. They had been together ever since Neville entered Merton College, Oxford, at the age of around twelve. Savile lectured in astronomy and later became Professor of Geometry at the college. He also travelled on the continent with the then young Neville for five years, where Neville helped Savile with his research into St. John Chrysostom – the Orthodox saint whose work is cited in Savile's preamble to the King James Bible. In other words, though King James sanctioned and patronised this translation of the Bible, it was always Savile (assisted quietly by Neville) who had carried out the groundwork. Also, it is worth repeating that the phrase 'I am that I am' was *first* used in the Authorised Version of the Bible: before that version, the Hebrew had been translated as 'I will be what I will be'. The Authorised version appeared in 1611 – two years *after* the publication of the Shakespeare *Sonnets.* How would Shakespeare of Stratford have been able to pre-empt this translation? He, unlike Neville, had no connection with the King James Bible.

Falstaff in the Sonnets: the linguistic physicality of Neville
Altogether, therefore, Neville actually names himself – strongly and unmistakably – in sonnet 121. However, the *physical* sense of a man like Falstaff is also hinted at in the sonnets, so we are surely left in no doubt about who the author really was. In the previous chapter, we looked at a sonnet in which the 'noted weed' of Falstaff is remarked upon. But there now remain one or

two sonnets which also dwell on the *weight* of the true author. I think this is most clearly seen in those sonnets which tell of the writer journeying away from his friend, and most clearly of all in sonnet 50:

> How heavy do I journey on the way,
> When what I seek (my weary travel's end)
> Doth teach that ease and that repose to say
> 'Thus far the miles are measured from thy friend'.
> The beast that bears me, tired with my woe,
> Plods duly on, to bear that weight in me,
> As if by some instinct the wretch did know
> His rider loved not speed being made from thee.
> The bloody spur cannot provoke him on
> That sometimes anger thrusts into his hide,
> Which heavily he answers with a groan
> More sharp to me than spurring to his side;
> For that same groan doth put this in my mind:
> My grief lies onward, and my joy behind.

The writer openly declares his heaviness is one of the spirit. But readers who know his true identity, and who have also read sonnet 121, are tempted to look back at those sonnets suggesting heaviness, and smile. They know Neville's physical girth. They therefore gain an extra, *physical* impression – and probably some amusement – when they review the sonnets, with their double meaning of 'heaviness'. They know that the author's heaviness of spirit is matched by his physical weight. They understand the *physical* reason why the author's horse cannot go any faster. The writer goes out of his way to ensure us that the reader has hints of his physical mass: the beast that carries him has to "bear that *weight* in me", and this is reinforced by the presence of the word 'heavy' in the very first line. One also feels the genuine sorrow of Neville in taking up a post (in France) which he does not want and which leaves his friend, "My grief lies onward, and my joy behind." In the very next sonnet, when he imagines returning to his friend, he knows his horse will simply not be able to go as fast as he wishes, "Then can no horse with my desire keep pace." I know the writer is primarily wishing to give a deep impression of his deep sorrow and reluctance to travel away, but the vocabulary he uses nevertheless also betrays a sense of his physical weight: "heavy, tired, plods, weight, heavily" are the words employed.

THE WRITER WHO CAN ONLY BE 'NE-VILE'

'Heavy' and 'heavily' are in fact used 9 times throughout the sequence.

In Sonnet 44, the writer's flesh is a 'dull' substance, and in the same sonnet we have 'heavy tears':

If the dull substance of my flesh were thought,
Injurious distance should not stop my way;
For then, despite of space, I would be brought,
From limits far remote, where thou dost stay.
No matter then although my foot did stand
Upon the farthest earth removed from thee,
For nimble thought can jump both sea and land
As soon as think the place where he would be.
But ah, thought kills me that I am not thought,
To leap large lengths of miles when thou art gone,
But that, so much of earth and water wrought,
I must attend time's leisure with my moan,
Receiving nought by elements so slow
But heavy tears, badges of either's woe.

Indeed, in this sonnet we see an incorporation of Sir Henry Neville's physicality with his situation in being reluctantly in France, where he is 'time's' servant, whose 'leisure' he must attend, "with my moan." Note too that the writer has travelled across the sea, which is re-inforced with the line "so much of earth and water wrought". (Shakespeare, as far as we know, never even saw the sea, let alone travelled across it – he had no passport.) And is it not also significant that this sonnet is numbered '44' and that there are 144 characters in the Dedication to the *Sonnets,* with Sir Henry's identity being revealed in its coding? Moreover, 144 was the code number representing King Henri IV of France. (I have dealt with some other aspects the 'significant numbering' of the *Sonnets* in *Sir Henry Neville and the Shakespeare Code.*)

Put all this together with a man who limps and is lame, and we definitely get an impression of Sir Henry Neville, with his weight and his gout, but also with his depth of feeling and quickness of wit which ill matches his 'dull flesh'.

'Not Veal' in *Love's Labour's Lost*

In my previous book, I pointed out some banter involving the character of Longaville in *Love's Labour's Lost.* I also described my reasons for concluding that some aspects of Longaville might well be Neville in disguise. Longaville has the following conversation with Katherine in Act V, Scene 2 of the play:

> **Katharine** What, was your visor made without a tongue?
> **Longaville** I know the reason, lady, why you ask.
> **Katharine** O, for your reason! Quickly, sir, I long.
> **Longaville** You have a double tongue within your mask,
> And would afford my speechless visor half.
> **Katharine** 'Veal' quoth the Dutchman. Is not 'veal' a calf?
> **Longaville** A calf, fair lady!
> **Katharine** No, a fair lord calf.
> **Longaville** Let's part the word.
> **Katharine** No, I'll not be your half.
> Take all, and wean it; it may prove an ox.
> **Longaville** Look how you butt yourself in these sharp mocks.
> Will you give horns, chaste lady? Do not so.
> **Katharine** Then die a calf, before your horns do grow.
> **Longaville** One word in private with you ere I die.
> **Katharine** Bleat softly then; the butcher hears you cry.
> [They converse apart.]
> **Boyet** The tongues of mocking wenches are as keen
> As is the razor's edge invisible,
> Cutting a smaller hair than may be seen,
> Above the sense of sense; so sensible
> Seemeth their conference. Their conceits have wings
> Fleeter than arrows, bullets, wind, thought, swifter things.

Without repeating the whole of the analysis of this scene, I'd like to point out that Boyet's speech at the end of the Longaville/Katherine dialogue is alerting us to the fact that there is something invisible' and 'Above the sense of sense' in what they have been saying. In other words, more senses are present in the dialogue than most people are aware of. This is surely yet another way of saying 'ecce signum'.[106] Some of the 'signs' pointing to Neville lie in the text itself. If we part the name 'Longaville' and give one half away we are left with 'ville'. The pun 'not veal' ["Is not veal a calf?"] then becomes a pun on the name 'Neville'. In German and Dutch, 'viel' means 'many' or 'much'. Neville was a large man, so the word 'viel' [veal] also made a comic sense which only those who knew the name of the true author would understand. Next, Katherine keeps repeating the word 'no' at the beginning of her phrases. When 'no' and 'veal' [no viel] are put together they become a variant on the name 'Neville' and also mean 'not much'.

The 'ox' and horns also come in for a mention in the dialogue: an ox head is one of the Nevilles' badges:

'Badge' bearing the inscription 'Nevill of Abergavenny'

(A 'badge' is a free-standing heraldic device.) Katherine is clearly saying she does not want to have any children by 'not veal' [Neville] because they will be as big as oxen! This, like the Falstaff references, is surely an allusion to Neville's size. Its 'not veal' reference is therefore an appropriate one to add to the 'ne-vile' of sonnet 121.

Since my initial writing about this, my research has uncovered even more connections between Neville and the themes of *Love's Labour's Lost*. As I've mentioned in my previous work, Longaville was a name in the Neville pedigree; but it now seems likely that Neville was privy to additional knowledge which inspired him to write this play and to choose the name 'Longaville'. Neville's father in law, Sir Henry Killigrew, had been the English ambassador to Scotland for many years. Neville and his wife were living for much of the year with Killigrew during the time the play was written. During the final two years of Killigrew's ambassadorship he would have come into contact with Mary of Guise, who was then in Scotland and who became the mother of Mary Queen of Scots. Mary of Guise had been married to the Duc de Longueville, so once again we are drawn into Neville's love of playing with names. John Knox's attack on 'The monstrous regiment [rule] of women' was aimed primarily at Mary of Guise. This would have both amused and angered Henry Neville, and especially angered Killigrew, as he was married to one Sir Anthony Cooke's daughters, who were known as the five most educated women in England. It is probable, therefore, that the agreement of three men to manage for three years without women in *Love's Labour's Lost* was partly a joke on Knox's misogyny.

Now knowing Neville's connections, we can therefore see the whole background to *Love's Labour's Lost* in a more revealing light. It looks likely that Neville was choosing to lampoon Knox, which is something that would hardly be investigated if one imagines Shakespeare as the author, as Shakespeare never visited Scotland and had no early connections to tell him about Knox and his speech. But Sir Henry Neville had stayed in Scotland early in his career (in 1583, on an official visit there with Walsingham and the Earl of Essex) so would have inevitably encountered discussions on Knox. Moreover, the women in *Love's Labour's Lost* are shown to be equally as well-read and witty as the men – highly relevant to Killigrew's and Neville's experience. And Scotland was linked with France by the Auld Alliance, which begins to explain the train of thought within the play, in which French noblemen are portrayed. Ferdinand of Navarre was a character in that same play. When Neville became Ambassador to France in 1599, King Henri IV (formerly Henri of Navarre) appeared to have already met him,[107] and we know that Henry went to France during his continental tour with Savile during the years 1578–83.[108] King Henri had overseen a translation of Plato's works, so 'Platonic Academies' were growing up in France at the time.[109] The Scottish and French quibbles about the presence of women in power may therefore very well have fused in Neville's mind. Thus we have a man with the perfect background experience to write the play.

Then there are incidents in the play which parallel even more incidents from Neville's real-life knowledge and experience. I have previously mentioned the instruction of the Princess in shooting a deer – the very thing in which Neville's father instructed Queen Elizabeth. I can now add to this the fact that Mary of Guise came by sea to Scotland, together with a great entourage of ladies, in the same way as the Princess of France and her ladies arrive in the play. Added to this, Killigrew had been secretary to Nicholas Throckmorton, the then French Ambassador, so he would have been able to relate many a relevant tale of France to his son in law. For instance, immediately before obtaining this official post in France, Killigrew had travelled to France from Germany in order to meet an old master of his who had now become governor of Calais. However, Sir Henry Killigrew's activities in France were viewed with suspicion by one very able French woman, Anne de Montmorency. She was constable of France and decided to detain Killigrew. He was only released and allowed to return home briefly, in 1559, before being given his new, *official*, French appointment by Queen Elizabeth. Soon after his arrival, Henri II was killed and the Catholic Guise family seized control.[110]

Next, there were incidents which brought Neville's knowledge of France, and subsequent dramatic references in the play, up to date. The Earl of Essex's and the Earl of Southampton's involvement in fighting for the then Protestant Henri of Navarre would have been followed closely by their friend, Sir Henry Neville. He was thus able to take the names of some of the main characters in the play from those he knew or knew about. For instance, the real-life Duc de Biron actually stayed with Henry Neville senior, and the others – de Longueville and the Duc de Mayenne (Dumain) – were also involved with Navarre, de Longueville supporting him and de Mayenne opposing him. Moreover, in addition to the arrival of Mary of Guise affording a pattern for the entrance of the Princess in the play, there was the more recent grand entrance of Marguerite de Valois. Marguerite was Henri of Navarre's estranged wife, and she arrived at Nerac in 1578 together with her female entourage. This was the year in which Neville began his five-year sojourn on the continent. In *Who Wrote Shakespeare?*, John Michell observed:

> In that idyllic period, the Court of Navarre was visited by an Englishman who afterwards wrote *Love's Labour's Lost*. Included in that play are scenes, characters and events, which only someone with intimate experience among those people at that place and time could have known about. Abel Lefranc was a specialist in that period. From contemporary records, particularly the *Mémoires* of Marguerite de Valois in which the life of the court is described in great detail, he proved that the author of *Love's Labour's Lost* was better informed on what went on there than any outsider could have been – at least until 1626 when Marguerite's book was published.

In more than one letter from France during 1599 and 1600, Neville voiced his opinions on Henri IV's womanising. He felt deep sympathy for Marguerite de Valois. (This of course unites the French and Scottish influences which can now be perceived in *Love's Labour's Lost*. Once again, knowledge of Neville as the writer illuminates the whole of this otherwise somewhat imponderable play.) Even the dream sequence of Catherine of Aragon [in *Henry VIII*] seems to be based on one experienced by Marguerite, as Catherine Duncan Jones declared in the 1960s.

Thus Henry Neville, the real Shakespeare, is revealed as having all the information, inclination and wit to write *Love's Labour's Lost*. Who else but 'not-veal' Neville could have written all this; and who else would wish to encode his own name in the works, inside so many astoundingly playful and mind-boggling linguistic stratagems?

The Turning Point: *Henry IV, part 2*, and Nevillian circumstances

The question so often posed in Shakespeare, i.e. "to be or not to be", came to its crucial resolution in Sir Henry Neville's own life when he returned from France in August 1600 and joined Essex in his attempt to solve the succession problem. Despite what is all too often written about the young Earl of Essex's hotheadedness and personal ambitions, there can be no doubt that his major concern was that Elizabeth I had made it treasonable for anyone to discuss the question of who would succeed her. The ban on this most important subject dismayed the aristocracy and populace alike. While this edict was in place, England was open to the scheming of ambitious and unscrupulous would-be monarchs. Essex, Neville, Southampton and other well-intentioned politicians finally decided to take matters into their own hands. Their motivation was concern over the possible civil warring that might break out at Elizabeth's childless death.

Shakespeare paints King Henry IV as having been faced by a somewhat similar situation. The surviving chronicles of Henry IV's time record Richard II as being an unbearable, ill-principled King, with little regard for the welfare of his people, who was therefore lawfully deposed by Henry Bolingbroke. Although there is some surviving evidence to show that this was probably not altogether true, that the usurpers 'doctored' the chronicles concerning Richard II's personality and deeds, and that the *rebels* could have been the unprincipled, ambitious parties in the conflict, Shakespeare nevertheless chose to portray Henry IV as a tortured, principled man. (That usurpers could also be principled was obviously a political message which would have appalled Queen

Elizabeth, or any other reigning monarch, so once again it can be seen that the true 'Shakespeare' had no choice but to write under a pseudonym.) Henry Neville viewed *himself* as acting in the role of a principled chaplain of power – a quasi-usurper – when he joined the Essex protest against the dangers he and his fellows saw as inherent in Elizabeth's intransigence. Was Neville's role in society 'to be or not to be?' Neville was faced with the choice of taking "arms against a sea of troubles" which Elizabeth's attitude heralded, or merely doing nothing and consequently leaving England to suffer "the slings and arrows of outrageous fortune". Henry Neville became a man as much tortured in spirit as his ancestor, King Henry IV.

Bearing this in mind, it is interesting to chart a certain development in the writing of *Henry IV, part 2* and note how it parallels Henry Neville's own life and own dilemmas. In the previous chapter, I explained how both the Henry IV plays encapsulated various 'signs' of Neville. But it is also uncanny how the actual sequence of the writing of part 2 meshes in with Neville's personal timetable and circumstances.

As noted, *Henry IV, part 2* was physically placed on the Stationer's Register during the very same stretch of time as Neville arrived back in England for his break of service in France, i.e. on 23rd August, 1600. But the first Quarto (which came out soon after this date) omitted one scene – the scene we now know as Act III, sc.1. This scene was published only in the second edition. Scholars have tried various explanations for this strange occurrence, but even the Arden edition of the play avers that no explanation seems satisfactory.[111] However, as always, put Neville into the equation and a most illuminating and plausible explanation is immediately forthcoming.

So let's look at this particular scene. It is very short. It is the scene in which King Henry begins by bewailing the fact that he cannot sleep, his first soliloquy ending with the famous line "uneasy lies the head that wears a crown." It is a scene in which the King talks of "...our kingdom, How foul it is, what rank diseases grow, And with what danger, near the heart of it." It is also – significantly – the one scene in the play which contains the word 'Revolution'. The King laments that his erstwhile great friendships have turned so quickly into a state of war; and that a Nevil (the Earl of Warwick) was better able to predict this turning of the tide than he. Indeed, it is the first scene in which the Earl of Warwick appears; and 'Shakespeare' makes the 'mistake' of calling him 'Nevil' when really it was a Beauchamp who held that title at the time. (No chronicle made this mistake, so who but a Neville writer would have made this meaningful confusion?)

My conclusions are therefore becoming clear: this scene was not present in the play when it was hurriedly registered by agents of its true writer, Sir Henry Neville, so we must ask "Why not?" Well, Sir Henry obviously knew by then that he, like King Henry IV, was going to be involved in some sort of action against the reigning monarch; that he, again like Henry IV, was going to break a number of old friendships by his actions, and that he, Neville, like Henry IV, was not going to be able to rest easy afterwards. Neville had reached a turning point: was the uprising 'to be or not to be?' Was the end in sight worth the means?

One possibility is that Neville wrote this scene while idly waiting for the Spanish representatives to agree to enter talks with him at Boulogne. Neville had had word of what was happening with Essex back in England – was indeed on such close terms with Essex that the Earl himself must have informed him about what he had in mind. So no wonder Neville was anxious to return home. This means that the text of that extra scene would then have suggested itself to Neville *at that particular point in his own life*. (Neville's great friend, Henry Savile, was later to write to Robert Cecil that the Earl of Essex had left a legacy in his will to "my trusted and unfortunate friend, Sir Henry Neville." This of course is yet another piece of evidence which gives the lie to Neville's statement at his Hearing – i.e. that he "hardly knew" the Earl.) As Neville wrote to Cecil when the Essex rebellion was nearing its moment, if the Queen did not give him permission to return from France, then he would do so without that permission and "live hermit in Ashridge or the Forest." Neville was clearly a desperate man, and a key one in Essex's plans.

Moreover, the overwhelming imagery in this added scene is that of the sea, which would be the case if Neville had begun it while in Boulogne and then put in the finishing touches immediately after returning to England. (It is worth noting again at this point that William Shakespeare is never known to have seen the sea.) When talking of his own lack of sleep in the scene, the King contrasts his own, physically-comfortable, state with extended images of those at sea, who are able to sleep despite their perils:

THE WRITER WHO CAN ONLY BE 'NE-VILE'

> Wilt thou upon the high and giddy mast
> Seal up the ship-boy's eyes, and rock his brains
> In cradle of the rude imperious surge,
> And in the visitation of the winds,
> Who take the ruffian billows by the top,
> Curling their monstrous heads, and hanging them
> With deafing clamour in the slipp'ry clouds,
> That, with the hurly, death itself awakes?
> Canst thou, O partial sleep, give thy repose
> To the wet sea-boy in an hour so rude,
> And in the calmest and most stillest night,
> With all appliances and means to boot,
> Deny it to a king? Then happy low, lie down!
> Uneasy lies the head that wears a crown.

Even the word 'revolution' – clearly pregnant with meaning for Neville – reminds King Henry of the sea:

> O God, that one might read the book of fate,
> And see the **revolution** of the times
> Make mountains level, and the continent,
> Weary of solid firmness, melt itself
> Into the sea; and other times to see
> The beachy girdle of the ocean
> Too wide for Neptune's hips; how chance's mocks
> And changes fill the cup of alteration
> With divers liquors! O, if this were seen,
> The happiest youth, viewing his progress through,
> What perils past, what crosses to ensue,
> Would shut the book and sit him down and die.

This is an insight into both the stage character's and the writer's frame of mind at such a moment in his own life. In the play, it is left to the 'Nevil' Earl of Warwick to put the King's mind at rest and assure him that the Kingdom will soon be healed:

> **Warwick** It is but as a body yet distempered,
> Which to his former strength may be restored
> With good advice and little medicine.

It is as if the writer Sir Henry Neville was seeking a Neville precedent to help him finally decide what to do. 'Good advice and a little medicine' was what Queen Elizabeth and the State now needed. This thing – this action – had 'to be'; and it is 'you', (Henry Neville), who must act; that it is a 'necessity':

> **Warwick** There is a history in all men's lives
> Figuring the nature of the times deceased;
> The which observed, a man may prophesy,
> With a near aim, of the main chance of things
> As yet not come to life, which in their seeds
> And weak beginning lie intreasured.
> Such things become the hatch and brood of time;
> And by the necessary form of this
> King Richard might create a perfect guess
> That great Northumberland, then false to him,
> Would of that seed grow to a greater falseness,
> Which should not find a ground to root upon
> Unless on **you**.
> **King Henry IV** Are these things then necessities?
> Then let us meet them like necessities;
> And that same word even now cries out on us.

The last line may even have sounded like a rallying call to those in the Essex circle who knew Neville, knew he was the writer, and understood the symbolism encapsulated in this scene. Who but Neville wrote it? Who but Neville would deem it politic to omit it from the first edition of the play? After all, King Henry even *names* the Earl of Warwick as 'Nevil' when he addresses him. Who but a Neville would have chosen a [falsely] 'Nevil' Earl of such wisdom – a wise Neville Earl who also possessed the power of rhetoric to goad a King into action? And who but a man who had just been tossed at sea would choose that precise and lengthy imagery of the ocean?

Chapter Six

THE RULE OF CHIVALRY: THE TEMPLARS, HOSPITALLERS, AND THE ORDER OF SION

If Sir Henry Neville had become tangentially involved in a minor revolution, then it was because his study of history had taught him a lesson: if all else failed, it was better to take preventative action than let old rivalries re-surface. One rivalry during Elizabethan days had persisted since Medieval times. It centred round the monarch and the chivalric, knightly nobles. Though ongoing contention between these three influential groups was often unspoken and hidden beneath a show of deference, it nevertheless grumbled away. True, its existence had been more pronounced before the Reformation, but its remnants still haunted the Court of Queen Elizabeth I. It is this rivalry which is illustrated in Shakespeare's *Henry VI* trilogy in particular, and touched on generally in all the History Plays. It therefore follows that any attempt to analyse the politics of this situation will illuminate meanings within the plays themselves and also provide further clues towards their authorship.

During Medieval days, the Church had been undivided – openly, at least – and it had been such a prominent landowner and holder of riches that the monarch was able to call on its financial resources for support. This meant the King had a degree of financial backing which was independent of the nobles. It also meant he could play the Church and the nobles off against each other, should either of them threaten his particular rule and lifestyle. (This rivalry between Church and some nobles was personified by Shakespeare in *Henry VI, part 1*, with his presentation of the deadly argument between Cardinal Beaufort and Good Duke Humphrey.) The Church, acting in consort with those nobles who had decided to go along with the Church faction, initially won out during the reign of Richard II. Thus the opposition of the Chivalric, *anti-Church* nobles became a fundamental cause of that King's deposition. However, this specific cause of the revolution against Richard II is not often written about because the nobles who won that particular Civil

War ordered previous records of King Richard's reign to be destroyed, and then re-wrote the Chronicles themselves.[112] Shakespeare's play of *Richard II* is anchored on the anti-Church, pro-chivalry side – he tells Richard's story from the perspective of the men who re-wrote the Chronicles.

The Roman Catholic Church in England could not but be weakened during the round of Civil Wars which kept erupting after Richard's deposition, and especially during the Wars of the Roses. To begin with, it is more difficult for any established Church, which is also a major landowner, to collect its rents in war time than in peace. Secondly, the Black Death and the wars during the 14th and 15th centuries depleted the number of men available to work on the Church's lands, so profit from agriculture was also reduced. Thirdly, as the strength and partisan support for particular warlike nobles rose, so the participatory gentry's support for the Church – financial and ideological – waned. During the time of the Wars of the Roses, for example, Richard Neville, Earl of Warwick, originally a leader of the Yorkist faction, became extremely powerful and popular. He was responsible for thousands of families on his estates, and it is said that none of them went hungry. He also staged great feasts for them at his own expense,[113] so it would be hardly surprising if many people decided to support their local knight more enthusiastically than their local church. In the short term at least, then, knights of chivalry actually gained from the spoils of war, while the Church lost out.

If such chivalric knights gained even from *Civil* war, how much greater were their gains from foreign broils. No wonder Richard Neville bewailed the loss of lands he had fought for in France: he had a share in the profits of the foreign land he won for the Crown. Besides, foreign war did not leave behind it a widely-perceptible trail of tangible and psychological damage for the chivalric knight to clear up, in full view of his own omni-present countrymen. It was not difficult for the Shakespeare plays, therefore, to steer the minds of the audience into believing foreign wars to be a good thing for the country and civil wars a bad thing.

But a Catholic monarch might well have had more cause to bewail *all* forms of war than did his chivalric nobles. Firstly, the monarch was always guaranteed a degree of financial support from the Church, during 'good behaviour', (and good behaviour meant going along with the Church's stratagems.) The Church itself received some revenue from its international connections, so the economic chain linking Foreign Revenue to the Church and the King was a strong one. War, however, could potentially break it.

'Good behaviour' on the part of the King also meant his favouring the Church's personnel, and its 'chosen' nobles too, and Richard II, for instance, did this. However, any monarch also had to be careful not to lose favour with his military-minded knights, because of their potentially threatening, warlike nature. He could best do this by passing on to them a share of his own and the Church's wealth, but this would obviously be easier to do in times when his own revenue was at its height. And there was the rub. The King's revenues were often boosted by spoils from foreign warfare which his military, chivalric nobles undertook. Consequently, the Church's aim of *peace* within the Holy Roman Empire did not always yield the level of profits a king might desire. The king was therefore bound to consider the interests of his *military* knights even though they might directly oppose the Church's policy of peace in Western Europe.

The situation of Thomas of Woodstock, Duke of Gloucester, was a case in point. Thomas was a relative and supporter of Richard II and carried the sceptre and the dove at his coronation in 1377. But his income of £1,000 per year – granted him on the eve of the coronation itself – was derived from the revenues of alien priories, which were at the King's behest only during the war with France. "Thomas thus had a vested interest in the continuation of the war."[114] One way or another, then, the chivalric nobles of England often had an interest in maintaining a state of war. But even if a King might gain foreign spoils from international warfare, he stood the risk of losing his Church's international support thereby.

To a large extent, however, this situation changed *after* the Reformation. Lands and Priories 'dissolved' by Henry VIII after his split with Rome were farmed out among those nobles who had supported his religious and marital stance. He and subsequent monarchs therefore became more dependent on his or her chivalric nobles than ever a previous monarch had experienced. Any foreign Catholic income and direct support from the Vatican was now cut off. This put the monarch in a weakened situation, which is perhaps why the Tudor monarchs became happy to torture or even execute any nobleman they suspected was not honouring them. Only by alternate striking and cajoling could he/she keep his chivalric knights in check: those who would not follow the monarch for love might at least do so out of fear.

This state of affairs must in turn have engendered a terrible tension within noble families under the Tudor monarchs. Even if they tried to follow and comply with the will of the King or Queen, they could be falsely denounced by rival nobles. To be sure, this had happened in pre-Reformation times too, but then there had at least been the sanctuary of the international Catholic Church, to whose moral, and even physical, protection a wronged nobleman or woman could appeal. After the Reformation, this protection was essentially lost, because the reigning monarch was now head of the Church in England. No fear of the Pope and his foreign power remained as an over-arching source of sanctions against the King of England.

How Medieval and Tudor politics affected the Nevilles

Shakespeare-Neville was well aware of all this political history, as I will demonstrate in later chapters analysing his Wars of the Roses plays. The Nevilles both suffered and benefitted under the new, Tudor situation. Sir Henry Neville's grandfather was beheaded for supposed complicity in a plot against Henry VIII, but his son was immediately re-instated and also became one of the King's favourites. It was as if King Henry VIII was giving out a three-fold message: 1) he was fearful of the Nevilles because he knew they had a better claim to the throne than the Tudors, should they ever wish to pursue it; 2) he was willing to live in harmony with them, so long as they never raised the question of their inheritance or took up arms against him, and 3) he would hold the Nevilles close to the Tudor monarchy because he liked them, but also because he feared them and felt he needed to keep an eye on their activities. Any monarch preferred the rich, powerful Nevilles' *support* to their *opposition*.

It was therefore under these three political arches that Sir Henry Neville was born and brought up. He showed that he was willing to know his place and keep it, so long as monarchs remembered their side of the implicit 'Neville bargain' too. But the first of these Tudor messages – that the Nevilles had a strong claim to the throne – must also have given Henry Neville a feeling of potential power, especially when coupled with his acknowledged academic and intellectual prowess, and his knowledge of weaponry. This feeling was surely derived from his ancestral chivalric knighthood too. The values of Chivalry were strong in every Neville. In his portrait at Audley End, Neville has his hand on his sword. But what were these Chivalric values, and how should they be played out in the new, post Reformation state of affairs?

Shakespeare and Chivalry

To begin with, in the Shakespeare History plays we can see the precise debate between the Church nobles on one side and the Chivalric nobles on the other being worked out. Those plays might speak of bygone days, but they were designed to contain lessons for the author's present day too. If their author had come from a lowly background, he would not have felt the keen edge of this debate, because it was a debate which was taking place in *privileged* circles. Nor would he have had access to its intricacies, which the playwright depicts so eloquently. Had the true writer of the Shakespeare Histories sprung from a family which supported the Church or were favourites of Richard II – such as the de Veres – he would have portrayed a very different political viewpoint from that put forward in the plays. As this book proceeds, therefore, it will become ever increasingly evident that a Neville's hand is behind their creation, and that Nevillian values and points of view predominate. These values, however, are not those of our own time, for Chivalry, in most of its forms, is now ailing if not dead.

I do not wish to make that last statement seem value-ridden or in any way reflective of the modern connotations which the word 'chivalry' holds. 'Chivalry' during and before Shakespeare's time denoted fighting in armour, usually on horseback. It had Elizabethan *connotations* too, but they were also rather different from those of today. There is so much talk of Chivalry and Knighthood in the Shakespeare plays and *Sonnets* that it is certainly necessary to try and understand something of what it had come to mean by Elizabethan times – and that meaning inevitably involved *political* overtones.

Chivalry had grown up with the Feudal system, but it liked to imagine its origins going right back to King Arthur. The Ideal was that Christian Knights of the Round Table were fighting for justice for all. These ideals spread around Europe. However, when it came to English Knights there always was a big anomaly. Though they considered themselves Knights of Christ, they carried a pagan hangover, because they also fought in the name of their lady, and for her honour too.[115] This is what has made them seem so romantic in modern eyes; but this romantic image turns out to be little short of the glamourisation of slaughter. Romanticisation of knighthood made room for a renewal of the pagan idea of glory in killing, which in France at least had indeed *preceded* the knightly pagan role of masculine 'courtesy' to women. What's more, Chivalry was always riddled with ideas of class – the 'courtesy' to females so valued in England and France was usually meant to apply only to women above a certain rank.

It was during the Crusades that glamourisation of the knight's role reached its peak. But it was at this time too that the military orders of knighthood – such as the Templars, Hospitallers, and the Teutonic knights – dominated all Europe and trained their men to fight in the Holy Land. This was the beginning of the *collective* military might of the nobles. For the very first time, they were a united multi-national force, fighting for a cause which was separate from their roles as individual knights setting out merely to please the King of their own country, and enrich themselves.

During the Crusades knights learned formalised techniques of horsemanship and the wielding of sword, and spear. (What better pseudonym than 'Shakespeare', therefore, for the true writer, who sprang from, and represented, the Knightly classes?) Because of the collective needs during this military campaign, social graces were standardised too. Romantic adventures of the knights on their journey to battle were recounted by French troubadours and German Minnesinger – 'Minne' being the old German word for 'love'. These tales became more and more elaborate and fantasised, so by the time Neville's father was devising Court entertainments, the knight had become a source of jokes too. Neville senior and his friend Henry Sidney staged mock knightly battles on hobby horses, and onlookers were also amused with Neville's sketch entitled 'Saving the Maiden at the Tilt'.

However, it was of course socially necessary for these now efficiently-trained military personnel to live by ideals that helped ensure they would not use their new skills aggressively in peacetime. The Knight was therefore trained to swear to honour God, the King and his Lady, and to wear the latter's favour in battle. He was also taught to recognise and respect rank and degree.

Our Sir Henry Neville, though not himself undergoing the complete medieval training in fighting and chivalry, was nevertheless brought up in a family where these traditions had persisted. He would therefore have been quite ready to accept knighting by the Earl of Essex at Cadiz in 1596. Neville was by then about thirty four years old. It has sometimes been thought that it was his cousin (also named Henry Neville, heir to the Lord

Bergavenny title) who was knighted at Cadiz, but this man was younger than twenty one at the time, so knighting him would have gone against the expected and accepted traditions of knighthood. It is therefore verifiable – based on this and other considerations – that it was indeed our Sir Henry who was knighted by Essex.

The knighting ceremony *before* the Reformation, and in time of peace was, however, a much more formal affair. It was surrounded by pomp, circumstance and an air of wonder induced by physical privation. The entrant had to fast, indulge in almost constant prayer and then spend a waking night meditating on religious mysticism. Next morning he partook in a mass, presented his sword to the presiding priest and then took an oath which included clauses calling on him to be true to the king, defend the church, protect women and the poor, to protect widows and orphans, and to 'fortify and protect justice'.[116]

The candidate for knighthood then knelt down and was touched on the shoulder by his knight with his sword, saying "In the name of God, of our Lady, of thy patron Saint, ... I dub thee knight; be brave, bold, and loyal."[117] In general, therefore, it was said that the knight was trained in 'love, war and religion'. But the meaning of 'love' encompassed friendship, kindness and grace, and it is in this sense that we see Sir Henry Neville using it in his letters, and, as 'Shakespeare', in his *Sonnets*. An old French knight's oath also included his promise to be 'Fair, kind and true'. We find this echoed **exactly** in 'Shakespeare':

Fair, kind, and true, is all my argument,
Fair, kind, and true, varying to other words;
And in this change is my invention spent,
Three themes in one, which wondrous scope affords.
Sonnet 105

When in the chronicle of wasted time
I see descriptions of the fairest wights,
And beauty making beautiful old rhyme
In praise of ladies dead and lovely knights,
Then, in the blazon of sweet beauty's best,
Of hand, of foot, of lip, of eye, of brow,
I see their antique pen would have expressed
Even such a beauty as you master now.
So all their praises are but prophecies
Of this our time, all you prefiguring,
Sonnet 106

This therefore means that Sir Henry, [and Sir Henry as 'Shakespeare'] though officially only a 'knight bachelor', had absorbed the family culture of courteous chivalry, and had also seen the *French* knight's oath. (By Neville's day, the title 'knight bachelor' was an honorary one bestowed by the monarch, though Elizabeth would certainly not have bestowed it on anyone totally unlearned in chivalric values and lacking the 'civil' rules of chivalry.)

If he was very lucky, the undergraduate knight might also have a tutor in classical languages, but this was not prescribed and so was by no means certain. It was this uncertainty, together with their lack of title, which probably decided Sir Henry's branch of the Neville family eventually to have their boys educated at University, rather than sending them to a noble family to be trained as military knights. However, Sir Henry must have been trained in the rudiments of horsemanship, falconry and hunting before he left home for Oxford, because we find him talking about these pursuits in his letters. But he was finally not really partial to them. He criticises King Henri IV for spending too much time at hunting and with his mistresses, and once he was past thirty years old he seems only to have hunted when in need of catching something to eat, not simply for sport.

It appears that all the branches of the Neville family – even the most ennobled – believed in education of the mind as well as the body, because Richard Neville, Earl of Warwick, is noted as exceptional in seeing to it that his daughters were educated well. One observer said of his daughter:

> "She was thereto courteous [i.e. in playing of instruments and reciting poetry], and free and wise, And in the seven arts learned withouten miss."[118]

(This is just the sort of tradition one would expect in the family of the true Shakespeare – the playwright who characterised strong, educated women in his plays.)

Yet despite further education and all their Christian vows, knights were known to be easily angered and often too easily tempted to use their weapons in a quarrel. For Queen Elizabeth I, unmarried yet in charge of men at Court who had been brought up by families trained in this tradition, the situation must sometimes have been terrifying. She therefore ruled with a rod of iron, protected by Walsingham and the Secret Service, and by the new professional ministers she was gathering around her, especially the Cecils. But even so, she sometimes drew the wrath of knights, who wore their swords at their sides, even in Court. On one famous occasion the Earl of Essex drew his sword, after the Queen had boxed his ears. For this he was of course banned from Court for some time, but he was a trained knight and his anger had been roused, so this incident may well have given him confidence to begin plotting to bring his envisaged rebellion/demonstration to fruition.

Sir Henry Neville had not received such a formal knightly training as an Earl, but he must nevertheless have had knightly skills passed on to him from his father (and perhaps even from his uncle Baron Bergavenny's family) because no one ever spoke of him in a formal situation without also uttering 'That noble knight.'[119] Again, he is also pictured with his sword in his portrait at Audley End House. It was traditional for any man, whether noble or not, to be pictured *without* his sword if he had taken holy orders. So being pictured *with* his sword may therefore have been a definite statement on Sir Henry Neville's part: he was a knight who was most definitely not connected with the Church faction.

The Nevilles had been among the greatest knightly families of times past, so there can be no doubt that Sir Henry was well aware of the specific training some of his relatives and fellow courtiers had undergone. Indeed, in times when his grandfather, Sir Edward Neville, was on good terms with King Henry VIII, he was especially chosen by that King to appear in a tournament alongside him. (A tournament was a sporting contest of jousting, in which the combatants usually used blunted weapons.) The following extract describes this precise event, which seems to have been performed as a celebration for the birth of Henry VIII's son.

> Henry displayed his joy at the birth of his son, Prince Arthur, by a solemn tournament. The court removed from Richmond to Westminster. The King himself determined to tourney, and he selected four knights to aid him. He styled himself "Cure Loial"; the Lord William Earl of Devonshire was called "Bon Voloire," Sir Thomas Knevet, "Bon Espoir," and Sir Edward Nevill chose for his tourneying name "Valiant Desire." These four noble spirits were called "Les quatre chevaliers de la forrest Salvigne." Their names were

written upon a goodly table [i.e. a placard], which was suspended from a tree, curiously wrought, the knights engaging to run at the tilt against all comers. Accordingly, by the prescribed time, a court in the palace was prepared for the games, and the Queen and her ladies were conducted to a gallery richly hung inside with cloth of gold, and on the outside with cloth of arras. A pageant preceded the sports of chivalry. [120]

Reading this extract leads one to make some remarkable parallels with the Shakespeare plays. To begin with, the suspending of name-placards on a tree is reminiscent of Orlando's suspending of Rosalind's name from trees in *As You Like It*. Edward Neville's tourneying name 'Valiant Desire' is also interesting. 'Valiant' is one of Shakespeare's favourite words – he uses it more than 160 times. And there is just one place – in *King John* – where 'Valiant' and 'Desire' are mentioned on adjacent lines. Moreover, they are mentioned in connection with the name Falconbridge. The Falconbridges were married into the ancestry of the Nevilles, and the Bastard Falconbridge in the play may well be an alter-ego of Henry Neville, given that Neville must have known about his parents not being married to each other when he was born. Henry – like Falconbridge – was an observer of those who ruled the land, because he had been an MP and a courtier from the age of twenty. It is therefore significant that this is the one instance where 'Valiant' and 'Desire' are used together, and that there is a Nevillian connection. Here is the relevant extract from King John:

KING JOHN - Scene 3. The Battlefield.
Alarums. Enter KING JOHN and HUBERT.
King John How goes the day with us? O, tell me, Hubert.
Hubert Badly, I fear. How fares your majesty?
King John This fever that hath troubled me so long
Lies heavy on me. O, my heart is sick!
Enter a MESSENGER.
Messenger My lord, your <u>valiant kinsman Falconbridge</u>
<u>Desires</u> your majesty to leave the field,
And send him word by me which way you go.

Altogether, therefore, Chivalric training generally helped advance the culture of the day. It was not purely militaristic and was at least a 'worldly' movement which could counteract the excessive influence of the Church in pre-Reformation England. As in ancient Greece and Rome, its development also led to a growth in the secular arts. All sorts of artistic presentations, culminating in an indigenous English theatre, sprang from the Troubadours telling their intriguing narratives of knights' adventures across Europe. Scarcely surprising then, when viewed in this light, that our greatest playwright stemmed from a family schooled in knightly training and romance. Unsurprising too that Sir Henry Neville's father and grandfather took active roles in these knightly entertainments.

However, even though by Elizabeth I's time the aspects of knighthood that were stressed were entertainment, courtesy and honour, the Queen decided that she rather liked the idea of their *militaristic* training being used also to bring foreign spoils home to her! But the knightly attributes had occasionally become more civilised by this time: we only have to look at accounts of the Earl of Essex's raid on Cadiz in 1596 to see this particular knight's civilisation in action. Even the King of Spain remarked that Essex did everything possible to prevent his men looting and pillaging after their victory.[121] This is surely echoed in *Henry V* where that king does not flinch at meting out the severest punishments for his soldiers who disobey his orders and indulge in looting. Henry Neville was the only possible Shakespeare author to have witnessed this 'grace' of Essex's at Cadiz. When we remember too that Essex is actually mentioned in this play as the 'General' now in Ireland, then we may reasonably assume that Neville based much of his characterisation of Henry V on the Earl of Essex's deeds and personality.

So in what other ways did the Nevilles' chivalric background translate itself into some of the Shakespeare plays? To begin with, the writer of those early plays exhibits a special interest in warfare itself. Anyone watching the *Henry VI* trilogy soon becomes sick of war and warfare. In just the same way, spectators of the early play *Titus Andronicus* become sickened by the personal violence of it. Whereas it can be feasibly argued that the playwright is purposely engendering a disgust with civil war in these early plays in order to fulfil the wishes of the new ministerial governors of England, especially the Cecils, one cannot escape the feeling that he is also facing up to his own ancestors' obsession with war and violence. Fighting and the mechanism of warfare is portrayed on the public stage in these plays as in no other which had preceded them. When one pictures the true author – Henry

Neville – behind all this then everything is explained. Moreover, at the time these portrayals of warfare were forming in his brain, Henry Neville had become the inheritor of a cannon works and the seller of armaments. This seemed a fitting fate for someone from the knightly Neville family, however much this particular Neville was eventually to hate the corruption involved in it. Altogether, however, it was as if the study of chivalry was transforming itself so as to fit in with the new Elizabethan commercial age, and helping to fight for the nation state rather than for the previous knightly ideals.

The ownership of weaponry was also encouraged by Neville's mother's family. Young Henry Neville's European Tour must have been funded and initiated by Sir Thomas Gresham, Neville's great uncle. The very rich Sir Thomas owned the cannon and ironworks in Mayfield, East Sussex, which Neville knew he would inherit. In 1578 – the year of Neville's departure – a ship bearing Gresham cannons to the King of Denmark had sunk, irretrievably, in the Thames estuary[122]. Gresham was old and ill and could not travel to the Danish King himself to explain what had happened and to arrange for a new consignment. But Henry Neville was young and energetic, and his tutor, Sir Henry Savile, was partially funded by Oxford University to undertake a European tour, accompanied by two of his best pupils, Henry Neville and Robert Sidney (younger brother of the great Sir Philip.) However, Oxford University only paid £6–13–4d towards this five-year continental sojourn,[123] which was less than a country vicar was paid for 5 months' work at the time, so it is obvious that only such a rich man as Thomas Gresham could have made up the sum needed for the group's five year visit! It would therefore have been incumbent on the young Henry Neville not to lose any opportunity of studying continental cannon-making while on this tour, and one of the places he researched was the Jewish Ghetto in Venice, site of the old Venetian cannon works.

Sir Thomas Gresham died in 1579 while Neville was still abroad, so he knew that he must take over the Mayfield cannon works on his return to England. This was to be delayed until 1583, so Neville had plenty of time to think things out. His uncle, Thomas Digges, had lectured at Merton, Neville's Oxford College, and had written a book on warfare strategies,[124] so Neville's mind would inevitably have been taken up with such studies. But the fact that Neville ran the Mayfield works for only two years before beginning to sell it off, that he refused to fit into the usual corrupt pattern expected from arms manufacturers of the time, that he complained to William Cecil about the corruption, and that he even risked fines and court action for selling off the cannon works (contrary to Gresham's will) illustrates the depth of Neville's *personal* antipathy to the *business* of war.[125] He happily took part in organising defences against the Armada in 1588 and in supplying the Cinque Ports and Lowlands with cannons to defend against the Spanish, but the whole *business* of warfare clearly disgusted him.

This disgust is certainly illustrated in the early history plays of Shakespeare. Neville was a 'Christian, inwardly,' as his father in law said, so must have found it difficult to glory in the business of war, try as he might. But fate and his ancestry had thrust upon Neville the necessity of his attempting to become familiar with the history of arms and warfare. He may very well have tried hard to see the glorious side of war by admiring individual acts of heroism, such as those portrayed in the plays. He was also never a supporter of international peace *on any terms*. The true writer of the Shakespeare plays did indeed view military action in defence of one's country as honourable and necessary. The *Henry VI* plays contain technical terms when it comes to cannonry, including the word 'linstock' which was used for lighting the cannon. They were *early* plays – written at the time Neville was working with weapons. It is significant too that another early play *Titus Andronicus* contains a most unusual reference to a steel 'gad', which was the miners' term for a wedge which helped to shore up the roof of a mine while the men were prospecting for ore. The word consequently also began to mean a steel chisel used to indent words on another metal. Yet the Oxford English Dictionary does not note any such use of this word before the eighteenth century – but there it is, nevertheless, in *Titus Andronicus*, Act 4, Sc.1:

> **Titus** ... I will go get a leaf of brass
> And with a gad of steel will write these words.

Looking at the history of warfare, then, Neville was also bound to have studied the history of the Crusades and wondered about the mental conflict between the fighters' butchery and their Christian ideals. Just such internal conflicts on the part of the author are evidenced in the texts of the early history plays: the **imagery** glorifying war and fighting chosen for the *Henry VI* plays is not Christian in origin, but *pre*-Christian. Neville must have seen that the Templars who went to fight in the name of Christ in the Crusades had faced these same internal conflicts, and the way in which they (secretly) justified what they were doing was very similar to the way in which civil war is justified by various noble knights in the *Henry VI* plays, namely fighting in defence of a bloodline.

This may at first seem a surprising statement. Surely the Templars – the then new knightly order created to defend Christian interests – were fighting for Christianity against Islam. But in Christian terms no such bloody conflict could be philosophically accommodated; yet the Templars still declared that they were Knights of Christ. The Templars, if they remained Christian at heart, must therefore have sought worldly means of justifying their actions. Even if they believed that one could not legitimately fight for the dominance of belief in Jesus (who preached turning the other cheek) they were worldly enough to believe that one could legitimately fight for other human beings and, specifically, for a bloodline. Whether or not the Templars had lighted on Gnostic gospels containing stories of the marriage of Christ and a subsequent bloodline spread through the royal families of Europe is not known for certain. What *is* known, however, is that this holy, knightly order was Earth-bound enough in their ideas to set up a King of Jerusalem, and once there was a recognised kingship then there could be a 'legitimate' need to protect that king and his descendants in title.

The writer of the *Henry VI* plays has demonstrated his knowledge of this development in the history of the Crusades by presenting Queen Margaret's father, René d'Anjou, as (among other titles) 'King of Jerusalem.' The writer also eventually has some of his characters poke fun at this title. It is by this means, surely, that he exposes the unresolved contradictions inherent within those who fought for dynastic rights in the Wars of the Roses: if the title of King of Jerusalem is meaningless, then *all* fighting for bloodline rights is meaningless. Shakespeare-Neville is pointing out an analogy between the un-Christian thinking behind those English civil wars and that same lack of Christian spirit pervading the Crusades.

Once this parallel is recognised, it is possible to see Templar symbolism in parts of the texts of the *Henry VI* trilogy. Further examples of that symbolism will follow, but the reference to the King of Jerusalem in the plays implies that the writer was consciously demonstrating *covert* implications. Sir Henry's politics were known, his plays were known (even though their authorship was not) but here I had seen something in the texts of all three parts of *Henry VI* which only a very privileged few would have understood, even at the time the plays were written: the 'King of Jerusalem' reference was certainly arcane.

Then I made another unusual discovery while researching the primary-source background to Sir Henry, a discovery which also connects with the Templars. This particular reference may actually have been directly connected with the strange decision of the author to mention the title 'King of Jerusalem' in the text of these highly political plays.

What I discovered was a direct, 16th century reference to the Order of Sion, and that Order is itself connected with the Templars. At the time, I did not know how unusual a discovery this was. However, my literary agent's chairman was the famous and much lamented Mark Barty King – the man who had published a book concerning the Priory of Sion some twenty or more years before I met him. He told me that the authors of that book, which concerned a supposed secret society based on the Templars, had never been able to find any primary source reference to prove that the Order of Sion had continued to exist after its known dissolution in 1314 and *before* the appearance of texts purporting to emanate from some supposed similar organisation in the 1950s. The question of whether these 1950s texts were genuine or not has been a vexed one, and the lack of any concrete evidence linking the Order with the Templars after their dissolution has understandably made historians very cautious about trusting the twentieth century documents. Even if the continued existence of an early Order of Sion were proven, then there still remains a lot of research to be done before the 1950s documents could begin to be viewed as having any possible connection with that *old* Order.

So, the **primary source** reference I found naming the Order in the sixteenth century certainly is rare. I found it among the letters of one Thomas Rogers – a man who indulged in a great deal of correspondence with Sir Francis Walsingham, whose profession was to enquire into secrets. Many unofficial government servants corresponded with Walsingham and were therefore labelled as spies. But they were always intelligent men, who had other interests and talents too. It is thus not surprising to find that Rogers regarded the Order of Sion as something worth looking into. Thomas Rogers (whose real name was Nicholas Berden) was a typically able servant of the Crown and would definitely have known Sir Henry Neville, because Rogers kept in close touch with Charles Paget – a spy whose services Neville used while in France, and whom he had already known in England.[126]

On 11th August, 1585, then, Rogers wrote to Walsingham, saying he had travelled with Charles Paget from Paris to Rouen. Paget told Rogers that Charles Arundel [whose name is present on the Northumberland Manuscript] was to have led an 'army' in England if the Spanish invaded. He also says that Paget is now "with Mr. Tresham and the Bishop of Ross [in Rouen] to see the profession of 2 Englishmen and 3 English women of the Order of Sion. I was invited, and intend to be there to hear their discourses."[127]

Unfortunately, I have not yet found any subsequent letter from Rogers reporting details of the meeting. Moreover, I have not been able to find any other primary or secondary sources recording the *ideas* and background of the Order of Sion in the 16th century. The old *Medieval* Order took its name from Mount Sion or Zion – a hill outside the Old City of Jerusalem. 'Zion' has also become a term symbolising the whole city of Jerusalem and the ideology of Israel. The 'Order of Sion' was, however, originally situated in the Abbey of Our Lady of Mount Zion, as it seems a small monastic order was founded there in the 12th century (and so must have had its origins in the early Crusades.) It had branches in Mount Carmel in Calabria and also in France.[128] However, the Abbey is reported as having been destroyed in an Islamic raid in the early 13th century, and the monks apparently then moved to Sicily. Any monks who remained joined the Jesuit Order in 1617. But none of this explains who they were and what they were doing in France in 1585, nor why both men and women were in the Order too. There is no recorded link between this Order and the Templars, though it would be very strange if they had not known and been protected by the Orders of Chivalry then present in the area.

Various conclusions can be drawn from Rogers' letter. Firstly, the Order existed but its 'professions' (beliefs) were not well known, otherwise Rogers would not have pointed out that this was what he and Paget were hoping to learn. Secondly, the Order could no longer have been officially affiliated to the Catholic Church, otherwise the Bishop of Ross (who accompanied Rogers to hear about the Order of Sion) would already have been aware of their beliefs. Thirdly, the Order of Sion was probably not an Order of monks or nuns, since Rogers does not say this: he merely describes the speakers as men and women. Indeed, women were considered capable of leadership in the old Order of the Templars, and we see this capability in the Amazonian Margaret of Anjou in the *Henry VI* plays. It may therefore be that either The Templars or the Order of Sion were always veering towards secularism, which was very probably one of the reasons the Pope wanted ultimately to annihilate the Templar Order. Moreover, *English* men and women were going to talk about it in Rouen, which means either the Order was English and some of the members were promoting it on the continent, or that it was not allowed in England, so the members had gone to the continent, either to join it, or to establish it there. We may also assume, however, that even if it existed in England, then it was a *secret* society, since Rogers and Walsingham clearly knew little about it, and they were among the most well informed men of their day. This all makes it even more frustrating that I have not yet located any further letter from Rogers explaining the Order's 'professions' [by which Rogers would have meant their 'beliefs'].

In 1585, when Rogers wrote his letter, Neville was about 23 years old, and Paget about forty. It was also the year after the publication of *Leicester's Commonwealth* (that text often ascribed to Paget.) Two annotated, manuscript copies of that work are to be found among Sir Henry's papers in the Worsley Collection in the Lincolnshire Archives. The Northumberland Manuscript also mentions *Leicester's Commonwealth* [noted close to Charles Arundel's name.] Rogers also states that the Papists are divided into factions, and that the Pagets and Thomas Throgmorton are on one side, with the Jesuits, including a certain Parsons, on the other, just as Neville later reported to Cecil.[129] It therefore appears that Neville had long been in possession of this information by the time he told Sir Robert Cecil about it (in a letter from France in 1599.) Once again, Neville is discovered as a man who did not automatically disclose any Intelligence he received to the highest authorities. This, then, suggests that he was indeed working within a deeper layer of society.

Rogers says that Paget and the Earl of Leicester are jealous of each other, which of course then gives further reason to suspect Paget of being the author of *Leicester's Commonwealth* – the book which slanders that Earl, or else lays bare his misdeeds, depending on how the individual reader views the situation.[130] It is also perfectly possible, given all the circumstances and double agents involved, that *Leicester's Commonwealth* was a creation under Walsingham's direction, because Walsingham, Sir Henry Neville senior, and the Cecils all distrusted the Earl of Leicester. In a later letter, Rogers says Paget is writing a book in answer to those against Throgmorton, in which he also states that the Earl of Northumberland's death looks like something more suspicious than suicide,[131] and: "Clitheroe, the priest here, doth help to pen it"[132] [in English and Latin.] Then, significantly, Rogers tells Walsingham that all the Papists in Rouen think Paget and Morgan are spies.

What can be said with certainty is therefore that, to have known Paget by the time he went to France, Neville must have had privileged knowledge of all this, and of just about everything that had gone on in the Walsingham circle. Whether he therefore subsequently also became involved directly with any secretive Order of Knighthood is not known. However, his friendship with Essex and his probable 'knighting' by that Earl[133] makes it highly likely that he was deeply cognisant of, and involved with, at least one Order of Knighthood. As a Neville, he would also have known about the Knights' code of chivalry, their myths and chansons – just as did Chaucer, his kinsman. It can therefore be no mere coincidence that reference to these Orders and myths are implied in a number of Shakespeare's works. It is also certain that Essex would not have chosen Neville as his hoped-for 'Secretary of State' had Neville not been inside Essex's personal circle of knighthood, by which he laid such great store, and about which Queen Elizabeth I was always troubled. When the Earl of Essex knighted many men 'in the field' after their campaign in Cadiz, Elizabeth complained so bitterly that it is probable that Neville, who was already in her bad books for selling so much ordnance abroad, decided to keep quiet regarding any Order of Knighthood with which he may have been associated. But this could well have been in vain, for Elizabeth had only to think about the others who had been knighted alongside 'Henry Neville' at Cadiz to realise that they sounded like a roll-call of our Neville's friends. Indeed, they even included such companions of his youth as Arthur Throckmorton, who had accompanied Neville on part of his foreign tour. It therefore becomes ever clearer why both Elizabeth and Cecil viewed Neville with some suspicion and not a little fear. Bearing in mind that Neville possessed knowledge of weaponry and its manufacture, one can easily understand the Queen's worries. If he was indeed also part of one of these secret yet powerful quasi-military Orders of Knighthood then he could become a very powerful rival, if the mood so took him.

It is also true that whomsoever the Nevilles supported throughout English Medieval history often became victorious in battle. Even the Tudors would have known them as 'Kingmakers' who could de-throne any monarch just as surely as they had placed him or her on high, should he or she give the Neville clan cause for too much concern. The *Henry VI* plays carried a non-too covert message in this respect. The Tudors must therefore have been caught between either favouring or slaughtering the Nevilles, in pursuance of their own safety. Henry VIII kept our Sir Henry's father contentedly on his side after slaughtering *his* father, Sir Edward Neville of Addington Park. Henry Neville senior was boisterous enough to amuse both Elizabeth and her father. But Elizabeth had never found it easy to fathom the *new* generation of Nevilles or Cecils. Perhaps this was partly because she naturally feared the new, young, energetic knights as she grew older. Perhaps too it was because they were able to read Italian books on political theory, and also *The Art of War*. These were pre-eminently the tracts of Machiavelli, which laid bare the machinations of Princes. However, she was right to feel safer with Cecil than with Neville, because Cecil's family was of newer blood and so would not be so deeply entrenched with the knightly Orders and family traditions as the Nevilles.

Returning, then, to the King of Jerusalem, what would this title have meant to Neville, from both historical and symbolic points of view? First of all, Neville must have known that anyone who held it had the powerful though hidden support of a quasi-military Order. This might explain why the Earl of Suffolk, in *Henry VI, part 1,* so readily gave Prince Regnier, King of Jerusalem, control of Anjou and Maine. What other explanations for Suffolk's strange actions can there have been? He was either afraid of some secret power the seemingly-impoverished Regnier possessed, or else perhaps he wished to enter some secret and powerful Order himself. Prince Regnier (René d'Anjou) was virtually penniless, and his daughter brought no dowry with her in her bid to marry Henry VI. Moreover, Richard Neville would have been receiving revenue from the French lands he had conquered, so Suffolk must have known he would have provoked the powerful Richard, Earl of Warwick's anger through the strange agreement he made with René. Suffolk would surely not have risked this unless either massive fear or expected prize had been lain before him.

In turn, if we consider the whole case of the Earl of Suffolk further, then we have proof once again of a Neville author at work: the writer goes out of his way to show up any injustices against Richard Neville, and at the same time ignores Suffolk's good side (which existed in historical records.) The point is that Richard Neville's enemy was that same Earl of Suffolk. Who but a Neville would have slanted his work in such a way? The unstated text is that Suffolk must also have *known* that *many* courtiers back in England would be angry with him for giving away the lands in France, for which so many of them had fought for so long. Only if he knew that he could call on the strong support of at least one powerful group as a result of his over-generous action, would Suffolk have agreed to such bad terms. It could perhaps be, therefore, that the Lancastrian support Suffolk finally obtained for his agreement with René was gained through a covert Templar connection the Lancastrians may have already been exploring. Added to this, the true writer of the *Henry VI* trilogy was making the worldly Richard Neville, Earl of Warwick, look much better than the churchy Suffolk. This not only bolstered the Neville family but also implied the following equation: Knights associated with Chivalry (especially those bearing the name of Neville) = good; Knights associated with the Church = bad.

Not only does all this betray the true writer as a Neville; it also betrays his anti-Catholic sympathy. This stance regarding religion is indeed reinforced throughout the *Henry VI* plays, as will be demonstrated during my detailed analysis in later chapters.

Templar subtexts surely abound in the *Henry VI* plays: Shakespeare-Neville (in *Henry VI, part 1*) showed the Wars of the Roses starting in the **Temple garden** in London, with the plucking of red and white roses. The London Temple Church was one of the Templar foundations which had by then passed into the hands of the Hospitallers. The Middle Temple and Inner Temple were Inns of Court with the Templar connection in their very name, and it is a *legal* point which the nobles are debating (in *Henry VI, part 1*) as they enter the Temple Garden. It is therefore also significant that just as the Red Rose represented the Lancastrians, so did the Red Cross represent the Templars. And just as the White Rose represented the Yorkists, so did the White Cross represent the Hospitallers. The clever staging of this scene would therefore have sent out **two** messages to members of Knightly Orders present in the audience: firstly, that this argument may have as much to do with the surviving Templars and the victorious Hospitallers as it has to do with rival English families; secondly, that the true author possessed inside knowledge of those Knightly Orders, and must therefore also have his origins in one of those noble families. No wonder Queen Elizabeth released the actor Shakespeare after questioning him about the performance and authorship of *Richard II* on the eve of the Essex rebellion – she herself was from a family who would have understood those messages encoded in even the earlier 'Shakespeare' plays. She would already have known that Shakespeare of Stratford could not possibly be the true author.

The Templars were cruelly burned in fourteenth century France. The post-holocaust phase of the Templars is associated with Scotland. This is because the Pope had sent out messages (as he believed) to all the countries of Europe saying that he had banned their organisation, but forgot to send such a message to Scotland. The remaining Templars had previously been based in, and then hunted in, France. The most logical place for them to hide, however, was in Scotland. Is there, then, a possible relationship between the Templars and the creation of the Scots Guard which later protected the French kings? Certainly, the Auld Alliance between Scotland and France is well known.

The writer of the Temple garden scene may of course simply be underlining his own perception of an association between the futility of the Crusades and the futility of the Wars of the Roses. But even on stage, the scene in the Temple garden is a mysterious and under-stated one. Richard Neville's declared reason for choosing a white rose rather than a red seems very flippant:

Warwick I love no colours, and, without all colour
Of base insinuating flattery
I pluck this white rose with Plantagenet.

We know from historical records that this Earl of Warwick had quarrelled with the Lancastrians over property inheritance; but this was a reason the author clearly did not wish to lay bare on the stage. The *true* cause behind Richard Neville's initial choice of sides in the dispute was ultimately a selfish one. Again, only a

Neville would have hidden his kinsman's true but somewhat ignoble motives. But by not giving any substantial reason for the Earl's choice, the author also left things open to all sorts of symbolic interpretations to do with 'colours'. It beggars belief that Richard Neville was really choosing the White Rose simply because he did not like 'colours'. Of course, the word 'colours' can signify warring sides or factions of various types, so Richard Neville might be implying that he does not welcome civil war. Yet he also shows later in the debate that he knows very well this business will inevitably lead to just such warring:

> **Warwick** ...
> And here I prophesy: this brawl today,
> Grown to this faction in the Temple garden,
> Shall send between the red rose and the white
> A thousand souls to death and deadly night.

We are therefore left in no doubt that the Earl of Warwick has stronger, unstated reasons for choosing the White Rose. Richard Neville even repeats out loud that they are in the **Temple** garden. He chooses white, however, which was the colour of the Hospitallers. In private, he tells Plantagenet, the Duke of York, that this is because he believes he has the better claim; but he does not say this in front of the other Knights. Indeed, once again, he is posturing with them, because he makes the excuse that he is no good at judging the finer points of law:

> **Warwick** Between two hawks, which flies the higher pitch?
> Between two dogs, which hath the deeper mouth?
> Between two blades, which bears the better temper?
> Between two horses, which doth bear him best?
> Between two girls, which hath the merriest eye?
> I have perhaps some shallow spirit of judgment,
> But in these nice sharp quillets of the law,
> Good faith, I am no wiser than a daw.
> **Plantagenet** Tut, tut, here is a mannerly forbearance.

The Plantagenet Duke of York with his 'Tut, tut' is in no doubt that Neville is merely posturing. Plantagenet therefore knows that there are some **hidden** reasons for Neville's reticence:

> **Plantagenet** Since you are tongue-tied and so loath to speak,
> In dumb significants proclaim your thoughts.

Let him that is a true-born gentleman
And stands upon the honour of his birth,
If he suppose that I have pleaded truth,
From off this brier pluck a white rose with me.

Plantagenet realises that Neville is loath to *speak* the reasons for choosing between him and Suffolk, so he makes it easier for Neville by suggesting he may speak in symbols only. Symbols are the means by which secret organisations must communicate, when forced to do so in public. It is surely not merely coincidence that red is the colour of the Templars' cross, and white that of the Hospitallers. The Nevilles had gained some erstwhile Templar lands and must have wished to keep hold of them, against any neo-Templar claims.

Throughout his long battles, and through all his changing of sides and 'colours', Warwick stressed the knightly precepts of birth and right, but above all he stressed the 'honour' that should go hand in hand with them. He was willing to change sides at a moment's notice, if a monarch let down him and the people in this respect. Yet at the very last he is telling us that land – and therefore home – are causes which he holds most dear:

My parks, my walks, my manors that I had,
Even now forsake me; and of all my lands
Is nothing left me but my body's length.
Why, what is pomp, rule, reign, but earth and dust?
And live we how we can, yet die we must.   *Henry VI,
  part 3*

Then, with his last breath, he talks of his greatest concern of all – friendship. He calls for his brother and favourite comrade, Montague, not knowing he is already dead:

...Ah, Montague!
If thou be there, sweet brother, take my hand,
And with thy lips keep in my soul awhile.

All these are the concerns of a worldly man, and one who was truly a Knight, with sworn oaths of friendship behind him. Warwick had felt true friendship for the old Duke of York himself, which he had never really felt for the Duke of York's sons. Friendship was his 'true soul', and the writer of the *Sonnets* entones this feeling too, throughout the sequence. There are remaining records of Sir Henry Neville having written and told two men that he bore them 'love' – and there is no doubt that he meant this in the knightly sense of 'Amours' and friendship. One of those towards whom he expressed such 'love' was Sir Ralph Winwood, and the other the an unnamed 'Noble Lord' to whom he dedicated his sonnets. This Lord was almost certainly Henry Wriothesley, Earl of Southampton. Wriothesley was actually a Knight of the Garter, as well as having been knighted by Essex, so he would understand the Sonnet which spoke of him as 'fair, kind and true', the attributes of a Knight. The Earl of Southampton was indeed the **one** Knight to whom Shakespeare-Neville dedicated all his poetry.

Therefore, the totality of the evidence suggests a writer who has himself taken some kind of knightly oath, and who is anxious not to give away this fact to all and sundry – even to the extent of leaving a very puzzling scene at the centre of *Henry VI, part 1* rather than allowing his ancestor to express in words a certain, *hidden* root of his antipathy to the Red Rose. Besides, this very symbolism of the Wars of the Roses was said to have been invented by 'Shakespeare'; yet it was referred to in annotations within manuscripts owned by Sir Henry Neville **before** the plays appeared, as I wrote of in my first book on Sir Henry, *The Truth Will Out*.

No doubt, however, Neville is also making the point that whatever the basis for civil war, it always ends in confusion, forcing men either to shift sides or else live with the consequences of their misplaced loyalties. Neville's political treatise shows first and foremost a concern that power should be balanced, not kept in the hands of one man or one faction. As such, he would also have studied and understood the interplay which had gone on for so long between Church, Knights, and Kings. Whoever wrote the History plays understood this too. In those plays, he promulgated political propaganda which effectively ruled out the Church as a reliable custodian of such power, thus leaving worldly power in the hands of the King and the Knights of Chivalry. (This truly echoes Neville's implied insistence on a split between religion and politics.) Formalising the relationship between the King and the secular 'Knights' of Parliament in the new, Stuart dynasty, and setting out a basis for harmony rather than discord between these two parties was therefore the aim of Neville's political treatise, and it is also the solution indicated in the plays but never achieved in Neville's own lifetime.

Chapter Seven

THE KNIGHTS' LEGACY: SECRET SYMBOLISM AND SECRET SOCIETIES?

Although Shakespeare's history plays never portray a truly equal partnership between a King and his Knights, they do give us a hint that the victory of Henry Tudor at the Battle of Bosworth Field (at the end of *Richard III*) promised just such a joint venture. The brief picture of Henry of Richmond as painted by Shakespeare presents a leader who seems to spring from the best of the knightly, chivalric tradition: he is at one with his men. Why 'Shakespeare' never went on to write a play about this first King Henry Tudor, the seventh of that name, has therefore often been the subject of debate.

Surely the foremost reason is that the writer did not wish to shatter this image of Henry VII as the 'Knight-King.' The severe problems of the times together with the psychological and physical wounds left by the Wars of the Roses inevitably necessitated a strict, absolutist rule by King Henry VII – and this is certainly something Shakespeare-Neville would never have wished to portray as a *successful* way to reign. Better to leave the Knight-King image of the Tudors in all its glory at the end of *Richard III* than shatter the dream. Anyway, it was altogether wiser not to present any play about a monarch whose granddaughter was still on the throne. Even though Shakespeare-Neville appears to have begun writing *Henry VIII* while Queen Elizabeth was still alive, it was not presented until after her death. Significantly too, this play ends triumphantly with the birth of Elizabeth herself. This was a wise decision: if Henry Neville had ever been discovered writing that play during Elizabeth's lifetime, then at least he would be able to prove the play was not in any way offensive to Queen Elizabeth.

However, the age and failing health of the Virgin Queen must have spurred Neville on to dare more in that play than he would have done, had she been younger: the play of *Henry VIII* risks dealing with the undertone of trouble between the Knights and the Church. The King – Elizabeth's father – is pulled first to one side, then the other. Cardinal Wolsey is portrayed as a dangerous, ambitious *politician* in Church costume. He opposes the King's 'knightly' favourites, especially the Nevilles' kinsfolk.

Indeed, Wolsey is cast almost in the role of Iago, misleading King Henry VIII and opposing his faithful wife, Catherine of Aragon. Being a Neville, the true writer therefore shows us which side of the fence he himself is on, viz., that of the Knights and not the then Church.

As he sided with the knights, however, Sir Henry had some cause to complain against the Henries of the Tudor dynasty. The first Tudor King had already weakened the power of his landowning knights by taxing them heavily. The Tudors generally established stronger *central* government, bringing many soldierly knights under the government's control, so the *military* basis behind the various orders of Knights diminished. The training of *Professional* soldiers began, and they used more modern weaponry, in addition to the sword.

On the positive side (as far as Neville was concerned), however, there was also truly a move towards secular civil society. Even the more successful of the mercantile classes were receiving knighthoods, which were now given as an 'honour' rather than a reward for fighting. During the reign of Queen Elizabeth I, knights eventually lost the right to knight others, the Privy Council being given the sole administration of this process.[134] Altogether, then, as a politician, Henry Neville approved – generally. But knowledge of precedence, ceremony and heraldry was still held within the knightly Orders, and therefore often led those members who understood such matters to become the organisers of Court entertainments based on the old chivalric traditions.

This is precisely the situation in which Neville's own father found himself. Henry Sidney and Henry Neville appeared together regularly in the Midsummer Revels[135], arranging hobby horse battles and staging mock tilting. This was therefore very Quixotic in nature – the Knights of Europe were clearly now becoming somewhat anachronistic. However, they still existed as cohesive, factionalist societies, and their cohesive nature, coupled with their riches, meant their voices were powerful. The obvious move was therefore for clever, civic, political leaders to emerge from their ranks. Indeed, the *Reformed* Church eventually gave them a chance to break openly with the old clergy and become nominally supportive of the new clerical reforms. Those old knightly families who became Protestants were enhanced by lands given to them at the dissolution of the monasteries. They were also able to carve out for themselves a new advisory role based on the new, civil, secularised society.

Nevertheless, those 'knights' who came to the fore as leaders would not always wish to reveal all their *progressive* ideas. They might well be loth to part with the identities of their supporters or supporting organisations too, so one immediately has the perfect ground on which to sow and nurture powerful secret societies.

Within the bounds of these secret societies, one might feel free to express unconventional and progressive ideas. Indeed, the Masonic Constitution of 1723 (which was itself based on earlier Masonic principles) said that those who were "Good men and True, or men of Honour and Honesty" could belong to the society, no matter what their "Denomination or Persuasion", and that Masonry thereby "...becomes the Centre of Union and the Means of conciliating true friendship among persons that must have otherwise remained at a perpetual distance."

Yet the society had to maintain secrecy. The societies' penalties for breaking an oath of silence were so severe as to offer greater protection than would be the case if divergent ideas were expressed within a more relaxed organisation. The glue which held – and holds – the societies together might well be shared secret signs, ceremonies and 'professions'. Indeed, it would have been very surprising if secret societies had *not* flourished in such repressive times, just as, later, the French Freemasons preceded and partly organised the French Revolution.

It is obviously also possible to look at the emergence of these secret societies in a more cynical, economic and practical light: their *practical* aims were doubtless major ingredients in the Masonic mix. (Every organisation involves itself with both infrastructural and superstructural concerns, and it is sometimes very difficult to draw a line between the two.) With the decline of the need for aristocratic, military knights, there was also a decline in the potential income awarded by the King to this previously 'protective' force. The knights' secret societies were therefore formed on the back of the Merchant and Livery companies, whose money was earned through trade. The old military knights began to re-focus their attention. If they were to trade profitably, rather than making their money from protection and warfare rackets, then they could surely best keep ahead of their rivals by maintaining *trade* secrets. The fact that the knights also knew about the latest developments in weaponry meant that they could call on their inherited skills to protect the newly-emerging, rich Merchant classes, and thereby *insure* their enterprises too. (It was indeed the

Templar Knights who had not only fought in the Holy Land but also protected the aristocratic knights' properties back home, while they were away fighting. The aristocratic knights would pay an arm of the Templars for this favour. If the knights were killed in battle, then their Templar protectors often inherited their property.) But, above all, new designs in shipping, time-pieces, arithmetical calculators, etc. would assist the new 'Merchant Knights' in their major aim of pursuing their new, *trading* source of income. In England – much earlier than the French Masonic societies – the Royal Society was formed, precisely to look into advancement through science; and it was formed predominantly from men who had centred themselves around the progressive ideals of the Protestant Gresham College. By investigating the natural world around them, as well as the universe viewed through their telescopes, these men were signalling that they were a new, Protestant organisation which opposed the Catholic Church's ban on many such activities. Consequently – through the advancement of science – they were completely able to set up an economic force to rival that of the international Catholic Church.

Gresham College had been instituted by Henry Neville's great uncle and benefactor, Sir Thomas Gresham. It involved itself with scientific investigation and disclosure, for it opened its doors to all interested in keeping up with new research and discoveries. Free public lectures were given by eminent scientists, mathematicians and humanist thinkers. Its professors and participating lecturers were freed from the restrictions of the old Catholic Church. Yet some of their thinking must also have gone beyond what even the new Church of England might be expected to tolerate, so it is little wonder that the inception of the Royal Society (with its attendant investigations into nature and into the nature of man himself) was said to have been formulated within emerging, secret Masonic-style societies.[136] Gresham College had been very clever: by maintaining an open, public face, and free lectures, it would encourage working people and entrepreneurs to turn their minds to practical developments in science and technology. But through its secret, Masonic, side, the College could ensure that the best, or most sensitive, of their developments were kept away from public gaze – probably by recruiting and paying entrepreneurs and forward-thinkers to join their secret society too.

Of course, it could be argued that there is no *direct* evidence of our Sir Henry ever having belonged to one of these secret societies. But this goes for many secret society members: they usually wished to keep their association with such 'underground' groups a secret. However, the circumstantial and, ultimately, written evidence points inevitably in favour of Neville's personal involvement in a secret society, as we shall see. The circumstances of Sir Henry's birth and position also argue that it would have been far more curious if he had *not* belonged to such a secret knightly organisation. He was a Neville and therefore from the family of Kings and Kingmakers, and from a family whose ancestors had fought in the Crusades. Thus, the Templar and Hospitaller side of Freemasonry became associated with Christianity. Whereas it was allowable to enter other branches of Freemasonry so long as a man believed in any Supreme Being at all, there was, and still is, a stipulation that the *Templar* degrees could only be embarked upon by Christians. This branch of Masonry is often known as 'The York Rite', so once again there is an inevitable connection with the Yorkist Nevilles. Our particular Neville owned and administered lands in Yorkshire. Altogether, then, there must have been a merging of Lancastrian, Yorkist, Templar, Hospitaller and Guilds which joined together after the Wars of the Roses, just as surely as the Lancastrian Henry VII merged the red rose with the white when he married Margaret of York.

Moreover, our Neville, newly released from the Tower at the beginning of King James I's reign, and still a courtier, would wish to stay in favour with the Scottish monarch – and this new Scottish monarch had already been initiated into the order of the Scottish Knights Templar, who are also associated with the York Rite.

King James I, just like Neville, named himself as one of the reformation Christians. Yet perhaps the association between the Templars and conventional Christianity is somewhat perverse. Fighting in the Crusades, at the heart of Christian territory, it is said that many knights learned that there was no evidence of *supernatural* activity in the places with which the Christian religion was associated. Instead of *strengthening* the Catholic Church, therefore, in line with the original aims of the Crusades, the Templar Christian fighters could be said to have weakened it. This Templar order was eventually drastically and cruelly dissolved and persecuted by the Pope himself, ending with their annihilation by a French King in 1308. Hugh de Neville (d.1234), however, chief forester under Kings Richard I, John, and Henry

III, had accompanied King Richard on a Crusade, and also become one of King John's chief advisors. Other Nevilles had been Crusaders too, and the Castle of St. Peter at Halicarnassus in Turkey still has an 'English Tower' bearing the Neville coat of arms (among those of other English knights) to prove it.[137] Even the Kingmaker Warwick's home – Bisham Abbey – was originally a Templar foundation, though they had lost it before it ever passed into the Nevilles' hands.

Altogether, therefore, it would have been impossible for Neville not to have been brought up with the tradition of Crusading Knights around him, and the Templars were precursors of Freemasonry. Neville's portrait's inscription 'everywhere without visible signs', also strongly suggests he was personally used to keeping secrets – secrets which might well have included his membership of emerging Speculative Masons. Even the Mitre Club to which he belonged bore just such an overtone too: besides being a Bishop's hat, a mitre can refer to the precise joining of material at right angles, such as is necessary in masonry. Indeed, the set square appears as a symbol of Freemasonry. Furthermore, Neville's involvement in the Essex conspiracy shows he certainly could keep the secret side of his life well and truly secure. He very nearly got away with everything. The fact that he did so proves that the Essex circle who protected him had valued him so highly that, whatever happened to the rest of them, they truly hoped Neville would survive.

Henry Neville's stepmother's half-brother, Sir Francis Bacon, took part in the trial of the Essex conspirators. Bacon was suspected of being connected with the secretive Rosicrucian society and he, as seen in Chapter 4, knew of Neville's writing and connections. Yet although Bacon had perforce to find Essex guilty, he never brought forward hard evidence against Henry Neville. Bacon also defended Sir Henry's son in a court case initiated by the French man, Jean Gandon.[138] Similarly, Robert Cecil never disclosed the Earl of Southampton's confession, viz., that Neville had been a key man in the conspiracy.[139] If the powerful combination of Bacon and Cecil therefore sought to protect Neville, then they must have had secret reasons for doing so.

Additionally, the Essex conspirators themselves protected Neville. They ensured that Neville took no **active** part in the uprising – that he was indeed known to be in a chamber, studying and writing all the time the action was taking place. But at the same time, Essex had named him as his projected first minister, should his plans succeed. Those who were executed after the uprising did their best to protect Neville with their very last breaths, declaring they were very sorry if they had unwittingly been the source of any trouble for "that noble Knight."[140] (Only after Neville's death did William Camden reveal the extent of Neville's involvement, writing about this in a further edition of his English histories.) Thus, even the very *manner* in which everyone made reference to Neville implies their perception of his knightly status and importance.

Neville was interested in chivalry, friendship and ceremonies, as witness his visit to Brussels to see a ceremonial procession there.[141] (Even though Neville had been disgraced by this time, he was still spoken of by the man who reported his presence at this ceremony as a person of 'quality'.) And why was there such unquestioning respect for Richard Neville, Earl of Warwick, in the *Henry VI* plays? Even after he has killed Richard Neville, King Edward IV merely says how he feared him, not that he ever felt disrespect or dislike for him. After he is dead, even Queen Margaret calls Richard Neville her 'anchor', yet she, above all the other spiteful characters in the play, invariably finds bad words to say about everyone else. The very fact that someone was born a Neville seems to have engendered respect, even fear – or, at least, this is the way the author of the History plays portrays the situation! For audiences to have accepted this kind of propaganda on stage, the idea must have had a ring of truth about it.

The above circumstances at very least add up to Neville's elevated, though secret, position within a certain faction. They also add weight to the evidence for his authorship of the plays. All the plays bear witness to knowledge of heraldry and other sources of family symbolism, and heraldry is the badge of chivalry. To begin with, Neville's own family held a significant array of symbols on their coat of arms. The Neville's main crest was a bull, but the branch of the Nevilles who descended from the Earls of Abergavenny also had a swan as their symbol, which was inherited from the Beauchamps, who had married with Neville's direct ancestors more than once.

The badge of the Beauchamps, which also became associated with the Nevilles.

Neville was thus a 'sweet swan of Avon' (Avon being the Celtic word for 'river'.) Henry IV and Henry V both had swans as their emblems[142], so the swan automatically suggested the name 'Henry' to anyone who knew their heraldry. Additionally, Neville's wife, Anne Killigrew, also had Beauchamp ancestry. It is thus small wonder that Ben Jonson chose to call the true writer 'sweet swan'. The Beauchamp chapel in Warwick contains a number of carved swans on the tombs of the Earls of Warwick, while the symbols of the bull and the swan are present in Shakespeare's plays, with Falstaff noting that both of them have been disguises for Jupiter, king of the gods:

> *Enter FALSTAFF disguised as Herne, with a buck's head on.*
> **Falstaff** The Windsor bell hath struck twelve; the minute
>   draws on. Now, the hot-blooded gods assist me!
>   Remember, Jove, thou wast a bull for thy Europa; love set
>   on thy horns. O powerful love, that in some respects
>   makes a beast a man; in some other, a man a beast. You
>   were also, Jupiter, a swan for the love of Leda.

The Neville's Bull and Swan symbols[143] therefore suggested the king of the gods. This meant that the Nevilles themselves, and all who could read the symbols, were persuaded to view them as natural leaders. However, as Neville was a known wit at the Mitre Club, one cannot help wondering if there might not also be the hint of a joke about all this too. Neville grew to Falstaffian proportions as he got older, so the lines from the play are probably meant as a joke against himself. Indeed, Ben Jonson would have enjoyed that joke. He too was a member of the Mitre Club, and calls Sir Henry

THE KNIGHTS' LEGACY: SECRET SYMBOLISM AND SECRET SOCIETIES?

merely 'Neville' in his epigram to him, suggesting a familiarity which bordered on open friendship.

Jonson was just the man to set the hints towards Neville's identity – hints which are contained in his poem 'To my beloved, the author, Mr. William Shakespeare and What he hath left us.'[144] In this poem, Jonson calls the author 'sweet swan of Avon', yet there were no swans on the *Stratford* section of the Avon at this time: they were royal birds, and were present at the section of the Avon which flowed through Warwick.[145] This was where the Beauchamps had their home, and where Richard Neville also owned the famous castle. (Towards the end of Sir Henry Neville's lifetime, the Earl of Warwick was Fulke Greville, whose mother was a Neville. This same Fulke Greville was the patron of William Davenant.[146]) The Beauchamps had been military knights who had fought alongside Kings of England in many foreign conflicts. But, unlike them, Sir Henry, their descendant, was a man of letters, and thus could be termed the *sweet* swan of Avon. Is there perhaps also a possibility that the identity of Anne Killigrew might be hinted at too, as she was a feminine, therefore 'sweet' descendant of the Beauchamps?

Yet the symbol of the swan has another association. It is found in a Templar myth. The first man to be offered the title 'King of Jerusalem' – Godfroi de Bouillon – became the subject of a chanson de geste. In this chanson – often sung by Trouvére – Godfroi's boat was pulled along by a swan. The Order of the Swan also existed in the Ardennes in Neville's day – and it is the Ardennes rather than Arden which is surely the setting for *As You Like It*.[147] The fact that a German doctor at the English Court, one Michael Maier, supported Neville's claim to become Secretary of State after Robert Cecil's death, may also indicate that Neville had the support of continental knights of various orders too, for Maier was also an alchemist well-known for his esoteric and continental associations.[148] The theme of the swan was famously taken up many centuries later by Richard Wagner in his opera, *Lohengrin*, proving the persistent strength of these 'swan' and Templar myths in continental Europe. It is also interesting to note that Robert Fludd (b.1574), who was perhaps the best-known occultist of the era, attended Oxford University (like Neville), which the Oxford Dictionary of National biography notes was well-known for its occult circles.[149]

Esotericism within the Shakespeare plays?
The work of Frances Yates and others has shown deep, symbolic connections between Shakespeare's later plays and newly emerging secret societies.[150] These societies descended from a combination of the chivalric orders and the trade guilds. (Sir Henry Neville was both a Knight and a merchant, his father having been a member of the Merchant Taylors Livery Company, and his Gresham relatives were leaders of the Mercers Company.) Yates maintains too that the Neoplatonist symbols within the later Shakespeare plays were also meaningful symbols in a Renaissance *Rosicrucian* society. Then, these same symbols were fused together with a deeper symbolism drawn from a knowledge of Judaism. (Neville knew of Judaism through one of his life-long friends, as will be revealed in my next book.) This fusion of ancient and Judaic beliefs into the fabric of Christianity would not have been tolerated in mainstream English or other European societies at the time, so we have yet another reason for the formation of *secret* societies.

However, some of the mythological references used in *Henry VI, part 1* imply that knowledge of **Egyptian** esotericism had also filtered through to Europe during the Renaissance. The Dauphin's reference to Rhodope in that play is an example of this influence. She was an Egyptian slave, and the reference will be detailed in following chapters. Renaissance knowledge of Egyptology came mainly from the works of the Greek historian, Herodotus. Neville was very fond of the Greek language and culture, and this fondness may well therefore also link up with a phrase which resulted from my decryption of the Dedication to Shakespeare's *Sonnets*. This phrase appears after the 'fourth setting' of this transformation code and reads THE WISE THOTH,[151] straight across the page, on row 9. [The columns of the matrix have been re-ordered in accordance with a recognised transformation system outlined in *Henry Neville and the Shakespeare Code*,[152] and this system is described in the 1974 edition of the Encyclopaedia Britannica]:

THE KNIGHTS' LEGACY: SECRET SYMBOLISM AND SECRET SOCIETIES?

```
T  N  O  H   E  O  L  I  E  T  B  E
T  O  E  T   E  R  F  T  H  G  E  S
N  N  I  S   U  I  G  S  O  E  N  N
S  X  T  Mr  W  H  A  L  L  E  H  A
I  S  P  N   E  S  E  A  N  P  D  T
T  R  A  E   T  E  N  I  T  H  I  E
O  E  R  M   I  S  D  B  Y  P  O  U
V  I  E  E   R  L  V  I  N  R  G  P
T  H  E  W   I  S  E  T  H  O  T  H
E  I  W  L   L  W  S  H  I  E  N  G
V  U  D  E   N  T  R  E  R  A  I  N
T  G  E  T   I  N  F  O  R  S  T  H
```

'Thoth' was the Egyptian god of wisdom and also of writing. Indeed, he is often called 'Hermes Trismegistus', or 'Hermes, the thrice-great', because he was said to have engaged in so many areas of philosophy and science. (The Greeks decided that Thoth was close to their god named Hermes, and thus often called the *Egyptian* god 'Hermes' too, rather than using his original Egyptian name.) Hermes was the messenger of the gods, and Neville was the messenger between the House of Commons and the House of Lords. Significantly, Hermes is also perceived as a Negotiator, and as a Trickster, both of which epithets probably fit Neville, in varying degrees! Albert G. Mackey, in his *Encyclopaedia of Freemasonry*, says that Thoth (or Hermes) was a priest, lawyer and philosopher. He is said to have written 36 books, including treatises on medicine, but all of them have been lost. Thoth is also said by Eusebius to have introduced the art of writing into Egypt. After his death, however, he became known as the god of Wisdom – hence the 'wise' epithet given in my decryption of the Sonnets' Dedication.

All this is of course too much to be mere coincidence: if I had decrypted things incorrectly, then none of these significant words would have occurred at all. The fact that they appear in sequence after applying a known decryption method absolutely

213

proves, once and for all, that I did indeed hit upon the **correct** methodology. Moreover, as I describe in my book on the Dedication Code, the words HE ONLIE BE OF THE SEIN, HENRY, POET, also appear symmetrically in another valid 'transformation'. When taken together with the positive naming of Neville in more than one of the Transformations of the Code, and in Sonnet 121, there can be no doubt as to the identity of this poet.

Additionally, there can therefore be little doubt that he would have been involved with some secret societies, as such societies are well known for their use and invention of Codes. Moreover, if THE WISE THOTH was indeed someone [or some *idea*] who HID THY POET [Neville], (metaphorically, that is, as the decoding above also suggests) then this strongly implies that Neville was a member of a society who used THOTH as its main guide to 'wisdom'.

Neville would have known about the *Masonic* links with Thoth/Hermes Trismegistus because a fifteenth century manuscript explaining it all still exists. Moreover, Neville was a founder member of the Society of Antiquaries,[153] so this document would not have escaped his special notice. It is known as the Cooke Manuscript, and of course the work would have seemed only as old to Neville as the works of Dickens seem to us now. Moreover, the document would have interested *our* Neville in particular, because it also contained reference to Tubal Cain, who it insisted was the first man to understand and develop metal working, including knowledge of how to forge iron.

It is said that some of the ancient papyri and hieroglyphs deal with Thoth's studies, which also included ritual and astronomy. Or at least, this is what some Renaissance scholars believed. In the end, it was the ancient Greeks who mediated Hermes Trismegistus (Thoth) to us during the second and third centuries AD.[154] Although the Greeks (who by then ruled Egypt) had not deciphered the Egyptian hieroglyphs, Egyptian priests began to reveal some of their ancient knowledge and beliefs to their Greek conquerors, fearing that their traditions might otherwise be lost.[155]

It appears that Neville was well aware of the line of transmutation between Egypt and Greece, and between Thoth and Hermes, for, besides the naming of Thoth in the Code, there is an oblique yet esoterically-powerful reference to Hermes in Sonnet 107:

THE KNIGHTS' LEGACY: SECRET SYMBOLISM AND SECRET SOCIETIES?

Not mine own fears, nor the prophetic soul
Of the wide world dreaming on things to come,
Can yet the lease of my true love control,
Supposed as forfeit to a confined doom.
The mortal moon hath her eclipse endured,
And the sad augurs mock their own presage;
Incertainties now crown themselves assured,
And peace proclaims olives of endless age.
Now with the drops of this most balmy time
My love looks fresh; and Death to me subscribes,
Since spite of him I'll live in this poor rhyme
While he insults o'er dull and speechless tribes:
And thou in this shalt find thy monument
When tyrants' crests and tombs of brass are spent.

Line 8 speaks of "olives of endless age" in connection with 'peace', which is a reference understood by all. But the next lines proclaim that there are 'drops of this most balmy time' and that 'Death to me subscribes'. The connection between olives and death is there in Hermetic mythology too, though not nearly so widely known as the one between olives and peace. Hermes carried a wand made from an olive branch. With drops of magic from his 'golden wand' he conducted souls on their forward journey into the afterlife, and occasionally brought the dead back to Earthly life. As Horace (one of Neville's favourite writers, and almost his alter ego) says:

Unspotted spirits you consign
To blissful seats and joys divine,
And powerful with your golden wand
The light unburied crowd command. *Hymn to Hermes*

Then comes the sonnet's reference to "o'er dull and speechless tribes" – they are the ones, not the writer of the sonnet, whom Death 'insults'. This too can be seen as referring back to the power of Hermes – the god whom Plato associated with power over speech and words (*logos*).[156] And – most relevant to Neville being the writer – it seems Plato regarded Hermes as much as an interpreter as a messenger. (Shakespeare-Neville, it would seem, therefore thought his luck in surviving was something of a gift granted to him as much through his power with language as through anything else.) Moreover, the Nassenes, an early Christian-Gnostic sect, also likened Hermes to the Saviour,[157] which would certainly have made him – and Thoth – a respectable god for the Christian Neville to study. In fact, some scholars maintain that the writings of Thoth originated from the period when Christianity was expanding over the Roman Empire, instead of being truly the writing down of oral records of wisdom created around the time of Moses.[158] In this case, the Hermetic documents could be seen as Neoplatonist manuscripts attempting to unite Christianity with pre-Christian philosophy, in much the same way as early European monks/missionaries grafted Christian feasts onto Celtic pagan celebrations. This aspect of Hermeticism therefore becomes most important when it comes to the writer of the Shakespeare canon, because the later, symbolistic plays are promoting precisely this Hermetic idea of Christian, non-Christian and pre-Christian beliefs all espousing the same ethics and lessons for life. Neville's grandson and namesake was the man who was brave enough to declare he was an atheist, that Cicero was more useful than the Bible, and also that there was nothing you could say about the Christian Bible that could not also be said for the Quran. Syncretism indeed! As we have seen, our Neville too was a man known for his attempts at uniting peoples and philosophies. He also was the man par excellence who would have known about Hermeticism, whereas thousands would not have had access to this knowledge, which was very restricted. Although Catholics were not expressly forbidden to join these Hermetic societies at the time, the Hermetic [i.e. Hermes Trismegistis] ideas and organisation grew up in England and Scotland alongside Protestantism. Presence of these Hermetic symbols in the Sonnets is therefore yet another pointer that 'Shakespeare' was not a Catholic.

Thoth was also associated with both the sun and the moon. In fact, he was the vice-regent to Re, the sun god. References to the sun and its imagery abound in the Sonnets, but here, in number 107, we have a reference to the moon too, as if the author's mind is definitely running along the lines of the Hermetic/Thoth tradition. There had been a real eclipse of the moon on 2nd March, 1603.[159] Queen Elizabeth died on 25th March and so Neville, as a keen astronomer, would quite naturally have used that particular image of the 'mortal moon' enduring the eclipse yet dying less than a month later. (Again, Catholics were not supposed to look into their telescopes, let alone study astronomy.) Of course, the non-esoteric reference to his no longer being "forfeit to a confined doom" becomes obvious (as Neville was still in the Tower when the Queen died.) Yet he cannot avoid linking this with the general covert, Hermetic background he suggests later in the poem, because any unexpected piece of luck was said by the ancients to be 'hermaion' – a gift from Hermes. No wonder Thoth – the Egyptian Hermes – is so prominently mentioned in the Dedication Code to these Sonnets, which ultimately become a testimony to Neville's unexpected survival. Queen Elizabeth, the "mortal moon" had endured her own personal eclipse in the sense that she had been conducted to the afterlife by Hermes. But to Neville, Hermes had been even kinder: he had brought him back to Earthly life.

As previously stated, the immortal imagery associated with this Hermetic philosophy is visible in Shakespeare's late plays, especially in *The Winter's Tale, Cymbeline, Pericles, Prince of Tyre* and *The Tempest*. Themes of Redemption and Resurrection are often thought of as exclusively Christian, but it is as if Shakespeare is saying in his later, symbolistic plays that these qualities are also to be found in pre-existing myths.

Such esoteric ideas obviously pleased King James I, who was inaugurated into Freemasonry in Scotland.[160] This means James would have been used to seeing the old Hermetic rituals acted out in the Scottish Masonic lodges. As Frances Yates avers, Freemasonry did not appear openly in England until the early 17th century,[161] but this is precisely the time during which James I came down from Scotland. Indeed, it is sometimes said that the Masques of the Jacobean Court were popular with James because they too included these old mythic elements, which were not yet performed in the halls of emerging Freemasonry in England.[162] We may recall, however, that Neville went to Scotland on a delegation to see King James in 1583, so may well have been invited to see some of these mythic re-enactments.

So, during James I's reign, symbolistic masques abounded, and were sometimes performed at the stately homes he visited, as is the case with the following example:

THE TRVE DISCRIP tion of a Royall *Masque*.

PRESENTED AT HAMP- ton Court, vpon Sunday night, be- *ing the eight of* Ianuary. 1604.

AND
Perfonated by the Queenes moſt Excellent *Majeſtie*, attended by *Eleuen* Ladies of Honour.

LONDON
Printed by Edward Allde, *and are to be* folde at the Long Shoppe, adjoyning vnto S. Mildreds *Church in the* Poultrye. 1604.

Copy of the front page of Samuel Daniel's masque *The Vision of the Twelve Goddesses.*

The true discription
Strange visions and vn-usual properties,
Vn-seene of latter ages, auncient rites;
Of gifts diuine, wrapt vp in Misteries,
Make this to seeme a Temple in their sight:
Whose maine support, holy religion, frame,
And wisedome, courage, Temperaunce and right:
Make seeme the pillors that sustaine the same,
Shadow some *Sibill* to attend the rites;
And to describe the power that shall reforte,
With the interpretation of the benefites
They bring in Cloudes, & what they doe importe,
Yet make them to protend the true desire
Of those that wish them, waking reall things;
Whilste I wil hoou'ring heere aloofe retire,
And couer all things with my sable wings.
    Som. Deere Mother Night, I your commandement
Obay, and dreams t'interpret dreames, will make
As waking curiositie is wonte.
Though better dreames asleepe, the dreames awake
And this White Horny wande shall worke the deed:
Whose power, doth figures of the light present,
When from this sable *Radius* doth proceede
Nought but confusde darke shewes to no intent:
And therefore goe bright visions, entertaine
All round about, whilste Ile to sleepe againe.
                                                   IRIS

A page from Samuel Daniel's *The Vision of the Twelve Goddesses* which seems to hint at the kind of language beginning to be used in masonic rituals.

It would appear too that the mathematical basis of stonemasonry and Freemasonry affected Neville from an early age, because Neville had already chosen to major in Mathematics and Astronomy at Oxford. As he was tutored there by Henry Savile, who became Professor of Geometry, Neville would have been well-grounded in this branch of mathematics, which closely concerned the old stonemasons and the Freemasons. Geometric theory underlay the building of the great Cathedrals, and Savile was always following two great religious aims. (It was as if Geometry had inspired this interest within him.) Firstly, he was writing a huge biography of St. John Chrysostom; and secondly, he was carrying out research in preparation for a new translation of the Bible into English. It was *his* work which underlay the King James' Authorised Version, of which translation Savile was indeed the co-ordinator. Thus did James' similarly dual passions for Religion and Freemasonry find their guardian in Henry Savile, Neville's best friend. Neville helped Savile in all his enterprises, and did not seek personal acclaim for doing so.

Those who have read my *Henry Neville and the Shakespeare Code* may also remember that I wrote of how the writer of *Hamlet* had clearly and demonstrably been reading the book of *Revelations* in the New Testament. Neville, who was used to employing ciphers in his diplomatic correspondence, could not but have been attracted by that book, which has so often been seen as popular reading for prisoners and the oppressed. (This was Neville's exact situation during the time *Hamlet* was written.) Neville, as a mathematician, would have been fascinated by the love of symbolic numbering displayed in *Revelations*. His introduction to Freemasonry in Scotland, together with his schooling in Geometry, would therefore naturally have led him to use numerical symbolism when building the code underlying the Dedication to Shakespeare's *Sonnets*. Is it any wonder, therefore, that this code is based on the precise numerology popular in *Revelations*? Firstly, there are 144 letters in the Code. 144,000 is the number of souls that *Revelations* predict will be saved. So well-known was the significance of this number that it is said to underlie some of the proportions in the building of the great Cathedrals. But in the case of Neville, may it not also symbolise the fact that he and his dedicatee unexpectedly survived the Essex affair and the Tower – **saved** by the death of Queen Elizabeth and an edict of James I, freeing him and Southampton? Twelve is also mentioned often in *Revelations* because of its connection with the twelve tribes of Israel. The 12 x 12 matrix is the basic setting of the Dedication Code. Four is also a significant number in that same book of the Bible, and it is the fourth setting of the Dedication Code which reveals THE WISE THOTH, and also, THE WISE THORP HID THY POET. (Thorpe was the publisher of the *Sonnets*.) No contender for the authorship of Shakespeare is ever known to have possessed this combined knowledge, nor these combined mathematical and linguistic skills.

144 was, incidentally, also the codeword which Neville used in his diplomatic correspondence to signify King Henri IV of France. Was it perhaps originally given to Henri because of his initial work to try and save the Huguenots in France, while he was Henri of Navarre? In other words, was that very code number itself, 144, chosen purposely to echo its salvatory significance in *Revelations*? Certain French intellectuals also showed a wish to bring religious strife to an end. Additionally, the French Protestant writer, Philippe Du Plessis Mornay was referencing Hermetic philosophy in his works. His *De la vérité de la religion chretienne* was published in Antwerp in 1581. Moreover, this publication was dedicated to the King of Navarre, who later became King Henri IV of France, whom Neville had met both as a student in France and again in 1599 when he became Ambassador there. As Frances Yates says, Mornay therefore became an example of how some influential writers and thinkers were turning to Hermeticism as an alternative to the religious Catholic/Protestant rifts and wars which ravaged Europe.[163] Neville as a politician, together with his Shakespearean pseudonymic dramas, has demonstrated his own syncretic aims. He was also skilled and experienced enough with the French language to have read Du Plessis Mornay's work. Perhaps it was this wish for peace and syncretism which inspired the Neoplatonists in England and on the continent. The Hermetica is generally a set of Neoplatonist documents, and the later works of Shakespeare really display an interest in this movement. It is interesting too that the number four was held sacred by Hermes[164], and there are four thanksgiving hymns in the Hermetica.[165] It was this number four which proved to be significant in solving the Dedication Code, so again the solution to the code ties in with its method of decryption, thereby assuring us that the correct method was used.[166]

Rituals and stage arts were seen as a means of spreading Propaganda against just such civil and international rifts as concerned Du Plesis Mornay. Stage arts had many of their origins in the Hermetic tradition, including the Eleusinian Mysteries of Demeter in Greece (reflections of which can be seen prominently in *The Winter's Tale*.) Mackey also asserts that some Masonic degrees originated with this same 'Mystery' too, while Frances Yates avers that Freemasonry in England had its predecessors, antecedents, traditions of some kind going back much earlier than the 16th century.

Many Freemasons hint that these myths were revived because their organisation existed primarily to unite people of different belief systems, and that the way chosen to do this was therefore to invent – and re-invent – rituals based on myths, which everyone *knew* to be myths telling a deeper truth, rather than to be taken as literally as religion tends to do.[167] Such an outlook was therefore able to unite men of different nations and different faiths, together with those who had no religious beliefs at all. It is probably also significant that Thoth generally took the part of the wise counsellor in many tales which grew up about him – significant because this is exactly the role which Henry Neville was carving out for himself.

Neville was indeed against religious divisions. I brought forward evidence for this in *Henry Neville and the Shakespeare Code*. To begin with, during the witch hunts following the Gunpowder plot, he was working with judges to soften some of the strict measures which were being enacted against lay Catholics. Secondly, he had many 'moderate' Catholic friends. Thirdly, he wrote to Cecil hinting that he agreed with Henri IV's stance on religion, namely that it was a subject best left to an individual's conscience, and that a truly Christian attitude was better shown by leading a good life and so setting a good example rather than forcing others into one's own belief system.[168] Fourthly, a whole branch of the Neville family (those associated with the Lords Latimer) remained Catholic. Yet links between the two sections of the family – Catholic and Protestant – were maintained. Neville also never displayed any animosity towards atheists – it has often been said that Robert Cecil and Walter Raleigh held no religious beliefs, and it is also noticeable that the Earl of Southampton never showed any keen interest in religion, though he (like Neville) supported the Protestant 'cause' against Catholic extremism.

For Neville, then, Protestantism held the best hope for reform of society and for a more liberal, scientifically-based philosophy, but he did not insist on his friends sharing this

THE KNIGHTS' LEGACY: SECRET SYMBOLISM AND SECRET SOCIETIES?

Protestant religion. So long as they acted ethically and posed no threat to society, he did not care what they believed. This was probably an attitude which he passed on privately within his family too, for his grandson famously became an openly-declared atheist who preferred Cicero to the Bible. The Shakespeare plays present history and myths as narratives and discussion papers for improving one's outlook. In just the same way, one object of Freemasonry and its staged rituals seems to be to wean people off their immovable belief systems and onto a view of all myths as being merely stories with a deeper meaning. The important thing was to realise how these stories could inform ethics, personal understanding, and one's conduct in life.

In the English Renaissance, therefore, it could also be said that reviewing the rather pagan ideas of Hermes Trismegistus may well have freed scholars from the dominance of the Medieval Christian Church. Furthermore, paganism was concerned with 'earth magic' which at least allowed for examination of nature, unlike the Catholic Church of the time, which condemned such investigation. Shakespeare's last plays therefore celebrate the rebirth of this 'earth magic'; but by implicitly undermining actual *belief* in it they look forward to a new age of scientific investigation. In *The Winter's Tale,* for instance, Hermione's statue comes to life and Leontes says, "If this be magic, let it be an art lawful as eating." But the whole point is that we, the audience, know that no such magic had occurred! (Hermione had been shut away and protected for fifteen years by Paulina. Leontes' belief that she had died and come back to life was erroneous.) Similarly, in the epilogue of *A Midsummer Night's Dream* we are told to imagine we have merely been sleeping, and in *The Merry Wives of Windsor* we know that the fairies who taunt Falstaff are not really fairies at all but children. Prospero too 'abjures' his 'rough magic'. This is surely Neville speaking. His 'rough magic' consisted of rustling up magical and historical beings, but they were only actors. Gresham College, founded by Neville's benefactor, Sir Thomas Gresham, had a 'secret' branch to it that became the basis of the Royal Society. Clearly, then, Neville and his cohorts were on the side of Galileo and investigating 'the Book of Nature.'

Altogether, therefore, it is highly likely that Neville associated himself with some form of early, emerging Freemasonry. Indeed, it would be very strange if he had not been drawn into such a movement, given his background and his propensity to join philosophical societies. Willie Schaw (steward to James VI of Scotland) had set up the Lodge system in Scotland just before Neville went there in 1583. Thomas Gresham and William Herbert, Earl of Pembroke, are said to have been early Grand Masters in England.[169] Herbert became a close associate of Neville during the reign of James I. Moreover, the Mitre Club (with its hint at right-angle joins, made with a 'mitre box') may even have been some sort of Masonic society. There is also the strange fact that Henry Neville's wife's family – the Killigrews – took for their seal the double-headed eagle, which is the sign of the thirty third degree in Freemasonry.[170] Added to this, the same sign is used for the Greek orthodox church, which Neville was helping Savile to research.

Who had more experience and knowledge of all these esoteric sources than Sir Henry Neville? The Rosicrucians (a secret society of the time so lauded and explained by Frances Yates) were even able to extend their symbolism for use in the foundation of the Royal Society. Sir Henry was the 'never-writer'[171] who could therefore protect his own and others' identities as the mainspring for these new ideas. Indeed, it is often said that the heads of these new societies were under oath not to publish anything under their own name. That way, the new ideas could plant themselves, unhindered by any prejudice which might ensue if the originators of the ideas were known and, perhaps, not liked in certain quarters.

However, another 'disguised' writer, Mr. Leon Davin[172], (who uses a pseudonym because he is a leading Freemason) denies that the origins of Freemasonry really go back so far as the Ancient Egyptians. While agreeing with him, I would argue that even though the organisational origins of *modern* Freemasonry do not stretch back to such distant times, *myths* purporting to come from those times were nevertheless used by Freemasons in order to teach moral and social lessons. I do not think Mr. Davin would argue with me on this point, as he quite rightly asserts that the Hiram Abiff myth (enacted during the ritual of the third degree) purports to stem from pre-Christian times but in fact parallels the life and moral lessons enshrined in Christianity. Mr. Davin also rightly points out that this was done in order to show that one can learn ethics from such myths, in just the same way as one can from the Christian story, without the necessity of perceiving any one of these stories (including that of Jesus Christ) to come from a **divine** origin. Indeed, he argues that the Catholic church long kept the

THE KNIGHTS' LEGACY: SECRET SYMBOLISM AND SECRET SOCIETIES?

people in a state of subjugation by teaching them to *fear* the 'divine'. A King or Priest was seen as a representative of the 'divine' on Earth; therefore the Catholic Church could teach the masses to fear the 'eternal' consequences of questioning or rising up against their masters. This being the case, it is not difficult to perceive why the emerging reformed church would have been rather more attracted to Freemasonry than the Catholic Church, (though it took several centuries for the Catholics to ban their members from becoming Freemasons.)

Now, Henry Neville was a follower of the Reformed Church, and his Gresham kinsmen were said to be leading lights in the newly-emerging organisation called Freemasonry. This means that it is perfectly possible that Shakespeare-Neville was using some new, Masonic symbolism in his plays – and most especially in his Sonnets and their Dedication. I say 'especially in his sonnets' because these were published after James I became King of England, and James was a Freemason. Neville could hardly have avoided meeting the King's Steward, Willie Schaw, while in Scotland – the man who set up the Lodge system and also had a hand in creating the symbolism in Rosslyn chapel. A good section of the *Sonnets* is taken up with contemplating the 'passage of the soul' (presented in either direct or symbolic form) – a major theme of contemplation in Hermeticism and the Neoplatonism to which it was closely related.

One cannot help noticing that Willie Schaw is another 'WS'. This may or may not be significant. However, another possible link between Neville and Freemasonry may be hinted at in the first two lines of the first of 'Shakespeare's *Sonnets*', though I freely admit that here I am stepping into the realms of speculation rather than purely logical conclusions:

From fairest creatures we desire increase
That thereby beauty's rose might never die...

Davin asserts that Hiram Abiff (whose story is enacted in the third degree of Freemasonry) should really be spelt 'Hiram Abith',[173] and that the 'TH' is a very cryptic Masonic sign. It may not therefore be purely coincidental that the alliterated double 'f' of the first line of the first sonnet is echoed by the alliteration of 'th' at the beginning of the second line. Moreover, I believe Arabic, like Hebrew, has an alphabet formed of consonants only, so the name THOTH (as seen in the ninth row of the Dedication Code) would have been originally spelt with the Arabic equivalents of THTH. Added to this, Canon Richard Tydeman[174] has pointed out that the Myles Coverdale edition of the Bible is the only one in which the name 'Hiram Abiff'/'Abith' can be found. This is doubtless a version Neville would have used right up until, and during, his time assisting Savile with the 1611 Authorised Version, because Coverdale was a leading reformer. Most interestingly too, we find 'Huram Abif' [II Chronicles 4:16] in the 1525 Coverdale edition described as 'Prince of Tyre', which therefore contains echoes of a very definite 'Shakespeare' work! In the later Coverdale edition of 1535, however, the exact name 'Hiram Abif' is used. Perhaps, then, the assertion of some 19th century freemasons – that 'Shakespeare' possibly had a hand in the Hiram Abiff story – might just have a grain of truth in it. Whether or not this is so, the use of a Coverdale Bible would certainly point to a Protestant writer, as would the phrase 'I am that I am', in Sonnet 121, which pre-empts its use in the Authorised Version by two years. (After all, the Authorised Version was a Protestant version and no Catholics were involved in its production.)

Neville and *Macbeth*

Now for yet another, more direct, link between Neville and a certain play – a link which presents itself through correspondents working for Francis Walsingham, Queen Elizabeth's spy master. An English spy, Thomas Rogers (discussed in the previous chapter), the man who wrote about the Order of Sion, also mentioned that the Bishop of Ross was in Rouen with Paget. At first sight, this may lead to the conclusion that Paget was indeed a fervent Catholic. But if he had been a truly fervent and devout one, I very much doubt whether he would have chosen that particular Bishop as a companion! John Leslie, the then Bishop of Ross, was rather better at politics than religion, for in the secular world he achieved the spectacular trick of pleasing both Mary Queen of Scots and William Cecil, Lord Burghley. Fond of bon cuisine and ladies, he was also the contented father of several illegitimate children.

But perhaps this over-worldly Bishop's most lasting *literary* achievement was his construction of a family tree linking King James VI of Scotland and I of England to the saintly Banquo, as portrayed in *Macbeth*[175]. John Leslie had published this family tree in 1578, cleverly realising that the son of such a controversial mother might very well one day need to invent a respectable pedigree. So Bishop John Leslie kindly spared his King the trouble. However, he wrote the book in which he publicised the King's supposed ancestry **in Latin,** which meant it would have been more for scholarly than popular consumption. What the play of *Macbeth* did, therefore, was to ensure this propaganda reached a wider audience. Again, however, we have the problem that the Bishop's book was not that widely available, especially to an impoverished actor who had left school at the age of 12. Once more, placing Sir Henry Neville in the picture absolutely overcomes all such problems: not only was he rich enough to purchase the book, but he would also have heard about Leslie and his works through their mutual acquaintances. King James I probably knew Neville was a concealed writer, otherwise he would not have stayed with him in Billingbeare, seeking advice on his own writing. And if the King knew Neville wrote plays, he would indeed have approved of the ancestral propaganda mediated in *Macbeth*. James, like Neville, would also have known that the effectiveness of this propaganda would be so much the greater, if the audience never suspected that it emanated from a politician who was in direct contact with the King himself.

There might even be an extra reason for Neville's decision to write such a play: he may very well have had a hand in the anonymous and now lost *Gowrie Conspiracy*. This was the play in which James I was portrayed as being involved in the murder of the Earl of Gowrie because of the latter's relationship with the King's wife, Anne of Denmark. Neville wrote of this event to Winwood as soon as it happened, voicing his suspicions of James' guilt, but quite obviously sympathetic with Gowrie and Queen Anne. Only a little later, James – the openly bisexual King – made his first visit to Neville at Billingbeare and, according to a hint given by Dudley Carleton, had his head 'busy with the young wenches.'[176] Neville might therefore have thought it politic to write a *favourable* propaganda play about the King's ancestry to redress the balance, because rumours of Neville's opinions regarding the Gowrie murder were bound to have spread around the court. It also strikes me that presenting the murder of the Earl Gowrie as a play, and actually having it performed at Court in front of the King, (which really happened) might have served the same function as does the play within the play of *Hamlet*: "The play's the thing wherein to catch the conscience of the King." Members of that court audience recall their fear while watching that and other politically-relevant plays,[177] but its author was never discovered. The Earl of Gowrie was greatly respected by Neville, and a good friend of his in France.

There is also perhaps a parallel to be made between *Macbeth* and the *Henry VI* plays. Surely Lady Macbeth echoes Queen Margaret. When the story of Queen Margaret's taunting of the Duke of York is related in *Leicester's Commonwealth*, Henry Neville writes 'such cruelty' in the margin. Richard, Duke of York famously accuses her of having a tiger's heart wrapped in a woman's hide, and the same could be said of Lady Macbeth. Moreover, both ladies are known to have lost their children. Margaret's cruelty on stage, however, occurs while her child is still alive, so she has not even got the partial excuse for her hardness that we might perceive in Lady Macbeth. (Lady Macbeth's child seems already to be dead by the time her cruel ambition becomes part of the drama.) The *historical* Queen Margaret is not known to have been especially cruel, but she certainly must have been strong to have involved herself so closely in the English civil strife. She follows hard on the heels of another strong French woman – Joan of Arc – whose deeds are related in *Henry VI, part 1*. In Portia, Rosalind, Viola, Beatrice and Helena, Neville had portrayed women who were both strong and good; in Margaret and Lady Macbeth he characterises strong yet flawed ladies, as he does with Joan of Arc, the tomboy. It is also notable how many of his 'strong ladies' have to dress as men before they can be allowed to act out a strong role, which must have been dictated by the cultural expectation of the times in which he wrote. However, if a woman is a Queen, like Margaret and Lady Macbeth, she need not become a transvestite before showing her strength, which is probably all due to the example of Queen Elizabeth I. But there again, the Templars sometimes had women leaders, so it was ultimately the knightly traditions that dictated that women could be seen to be women and yet still be strong, so long as they had already achieved an elevated position in society.

The man known as Shakespeare was dealing with the status of women throughout his plays. Small wonder, then, that he collaborated with a playwright whose theme ran that way too. This was John Fletcher, who collaborated with Shakespeare on the later plays. Neville was both a Mitre companion of, and related to, Francis Beaumont (who wrote with Fletcher). Beaumont certainly had enough connections with Orders of Knighthood to become associated with Neville through these channels too. Beaumont's aunt Elizabeth died young; she was married to William, third Lord

Vaux, who subsequently married Mary Tresham. Mary was the granddaughter of John Tresham (d. 1559) who was the Grand Prior of the Order of St. John. Richard Neville, brother of George, third Baron Bergavenny (d.1535) also belonged to the Order of St. John.[178] Thus the Neville Hospitaller connection with the Treshams was strong, and Neville, while Ambassador to France, was promoting the interests of a 'Mr. Tresham' and his friend Charles Paget.[179] Again, therefore, we encounter the connections between the Nevilles, the white rose of York and the white cross of the Hospitallers.

The Hospitallers were the Order of Knighthood who received the Templars' property after their disbanding, so it must appear that they were then more in favour with the Catholic hierarchy. It might therefore seem surprising that Sir Henry, as a strong Protestant, had been involved with them in any way. However, the drawing of straight lines between the Protestants and Catholics in post-Reformation Europe has often been presented in too reductionist a manner. *Every* Catholic had Protestant friends and relatives, and vice versa. Added to this, there was the complex interplay of land ownership within those families. Some of the Nevilles' property had once been owned by the Templars, but had only come to the Nevilles by way of the Hospitallers, and this situation must have been repeated hundreds of times within tens of families. There must therefore have been both emotional and 'sworn oath' bonds between these families and the Hospitallers at some time during their history. When the religious Reformation occurred Catholic lands owned by monks passed into Protestant hands. The more 'secular' branches of the Hospitallers must have been numbered amongst those who benefited, while devotional Hospitallers may have lost out. So *which* allegiances then took preference – those grounded on the new Protestant cause, or the more ancient ties between the old Catholic Hospitallers and many of the English aristocracy? Such dilemmas were not new, and such problems were ongoing and insoluble, as expressed by the deposed King Henry VI, in the third of the plays by that name. Two forest keepers see the deposed, escaped King Henry VI and know that they are under instructions from the *present* King – Edward IV – to arrest him, because all Englishmen have now taken an Oath of Allegiance to the new King. But Henry VI points out these men's dilemma. He was the King to whom the keepers *first* swore an oath of allegiance, and yet they are now breaking that oath:

> **1st Keeper** Ay, here's a deer whose skin's a keeper's fee:
> This is the quondam king; let's seize upon him. ....
> **2nd Keeper** Well, if you be a king crowned with content,
> Your crown content and you must be contented
> To go along with us; for, as we think,
> You are the king King Edward hath deposed;
> And we his subjects, sworn in all allegiance,
> Will apprehend you as his enemy.
> **King Henry** But did you never swear, and break an oath?
> **2nd Keeper** No, never such an oath; nor will not now.
> **King Henry** Where did you dwell when I was king of
>   England?
> **2nd Keeper** Here in this country, where we now remain.
> **King Henry** I was anointed king at nine months old;
> My father and my grandfather were kings,
> And you were sworn true subjects unto me:
> And tell me, then, have you not broke your oaths?
> **1st Keeper** No, for we were subjects but while you were
>   king.
> **King Henry** Why, am I dead? Do I not breathe a man?
> Ah, simple men, you know not what you swear.
> Look, as I blow this feather from my face,
> And as the air blows it to me again,
> Obeying with my wind when I do blow,
> And yielding to another when it blows,
> Commanded always by the greater gust;
> Such is the lightness of you common men.
> But do not break your oaths; for of that sin
> My mild entreaty shall not make you guilty.
> Go where you will, the king shall be commanded;
> And be you kings; command, and I'll obey.
> **1st Keeper** We are true subjects to the king, King Edward.
> **King Henry** So would you be again to Henry,
> If he were seated as King Edward is.

In the same way, the Hospitallers – to whom the Nevilles were at one time bound in some way or other – still 'lived'. So did the Nevilles' Catholic friends and relatives. For the Nevilles to have forsworn them entirely would have been neither honest nor honourable, nor would it have been in their own best interests. New rulers and new ideas may attempt to dictate entirely new civil relationships; but it cannot entirely replace nor overcome the forces of history.

THE KNIGHTS' LEGACY: SECRET SYMBOLISM AND SECRET SOCIETIES?

It was not in the best interests of the State that the national and international old alliances of Knights should be entirely lost, simply because of *religious* conflict. The Orders and their subsequent organisations must have built up a great store of political, military and commercial knowledge which was by then only loosely attached to their original religious base. These secular aspects of their existence could therefore surely be separated out from religious and other factional differences, so that a meeting of Knights within the framework of a now *secret* Order could provide a very useful conference table in times of conflict. There was nothing Sir Henry loved more than negotiations and reconciliation. Similarly, the themes of reconciliation and redemption are strong and openly stated within Shakespeare's later plays. The Phoenix had always been a symbol of resuscitation, regeneration and redemption within the early works.

All the Shakespeare plays and poems are concerned with the treatment and status of women and the welfare of the State. Philosophically, historically, artistically and emotionally, therefore, Sir Henry was in sympathy with the old chivalric ideals of the friendship, honour and courtesy pertaining to Knighthood. Altogether, it is unthinkable that Sir Henry would not have retained close links with the once-open, religiously-allied, now more secretive, mercantile, political and independent Orders of Knighthood. The respect in which he was held by his contemporaries, their constant prefixing of his name with 'that noble knight', together with the secrecy on which he so often insisted[180] suggest his high office in at least one of their Orders.

The discovery of Sir Henry Neville as the most likely author of the Shakespeare works has thus provided us with a chance to ask questions about the plays which have rarely been asked and answered before. Understanding Neville's *personal* obsession and profession within the business of warfare at the time he wrote the History plays now opens our eyes to other references within the plays themselves. But the personal knowledge and interest displayed about René d'Anjou (so significantly declared as 'King of Jerusalem') also now needs to be questioned. How could the Stratford Shakespeare have obtained this 'esoteric' knowledge? Why would he have been interested enough in René to have his title of 'King of Jerusalem' even mentioned? Perhaps we have come somewhere near to answering these questions, but the answers have perforce involved Neville rather than Shakespeare of Stratford.

How King René and the Knights bring signs of Neville's authorship

In addition to his long list of titles, René of Anjou – Count of Provence, Duke of Anjou, Bar and Lorraine, and King of Jerusalem and Sicily – was also a writer, and patron of the arts. Added to this, he was known as a soldier, administrator and statesman. He lived through Henry V's conquest of Normandy, and its recovery by Charles VII. Besides his French relatives, he was related to the royal families of England and Spain. But his fighting career was ultimately unsuccessful, his lands and titles being eventually won back by the King of France.

René's background and career ran quite a parallel course to Neville's, because King René turned to writing even more strongly at times when his political career waned. This is very close to Neville's declaration of his thoughts and intentions when he was out of office during part of James I's reign:

> But I am out of my proper Orb when I enter into State Matters; I will therefore leave these Considerations to those to whom they appertain, and think of my husbandry in the Country, which puts me often in mind of that Beatitude which Horace so much commends...[181]

(The 'Beatitude' Horace referred to was writing. Neville was telling Winwood, that he was now concentrating on his writing.) Besides three prose works – the *Mortiffiement de Vaine Plaisance*, a religious allegory (1455); the *Livre du Cuer d'Amours Espris*, (a romance, 1457); and the *Forme et Devis d'un Tournoy*, a practical treatise on how to hold a tournament (1460) – René also wrote poetry. True to his international background, his Tournament book calls on the traditional forms of the art held in France, Germany, and the Low Countries. (This is surprisingly similar to the interests held by Neville's father, who arranged tournament entertainments for Queen Elizabeth I and her father. But the point is that it was from the secular chivalric knights that such entertainment stemmed. This means that the close interest in chivalric knighthood, plus the depiction of real fighting in the *Henry VI* trilogy, and the staged 'trial by tournament' in *Richard II* would have been written by a writer with Sir Henry's background rather than by a country boy like Shakespeare, with no such connections.)

THE KNIGHTS' LEGACY: SECRET SYMBOLISM AND SECRET SOCIETIES?

The echo of the Templars and the Order of Sion which exists in the *Henry VI* plays is an implication only, and it is a passing reference only, yet it is one which is repeated in each of the three plays. Moreover, that echo itself comes about through the references to the 'King of Jerusalem'. To the groundlings in the audience, this title would have sounded like just another unfathomable link in René's ancestral chains. But to those who came from similar knightly ancestry to that of the true author, it would definitely have resonated with meaning. All other of the Regnier titles signalled his inheritance of tangible territories: Duke of Lorraine, King of Naples and King of Sicilia. However, the Kingship of Jerusalem had ceased to be a reality over one hundred years before the time in which the Henry VI plays were *set*, (i.e. the 1440s to 1460s,) and over three hundred years before they were *written*. Jerusalem had been lost to the Europeans and, in any case, the title had been conferred only when the Knights Templar held sway in that city; the Knights Templar had been officially disbanded, persecuted and chased away at the beginning of the 14th century.

To a convinced Stratfordian, it might appear that here we have just another instance of the uneducated boy, William Shakespeare, getting his history wrong. But this is certainly not the case. The problem is, however, that all this would have been known only in a very restricted circle. The kingship of Jerusalem soon lost its meaning, because the Christians had only a short-lived hold over the city. The Templars were the military Order of Knights who held sway during the Christian presence there; but they clearly continued as an Order throughout Europe even after the expulsion of the Christians from the Temple of Jerusalem – the site from which the 'Templars' took their name.[182] The title of 'King of Jerusalem' was subsequently awarded by these *European Knights*, even though there was no longer any territory attached to it. So the title itself must have conferred prestige on its holder, and in order to do this it must have been still recognised in some influential circles. It must have been recognised in some circles in England too, otherwise Shakespeare/Neville would hardly have thought it worth mentioning on the English stage.

The Templars had been specifically abolished by the Pope. True, there are references to the Templars running a courier service in Medieval England, even after their disbanding, but, once again, this would not have been generally known among the mass of the people, and would scarcely have been associated with the

'King of Jerusalem' in the public mind. So why did the author of the *Henry VI* plays mention the title at all? This was probably because he was consciously sending out a message to one specific strata within his audience. It was necessary to include esoteric material for the more privileged, educated spectators – it must have helped them feel superior. It also helped to send the message that the plays were written by someone from their own class. As I mentioned in my previous book, stage plays were considered a 'lower' form of art than poetry. If the printed versions of those plays were to sell to the richer members of society, there needed to be a 'higher' reason to buy them, such as esoteric knowledge within them and the perception of a more elevated provenance. This improved provenance was obviously helped if the richer members of the audience realised that one of their own strata had written the works. Such was the reality of the snobbery and class divisions existing in the Shakespeare-Neville era!

By 1314 the Templars appear to have been either slaughtered or completely expelled from their then French homeland, with orders sent out to every country in Europe [with the exception of Scotland], that they were not to be sheltered and not to be granted ownership of the lands which they had gained internationally. All that had now to be handed over to the Hospitallers of St. John. Much has been written about the cruel way in which the Templars were pursued but, unfortunately, it has all become very mixed up with their supposed adherence to Satanism and/or other distasteful movements. Regrettably, therefore – due to the then Church's extraordinary accusations, and to sensationalist literature since – even *legitimate* research and study of their Order has sometimes met with scorn. To add to this problem, the 1950s 'Prieuré de Sion' documents really do appear to be of more recent manufacture, so some readers have tended towards the view that the whole Order of Sion, together with everything written about the Orders of Knighthood, may have been a matter of myth rather than reality.

But to the real playwright, living in his own time with its different cultural references, the orders of knighthood were within his scope of specialist knowledge, and highly relevant to the political message he was attempting to present. That message definitely concerned the identification of the split between those noblemen who supported the Church and those, like Richard Neville, Earl of Warwick, who represented the secular, progressive faction. At the time 'Shakespeare' was writing, a Protestant

Reformation had swept the country, but it still felt itself threatened from Catholics, both at home and abroad. It is little wonder, then, that the real Shakespeare – who is so obviously a young, *Protestant* writer of the *Henry VI* trilogy – should wish to portray the Catholic Church as *always* in the wrong. This aim the playwright spectacularly achieved, notwithstanding the fact that he had sometimes to twist the historical record in order to do so.

One would think from Shakespeare's account of Cardinal Beaufort, for instance, that that clergyman had always acted contrary to the good of England, and that he was a proven murderer. But this is not the case in the historical records. In fact, he ultimately supported Henry V's campaigns in France with some of his own personal wealth, and was subsequently made executor to that King's will. Though he was known as an opposer of the Duke of Gloucester's hold over the young King Henry VI, Beaufort is never noted as being the murderer of 'Good' Duke Humphrey. Thus, the only cause the playwright could have wished to promote through his complete denigration of Beaufort in the *Henry VI* plays was the promotion of anti-Catholic sentiment. Perhaps our Neville even saw Beaufort as a traitor to the family in becoming a prominent churchman. The Beauforts were an illegitimate line of the Nevilles, and this particular writer was a Reforming, *Protestant* Neville.

One thing an Elizabethan Protestant writer could never forgive Cardinal Beaufort having done, however, was leading the anti-Hussite faction in Bohemia.[183] (Jan Huss was the cornerstone of the Protestant reformation in Europe.) And as if to seal the author's anti-Catholic bias, Shakespeare never once showed some of the just causes behind Cardinal Beaufort's animosity with Gloucester, such as Gloucester's attempt to deprive him of the see of Winchester. Only in the sixteenth century was a Protestant stand made *against* Cardinal Beaufort's reputation in any written prose work. The writer of the plays would have had access to more than this one source, however. He could easily have taken up some of the *pro*-Beaufort chroniclers. Yet it is the *Protestant* stance – taken by Edward Halle in his Chronicles of 1547 – which 'Shakespeare' chose to follow. Hardly the choice of a *Catholic* writer!

The writer's idiosyncratic portrayal of the Earl of Suffolk is one further aspect of the *Henry VI* trilogy that, above all, demonstrates his Protestant stance. In the trilogy, this Duke is an over-ambitious nobleman with less thought for his monarch and his country than for his own interests. He is even termed pejoratively in the play as 'the Queen's paramour'. Yet no historical support for Shakespeare's view of him is to be found anywhere in the *official* chronicles. According to all historical records, Suffolk was a careful advisor to the young King. It is true that he was the man responsible for bringing back the daughter of King Regnier from France – the King with more titles than wealth or land – but it is nowhere recorded that he became the Queen's lover (nowhere, that is, except in the **banned** *Leicester's Commonwealth,* copies of which, complete with annotations by Henry Neville, can be seen in the Lincolnshire Archives.)

Suffolk was also a careful organiser and manager, so why did the writer never bring out this side of his abilities? The only answer can be that the Earl of Suffolk was a known supporter of the [then Catholic] Church faction. It was he and Beaufort who were largely responsible for making the young King Henry VI so 'spiritual'. It was the Earl of Suffolk who set up, and laid the first foundation stone for, King's College Cambridge, and – significantly – its *chapel* was the largest and finest of all. He also founded a new college in honour of the King at Eton, but neither of these two achievements is mentioned in the plays. By instituting these new colleges, Suffolk probably hoped to demonstrate to all the educated population of England that the King had come of age and was in control. But it was still an *adolescent* control, needing the support of different departments of the Court, and effectively therefore uniting courtiers, clerks and bishops in a 'spiritual enterprise.'[184] This was obviously not the kind of union which pleased our secular playwright, otherwise the Duke's achievements would have been stressed in the trilogy. The real Shakespeare was therefore not even a *covert* Roman Catholic, otherwise he would certainly have taken the opportunity to point out some of Suffolk's positive achievements. There would have been no danger in doing so. One must conclude that it was the playwright's personal, anti-catholic choice not to mention these 'good deeds'.

We are therefore building up a true picture of the true, humanistic, Hermetic and Protestant, playwright – backed by both the internal textual evidence of the plays, and by extraneous evidence, such as the Dedication Code. It is evidence based on solid textual existence, not on myth or fancy. The next chapters will continue with just such solid evidence.

Chapter Eight

RELIGION, HENRY VI, AND THE GREEK CONNECTION

Some Greek Influences
Returning for a while to the politics of Shakespeare/Neville, we saw in Chapters 1 and 2 how Neville's writing style and choice of allegorical references betray his interest in ancient Greek language and culture. Reinforcing this, we have the Greek inscription on the painting of Sir Henry Neville, housed at Audley End House, as discussed in earlier chapters.

In the later Shakespeare plays, such as *Timon of Athens, Pericles, Prince of Tyre, The Winter's Tale, Troilus and Cressida,* and even in the early plays, *The Comedy of Errors,* and *A Midsummer Night's Dream,* there are overt Greek settings. Additionally, there are many Greek references within all the works of Shakespeare. Although placed in an English setting, *Cymbeline,* for instance, has the Greek work, *Chaereas and Callirhoe* by Chariton of Aphrodosia as one of its sources, even though that work was only available in a 13th century codex. Moreover, the work was not translated into any other language until the eighteenth century. Sir Henry Neville had travelled to, and resided in, Venice, where he and his tutor, Sir Henry Savile, were viewing the Greek texts which were then arriving in that city by the shipload. Sir Henry Neville's interest in Greek therefore immediately becomes yet another piece in the jigsaw linking the Shakespeare works with Neville.

Although many of Shakespeare's tragedies do not share with Greek theatre the idea of a unity of theme and a single movement of ideas towards a predictable end, there are one or two which are more 'Greek' in this respect, notably *King Lear* and *Othello*. The high register of language used in the Shakespeare plays, making them susceptible to tip over into poetry, is yet another influence drawn from the Greek model. Moreover, the rhetoric of Shakespeare is influenced by theories expounded by the ancient Greeks. Ben Jonson was indeed later to argue that Shakespeare's poetic, rhetorical style made his work more poetic than was suitable for the stage, and if we are honest, we have to admit that the plays' intricate language cannot be fully appreciated on the stage without previous study.

It is noteworthy, however, that the *English* theatre was already separating itself from the Greek in many of these respects during Shakespeare's lifetime: speeches by *other* playwrights were becoming shorter, allusions (as in Ben Jonson) more topical, the action much slicker. Yet Shakespeare did not move with the times in this way, which suggests that Shakespeare's plays were not written by a full-time theatrical practitioner but by someone learned in Greek, and in all classical philosophy.

The writer also occasionally betrays a greater interest in classical Greek rhetoric than in theatrical characterisation, in that he sometimes allows his lowly characters to speak as if they had a degree of learning that was impossible for them in Elizabethan times. The Greek playwrights, such as Euripides, shared this rather unrealistic trait. In Shakespeare, one thinks immediately of the servant Lancelot Gobbo in *The Merchant of Venice,* or some of the shepherdess Phoebe's pronouncements in *As You Like It.*

Then there is the widespread use of Greek references and Greek imagery within all the plays, including all the *English* History Plays. What James Emerson Phillips says always holds true too: Shakespeare's conception of Ancient Greece was **political**, as were his perceptions of Medieval England. Phillip's pronouncement concerning Shakespeare's essentially *political* conception of Ancient Greece is therefore now explained: the real Shakespeare was a politician who was greatly interested in the politics of the Classical world, and Sir Henry Neville is the *politician* named in the Sonnets' Dedication Code.

In an age when one might expect *Christian* imagery to be used in political rhetoric, it is noteworthy that the stage works of 'Shakespeare' and the political works of Neville both display a preference for references drawn from the Ancient Classical World. The reasons for this are many and varied, but they obviously begin with the fact that neither Kingship nor War fit easily inside a Christian framework. Yet Kingship and War were primary concerns of both Neville himself and of the Shakespeare plays. It is therefore logical that the real playwright finds it necessary to call on his knowledge of non-Christian imagery to make his political points, whether in Parliament or on the stage.

It necessarily follows too that Shakespeare-Neville's political outlook was generally influenced by the ancient Greek model. Neville's late treatise, with its parable drawn from a Greek source, shows that this influence was present with him all his political life. So too were his links with theatricality for, although not a theatre practitioner, it has to be remembered that Neville was born and brought up in Blackfriars, London, next to the Office of the Revels, and on the site of what became the first Blackfriars theatre. This theatre was actually formed in premises rented from Neville's father, and his father was a deviser of Court entertainments. Overlaying this early theatrical contact, Greek influences on the plays were always bound to be present, given Sir Henry's later education. The works of Aristotle, Euripides, Herodotus, Josephus Flavius (who wrote in Greek), Homer, Lucian of Samosata, Thucydides, Aesop and Aristotle are just some of the authors 'Shakespeare' displays knowledge of in his works, even though they were not all available in translation during his lifetime, and even though he would not have heard more than passing reference to them within his limited education.[185]

Even the *first* of the English History Plays in the accepted Shakespeare canon, *King Henry VI, parts 1 and 2,* exhibit a number of Greek references, while at the same time engaging in political debate. For Shakespeare-Neville, Greek influence and political debate therefore seem inseparable. But the Greek mythological/theological references are carefully placed, so that in addition to the political dimension of the plays, the Greek references provide essential clues to other aspects of the playwright's inner philosophy too. When taken together with the less frequent, overtly Christian and Pagan references which are also occasionally present in *Henry VI part 1*, these clues appear to add up to a warning from their writer that *all* unquestioned belief-systems are potentially dangerous and should be handled with great care. The plays consequently emphasise the great danger to everyone when a country's *leaders* become carelessly obsessed with their own, *unquestioned,* beliefs based on tradition or religion.

Religion and some of its personal and political implications in the Shakespeare plays

The only people who had power to bring about social progress in Medieval and Renaissance England were the Church, the Monarch and the politicians. However, the politicians themselves were then inevitably drawn from the aristocracy and gentry, especially the Barons, so the belief-systems which influenced the Lords and Gentlemen of the land were entirely relevant areas for any politician to analyse. Exactly this kind of analysis is implicitly conducted by the writer in the first *Henry VI* play, and the message comes through loud and clear that only humanism, fellowship, learning and logical thought patterns (freed from the yoke of any dogma) can liberate the mind and thus herald true human progress.

One of the unmissable messages from *Henry VI part 1* is that it is in order to be *aware* of tradition and religion, but that human necessities and humane, pragmatic judgement should come to mind *before* reliance on these beliefs. Neville was a Christian 'inwardly'[186] and to him that was enough: he tried to make his actions spring from his basic Christian ethics without ever discussing his inner religious *beliefs* or doubts. For Neville, to act otherwise would be mere hypocrisy. The word 'hypocrisy' itself comes originally from the Greek *hupokrisis* ('acting a part') but Neville had also been in Germany long enough on his European tour to know that the German equivalent is 'Scheinheiligkeit' – feigning holiness – which was a quality 'Shakespeare' could not endure. We encounter abhorrence for the Germanic slant on 'hypocrisy' in all the Shakespeare plays: those characters who rely on their own proclamations of their personal Christianity to gain respect are repeatedly portrayed as reprehensible. Conversely, the **heroes** are the characters who strive (inwardly) to live up to the Christian ethic in a world that proclaims itself Christian yet acts hypocritically and cruelly. Hamlet and Portia exemplify such *inwardly* Christian characters, and we need to bear in mind their *active* version of Christianity in order to compare and contrast their characters with the 'scheinheilig' characters portrayed in the *Henry VI* plays. Hamlet's and Portia's strivings in the Christian direction may not always be successful, and they certainly do not always get it right, but it is their ethical, true-hearted Christian struggle which counts. For Shakespeare, outward Christian 'show' without heart is meaningless and, at worst, even sinful and dangerous.

It is not merely coincidence that the heroes and heroines of all the Shakespeare plays use the least possible *religious* imagery in all their utterances, while villainous characters often use the most. This holds true not only in the History plays and for Christianity alone. Shylock, for instance, uses old testament references in his speeches, and he – not the Christians in the play – is actually seen preparing to go to his house of religion, i.e. his synagogue. Yet he is shown to be merciless and of murderous intent. It is not because he is a Jew that he is murderous, any more than Bishop Winchester's murdering, ambitious nature (as portrayed in the first two parts of *Henry VI*) is caused by his being a Christian. But what Shylock and Bishop Winchester have in common is that they *proclaim* their supposed religiosity and *profess* to understand and live by its creeds, even when they know they are acting quite contrary to their religion's laws. Portia, on the other hand, preaches the philosophy of mercy in the speeches she gives in court, but she never once uses Christian imagery or talks of personally going to church to pray. Bassanio and Antonio – the true friends – are ultimately the male heroes of the play, each willing to sacrifice himself for the good of the other. But they have no need to bring in Christian imagery to demonstrate their goodness. Indeed, when Bassanio chooses the lead casket he gives a speech which sums up the writer's attitude to religious, and all other, outward, shallow show:

> So may the outward shows be least themselves.
> The world is still deceived with ornament.
> In law, what plea so tainted and corrupt
> But, being seasoned with a gracious voice,
> Obscures the show of evil? In religion,
> What damned error, but some sober brow
> Will bless it and approve it with a text,
> Hiding the grossness with fair ornament?
> There is no vice so simple but assumes
> Some mark of virtue on his outward parts.
> How many cowards, whose hearts are all as false
> As stairs of sand, wear yet upon their chins
> The beards of Hercules and frowning Mars,
> Who, inward searched, have livers white as milk?
> And these assume but valour's excrement
> To render them redoubted. Look on beauty
> And you shall see 'tis purchased by the weight,
> Which therein works a miracle in nature,
> Making them lightest that wear most of it;

We even have the word 'inward' here – 'Who, inward searched, have livers white as milk'. 'Inwardly' was the very word Neville's father in law used to denote how Sir Henry wore his own Christianity. For Neville, that which is 'inward' counts most. He therefore saw no need to use Christian imagery when he spoke in Parliament. If a man is a good Christian – inwardly – he will automatically produce an ethical policy. (Shakespeare uses the word 'inward' to denote this difference between 'Schein und Sein' [to seem and to be] more than 40 times. As with Neville, it is clearly important to him.)

Given the surrounding culture of the times, this is a very **Protestant** stance concerning Christianity: it pervades Neville's life and Shakespeare's works. Yet Shakespeare-Neville always fought shy of condemning Catholic laity, even though he frequently criticised catholic leaders, both in his personal correspondence and in his plays. Religious intolerance, however, was to impinge increasingly on the political scene after Neville's death, when his dire warnings concerning the separation between King and Parliament, Catholic and Protestant, were to become a catastrophic reality. In the ensuing Civil War, Christian rhetoric was to merge with political rhetoric in a most disturbing way. Examining Shakespeare/Neville's stance on religion could very well, therefore, bring us to the heart of his **political** ideology.

Connections between Religion and Politics in the *Henry VI* trilogy

The political points made in the plays – Shakespeare's viewpoint – surely stem from a writer who is well aware of, and initially in sympathy with, the aristocratic/chivalric tradition. *Henry V* portrays the most complete, successful monarch in all Shakespeare's English history plays. But we have to face the fact that this monarch's glory is mediated (by the writer) through his success in international warfare. "Busy giddy minds with foreign quarrels," was advice given to Prince Hal by his father, the usurping King Henry IV. And that King himself came from the knightly, chivalric, aristocratic class who had – arguably – overthrown the peace-loving Richard II simply because they had not been able to profit by foreign wars during Richard's peaceful, cultured reign.[187] If the true writer had not sprung from chivalric family origins, and thus come under this military rather than Church influence, he would have been more pejorative in his writing of the Henry IV character. The fact that the author presents this usurping king as a moral man, that he portrays Richard II as an inept leader who spent time with his favourites rather than on the serious issues of State, and that he emphasises the political prowess of chivalric knights such as John of Gaunt, surely displays 'Shakespeare' as siding with the chivalric faction. Henry IV's outlook was chivalric and military, therefore scarcely

RELIGION, HENRY VI, AND THE GREEK CONNECTION

Christian, or at least not 'Churchy'. For Medieval knightly families like the Nevilles and the Beauchamps, the chivalric tradition was much more powerful an element in their upbringing than the Roman Catholic version of Christianity – which was the only Church available to them at the time. Little wonder, then, that the warring, catastrophic reign of Henry VI should have to be peppered with Greek and Roman rather than *Christian* imagery. The chief representative of the Catholic Church in the *Henry VI* trilogy is Cardinal Beaufort, Bishop of Winchester, and he is portrayed as a villain.

Plot summary of Henry VI, part 1.
There is no definite documentation of the staging of this play, though it may have been performed at the Rose Theatre in 1592.[188] It would have drawn an intellectual, politically-aware audience as well as groundlings. It did not, however, appear in a printed version until its inclusion in the First Folio of Shakespeare's works, 1623.

The play opens with the funeral of Henry V, during which we witness the obvious tensions and divisions caused by the necessarily problematic succession of the infant king, Henry VI. (However, the writer does not present us with this infant king. We see Henry VI on stage as an adult later in the play, and the whole drama ends with his controversial marriage to Margaret, daughter of King René d'Anjou.)

As the play proceeds, we become aware of the various layers of divisions between the King and the knightly/parliamentary class then governing the realm, and between the individual knights themselves. The first division comes about through the young King not maintaining his hold on the French possessions, so dearly won by his father. Knights like Richard Neville, Earl of Warwick, are incensed by the loss of these possessions, which they had fought so hard to win. It is Knights like the Earl of Suffolk – the 'Church faction' – who have been involved in virtually giving away some of those lands. (This division between the the two 'sets' of knights would have been immediately perceived by an aristocratic audience of the day.)

The English attempt to re-take their losses in France, but 'La Pucelle' (Joan of Arc) is urging the Dauphin to resist. The English army led by Talbot (Sir John Talbot, 1st Earl of Shrewsbury) is consequently defeated.

Meanwhile, at the English Court, there is an ongoing struggle between Henry Beaufort, Bishop of Winchester, (later Cardinal) and Gloucester, who is called 'good Duke Humphrey' – Protector of Henry VI. The entry of Richard Neville, (the 'Kingmaker'), into the proceedings is strongly portrayed, and he is caught up in, and comments on, a dynastic argument which begins the troubles between the Houses of York and Lancaster. The discussion in the Temple Garden, ending in the plucking of the Red and White roses extends the use of the term 'The Wars of the Roses' to symbolise these civil wars. Richard Neville sides with the Yorkists.

King Henry VI is politically immature, being subjected to the views of first one, then another, advisor. Swayed by the Lancastrians and ultimately choosing their red rose, he falls under their influence. Edmund Mortimer has been a long-term Yorkist prisoner in the Tower of London, and he declares Richard Plantagenet, Duke of York, is the *true* heir to the English throne.

While in France, Talbot and his English army are trapped in the castle of a French countess, in what becomes the only comic scene in the play. Talbot escapes, but is eventually killed in battle. It is Richard Plantagenet, Duke of York, who finally captures Joan of Arc, and she is sent to the stake. Cardinal Beaufort arranges a truce, but the Duke of York is angry because he believes he could have obtained a complete victory, had Beaufort not interfered.

The Earl of Suffolk, meanwhile, captures Princess Margaret of Anjou. He and she truly fall in love with each other; but this does not stop the scheming Suffolk from taking her back to England and arranging a marriage between Margaret and the innocent King Henry VI. In a soliloquy, Suffolk declares that he will now be able to control the King through her. His declaration of foul intent comes at the very end of the play, and one is left with the feeling that trouble between him and the Neville/Gloucester faction is bound to grow, because the latter has favoured a different French princess from a more powerful lineage for King Henry's bride.

Even from this summary it can be readily appreciated that Shakespeare-Neville was not siding with the 'Church nobles.' The same religious/political stance is repeated throughout the three plays, and an understanding of this helps us to set the *Henry VI* plays in a wider context. (This will be useful to bear in mind when reading my next chapter on the imagery in the Henry VI trilogy.

RELIGION, HENRY VI, AND THE GREEK CONNECTION

Frances Yates notes that the French Academies actually taught playwrights to hide political statements in symbolic, mythological constructions, and this is clearly demonstrated in all the Shakespeare-Neville history plays, but especially in the earliest ones, which were written just after Neville's continental tour.)

Though it may be argued that the existent, anti-Ricardian Chronicles emphasise Richard II's political incompetence as the cause of his downfall rather than the chivalric/monarchical divisions of the time, it is notable that the Chronicles do not cast Cardinal Beaufort in the villainous role which 'Shakespeare' chooses for him in *Henry VI*. There is therefore definite personal selectivity on the part of the author when it comes to his choice of characterisation. The Roman Catholic Cardinal is portrayed as an out and out villain. Thus it cannot be denied that he and only he, the writer, is choosing to slant things in favour of the chivalric classes and against the Catholic Church. Amidst such evidence in this and other plays, one therefore definitely senses the playwright's Protestant stance. [189]

But a stance which (even partially) supported the worldly, warring knights would necessarily cause an 'inward' Christian like Neville a great deal of internal conflict. He would find his chivalric family's pageantry attractive, but their warring abhorrent. Such an ethical Christianity as his would therefore have caused just the kind of Angst between ideals of military glory and the gentleness inherent in the Christian message so clearly displayed in the *Henry VI* trilogy.

By the time he wrote *Henry V,* [a later play] the playwright appears to have come to terms with this contradiction, in some measure at least, because he has the King himself sanction such irreconcilable ambiguities for his Christian fighters. "Modest stillness and humility" are Christian traits, but war demands that the soldier leave these behind when in action:

France. *Before Harfleur:*
King Henry Once more unto the breach, dear friends, once
 more;
Or close the wall up with our English dead.
In peace there's nothing so becomes a man
As modest stillness and humility;
But when the blast of war blows in our ears,
Then imitate the action of the tiger:
Stiffen the sinews, conjure up the blood,
Disguise fair nature with hard-favoured rage;

> Then lend the eye a terrible aspect,
> Let it pry through the portage of the head
> Like the brass cannon, let the brow o'erwhelm it
> As fearfully as doth a galled rock
> O'erhang and jutty his confounded base,
> Swilled with the wild and wasteful ocean.
> Now set the teeth and stretch the nostril wide,
> Hold hard the breath, and bend up every spirit
> To his full height. On, on, you noblest English,
> Whose blood is fet from fathers of war-proof;

In the remainder of this chapter I shall, however, be examining only *Henry VI, part 1*, in some detail, because it begins a trilogy of plays which essentially form discussion papers on various types of war. In doing so, it will become clear that a somewhat concealed layer of Greek scholarship pervades throughout, giving an insight into the true writer's conscious and sub-conscious mind. It will also give an unmistakable insight into the writer's tussle with religion and, indeed, with all unquestioned belief-systems.

Reading between the lines
Unlike the other two *Henry VI* plays, *Henry VI, part 1* begins and ends with references to ancient, pre-Christian beliefs. Moreover, the imagery from these sources returns again and again within the play. The play is therefore framed by an examination of 'belief' and superstition, all set within a very political structure. The writer seems to be on a mission to reform, instruct and inform his audience in these matters – just as a professional politician tries to influence his fellow MPs and his electorate. He is also skilled enough to do this by hidden persuasion and almost subliminal suggestion, just as the French were taught in their academies.[190]

The outward purveyors of *Christianity* in the play are the churchman Bishop Winchester, (later to become Cardinal Beaufort), and King Henry VI himself. Winchester is learned in the Christian faith and obviously professes (or pretends) Christianity; but he is consciously corrupt. Henry VI has learned his Christianity by rote, but he is too simple to have fully internalised it or successfully put it into practice, even though he is never *intentionally* corrupt or hypocritical. Christianity in the hands of both Winchester and King Henry is therefore shown as being hopeless and helpless in all the warlike and practical political situations in the play. Civil war is erupting, and the writer ensures that this is ultimately seen as a 'bad thing' in each of the *Henry VI* trilogy of plays. However, the first part of *Henry VI* seemingly glorifies the practical situation of war when it is against a foreign power, which is of course not a *Christian* stance. Only Pagan and Ancient World imagery can find its place in this situation, as will be illustrated. *Civil* war, however, being viewed from a completely inglorious standpoint, allows the writer to bring some *practical* meaning into the rote-Christian utterances of King Henry VI. It is as if most characters are seeking support in their decision-making processes by accessing their knowledge of renowned ancient examples, Christian or otherwise, but are all 'getting it wrong' – wilfully or otherwise, depending on their intrinsic character.

The characters brought out by the writer as the most honest ones in the play are the most logical, straightforward, unsuperstitious thinkers. These are led by 'good' Duke Humphrey of Gloucester and Richard Neville, Earl of Warwick. Yet even these two men have their otherwise clear vision held back by their one, unquestioned, traditional belief in a leadership founded on purely dynastic, inherited grounds. This unquestioned *illogical* idea that dynastic right is worth fighting and dying for brings about their downfall. Most importantly too, the fact that those in high office hold such a dangerous, unquestioned belief inevitably spawns civil strife and bloodshed for all the English. Although Richard Neville and Duke Humphrey are politically motivated, honestly seeking the best and most beneficial government of the country, their unquestioning **belief** in the monarchical system of government is nevertheless preventing them and the country from being at peace with itself. They are politicians who have power and influence in the country; yet they simply do not realise that their absolute belief in dynastic succession is standing in the way of both personal and social progress. This unquestioned belief is blinding them to other possible political solutions. Thus is 'Shakespeare' making us question the foundations of *all* our unquestioned beliefs in this often-underrated play. Thus, too, one can see Sir Henry Neville's political hand at work.

Yet at least Warwick and Gloucester are ultimately more flexible, logical and altruistic than those characters who, like Winchester, openly flaunt and profess an adherence to religion, whether Christian or otherwise. Gloucester and the Earl of Warwick gradually learn lessons by bitter experience as the trilogy progresses. They are also struggling for what they think are public rights rather than merely private gains. (All this, by the way, seems to be out of line with chronicled history, so it is difficult to imagine anyone but a Neville presenting another Neville in such a whitewashed manner.)

In the play, the Duke of Gloucester is murdered by his rival, Bishop Winchester, which was not included in the Chronicles. The Earl of Warwick learns all too late that his goal – placing the 'rightful' heir onto the throne – may not justify the means, and that it may not, in any case, have been the right goal in the first place. The implied political message is that all Englishmen should try to unite around their present figure of the monarch and work with him or her. What they should *not* try to do is change the situation merely because of perceived inherited rights. However, those more privileged, learned members of the audience may have gone away discussing another possible solution not mentioned in the play – that of Republican rule. All learned Elizabethan men read about Republicanism, because it was an aspect of Renaissance studies: the Roman Republic always came in for much discussion among the intelligentsia of the day.

The unhappy fates of Gloucester (and, later in the trilogy, of Warwick too) occurred because they were caught in a web of ideology woven in their own times by their own social class. They could not – as true politicians should – step out of their time web and examine the situation dispassionately. Dynastic squabbling and pointless battles had been the order of their day. Richard Neville, Earl of Warwick, wasted the earlier portion of his life through not examining the grounds of his own beliefs. He was highly intelligent and was in a position to help bring about good government, so the message in the *Henry VI* plays is that he should have turned his energies to achieving good government rather than arguing about his belief in dynastic succession. (It could be argued that Sir Henry Neville himself attempted to redress his ancestor's faults and to put his political ideas into action when he joined the Essex rebellion, doubtless in the hope of pre-empting what could have been a **vacuum** after the death of the childless Queen Elizabeth – a vacuum which may once again have been filled by civil war, bearing in mind that many of the same family divisions and ideologies as in Henry VI's reign were still present in 16th century England.)

However, even though he comes to his conclusions much too late in the day, at least Warwick is portrayed as having left to posterity one idea capable of positive development. His honesty and willingness to change his position – and to change his dynastic adherence – in the light of experience, eventually leads Henry VI to accept that he cannot govern on his own, and, in particular, that he needs a Neville's help! (Who but a young Neville would have included such a message in his plays?)

Richard Neville (as portrayed in the play) at least *sets out* on an honest path towards enlightenment which, unlike many other characters in the play, is not one paved with self-seeking ambition. His rhetoric is consequently never clouded or overcrowded with use of Christian imagery, nor even with pre-Christian citations. This is noteworthy, because Richard Neville's absence of reliance on such imagery announces him as an unprejudiced a politician as one was likely to encounter in those overwhelmingly prejudiced times. The self-seeking Earl of Suffolk, however, stands in direct contrast with Richard Neville. Suffolk seeks to support his own ignoble ambitions by reference to ancient Greek example, and thus comes to a sticky, dishonourable, unrepentant end (later in the trilogy), while Richard Neville dies 'honourably' in battle. Even so, Neville's dying speech (later in the trilogy) is disproportionately long, leaving us with his tragic, too-late realisation that glory in *civil* war counts for nothing:

> These eyes, that now are dimmed with death's black veil,
> Have been as piercing as the midday sun,
> To search the secret treasons of the world;
> The wrinkles in my brows, now filled with blood,
> Were likened oft to kingly sepulchres;
> For who lived king, but I could dig his grave?
> And who durst smile when Warwick bent his brow?
> Lo, now my glory smeared in dust and blood!
> My parks, my walks, my manors that I had,
> Even now forsake me; and of all my lands
> Is nothing left me but my body's length.
> Why, what is pomp, rule, reign, but earth and dust?
> And live we how we can, yet die we must.
> *Henry VI, part 3, Act5 Sc.2*

"What is pomp, rule, reign, but earth and dust?" Poor Warwick, he realises at last the meaningless cause for which he has been fighting. In his dying hour, Warwick declares his own assessment of his *best* purpose in life – "To search the secret treasons of the world;". The murder of his friend and kinsman, good Duke Humphrey, had surely been one of those 'secret treasons', and Warwick had detected the manner of his death, and worked out the identity of the killer, in a logical analysis worthy of Sherlock Holmes:

> **Warwick** See how the blood is settled in his face.
> Oft have I seen a timely-parted ghost
> Of ashy semblance, meagre, pale, and bloodless,
> Being all descended to the labouring heart,
> Who, in the conflict that it holds with death,
> Attracts the same for aidance 'gainst the enemy;
> Which with the heart there cools, and ne'er returneth
> To blush and beautify the cheek again.
> But see, his face is black and full of blood,
> His eyeballs further out than when he lived,
> Staring full ghastly like a strangled man;
> His hair upreared; his nostrils stretched with struggling;
> His hands abroad displayed, as one that grasped
> And tugged for life, and was by strength subdued.
> Look on the sheets, his hair, you see, is sticking;
> His well-proportioned beard made rough and rugged,
> Like to the summer's corn by tempest lodged.
> It cannot be but he was murdered here;
> The least of all these signs were probable.
> *2, Henry VI,* Act 3, Sc.ii

Warwick is therefore a hero for precisely the same reason that Hamlet is a hero: both characters search for openness and truth. This is why we, the audience, love them, warts and all. Truth can only exist outside personal ambition, and those who search for it stagger through miles of darkness to find it, usually to their own detriment.

But their quest, even with its mistakes, nevertheless teaches posterity important lessons. The characters who are image-touting and hypocritical in the Henry VI plays, in contrast, fail to leave behind them any fruitful lessons. They use examples from the ancient world only to help justify their own actions instead of using them to advance political philosophy, in aid of mankind.

Richard Neville is ultimately the man who, like Sir Henry Neville, his kinsman and secret chronicler, contributed a political **idea** which could be developed for the benefit of society: it was Richard Neville who eventually demonstrated that it might be possible to be a Kingmaker yet at the same time not glory in this role. Instead of killing or protecting Kings, Nevilles could guide and work in partnership with monarchs who, left to their own devices, might cause economic and social collapse. Moreover, it would then not matter who this monarch was, nor what were his dynastic rights, so long as the monarch himself was unprejudiced enough to agree to work in partnership with Parliament and his advisors. Richard Neville's and the country's tragedy was, however, that neither he nor King Henry VI came to this realisation in time to halt the Civil Strife which Warwick's previously uncompromising *beliefs*, in parallel with the King's indecision, had both helped to set in motion.

Chapter Nine

SUPERSTITION AND IMAGERY IN *HENRY VI, PART ONE*

The mind of a politician is clearly at work in the Henry VI plays, and Henry Neville had been a *politician* since he was twenty years old. But he had been a *scholar* even before then. *Henry VI, part 1* was written when Neville was about 28 years old, so his varied experience of politics and ancient learning are evident within the play. Noted by Richard Edes for his 'book-learning'[191] Neville had majored in Astronomy at Merton College, Oxford. Astronomy and astrology (the latter being an ancient belief-system) were linked together in Elizabethan days, and it was one of Neville's fellow-students and best friends, George Carleton, who wrote a great treatise separating superstitious astrology from the scientific study of astronomy. (Carleton later married Neville's widow.)

Neville, like Carleton, was one of the *new* astronomers. Carleton and Neville studied Copernicus as well as Ptolemy, so both men must have come to an early realisation that the old Astrology was based on superstitious, pre-scientific beliefs, which had unfortunately got mixed into the 'common sense' of Renaissance Christianity. Neville was just the man, therefore, to be able to wield both the astrological and astronomical references and imagery in the 'Shakespeare' works. Having come under the influence of French and Italian learning, he was also just the man to be able to hide various 'truths' in his chosen symbolism.

Despite its unchristian messages, Astrology remained one of the traditional beliefs which contributed to the mass survival of various superstitions in both Henry VI's and Queen Elizabeth's times. Shakespeare/Neville, trained to ponder such matters, opens *Henry VI, part 1* with a strange Christian/astrological mixture of images. But, as we shall see, the writer implicitly undermines the astrological imagery just as surely as he later undermines Beaufort's and other hypocrites' *Christian* imagery. By extrapolation, therefore, the writer is immediately setting up a position from which the audience can be led to question their own traditional beliefs – including that of monarchical dynasties. This was a very daring political viewpoint to put forward at the time, so the writer presents it almost subliminally. (No wonder he also presents these dangerous ideas under a pseudonym!)

Henry VI, part 1 opens with the funeral of King Henry V:

Westminster Abbey
Dead March. Enter the funeral of KING HENRY THE FIFTH, attended on by the DUKE OF BEDFORD, Regent of France, the DUKE OF GLOUCESTER, Protector, the DUKE OF EXETER, the EARL OF WARWICK, the BISHOP OF WINCHESTER

BEDFORD. Hung be the heavens with black, yield day to night!
Comets, importing change of times and states,
Brandish your crystal tresses in the sky
And with them scourge the bad revolting stars
That have consented unto Henry's death!
King Henry the Fifth, too famous to live long!
England ne'er lost a king of so much worth.

The Duke of Bedford thus uses the ancient astrological beliefs in this, the opening speech of the play, whereas the Duke of Gloucester (who speaks next) is content to say more by using less imagery, full realising that Henry V fashioned his skills as a monarch and fighter by his own means, not with the help of anything supernatural:

GLOUCESTER. England ne'er had a king until his time.
Virtue he had, deserving to command;
His brandish'd sword did blind men with his beams;
His arms spread wider than a dragon's wings;
His sparkling eyes, replete with wrathful fire,
More dazzled and drove back his enemies
Than mid-day sun fierce bent against their faces.
What should I say? His deeds exceed all speech:
He ne'er lift up his hand but conquered.

The Duke of Gloucester is portrayed as an able politician and Protector to the King. The only image he conjures up in this speech is that of the dragon, which is far more practical and appropriate than Bedford's astrological/pseudo-religious imagery. The writer is therefore leading us to assess politicians by their practical perception rather than their adherence to any supernatural belief. Henry V's reputation as a fighter bears *appropriate* comparison with just such a fiery creature as a dragon. In exactly the same way, Henry Neville chose appropriate, worldly rather than supernatural examples to illustrate his meaning in his political treatise. Gloucester's image of the dragon also brings to mind the very English reference to St. George and the dragon. As Gloucester is painted in such a positive light generally in the play, one is left to conclude that the writer is therefore quite a patriot, politically speaking. Neville considered himself a true patriot of England, putting his country's interests before all personal considerations, and only mixing the two when it would not harm his countrymen!

The next to speak at Henry V's funeral is the Earl of Exeter. He too is concerned that Bedford's speech may be misattributing cause and effect. He takes it that Bedford might be suggesting the stars had something to do with the dead king's early demise. However, instead of denying outright that this could have been the case, Exeter leaves a question hanging in the air, and he allows that question to contain a reference to the pre-Christian belief in magic:

> **EXETER**. We mourn in black; why mourn we not in blood?
> Henry is dead and never shall revive.
> Upon a wooden coffin we attend;
> And death's dishonourable victory
> We with our stately presence glorify,
> Like captives bound to a triumphant car.
> What! shall we curse the planets of mishap
> That plotted thus our glory's overthrow?
> Or shall we think the subtle-witted French
> Conjurers and sorcerers, that, afraid of him,
> By magic verses have contriv'd his end?

It is obvious that belief in both these superstitions – astrology and magic – was still alive in Medieval England, and also in the early modern, Tudor period. Otherwise the writer would hardly have given voice to these ancient beliefs on stage. (Such beliefs are thrown further into question, and subjected to implicit disapproval, during the course of the *Henry VI* trilogy. Both Gloucester's wife and Joan of Arc are portrayed as holding on to ancient, pagan 'magic', and both receive their comeuppance for it.)

SUPERSTITION AND IMAGERY IN HENRY VI, PART ONE

Next to enter is the Bishop of Winchester. He attempts to give a Christian view of the King's death, even though he is soon to be clearly ear-marked as a villain:

WINCHESTER. He was a king bless'd of the King of kings;
Unto the French the dreadful judgment-day
So dreadful will not be as was his sight.
The battles of the Lord of Hosts he fought;
The Church's prayers made him so prosperous.

The writer has obviously set out to make the churchman and his Christian words look immediately ridiculous. In the old pagan magic religions warfare was glorified. It cannot, however, be legitimately glorified in Christianity; yet here is a Catholic Bishop attempting to do so. Neither does this Bishop stop at military glorification; he extends the matter by saying that Henry V's military victories were due to the Church's prayers!

It does not take long for Gloucester, the practical politician, to point out some of the obvious illogicalities in what the Bishop is saying. Gloucester is definitely unwilling for the late King Henry's reputation and memorial to be commandeered by the Church and their superstitious claptrap:

GLOUCESTER. The Church! Where is it? Had not churchmen pray'd,
His thread of life had not so soon decay'd.
None do you like but an effeminate prince,
Whom like a school-boy you may overawe.

Winchester clearly has neither the wit nor wisdom to dispute with Gloucester, so scurrilously changes the subject, attacking Gloucester personally instead of engaging with the point of Christian philosophy now opened up by Gloucester:

WINCHESTER. Gloucester, whate'er we like, thou art Protector
And lookest to command the Prince and realm.
Thy wife is proud; she holdeth thee in awe
More than God or religious churchmen may.
GLOUCESTER. Name not religion, for thou lov'st the flesh;
And ne'er throughout the year to church thou go'st,
Except it be to pray against thy foes.

UNDERSTANDING THE INVISIBLE SHAKESPEARE

Thus is the focus now taken into a personal context and it is Bedford who takes on the role of peacemaker:

> **BEDFORD**. Cease, cease these jars and rest your minds in peace;
> Let's to the altar. Heralds, wait on us.
> Instead of gold, we'll offer up our arms,
> Since arms avail not, now that Henry's dead.
> Posterity, await for wretched years,
> When at their mothers' moist'ned eyes babes shall suck,
> Our isle be made a nourish of salt tears,
> And none but women left to wail the dead.
> Henry the Fifth, thy ghost I invocate:
> Prosper this realm, keep it from civil broils,
> Combat with adverse planets in the heavens.
> A far more glorious star thy soul will make
> Than Julius Caesar or bright –

> *Enter a MESSENGER*

We shall never know what other, non-Christian, image Bedford was about to invoke before he was interrupted. Bedford, was the French Regent at this time. He realises that if he is to keep order abroad, he must preach against 'civil broils' at home. Yet he seems unable to do this without once again reverting to his astrological imagery. Then he makes it clear that his military pattern is 'Julius Caesar' as the embodiment of military glory. He would have doubtless gone on to mention other pre-Christian examples, had his speech not been cut short by the entry of a messenger. Bedford too – even if only subconsciously – is aware that Christian rhetoric cannot accommodate military action.

It is clear that the writer does not wish to become further embroiled in this mythological/religious debate, because the interruption of Bedford encourages the audience to start to ponder on practicalities rather than the abstract philosophy of the day. This is just the kind of situation Neville engineered at the 'surprise' reading of his political treatise. (One simply cannot escape the feeling that mischievousness and humour are other strong qualities in the Shakespeare plays and Neville's politics!)

In these few opening lines, then, the writer has immediately and efficiently marked out the shortcomings of all supernaturally-based belief systems. With doing so, he has also implied that there are shortcomings inevitably woven into the fabric of the

Renaissance ideal. By reviving the study of ancient literature, intellectuals of the time were also reviving the ancient superstitions. Shakespeare/Neville would have been the last person to wish to throw out the baby with the bath water. Yet by writing lines which showed (the ultimately incompetent) politicians of the day filling their minds full of superstition, is he not trying to make the audience push their leaders into a more rational, more discerning state of mind? This cannot have been done by accident. *All* supernatural-belief imagery (including that of Christianity) is portrayed as being unable to impart meaning to the life of Henry V. It is also unable to bring peace between the jarring factions at the head of the State. Old, pre-Christian belief systems are based on supernatural, unscientific explanations of natural phenomenae. But neither Henry VI's nor Beaufort's *Christian* imagery brings peace. The writer is therefore surely telling us not even to be prejudiced by Christianity on the basis of it being a supposedly divinely-ordained, supernatural system. Just as in Sir Henry Neville's Treatise, therefore, the writer of this play is impliedly arguing for a separation between religion – of any sort – and politics.

The ease with which the aristocrats mix superstition with Christian imagery as the play progresses demonstrates that an unthinking belief in Christianity can easily be made to tip over into a belief in pagan and other ancient ideas, even though these ideas are clearly destructive to humanity. By extrapolation, then, *any* fixed, supernatural belief can prevent the believer from looking objectively at a human situation and coming to the best, most *humane,* conclusions and solutions. The only possible hope of salvation left to us, the 'governed', after this kind of rhetoric, lies in an individual politician's internalised Christian *ethics*. Outward devotion is meaningless. (This surely implies that any Roman Catholic view on the part of the author is utterly impossible.) When ambassador in Catholic France, Sir Henry Neville arranged 'Sermons' at his home rather than attending a Catholic Church on Sundays.[192] Once again, outward religious show meant nothing to him, which is precisely what we would expect Shakespeare's attitude to be, when we look at the message given by the text of the plays.

Shakespeare's characterisation of Joan of Arc
It is within the character of La Pucelle, or Joan of Arc, par excellence, that 'Shakespeare' illustrates the dangers of

supernatural belief. La Pucelle embodies the problem of what can become the thin margin between Christianity and ancient, anti-life beliefs. Her progress from Christianity to sorcery wanders its way through various passing references to other religions, throughout the play.

During her first appearance, however, Joan introduces herself to the Dauphin as a **Christian.** Yet at the same time, she credits the virgin Mary with having performed a miracle on her, which immediately makes her seem either fanciful or manipulative:

> **PUCELLE.** Dauphin, I am by birth a shepherd's daughter,
>   My wit untrain'd in any kind of art.
>   Heaven and our Lady gracious hath it pleas'd
>   To shine on my contemptible estate.
>   Lo, whilst I waited on my tender lambs
>   And to sun's parching heat display'd my cheeks,
>   God's Mother deigned to appear to me,
>   And in a vision full of majesty
>   Will'd me to leave my base vocation
>   And free my country from calamity
>   Her aid she promis'd and assur'd success.
> In complete glory she reveal'd herself;
>   And whereas I was black and swart before,
>   With those clear rays which she infus'd on me
>   That beauty am I bless'd with which you may see.
>   Ask me what question thou canst possible,
>   And I will answer unpremeditated.
>   My courage try by combat if thou dar'st,
>   And thou shalt find that I exceed my sex.
>   Resolve on this: thou shalt be fortunate
>   If thou receive me for thy warlike mate.
> **CHARLES.**[the Dauphin] Thou hast astonish'd me with thy
>   high terms.
>   Only this proof I'll of thy valour make
>   In single combat thou shalt buckle with me;
>   And if thou vanquishest, thy words are true;
>   Otherwise I renounce all confidence.
>   *{ACT1|SC2 }*

The only other character in the play who has previously relied on his Christian beliefs to impress his hearers is the scurrilous Bishop of Winchester, so the writer has by now put us in the mind-frame of viewing Joan with care and scepticism.

SUPERSTITION AND IMAGERY IN HENRY VI, PART ONE

Doubtless the audience would have been hoping the Dauphin would ask Joan to summon up divine proof of her supernatural gifts. It would perhaps have made for some spectacular stage effects. But the writer chooses to produce a different sort of stage effect: that of fighting. The Dauphin requests he might try Joan's professedly-divine skills by sparring with her. Any member of the audience who has absorbed the Christian/military conflict outlined subtly in the play so far will therefore already mistrust Joan and the Dauphin – subconsciously, at least. But in the absence of proof divine, the sheer fun of a woman fencing with a man in Elizabethan times must have been amusing, and perhaps slightly shocking.

It is the *amusing* side of the spectacle, however, which is immediately re-inforced by Joan's words. Even then, she can't help backing up her claim of divine powers by mentioning St. Katherine's churchyard and 'Christ's mother':

> PUCELLE. I am prepar'd; here is my keen-edg'd sword,
> Deck'd with five flower-de-luces on each side,
> The which at Touraine, in Saint Katherine's churchyard,
> Out of a great deal of old iron I chose forth....
> Christ's Mother helps me, else I were too weak.

Later, after the Dauphin has shown his admiration for her skills, and almost declared his love for her, the Christian imagery suddenly changes itself into similes involving ancient Rome:

> PUCELLE. ...
> Glory is like a circle in the water,
> Which never ceaseth to enlarge itself
> Till by broad spreading it disperse to nought.
> With Henry's death the English circle ends;
> Dispersed are the glories it included.
> Now am I like that proud insulting ship
> Which Caesar and his fortune bare at once.

Joan has now dared to bring in this non-Christian imagery. But alongside it she also implicitly expresses her unquestioning belief in the power of inherited dynasties: "With Henry's death the English circle ends." The Dauphin now goes one step farther with his own mixed imagery:

> **CHARLES.** Was Mahomet inspired with a dove?

> Thou with an eagle art inspired then.
> Helen, the mother of great Constantine,
> Nor yet Saint Philip's daughters were like thee.
> Bright star of Venus, fall'n down on the earth,
> How may I reverently worship thee enough?
> {*Act 1, Sc.2*}

The Dauphin has become the epitome of superstitious religiosity: he passes through Islam then on to the eagle, which could be a reference to the Roman Empire or (if it is a double-headed eagle) to the Eastern Orthodox Church. He then extends this into mention of the Emperor Constantine, briefly moves back to Christianity, then on to mention the Roman goddess of beauty, finally declaring that he is ready to worship Joan herself. This is not an illustration of profanity: it is a demonstration of how *all* 'divinely-based' belief systems can ultimately get lumped together in the human mind, leading the judgement astray. It is doubtless also nationalistic in purpose: it defines the French as even more heretical than the English!

After one of Joan's great triumphs, the Dauphin again praises her by reference to Greek mythology. But it is interesting to see that Duke Reignier then counters this reference by attributing her victories to what seems to be a Christian God. Reignier is the father of Margaret of Anjou, and it is this same Margaret who later marries King Henry VI and then goes on to lead a faction in the English Wars of the Roses. This, then, may have been one good reason for the writer giving Duke Reignier Christian rather than pre-Christian utterances. He cannot, after all, make a lady who becomes an English leader seem as bad as the *French* military leader, Joan of Arc.

Charles (the Dauphin), however, mentions Astraea, who was the Greek goddess of justice, thus illustrating how all these mythological/religious concepts could be used by any *scurrilous* character, whether English or French, in order to make themselves look more glorious by example, with no reference to the true situation:

> **PUCELLE**. Advance our waving colours on the walls;
> Rescu'd is Orleans from the English.
> Thus Joan la Pucelle hath perform'd her word.
> **CHARLES**. Divinest creature, Astraea's daughter,
> How shall I honour thee for this success?
> Thy promises are like Adonis' gardens,

That one day bloom'd and fruitful were the next.
France, triumph in thy glorious prophetess.
Recover'd is the town of Orleans.
More blessed hap did ne'er befall our state.
  REIGNIER. Why ring not out the bells aloud throughout
    the town?
Dauphin, command the citizens make bonfires
And feast and banquet in the open streets
To celebrate the joy that God hath given us.
{ACT1/SC6}

Then, in Act 1, Scene 5, Talbot, the great English leader, meets with Joan and declares her a witch. Pagan earth-magic is now thrown into the supernatural melting pot – and this belief is held by a Christian English gentleman! The overall message is surely that it was no wonder England was so generally sown with civil strife, when its educated gentlemen and leaders were themselves so mentally mixed up and unquestioning of their own contradictory philosophies.

Yet, despite all this, *after* Joan's initial military victory, the Dauphin turns back again to Christian imagery when talking of her to the other French combatants. But he preludes even this speech with mention of ancient Egyptian history, as mediated through the Greek historian, Herodotus:

CHARLES. 'Tis Joan, not we, by whom the day is won;
  For which I will divide my crown with her;
  And all the priests and friars in my realm
  Shall in procession sing her endless praise.
  A statelier pyramis to her I'll rear
  Than Rhodope's of Memphis ever was.
  In memory of her, when she is dead,
  Her ashes, in an urn more precious
  Than the rich jewel'd coffer of Darius,
  Transported shall be at high festivals
  Before the kings and queens of France.
  No longer on Saint Denis will we cry,
  But Joan la Pucelle shall be France's saint.
  Come in, and let us banquet royally
  After this golden day of victory. *Flourish. Exeunt*
{ACT1/SC6}

Herodotus wrote of Rhodope, who was a courtesan of Greece and a fellow-servant with Aesop at Samos. She was carried to Egypt by Xanthus, and her liberty was eventually bought by the brother of Sappho, who married her. She is said to have erected one of the pyramids ['pyramis'] of Egypt. It may of course be that the Dauphin is here suggesting that La Pucelle, like Rhodope, is a whore. But whatever its meaning, there is no doubt that the writer was aware of the Greek references in this speech. This extract also makes us aware that the writer was familiar with Egyptian mythology too – a subject I shall deal with in a later chapter. (A direct and unmistakable reference to the Egyptian god, Thoth, occurs in the decryption of the Dedication Code.)

Joan of Arc's personally-proclaimed, pretended, hypocritical Christianity did not stand the test of battles and the bantering of men. Predictably, then, in the play, Joan's allegedly Christian divinity cannot survive her defeat. The minute she is in danger of being captured by the English she cries on pagan – not Christian – powers for aid:

> **PUCELLE**. The Regent conquers and the Frenchmen fly.
> Now help, ye charming spells and periapts;
> And ye choice spirits that admonish me
> And give me signs of future accidents;   [Thunder]
> You speedy helpers that are substitutes
> Under the lordly monarch of the north,
> Appear and aid me in this enterprise!-
>   *Enter* **FIENDS**-
> This speedy and quick appearance argues proof
> Of your accustom'd diligence to me.
> Now, ye familiar spirits that are cull'd
> Out of the powerful regions under earth,
> Help me this once, that France may get the field.
>   [*They walk and speak not*]
> O, hold me not with silence over-long!
> Where I was wont to feed you with my blood,
> I'll lop a member off and give it you
> In earnest of a further benefit,
> So you do condescend to help me now.
>   [*They hang their heads*]
> No hope to have redress? My body shall
> Pay recompense, if you will grant my suit.
>   [*They shake their heads*]
> Cannot my body nor blood sacrifice
> Entreat you to your wonted furtherance?
> Then take my soul-my body, soul, and all,
> Before that England give the French the foil.

SUPERSTITION AND IMAGERY IN HENRY VI, PART ONE

> [*They depart*]
> See! they forsake me. Now the time is come
> That France must vail her lofty-plumed crest
> And let her head fall into England's lap.
> My ancient incantations are too weak,
> And hell too strong for me to buckle with.
> Now, France, thy glory droopeth to the dust.   *Exit*
> *{ACT5|SC3 }*

Of course, this would all have been very nationalistic stuff too, as far as the English Elizabethan audience was concerned. Shakespeare-Neville was an Elizabethan English politician who had already visited France during his European tour with Henry Savile, but he knew where his and his audience's loyalties lay. The spectacle of a defeated French military leader calling on pagan forces for aid, and failing, must have heartened English audiences of the day. The *surface* message for the audience is that pagan spirits cannot prevail against true Christian Englishmen. But when one contrasts this scene with Joan's original protestations of 'Christ's mother' being her divine aid, the message of one misguided belief being prone to slip into another, worse one, cannot be missed by anyone who analyses the text. The writer is also clearly saying it is all too easy for anyone to put two and two together and make five, when it comes to attributing their own, or anyone else's, good fortune to God – and Christ – being on their side. After all, Christ himself was not blessed with a happy, successful life, or with a painless end, yet no Christian suggests that God was therefore not on his side! Those who consider themselves (on stage) able to know and declare the will of God or the saints are therefore much mistaken in their (inward) Christian understanding. By extension, therefore, they are the very last people who should be trusted as leaders of their community in any capacity whatsoever. This is surely the crux of the playwright's meaning when he makes scoundrels like Cardinal Beaufort (Bishop Winchester) suggest that they can read signs of a Christian God taking sides. This is also surely why Neville did not bring any Christian imagery into his own political treatise.

None of the *English* characters in the first part of the *Henry VI* trilogy goes so far as to use the nomenclature of sorcery in their imagery unless they are specifically talking about Joan of Arc or the French. But many of them make references to examples from ancient mythology, even though they think of themselves as Christians. Talbot is the military hero of the play, though the writer cleverly includes him in comic scenes too. Even his troops' battle cry – 'A Talbot' – marks him out as something of a comic hero. A talbot was the sixteenth century name for a breed of dog [now extinct.] It was a large hound with long ears and a pale coat, and was so called because the family of Talbot used it as one of its heraldic emblems. But in the comic scene where Talbot speaks with a French Countess, he is clearly shown to be anything but 'large':

> **COUNTESS.** Is this the scourge of France?
> Is this Talbot, so much fear'd abroad
> That with his name the mothers still their babes?
> I see report is fabulous and false.
> I thought I should have seen some Hercules,
> A second Hector, for his grim aspect
> And large proportion of his strong-knit limbs.
> Alas, this is a child, a silly dwarf!
> It cannot be this weak and writhled shrimp
> Should strike such terror to his enemies.
> *{ACT2|SC3}*

In real life, Neville was shown to befriend men, like Robert Cecil and Thomas Edmondes, who were small and/or deformed, but nevertheless capable of good political management, so he is certainly not siding with this Countess' value systems, either on or off-stage. By adding this joke, he is merely showing up this French countess for what she is – shallow. (Like Touchstone's predilection for the unusual-looking Audrey, Neville liked people who were in some way 'different'. Ralph Winwood – with whom Neville was the best of friends – had a quick temper and a harsh tongue, yet Neville never doubted the man's inner integrity. Once again, Neville and Shakespeare therefore display the same viewpoints.) In laughing at Talbot, the English are surely also showing a willingness to laugh at themselves. Laughter, as the playwright knew, defuses many a tense situation.

So Talbot, though not large and not boastful, gets compared – by an *English* Lord – with Alcides, which was, significantly, the less well-known Greek name for Hercules. (Shakespeare was not taught Greek, even if he attended Grammar School, but Neville learnt the language and its culture from childhood onwards. How much more likely, then, that Neville, not Shakespeare, would use the more obscure Greek name, even though the Latin, Roman equivalent was better known to those in his audience who had perhaps gone through the local grammar school education.)

> **LUCY.** But where's the great Alcides of the field,
> Valiant Lord Talbot, Earl of Shrewsbury,
> Created for his rare success in arms
> Great Earl of Washford, Waterford, and Valence,
> Lord Talbot of Goodrig and Urchinfield,
> *{ACT4|SC7}*

(One may also note that Lord Lucy, who talks with such Greek imagery, is portrayed sympathetically in this play, even though one of his descendants is credited as being an enemy of William Shakespeare, who is said to have poached deer from the Lucy's land at Stratford.)

One of the greatest **villains** of the play is undoubtedly the Earl of Suffolk. He uses references to ancient Greece as pre-emptors for the villainy he is about to foment in the second part of the *Henry VI* trilogy. His are the ominous closing words of *Henry VI, part 1:*

> **SUFFOLK.** Thus Suffolk hath prevail'd; and thus he goes,
> As did the youthful Paris once to Greece,
> With hope to find the like event in love
> But prosper better than the Troyan did.
> Margaret shall now be Queen, and rule the King;
> But I will rule both her, the King, and realm.

Cardinal Beaufort, Bishop of Winchester is portrayed as being equally as bad as Suffolk, even though his references are to the Christian canon, and even though he is so obviously a declared Christian. Considering Beaufort and all other Cardinals in the plays (e.g. Cardinal Pandulph in King John) are portrayed as overwhelmingly bad, it has always puzzled me greatly that some scholars try to argue that 'Shakespeare' was a crypto Catholic! However, the perceptive Frances Yates argues in *Shakespeare's Last Plays* that *Henry VIII* is a play which celebrates the triumph of Protestantism. As she also asserts, the 'Bohemia' in *The Winter's Tale* is portrayed as an idyllic land – in celebration of the writer's support for the Palatinate Prince who then resided there with his wife (James I's daughter) and around whom the Protestant hopes for Europe were centred. This is the Prince to whom the Earl of Southampton gave financial support.

Altogether, then, my statement that Shakespeare is not a Catholic is shared, and also not merely subjective: when it is realised that Cardinal Beaufort was in real life a much more helpful and sympathetic character than he is portrayed by Shakespeare, then it becomes a completely logical, *objective* conclusion that the writer was definitely not in sympathy with the Catholic Church. Indeed, he underlines his lack of sympathy for the Catholic hierarchy by showing how corrupt and self-seeking Beaufort is even *before* he is promoted to the position of Cardinal. The logical inference is that if the Catholic hierarchy had been honestly concerned to promote true, honest people, then it would have found someone better to champion than Beaufort, Bishop of Winchester. Whichever way one looks at it, therefore, Shakespeare was openly pejorative to the purveyors of Catholicism. What's more, even if we suppose Shakespeare, the writer, was the man from Stratford and also suppose that Henry Wriothesley, third Earl of Southampton, was his patron, then we must surely conclude that this 'Shakespeare' was therefore unlikely to be a Roman Catholic. Besides being brought up by the Protestant Lord Burghley, Wriothesley actually fought for both French and German Protestants, as well as sending funds to the Bohemian Prince Frederick (husband of James I's daughter) who was seen as the great Protestant hope in Europe.

Along with other characters in the play who hide their true motives when expressing their ideas in front of others, Beaufort declares his bad aims in his soliloquies. Just as Suffolk ends the whole play with a soliloquy declaring his dishonourable motives, so does Winchester end Act 1, Scene 1 with his own disreputable declaration:

> **WINCHESTER**. [Aside] Each hath his place and function
>   to attend:
>   I am left out; for me nothing remains.
>   But long I will not be Jack out of office.
>   The King from Eltham I intend to steal,
>   And sit at chiefest stern of public weal.   *Exeunt*

Just to underline his perfidy further, Shakespeare affirms Winchester's place as a **hypocrite** too, because, on his very next appearance, he charges Gloucester with being ambitious, which is precisely what we, the audience, now know to be a fault of Winchester's own:

> **WINCHESTER.** How now, ambitious Humphry! What means this?
> **GLOUCESTER.** Peel'd priest, dost thou command me to be shut out?
> **WINCHESTER.** I do, thou most usurping proditor,
> And not Protector of the King or realm.
> **GLOUCESTER.** Stand back, thou manifest conspirator,
> Thou that contrived'st to murder our dead lord;
> Thou that giv'st whores indulgences to sin.
> I'll canvass thee in thy broad cardinal's hat,
> If thou proceed in this thy insolence.
> {ACT1|SC3}

The audience also becomes aware later on in the play that Winchester is likely to be promoted to the position of a Cardinal, so this is where we actually witness the writer implicitly maligning the Catholic Church. Moreover, in Gloucester's retort to Winchester the writer has shown that he knows about the Lutheran charge of the corrupt sale of indulgences – something of which Neville would have been made very aware during the two years he spent in Germany while travelling on the continent between 1578 and 1583. It is no Catholic writer speaking here but one most definitely rooted in Protestantism.

It is worthy of note that the author has not chosen to characterise a strikingly good Christian character within the play. The nearest he comes to this sort of portrayal is with his characterisation of King Henry VI himself. But this King ultimately disappoints in a Christian as well as in every other direction. He knows his Bible and he never ceases to preach in an endless series of homilies. The writer thus leads the audience on to expect more of him than he ultimately delivers, because the first homily he utters – against civil war – is the truest:

> **K. HENRY.** Uncles of Gloster, and of Winchester,
> The special watchmen of our English weal,
> I would prevail, if prayers might prevail,
> To join your hearts in love and amity.
> O, what a scandal is it to our crown,
> That two such noble peers as ye, should jar!

> Believe me, lords, my tender years can tell,
> Civil dissention is a viperous worm,
> That gnaws the bowels of the commonwealth.

But when Gloucester and Winchester come to actual physical sparring it is not King Henry VI nor anyone who professes religiosity who puts an end to the broils. It is none other than Richard Neville, Earl of Warwick. He is from the Knights' faction at court, and not allied with any Churchman. He uses no religious imagery at all to make his point:

> **WARWICK.** Yield, my Lord Protector; yield, Winchester;
> Except you mean with obstinate repulse
> To slay your sovereign and destroy the realm.
> You see what mischief, and what murder too,
> Hath been enacted through your enmity;
> Then be at peace, except ye thirst for blood.
> {ACT3|SC1}

Altogether, therefore, it is reasonable to assume that the writer is arguing for the secularisation of politics. The evidence surely points in this direction, and this direction only. Richard Neville, the Kingmaker, though flawed, is the ablest, most honest politician in the play.

Of course, there is neither coincidence of philosophy nor of personality here! Richard Neville, the Kingmaker, was Henry Neville's ancestor, and shared his name. What else could have made the author present this ambitious nobleman in so favourable a light? When we realise too that the placement of Richard Neville here as the Earl of Warwick at this early point in Henry VI's reign is entirely anachronistic, then the evidence for Henry Neville's authorship again scores an extra point. The real Earl of Warwick at the time was Richard **Beauchamp**, Richard Neville inheriting the position at a later date.[193] Yet we can be sure that it is Richard *Neville* who is meant here, because the Duke of York, in a soliloquy, declares Warwick and his father (who is named as the Earl of Salisbury in the play) to be 'Nevils':

> A day will come, when York shall claim his own ;
> And therefore I will take the Nevils' parts,
> And make a show of love to proud duke Humphrey,
> And, when I spy advantage, claim the crown,
> For that's the golden mark I seek to hit : ...

SUPERSTITION AND IMAGERY IN HENRY VI, PART ONE

It is noticeable that although the Duke of York has a harsh word to say about Humphrey, Duke of Gloucester, he utters no such pejorative statement concerning the Nevils. There is clearly a Neville writing this script.

Eventually, the audience is bound to tire of King Henry VI's words with no action to support them. Yet if we watch or read the three plays in succession, we certainly warm to Henry VI by the time we reach *Henry VI, part 3*. The writer has constructed the plays with the purpose of making us sick of civil war, so by the end of his trilogy it becomes obvious to us that only King Henry VI himself is consistently preaching a message of peace. It is significant that in his constancy to this ideal the King therefore expresses a wish to be king no more. Ironically, this is the first time we perceive Henry VI as the man who really *should* be King, and we begin to think that he may at last have gained the maturity necessary for the post.

The author surely intended this ironic situation to point out the ultimate contradiction inherent in kingship. Those who least long for the crown are the most fitted to wear it, while those who strive ambitiously and ruthlessly to gain it from another are the last people who should have it. First of all, though, before eventually relinquishing his kingship under pressure from the Yorkists, King Henry asks Richard Neville, Earl of Warwick, to take on the political leadership of the country:

> But, Warwick, after God, thou sett'st me free,
> And chiefly therefore I thank God and thee;
> He was the author, thou the instrument.
> Therefore, that I may conquer fortune's spite
> By living low, where fortune cannot hurt me,
> And that the people of this blessed land
> May not be punished with my thwarting stars,
> Warwick, although my head still wear the crown,
> I here resign my government to thee,
> For thou art fortunate in all thy deeds.

At first, Neville graciously declines the King's offer, saying that the Duke of Clarence should be Henry's 'Protector'. Once again, the writer is pointing out that any office of state should be thrust upon a person by others, not aimed at ambitious and go-getting individuals. This truly mirrors Henry Neville's own attitude when he did not gain the office of Secretary of State. He had a wide range of support, and truly hoped for the office. But when his best friend – Sir Ralph Winwood – got the position, he was content to work with him. Neither would Neville accept another post, which the King's favourite, Robert Carr, offered to purchase for him. Neville knew he was not the right man for that particular job. He also declared he was not prepared to let someone 'buy' him an alternative office.

In the play, however, Clarence himself insists that Warwick is the better candidate for the post of chief advisor to the king. So, in the end, King Henry himself joins Richard Neville and the Duke of Clarence (Neville's brother in law) in an alliance resembling a mini Parliament, or Privy Council, to advise the Crown and therefore govern the land:

> **King Henry** Warwick and Clarence, give me both your hands:
> Now join your hands, and with your hands your hearts,
> That no dissension hinder government.
> I make you both protectors of this land,
> While I myself will lead a private life,
> And in devotion spend my latter days,
> To sin's rebuke and my Creator's praise.

It is this kind of arrangement which we see advocated in Henry Neville's political treatise, even though it is not *precisely* the one Sir Henry had in mind. In this less than *ideal* arrangement, King Henry VI has actually devolved government onto Neville and Clarence. He has therefore gone one stage farther than Neville suggested in his treatise addressed to James I. This difference in approach between the two kings is accounted for by their very different personalities and backgrounds. Henry VI was a child king and so had been perforce accustomed to being ruled by his protectors and by Parliament, whereas King James I had always wished to rule single-handedly, if only Parliament would allow him to do so. In the case of 'simple' Henry VI, therefore, Henry Neville would clearly have preferred the king to take on more decision making; but he wished the arrogant James I to step back occasionally and become a partner, not a ruler, of Parliament.

King Henry VI's crime of omission – almost amounting to abdication – makes him seem almost as bad as the feuding warmongers who lead the rival families in these Wars of the Roses plays. A King should not opt out while it is humanly possible for him to play an active part in politics. Henry VI's peaceful philosophising would have been a useful ingredient for all the warring factions to consider. In such a situation, it was only the King who could achieve unity within his Parliamentary 'family' (as Neville termed it in his treatise.) But Henry VI palpably refused to grow up and assume his role as father of Parliament, and father of the nation. The writer of the play does not suggest a way out of this situation, but the audience would surely put two and two together: the only possible way forward in such a circumstance would be for the King to agree to present an outward show of authority to the people, and for his chosen ministers to govern the land quietly, insisting, however, that the King should still form and express his ideas and that the ministers take these into account. Abdication of a monarch was not an option, because this would leave a space which could once again become a focal point for civil war.

In his political advice to King James I, Sir Henry Neville likened the ideal relationship between King and Parliament to relationships within the family. To Sir Henry, a member of Parliament with eleven surviving children, family and methods of good government were of prime concern, and he obviously saw the two subjects as inseparable: the family was for him a microcosm of government and society at large. It could well be, then, that these very political plays sprang from Sir Henry's personal outlook. With such thoughts in his mind, it is no wonder he therefore looked into his own great family's past history, assessing their successes, failures and, above all, their fatal mistakes. King Henry VI was descended from a line of Plantagenets, just as was Sir Henry Neville. But instead of taking on board the responsibility which such a descent gave him, along with the privileges, Henry VI simply refused to attempt to govern. He was a King who held such a dangerous, unquestioning reliance on faith and religious *belief* that he failed to act. Richard Neville, Earl of Warwick, on the other hand, only mentions God towards the end of his life. He was therefore portrayed as a man of action without a firm enough philosophy of life on which to anchor himself, except on what he ultimately discovers to be the worthless anchor of belief in dynastic succession. Perhaps Sir Henry saw it incumbent upon him – as a Neville – to lead men away from this past error committed by a member of his own broader family.

What effect might watching performances of the *Henry VI* trilogy have on their audiences? They are very bloodthirsty, ruthlessly hegemonic plays concerning *English* history, which would certainly have led educated members of Shakespeare's audience to make comparisons with *Roman* history. (Both the highly and lowly educated members of the audience would have studied this.) Rome had seen these dynastic squabbles over a thousand years before English patricians were making the same mistakes. It's even probable that the plays were actually designed to encourage politicians in the audience to try to learn lessons from history. The Dauphin's reference to the Emperor Constantine (in *Henry VI, part 1*, Act 1, Sc.2,) is very apposite, because Constantine was the Roman Emperor who is credited with having established Christianity in Europe. Yet his ascendancy was marked with battles, civil war, and bloodshed, and with family member killing family member. The parallels between the birth of the Christian Church and the Wars of the Roses are all too true to be good, and it looks very much as if the playwright is surreptitiously directing us to make these parallels. He is forced to do this indirectly, by the use of imagery and passing references. To have spelt it all out in plain terms to a superstitious Elizabethan audience, indoctrinated with Christianity, and legally obliged to attend a Christian Protestant Church at least once a week, would have meant committing literary suicide. The Dauphin has just sparred with the warlike Joan of Arc when he makes his reference to Constantine. He does not, therefore, mention this Christian Emperor in the context of Christian *peace*. This inevitably makes us think of the origins of the Christian Church, and reflect that it was not born in peace but in war. By these precise, 'French–style' literary devices, the writer is therefore once again warning against supernatural, unquestioned beliefs, and hoping to encourage us to examine their historical origins. Put this together with his portrayal of Churchmen (especially Roman Catholic ones) as villains, and one cannot escape the writer's message that the Christian Church – born in blood – is not to be confused with Christian ethics and humanist morality. Because of its *new* philosophy and lack of such a bloodthirsty past, the *Protestant* church is therefore being implied as a possible solution to society's ills, based on Christian ethics.

The total effect of the Henry VI trilogy on the audiences of the day must therefore have been considerable. Many of them would never have seen drama before, so to see the enactment of conflict and warfare must have affected them profoundly. Human nature can change with nurture, but for most of the audience – especially the women – it must have seemed obscene to hear the aristocrats' conflicts and battles supported by imagery and references from Christian and other mythical sources, which most of them had been schooled to respect. The suggestion of a Christian God favouring one side rather than another in either civil or international wars must also have failed to ring true with many of the logical thinkers in the audience. The playwright, however, must have predicted these effects and have been totally aware of what he was doing. He was educating the population and teaching them to think for themselves. There is later evidence that aristocrats in the audience did indeed object to having their class and their customs paraded on the stage – as if they knew very well that the Shakespeare plays were the work of an unidentified 'insider' who was purposely laying bare the schemes, rituals and motives of the aristocratic class.[194] De-mystifying what went on at the top was certainly a *political* move.

The play of *Richard III* is a rounding-off of this whole dynastic, aristocratic family tragedy. So much war and bloodshed has been expended in pursuit of the crown that Richard sees nothing wrong with using more war, bloodshed, infanticide, and even attempted incest, to gain it for himself. Neville's solution of a partnership between King and Parliament therefore becomes the *only* solution to the problem of Kingship. If Kingship is so absolute that it gives absolute power, then ruthless men, without morals, ethics or principles, will see it as something worth fighting for, no matter who suffers in the process. If, however, Kingship affords little power – because all a monarch's would-be enactments are subject to the will of Parliament – then it will no longer be worth fighting for. In order for such a balancing of power to come about peacefully, it would have been necessary to set up a written constitution, and there is little doubt that Neville would have made moves towards this, had he not died so soon after producing his initial treatise.

If we are still seeking for really convincing evidence that a Neville wrote these plays, then we need go no further than analysing the fantasised portrayal of Richard Neville, Earl of Warwick. He is characterised as having been initially motivated solely by his *belief* in inherited Kingship. But this portrayal does not correspond with the historical record. In reality, one major reason for Richard Neville's opposition to Somerset's Lancastrian cause was that Neville was in personal dispute with Edmund, Duke of Somerset, regarding the inheritance of some really big property. There is no evidence of Richard Neville's sympathy with the Yorkist cause before this date![195] Yet the writer of the play fails to bring out this fact, inserting instead the memorable scene of what may reasonably be called a 'declaration of pure belief' in the Temple Garden, where the participants are portrayed as choosing their roses out of pure pursuance of the 'rightful' heir to the throne:

> **Somerset** Judge you, my Lord of Warwick, then, between us.
> **Warwick** Between two hawks, which flies the higher pitch?
> Between two dogs, which hath the deeper mouth?
> Between two blades, which bears the better temper?
> Between two horses, which doth bear him best?
> Between two girls, which hath the merriest eye?
> I have perhaps some shallow spirit of judgment,
> But in these nice sharp quillets of the law,
> Good faith, I am no wiser than a daw.

So Warwick has already manifested his ignorance of the law, (though this may be mere posturing on his part – playing for time in order to get the oppositional parties to show more of their characters and intentions.) But if the law really does not motivate these Lords in their choice of sides, what does?

> **Plantagenet** Tut, tut, here is a mannerly forbearance.
> The truth appears so naked on my side
> That any purblind eye may find it out.
> **Somerset** And on my side it is so well apparelled,
> So clear, so shining, and so evident,
> That it will glimmer through a blind man's eye.
> **Plantagenet** Since you are tongue-tied and so loath to speak,
> In dumb significants proclaim your thoughts.
> Let him that is a true-born gentleman
> And stands upon the honour of his birth,
> If he suppose that I have pleaded truth,
> From off this brier pluck a white rose with me.
> **Somerset** Let him that is no coward nor no flatterer,
> But dare maintain the party of the truth,
> Pluck a red rose from off this thorn with me.
> **Warwick** I love no colours, and, without all colour
> Of base insinuating flattery

SUPERSTITION AND IMAGERY IN HENRY VI, PART ONE

I pluck this white rose with Plantagenet.
Suffolk I pluck this red rose with young Somerset,
And say withal I think he held the right.
Vernon Stay, lords and gentlemen, and pluck no more,
Till you conclude that he, upon whose side
The fewest roses from the tree are cropped,
Shall yield the other in the right opinion.
Somerset Good Master Vernon, it is well objected:
If I have fewest, I subscribe in silence.
Plantagenet And I.
Vernon Then, for the truth and plainness of the case,
I pluck this pale and maiden blossom here,
Giving my verdict on the white rose side.
Somerset Prick not your finger as you pluck it off,
Lest, bleeding, you do paint the white rose red,
{*ACT II, SC.iv*}

So, the *surface* picture is one of whimsical Lords who are patently able to afford the luxury of shallow thinking. Our Neville would surely have met just such courtiers already and now wished to display to the audience that privilege of birth can indeed bestow its blessings on unworthy men. Not only is this a brilliant piece of theatre, but the political and personal implications of this fanciful scene are vast. First and foremost, Richard Neville denies any learning to back up his decision: he is motivated only by belief. Secondly, there is no mention of the huge dispute he was having with Somerset at the time in reality – a dispute which had by then led to actual fighting between them, plus the seizure of a couple of castles by Neville in order to prevent Somerset taking them. The writer is therefore crediting a Neville with more honour than he had in reality, even if he is willing to admit that there is a side to Richard Neville which can be either shallow or posturing. Yet the writer is also saying, "Beware the Nevilles: one never quite knows whether they are serious or just good actors." Indeed, all this occurs before the murder of Gloucester, when the star of Richard Neville truly begins to shine out brightly to the audience, because it is Neville, like a true detective, who analyses the corpse and the whole circumstances of Gloucester's death, proving that a Neville is not as shallow as he might at first seem. A Neville, therefore, stands out above the rest. At the same time, the writer is including something which knocks at the centre of power in the State: he is at the start of his demonstration of how destructive a thing inherited monarchy can be, per se. As the trilogy proceeds, this latter aspect of these shallow Lords' fateful decision is reinforced with the depiction of war and bloodshed to which this idea of Kingship leads. All this, therefore, provides evidence not only of how the writer is making us analyse unreasonable beliefs, but, by omitting to show Richard Neville's baser motives, he is also providing evidence that a politically-motivated member of the Neville family is behind the authorship of these plays.

Neville himself was a Parliamentarian who knew he had something great to offer towards a peaceful political solution when it came to managing the government of an advancing society. As a Neville, he would therefore have seen it as his duty to attempt to bring about this kind of peaceful society. Did he therefore write these plays with this dutiful aim in mind? Also, was the main reason for his pseudonymous identity a selfless wish to see the ideas he presented in them discussed and put into action? It seems likely, because he must have known that his audience/readers might well become cynical about the ideas themselves, if they suspected that Sir Henry, the courtier and politician, was the true author who could therefore seem to be promoting the ideas for his own personal reasons rather than the good of the state. By keeping his authorship secret, he avoided such a cynical conclusion, leaving the ideas to speak for themselves. This is an entirely plausible and reasonable scenario, and if it illuminates the plays and their selfless motivation then it is also a helpful and inspirational discovery.

Henry Neville's vision of a new order (as given in his pseudonymous plays) also proposes that the Knights of Parliament should be at peace with each other so as to present a united front to the King. Only if they felt themselves to be united and equal, and put aside their ambition to be Kings themselves, would Neville's solution work – and he must have known this. The best of the Knights (like Talbot) in the *Henry VI* trilogy therefore exhibit an 'all for one and one for all' mentality (which actually happened to be the motto of the Earls of Southampton too.) It was this attitude, together with the 'chivalrous' side of knighthood which Sir Henry wished to foster.

In presenting my evidence for Shakespeare/Neville's symbolism suggesting the rejection of superstition and fixed beliefs, I am aware that Frances Yates makes arguments which suggest otherwise. Yates claimed the later plays were imbued with some sort of *belief* in magic. I disagree. The evidence of the texts points to a writer who *knew* about these beliefs, but who wanted his audience to *question* them. However, I have dealt here with the *earlier* plays, which were written before the emergence of a formalised set of Rosicrucian ideals, whereas Yates expressed her opinion from evidence in the *later* plays. But even in those later dramas there is surely a sense where the 'magic' is undermined by what the author has his characters say, and undermined also by the diegesis itself.[196] For instance, even in *The Tempest*, Prospero voluntarily says goodbye to the old belief systems. He abjures the 'rough magic' with which has presented the audience, and this play contains the same sort of philosophical reverie as that within *A Midsummer Night's Dream*. Moreover, *The Dream* itself ends by asking the audience to think that they have merely been asleep while watching the play! It is surely more as if the writer is treating the old beliefs as some sort of beguiling, informing myth. So we come full circle: the secret societies, formed by a fusion of romantic notions of knighthood combined with the rituals, and *practical* ingredients, of the Guilds, began performing these myths but also showing them up for what they were: fables only, which should be treated as educational parables, not accepted as literal truths. Surely this is exactly the attitude towards magic and belief that Shakespeare-Neville was trying to engender in his plays. He was certainly not suggesting that there could really be some truth behind the astrological and alchemical nonsense of the times. The abjuration of magic, the outspoken criticism of astrology we find in *King Lear*, the natural, not supernatural, preservation of Hermione's life in *The Winter's Tale* all point in one direction: that a 'new-age' scientist is behind the plays, not a practising mystic.

Chapter Ten

NEVILLE'S GRANDFATHER IN THE WIDE SEA OF WAX – A TRANSGENERATIONAL WARNING

> **Poet** You see this confluence, this great flood of visitors.
> I have in this rough work shaped out a man
> Whom this beneath world doth embrace and hug
> With amplest entertainment. My free drift
> Halts not particularly, but moves itself
> In a wide sea of wax. No levelled malice
> Infects one comma in the course I hold,
> But flies an eagle flight, bold and forth on,
> Leaving no tract behind....
> **Timon of Athens,** Act 1. Sc.1

There are signs that Sir Henry Neville's grandfather's experiences affected him deeply and became a lesson from history in many diverse ways. Reflections of his grandfather are therefore visible in his plays, as well as becoming lessons for his everyday life. Yet Shakespeare-Neville was moving in such a "wide sea of wax" that it was difficult for anyone who did not know the true identity of the author to tease out resemblances between the stage characters he created and those whom he knew – or knew about – in real life. Added to this, as with all writers of the time, Shakespeare-Neville was able to combine the personalities and experiences of at least two real people when he created any single character in his plays. Timon of Athens therefore appears to be a combination of Sir Henry's own experiences, with some of his grandfather's mixed in.

Our Henry Neville, like Timon, sank into deep debt after he spent his own money on his expenses while Ambassador in France, and doubly so after he was fined for his part in the Essex rebellion. Like Timon too, he was then put under house arrest for a time. But Timon is portrayed as once having been the life and soul of every social gathering, whereas Henry Neville was a very private man. It was his grandfather's life rather than his own on which he drew for that side of Timon's behaviour. For instance, our Henry was known to be ambitious for high office, but it was remarked upon that, nevertheless, he did not often appear at public ceremonies.[197] This was surely in conscious contrast to his grandfather Edward's decision to be always on show, always with the King, jousting, dancing, singing, quipping and merry-making. This was the side of Edward's character, therefore, that was incorporated into the character of Timon. But Sir Edward Neville's career was nevertheless to end in a massive fall from favour, like Timon's. Indeed, Edward's fate was even sadder than Timon's because it ended with his execution, so it is little wonder that his grandson decided to take a much quieter path towards political promotion.

My contention is, however, that Sir Edward Neville's experiences also found themselves mirrored, and/or re-worked, in more than just one play – more than in *Timon of Athens* alone. In fact, a set of web-like connections within the great Shakespeare History plays shows Henry is cognisant of Edward and his circle, and that the writer may be attempting the difficult task of settling old scores by vilifying some characters from history whose very names stir up painful memories for the Nevilles generally and for our Sir Henry in particular. This chapter will therefore firstly be concerned with an exposition of the life of Sir Edward Neville (1482–1538) incorporating an examination of where his experiences are echoed in the Shakespeare plays.

Sir Edward Neville was born at Addington Park, near Maidstone in Kent. He was a younger son of George Neville, second Baron Bergavenny. Edward's older brother George, to whom he remained close, became the third Baron Bergavenny. In fact, Edward's popularity with King Henry VIII was connected with the respect in which he held George, and also another brother, Sir Thomas Neville, who became speaker of the House of Commons in 1515. (Thomas' career therefore already marks out the fact that the younger, male, untitled members of the Neville family invariably became involved in politics.)

As a squire of the body, Edward Neville attended Henry VII's funeral in 1509, and he eventually became a gentleman of the privy chamber. There must therefore have been a certain amount of rivalry between Thomas Wolsey – the ambitious churchman – and Edward Neville when it came to winning the King's favour. Edward was popular with the King because of his wit and boisterous good humour. But Wolsey gained popularity with the King in a very different manner. He did so by cutting through a lot of the administrative red tape that kept some of the

King's wishes in check. Until a number of seals were present on a document, the policies outlined in that document could not be enacted. Consequently, Wolsey pleased the King by changing this procedure, allowing Henry a much freer rein. Yet such changes must have taken Wolsey time and serious discussion to enact, so he would have been aware that he was actually losing face to face contact with the King while he set about this business. This, then, may have been why Wolsey perceived young, good-time noblemen like Edward Neville as a threat.

Wolsey therefore attempted to become fun-loving too, arranging banquets to which he invited the King. Edward Neville, however, does not seem to have appeared on Wolsey's guest lists – after all, his somewhat riotous good company, singing and composing ad hoc quasi-satirical verses at the drop of a hat would very possibly have outshone Wolsey's abilities. So Edward and his friends devised a ruse for gate-crashing one of Wolsey's banquets.

Edward was among a group of masquers who arrived unexpectedly at a Wolsey party, at which the King was a guest. Edward took advantage of the moment by disguising himself as King Henry VIII. (Before Henry VIII became seriously overweight, he had indeed resembled him.) Wolsey was apparently taken in at first by Edward's disguise, though he seems to have glossed over the incident by ultimately unmasking him in front of the whole company, probably thereby hoping no one would make fun of his initial mistake.

This would have been a marvellous incident to have elaborated upon in Shakespeare's *Henry VIII,* as Shakespearean scholars have since pointed out. Yet the playwright left out specific mention of Sir Edward Neville and did not make as much of the whole charade as he might have done. It would surely have extended the masquing scene in a play which is otherwise so political that it needed to make the most of every diversion that could possibly be included. My contention is that the only reason the playwright did not milk it for all it was worth is because the real author did not wish to leave a 'tract behind' – he still wanted his sea of wax to be moulded to fit many possible authors, not to leave such an identifiable Neville footprint in it.

Edward's jousting and hunting abilities added to his lively image so it was only Wolsey, not Henry VIII himself, who took offence at the masquing incident. Indeed, the young Henry VIII must have thought he had truly found a soul mate in Sir Edward.

Under his tourneying name, 'Valiant Desire', Edward played in several pageants, sometimes a little too enthusiastically, for he once almost killed his opponent. Unfortunately, this victim had, for a moment, been thought to be the King himself. (Jousting armour hid identities very effectively. Is this yet another reason why the real author chose the image of a knight's 'shaking spear' for his pseudonym?)

By chance, this unfortunate jouster (William Compton) had also been a friend of Thomas Wolsey, and Wolsey became guardian of Compton's son after William's death. (One already sees a pattern of Wolsey rounding up against his enemies, as later described in Shakespeare's *Henry VIII*.)

Edward was present at the capture of Tournai in 1513, for which he received his knighthood, so it is beginning to look as if he may even have been one model for the military side of Richard Neville, Earl of Warwick, in the *Henry VI* trilogy. He was also chosen by Henry VIII to represent him at tournaments given outside Paris prior to his sister's [Princess Mary] coronation as queen of France, in 1514, following her marriage to Louis XII. Henry VIII then became godfather of Edward's son, Henry, (who was our Henry Neville's father.) Even the *young* Henry Neville must therefore have felt the truth of the Biblical adage 'put not your trust in princes' because, clearly, having a king as a godfather to one's son did not protect you from eventual disfavour and execution. In 1520, Edward was present at the Field of Cloth of Gold celebrations with Henry VIII and Francois I of France, so it was certainly a case of the mighty falling when Edward Neville tumbled from grace.

Following the pageantry of the Cloth of Gold, Edward fought twice under the Earl of Suffolk, in 1523 and 1526, and it may well have been that Shakespeare/Neville was alerted to an Earl of Suffolk's womanising tendencies partly through tales his grandfather told of the particular Earl of Suffolk whom he knew personally. (Stories and names passed down families are often redolent with meaning for playwrights.)

The particular Earl of Suffolk known to Edward Neville was Charles Brandon. Brandon's promotion to the title of Duke of Suffolk was attained through the personal desire of King Henry VIII, but much criticised throughout the Court. It was rumoured that the promotion had been given in order to enable Brandon to marry Margaret of Austria, regent of the Netherlands. Brandon – rather like William de la Pole, Earl of Suffolk, in the Henry VI plays – had been openly flirting with this lady during Henry's visits to her court in 1513. But, unlike Margaret of Anjou in the plays, Margaret of Austria was having none of it. She even demanded that the king should cancel Brandon's projected visit to the Netherlands in order to put a final end to the rumours of any possible marriage between her and the Duke. No wonder Margaret reacted in such a manner: Brandon was then actually engaged to Lady Lisle, while he had also been married twice between 1503 and 1510.

Moreover, there was a Shakespearean-Nevillian connection with Brandon's first wife, Anne Browne, and Anne Browne's mother had actually been a Neville. Shakespeare's patron is often said to have been Henry Wriothesley, third Earl of Southampton, and although there is no evidence to that effect, what we do know is that Southampton was *Sir Henry Neville's* friend, 'champion' and Tower companion. There is therefore no way that Neville would not have heard about Brandon's marital adventures, through both the Nevilles and though Southampton himself, because Anne Browne was daughter of Sir Anthony Browne, and Sir Anthony Browne was Southampton's great, great grandfather. Scandalously, Brandon had secretly married Anne Browne, but when she became pregnant he abandoned her. Even more reprehensibly, he went on to marry her aunt as his second wife, so both the Wriothesleys and Nevilles must have been buzzing with Brandon's name . Anthony Browne, Anne's father, was married to Lucy Neville, daughter of Sir John Neville, 1st and last Marquess of Montagu, so the reasons behind the true playwright's wish to label the name of 'Suffolk' with womanising becomes overwhelmingly clear. No other authorship candidate has such potent reasons for characterising the Earl of Suffolk so disparagingly in the plays.

The Love/Hate relationship between the Nevilles and the Tudors

The Tudors knew very well that the Nevilles should probably be the true inheritors of the Crown, as far as correct dynastic succession was concerned. It is therefore not surprising to see that Henry VIII seemed to be constantly pursuing some argument or other against members of the Neville family, even while outward appearances proclaimed him to be on good terms with Edward Neville. One quarrel he had was with George Neville, Baron Bergavenny, Edward's brother. George had supported his father-in-law over the course of a long argument he had with the king. George Neville was Edward Stafford's (Duke of Buckingham's) son-in-law, and his support for Buckingham impelled Henry VIII to ban poor George from his presence. From an outsider's view, it looks very much as if Henry VIII might have fomented a quarrel with Stafford, perhaps to gain some of the manors and land which his father, Henry VII, had put into Stafford's hands. But whatever the true cause, it led to a rift between Stafford, the Nevilles and King Henry VIII, from which the King and Wolsey had everything to gain (materially speaking) and the Staffords and Nevilles everything to lose.

Buckingham's story was told in *Henry VIII* – and told from a Nevillian point of view in that the writer's sympathies were clearly with Buckingham. His title and different surname obviously made it safer for the true Neville author to pursue Buckingham's cause rather than that of his own grandfather. The Duke of Buckingham was a *cloaked* Nevillian, whereas Edward Neville would have to have been openly named. Whereas this Nevillian naming of characters had been just about permissable before the writer's 'disgrace' and imprisonment, things were now completely different.

Yet, in real life, Henry VIII must have missed the Nevilles' presence, because ten months after the incident various family members were re-instated at court, though with a little more reserve on the King's part than heretofore. One can perhaps understand Henry VIII's guarded reservations. He must have had concerns about what the wider Neville 'clan' was up to. The Bulmers, for instance, were inter-married with the Nevilles, and one of them seems to have openly displayed his loyalty to the out-of-favour Duke of Buckingham – *too* openly for the King's liking. Sir William Bulmer appeared in the King's presence wearing Buckingham's livery. This was a dangerous enough action, given the Duke's outcast situation, but there was an added insult: Sir William Bulmer was a member of the King's household and should therefore have been wearing the *King's* livery. It was a *doubly* intentional action on Bulmer's part, since the father in law of *Edward* Neville – Bulmer's kinsman – was keeper of the Great Wardrobe. This meant that Edward Neville's father in law could easily have provided Bulmer with the King's livery, and indeed it was ultimately his responsibility to see that Bulmer wore it. So in 1519, Bulmer was actually charged in the Star Chamber with this open offence. It was even noted in Halle's Chronicles that the

King remarked "he would none of his servants should hang on another man's sleeve."

On top of this, Buckingham himself began to complain that the King's love of pageantry was hitting his own purse. (Buckingham, like Edward Neville, was involved in the great expense of accompanying the King at the Field of Cloth of Gold in 1520.) Moreover, Buckingham apparently also angered Wolsey around the same time by openly defending Katherine of Aragon when Wolsey had just rebuked her. The result of all this was that Buckingham was executed in 1521, which must have made Edward Neville's relationship with the King rather uneasy from that time onwards. After all, the king was well aware that Buckingham was a Stafford, and that they were long inter-married with the Nevilles. (Buckingham was father in law to George Neville – our Sir Henry Neville's great uncle.)

It is doubly interesting, therefore, that Buckingham was later to feature prominently in Shakespeare's *Henry VIII*. To a Neville-writer, it would seem a lot safer to place Buckingham in the play rather than a character openly-named 'Neville'. But if it were anyone other than a Neville writing the play, the inclusion of Buckingham and the exclusion of Edward Neville is totally inexplicable.

This exclusion of the Neville **name** was of course in contrast to the very earliest of the History Plays – the *Henry VI* trilogy – in which the Nevilles were mentioned by name and played a prominent role. And it isn't hard to see the reason behind this change. At the beginning of Elizabeth's reign, the old Sir Henry Neville was really in favour with the Queen, teaching her and her ladies how to hunt, devising court entertainments, etc. His son would therefore have less to fear in naming past Nevilles, at this particular point in his life. But by the time he wrote *Henry VIII* – a project which he began while imprisoned in the Tower of London[198] – our Henry had been disgraced, and felt he had disgraced the Neville name. Even though a new dynasty was on the throne when *Henry VIII* was completed, Henry Neville had had his problems with this new monarch too, as seen in previous chapters, so it was definitely wiser for a Neville writer not to portray the misdeeds and execution of his own direct ancestor on stage.

When all the evidence is put together, it appears, therefore, that Henry VIII may have perceived the gathering together of the wider Neville clan as a possible 'conspiracy'. Was he justified in his suspicions, or was he putting two and two together and making five? We shall probably never really know, but it is nevertheless interesting to see what effect all this seems to have had on Neville's own father and, in turn, on his son, our Henry.

First and foremost, it will be noticed that Henry Neville senior married into the bourgeoisie rather than the aristocracy. His first fiancée/wife was Winifred Losse, daughter of Henry VIII's surveyor; his second a Gresham – Elizabeth Gresham, who stemmed from a family who were financiers and a major trading house. Our Henry, his son, followed suit. He married Anne Killigrew, daughter of a Cornish gentleman, whose family was only just beginning to be recognised as 'genteel'. Indeed, the wider Killigrew clan in Cornwall still included free-booters, and even pirates.

The point is that none of these wives brought with them any 'white rose' history – or, at least, not openly so, for their names were still new in courtly circles. Henry Neville senior made friends with the Sidneys, Killigrews and the Cecils, who were not, at the time, perceived as any threat to the monarchy. Our own Henry Neville similarly chose to be seen with non-dynastic companions, prominent among whom were scholars (like Henry Savile) and emerging middle class gentlemen, such as Ralph Winwood and Thomas Edmondes. In fact, his only initial variation from this rule was his friendship with the Earls of Southampton and Essex, which he did his best, however, to keep secret (probably suspecting that open friendship with them might one day look like a dangerous Plantagenet alliance.) He did not become openly friendly with the Herberts, including William Herbert, Earl of Pembroke, until it became absolutely clear that this family too were liberally-minded and against absolute monarchy.

Through his Gresham ancestry, Henry Neville also became interested in trade and politics, rather than just a career at court. By becoming interested in the arts, especially plays and the public theatre (as witness his reading of Beaumont and Fletcher[199]) he was distancing himself from those courtiers who took up the truly 'courtly' pastime of jousting. Some of his social life seems to have centred around the Mitre Club and its literary frequenters, who were not prominent at court. As well as following his own interests, therefore, Neville was surely absorbing yet another lesson from his grandfather's sad history: closeness to the monarch could mean (for a Neville) that the monarch might begin to perceive ulterior motives for the friendship.

Edward Neville and the King's Wardrobe
In 1532, Edward Neville was in France again with the King. Edward was then sewer at the coronation feast of Queen Anne Boleyn, whose coronation was portrayed in *Henry VIII*, with that very scene having been pre-figured in our Henry's 'Tower Notebook'[200]. In 1533 Edward was nominated to be a 'knight for Kent' – just as his young grandson was later to become a knight for Sussex.

Edward Neville was particularly fortunate in his marriage, and his choice must have been especially interesting to a grandson who became a playwright, for his wife was the daughter of Andrew, first Baron Windsor, keeper of the Great Wardrobe. This was an important office which must have brought Andrew into contact with just about every courtier and court event, because Baron Windsor oversaw the provision of cloth and craftsmen to create not only the king's wardrobe but the costumes of all those who surrounded him in his pageantry. Even the dressing of the horses for jousting was ultimately the responsibility of the keeper of the wardrobe, as can be seen from the account books:

> Warrant to the Great Wardrobe to pay Th. Foster, "one of our broderes," for embroidering horse harness, &c. Greenwich, 12 Jan. 3 Hen. VIII.[201]

And the king's trumpeter was similarly provided for:

> Warrant to the Great Wardrobe to deliver John Blak, "our trompeter," a gown of violet cloth, &c., including a bonnet and a hat, "to be taken of our gift against his marriage." Greenwich, 14 Jan. 3 Hen. VIII.[202]

The King's bounteous costume budget even stretched to providing favourite courtiers with their wedding outfits:

> Warrant to the Great Wardrobe to deliver Ric. Mayre, "one of the yeomen of our Ewery, for his wedding apparel, a gown cloth of violet containing four broad yards

and as much black Irish lamb as will suffice to fur the same," also tawny chamlet for a jacket, and for his wife "three broad yards of violet cloth for her gown." Greenwich, 12 Jan. 3 Hen. VIII.[203]

Indeed, Henry VIII's wardrobe became one of the earliest ways in which he broke with the comparative austerity of his father's court. He was a lively, impressive 18 year old when he succeeded to the throne in 1509, another reason why theatricality became the order of the day, and why the young king encouraged artists and designers, who eagerly now pressed to gain influence at the court. A papal emissary came to London in 1515 and reported on the new magnificence of the English court. This, it seems, then encouraged continental kings to try and follow suit. The splendour of the Renaissance was truly stretching northwards, and the people were beginning to expect an outward show from their leaders. A drastic expansion of the 'Great Wardrobe' (as the court office responsible for the management of all this splendour was named) was therefore necessary. It began to extend along a whole street by the Thames, employing five officers under Baron Windsor (Neville's great grandfather), keeping an eye on the standards of the craftsmen they contracted. Altogether, therefore, it is easy to see how noblemen fitted out so lavishly from this office were able eventually to pass on their out of date but beautiful and hard-wearing costumes to the Globe actors for their plays. Also worthy of note is the fact that our Henry Neville was born and baptised in this vicinity and had such a family history of costume and pageantry behind him.

Edward Neville's break with the King
As we have seen, Edward Neville had been somewhat under the thumb of his older brother, Baron Bergavenny, when it came to marital and other alliances he made at court. These included the Courtenay and de la Pole families but, unfortunately, they were the very ones who began to oppose Henry VIII after the death of George Neville in 1535. At the same time, Edward Neville was noticing a change for the worse in the king, as the latter set out on his ruthless marital adventures. Catherine of Aragon was actually related to the Nevilles (through their common descent from John of Gaunt), so it is not surprising that his attitude was therefore going to be doubly condemnatory. "The King is a beast, and worse than a beast." he was heard to declare. And he

also let it be known in no uncertain terms that he did not like the king's choice of new members of the privy chamber, "The king keepeth a sort of knaves here that we dare not speak; and if I were able to live, I would rather live any life in the world than tarry in the privy chamber."[204]

Such utterances were not going to maintain Edward's same old position with the king, but they were inspired by the king's own actions and a seeming change of tactics. Henry VIII's youth was characterised by a dominant wish for open friendship and enjoyment, based on a policy of 'forgive and forget' as far as past Wars of the Roses family alliances were concerned. But this seems to undergo a sea change during the time in which the controversy surrounding his divorce from Catherine of Aragon was taking place. Perhaps his new attitude was partly brought on by a realisation that Catherine was related to the Nevilles (who had been predominantly of the white rose faction in the Wars); but if so, then it demonstrated a confusion on the king's part about what was now really happening in the land. New alliances were being forged, old ones breaking down, mainly because the question of the divorce was beginning to throw people into Protestant v. Catholic stances, thus inevitably changing some of the old family allegiances.

Henry VIII may also have overlooked the fact that other families in addition to the Tudors had already been consciously trying to make alliances with families of opposing colours in the old wars. For instance, the de la Pole dukes of Suffolk had been of the Red Rose faction in the Wars, but they were now inter-marrying with the white-rose Nevilles. Yet in his next set of actions, the king seems to have been hardly aware that this rather momentous peace-making was going on. He began to move suddenly and brutally against the old white rose faction. The punishments he meted out to them were far harsher than to others concerned in the same 'conspiracies'. This was the discrimination of which Sir Edward Neville – our Henry Neville's grandfather – was to fall foul.

The story of Edward Neville's final downfall goes alongside that of the Pole family – traditionally the dukes of Suffolk. It was this red-rose family of Poles who were now rebelling; yet they did not receive as much punishment as their white-rose kinsmen. There seems little evidence that Edward Neville was really fully involved with the Poles and their conspiracy. Still, nevertheless, it was Edward who was ultimately executed, not the leading Pole in the business. Reginald de la Pole was a cardinal who wrote against Henry VIII's divorce from Catherine of Aragon, and it was his brother, Geoffrey, (who seems to have been a one time friend of Edward Neville's) who ultimately brought about Neville's execution. Yet Edward Neville had shown no sign of animosity to Anne Boleyn, even though he considered the king himself was behaving like a beast, and even though he was far from being the only courtier to voice such an opinion. Indeed, Anne Boleyn had agreed to grant Edward Neville a keepership on one of her Kentish manors, which she would hardly have done, had she thought him any kind of personal enemy.[205]

In the end, Reginald de la Pole resided safely in Italy, though he was seriously worried that the King might take out his vengeance on his mother and brother. Yet King Henry did not do so. Instead, he inappropriately targeted Sir Edward Neville. Only the memory of old red rose/white rose allegiances could have prompted such an action. Even those Poles who were finally put to death over the matter had a Neville connection. Edward Neville had two sisters, Jane and Elizabeth. Jane was actually executed in 1539 along with her husband Henry Pole, 1st Baron Montagu, as he was the elder brother of Reginald Pole. Our Sir Henry therefore lost his great aunt, as well as his grandfather, to the axe, though even Thomas Cromwell – Reginald Pole's chief accuser – said that Jane and Henry Pole had really not 'offended' at all, except by being Reginald's kin. This is of course all rather inexplicable, unless one understands that any new dynasty after the Wars of the Roses would be bound to fear the Nevilles, and thus to harbour a latent yet constant desire to curtail their power and influence. Perhaps this followed in the wake of Richard Neville, the Kingmaker's, energy, popularity and power; or perhaps it was simply because the Nevilles were always able to claim a good dynastic right; or perhaps it was simply jealousy of their wealth, wit and possessions. But whatever the reason – or combination of reasons – the upshot was that no Neville could consider himself safe, which already says enough to explain our Sir Henry's determination to hide behind a pseudonym.

The marked difference between the treatment of the erstwhile white rose faction can surely only be explained by the Tudor king's sense of grumbling dynastic rivalry with the Neville family. But our Sir Henry doubtless also perceived the trouble as having been caused partly by Catholicism, and the de la Poles had remained firmly Catholic. Once again, it has to be noted that any supposed link between the Shakespeare texts and Catholicism has no textual evidence behind it. Indeed, even those who consider Shakespeare of Stratford to be the true author display an illogical step in their reasoning if they consider that same Shakespeare was a Catholic. All those who consider Shakespeare might have been a Catholic also seem to say that there is no doubt that the third Earl of Southampton was his patron. Yet the third Earl of Southampton was so strongly Protestant (as far as he showed any religious interest at all) that he fought alongside the Earl of Essex for the right of the then Protestant Henri of Navarre to succeed to the French throne. What's more, Southampton fought on the Protestant side in at least two other continental wars, and is even said to have given money to Frederick, the 'lost' Prince of Bohemia, who was considered the great hope for continental Protestantism during King James I's reign!

But, leaving religion aside for the moment, it should by now be becoming clear that Neville's grandfather was the epitome of the situation described by *Timon of Athen*'s Poet. Sir Edward Neville had been a favourite at court, lauded by the King, the life and soul of every party, till Fortune turned her wheel and crushed him. Even the image of Edward's well-known skill at horse-riding – his foot in the stirrup – is present in the imagery of the Poet's speech from *Timon*:

> All those which were his fellows but of late,
> Some better than his value, on the moment
> Follow his strides, his lobbies fill with tendance,
> Rain sacrificial whisperings in his ear,
> Make sacred even his stirrup, and through him
> Drink the free air.
> **Painter** Ay, marry, what of these?
> **Poet** When Fortune in her shift and change of mood
> Spurns down her late beloved, all his dependants,
> Which laboured after him to the mountain's top
> Even on their knees and hands, let him slip down,
> Not one accompanying his declining foot.

The Poet cleverly transmutes the meaning of 'stirrup' from 'stirrup **cup**' (with its associations of horsemanship as well as drinking) to a man alone on his 'declining foot', thus bringing in the image of a man slipping from his horse. Moreover, we see Timon being abandoned by his 'dependants' in the same way as

Edward Neville suffered for the Pole conspirators, all of whom finally escaped, except for those with a direct Neville connection.

Edward Neville and Some Forgotten Sources of *Richard III* and *Henry VIII*

The Edward Stafford (1478–1521), who was a relative of the Nevilles and was alive during the reign of Richard III, actually rebelled against that monarch. The Duke of Buckingham even said that his father (Stafford) had planned to stab Richard III to death: so here's where Henry Neville's stories of that 'bad king' may have begun to be passed down the Neville family. Added to this, one of Richard Neville, Earl of Warwick's daughters was married to the Duke of Clarence, who was murdered on the King's orders by being 'drowned in a butt of Malmsy wine'; so once again we can see where the true writer of the plays had rooted his point of view, even though his friend, the Earl of Southampton, held a very different opinion of that King. (For Southampton, Richard III was a man much maligned by Tudor history. Southampton therefore sent a treatise concerning this to Sir Henry Neville.[206])

Sir Geoffrey Pole, (d. 1558), who was related to Edward Neville, owned a manuscript of Sir Thomas More's History of Richard III. This is the manuscript which, above all, recounts the evil of that king, and therefore the work on which Shakespeare's play was based, more than any other. Although some of it appears in some form in Halle's Chronicles, Rastell – the first publisher to print More's original work in 1557 – makes the point that Halle's version had greatly altered the original. Rastell's publication was limited in number and not widely available. Indeed, it was only part of a huge folio edition of More's works, which was rare and expensive, so some Shakespearean scholars' bland assertion that Shakespeare would have had access to it fails to be substantiated. Yet, for all that, Shakespeare's play follows More's text extremely closely, even recounting (in dramatic form) some of the smaller incidents. Moreover, Rastell's version leaves blanks for the names of some of the protagonists,207 yet 'Shakespeare', inexplicably, seems to know them!

More such amazing anomalies occur between Shakespeare and the authorship of *King Henry VIII*. This play has received scant attention, probably due in part to its very political (rather than strikingly dramatic) nature. But it may also be due to the fact that Tennyson declared he thought it to have been written partly by

John Fletcher (though with very little evidence)[208] . It was, however, entirely possible for Fletcher to have assisted Neville in writing the play, since the Fletchers – like Neville – worked in the diplomatic service, and since John Fletcher's father had lived near the Mayfield estate where Neville, his great uncle Thomas Gresham, and his father all had a hand in ironworking. As detailed in my previous books too, Beaumont and Fletcher sent our Neville their plays for assessment. Yet for all that, Neville could have written the play alone. After all, *Henry VIII* fits in with the very political nature of some of the other late Shakespeare plays, especially *Coriolanus,* so there is no real reason to see any other hand in it.

Curiously, although Shakespeare's *Henry VIII* pretends – by its title – to be about that king, it is far more concerned with Thomas Wolsey, his downfall and his influence on King Henry. And Thomas Wolsey was a politician, despite his religious titles and pretensions. So why did the author call it 'Henry VIII' ? Perhaps titling the play after a politician would have given more of a clue to its true authorship. Titling it *Thomas Wolsey* would also certainly have given a clue to its major source, which was not available to Shakespeare of Stratford.

The play also follows closely a text by George Cavendish (1494 – c. 1562), entitled *Thomas Wolsey, Late Cardinall, his Lyffe and Deathe.* The Oxford Dictionary of National Biography describes this as the "most important single contemporary source for Wolsey's life", and that work also details the King's divorce from Catherine of Aragon. Yet Cavendish's work remained exclusively in handwritten manuscript form until 1825. However, the Nevilles, who were so near the centre of government, would have been among those who possessed a copy, even though it could not be widely circulated for many years after it was written, due to the sensitive nature of its material content. Even in Queen Elizabeth's days, it would have been thought less than 'proper' to possess openly a copy of a text which detailed her own controversial parentage. Samuel Weller Singer was the publisher of the 1825 edition, and he said that Shakespeare "merely put Cavendish's language into verse." Altogether, therefore, my contention is that Neville had the motives, opportunity, family knowledge and political inclination to write this play; the least likely author of all is William Shakespeare of Stratford.

In looking at Neville's grandfather alongside *Henry VIII*, I did not wish to convey the idea that Neville wrote this play simply as a catharsis. Far from it. The play carries a number of *political* messages, one of the main celebrations in the play being the final triumph of the Protestant religion in England. It is this note which ends the play, surely: we see Henry VIII in triumphal mood, having won against the Pope, and having become the father of the new, glorious, Protestant Queen Elizabeth. The praise of her and that king yet to come – the 'star' who will follow Elizabeth – are therefore declaimed too. This firmly puts King James I alongside Henry VIII and Elizabeth I as the embodiment of the continuation of the Protestant line. A very Nevillian ending.

> Richard duke of Glou=
> cester the thirde sonne(of whiche I must moste en=
> treate)was in witte and courage egall with the o=   *The discri=*
> ther,but in beautee and liniamentes of nature far   *ption of Ri=*
> vnderneth bothe, for he was litle of stature, eiuill *charde the*
> feautered of limnes, croke backed, the left shulder *thirde.*
> muche higher then the right, hard fauoured of vi=
> sage,suche as in estates is called a warlike visage,
> and emong commen persones a crabbed face. He
> was malicious, wrothfull and enuious, and as it
> is reported, his mother the duches had muche a
> dooe in her trauaill, that she could not bee deliue=
> red of hym vncut, and that he came into the world
> the fete forwarde, as menne bee borne outwarde,
> and as the fame ranne, not vntothed, whether that
> menne of hatred reported aboue the truthe, or that
> nature chaūged his course in his beginnyng, whi=
> che in his life many thynges vnnaturalli commit=
> ted, this I leue to God his iudgemente. He was
> none eiuil capitain in warre, as to whiche, his dis=
> posicion was more enclined too then too peace.

Copy of a page from Sir Thomas More's Richard III. The description of the King is very closely followed by 'Shakespeare', yet the work was not widely available.

Chapter Eleven

SIR HENRY NEVILLE AND THE SONNETS IN THE TOWER

In this chapter I shall be examining some of the letters concerning Sir Henry Neville, now present in the library of Hatfield House. These consist mainly of his correspondence with Sir Robert Cecil, written while Neville was imprisoned in the Tower of London. The library also contains the letters of Anne Neville, née Killigrew, begging Cecil to sue for the release of her husband, together with letters from others relating to Sir Henry at this time. They are necessarily sorrowful documents, but at the same time revelatory. They link up with the Shakespeare works, most especially with a whole section of the Sonnets.

The earliest of them contains a record of Neville's journey from Boulogne back to Dover. Neville had been attempting to negotiate a peace treaty with the Spanish but had been devastated by the way he was treated. Argument after petty argument ensued. It even became comic: the Spanish princes (chosen to represent Spain at the negotiations), finally declared they thought their country superior to England – in God's eyes! [209] They were also not prepared to talk to an untitled person like Henry Neville, but Neville retorted that they clearly feared his professionalism.

When the negotiations therefore unsurprisingly broke down, the Queen finally allowed all her commissioners over there to return to England. But Sir Henry was not allowed to accompany them. She asserted that he was engaged to remain in France, having about another two years to spend there in order to complete his term as Ambassador. She also ordered him to remain for the next 60 days in Boulogne, in case the Spanish decided to come back to the negotiating table.

This greatly annoyed Neville, who was longing to return to England. The secondary sources often say he made the excuse that he was becoming increasingly deaf and so would be of little use in his post in France until he had rested in the hope that his full hearing would return. However, the *primary* sources – the letters at which I was now looking – suggest a somewhat different story. Before being appointed Ambassador, Neville had protested that he really did not want the job. In May 1598 he had begged Cecil initially to intercede with the Queen for at least a 'respite' before taking up his post as Ambassador in France, and one of the main reasons for this was that his wife was suffering from a life-threatening illness. After this *she* – not Sir Henry – became deaf. He even said that his wife was "in great extremity, as her Majesty's physicians... can inform you;" and "ready to attend the pleasure of God for her last hour... ."[210] [It is interesting that the exact phrase 'in great extremity' appears once in the Shakespeare canon, viz. in *Henry VIII*, for which play Neville was making notes while imprisoned in the Tower, two and a half years later.[211]] In that same letter, Neville also explained that he had sold his land in Sussex in order to buy some extra land around his Berkshire estate. This land had been owned by his friend and neighbour, Sir Henry Unton, who had recently died while on diplomatic service in France. (This is the Henry Unton whose wedding festivities appear in a famous painting. It was probably Unton's wedding which inspired the final act of *A Midsummer Night's Dream*.) However, Neville argued that if he were to go to France then he would be hard pressed to complete this contract with Unton, and its neglect would then endanger the size of his "poor estate."

In her letters to Robert Cecil, Anne Neville later made it clear that her deafness was increasing, so this might be one cause of Queen Elizabeth's eventually taking a softer line when Neville begged to return home from Boulogne. However, the Queen was rarely softened, so I imagine it might also have been Neville's threat of returning and becoming an outlaw "in Ashridge or the Forest" which was the most persuasive factor in her decision. Neville knew about weaponry; he was so intelligent that he would probably have become another Robin Hood type of leader, had he returned under these conditions. Also, Elizabeth would never have wished the King of France to find out that a man she had entrusted in high office in his kingdom had now become a criminal. So, whatever the cause, the Queen suddenly granted Neville, his wife and all his children, the requested return permission, even though he had served only 15 months of his two year contract as Ambassador in France.

Anne had also been pregnant with her ninth child when she travelled to France in May, 1599. She must therefore have been quite weak when the child was born, and perhaps grown even weaker with subsequent sad events. The severity of the illness from which she had suffered only one year earlier makes it likely that 'Falstaff's' baby boy with a great head "and a very litel body" (as reported by the Countess of Southampton) was indeed the child Anne was carrying and who died in September of the same year. One thus begins to build up a picture of incremental reasons for Neville's feelings against Queen Elizabeth. Even after Neville and his family arrived back in England, and after he had been placed in the Tower, Anne's deafness was continuing to increase, as will become clear when we look at her letters. Sir Henry must have sometimes blamed the Queen for Anne's continuing ill health.

When I wrote my previous book, I was not aware of the date on which Sir Henry and his family had finally arrived back in England for a break in his Ambassadorial service. I have now found that they arrived home in early August, 1600. He was actually back in London by August 6th.[212] This means that Neville had plenty of time to place the 'Shakespeare' plays in the Stationer's Register on 23rd August. (This is the first time the Shakespeare name appears in the Stationer's Register.) In that same letter to Robert Cecil, incidentally, Neville mentions Mr. Secretary Herbert. He was Sir John Herbert, a Welshman who was Cecil's secretary but who came over to Boulogne to assist Sir Henry Neville in his negotiations there. He had long been a friend of the Cecils, so would have known Neville too, even before they worked together in France. (As he was fluent in Welsh, one wonders whether Herbert assisted Neville in the writing of the Welsh episodes in *Henry IV, part 1*. Yet again, it is demonstrated that those who knew about his writing during Elizabeth's reign belonged to a very powerful, close and secretive circle.)

Neville and his family seem to have stayed in Dover castle for a couple of nights before travelling onwards to London, (and it will be remembered that Sir Anthony Dering, who was keeper of the Tower during Neville's incarceration, was the owner of this castle, and that it was there where an original manuscript compilation of *Henry IV, parts one and two* was found.) Another visitor in that same castle at the same time was Sir Thomas Fane, who wrote to Lord Cobham, warden of the Cinque Ports, about Neville's arrival, and who was also married to a Neville. Sir Thomas wrote[213] "Here arrived this evening from Bolloigne, Sir Henry Neville, with his wife and family, and also Mr. Secretary Harbert [Herbert], with the rest of the Commissioners late employed for the treaty there." [214]

There has certainly never been a case of so many connections between a Shakespeare authorship candidate, the Shakespeare works and the extant documents as that presented by

Sir Henry Neville! Synchronization of place, time, circumstance and texts keeps rolling in with such astounding regularity that it beggars belief and statistical expectation that the events can be *merely* coincidental.

I have already related part of the story of what happened next between Neville, Essex and Southampton in *The Truth Will Out*. Neville was now in London, but the Queen was insisting he should return to France as soon as possible. Clearly, Neville was negotiating with the two earls and trying to delay his return to foreign duties, thus allowing him time to partake (passively) in the Essex uprising. (He was in fact shut in a room waiting for Essex's call for him to come and take over the reins of government.) William Camden wrote about Neville's involvement, but only after Sir Henry's death. For obvious reasons, Neville tried to maintain *publicly* throughout the rest of his life that he had never known the protagonists very well, that he was never really party to their plans, and that his only guilt was that of omission, in his not informing the Queen about what he had 'heard'. But Camden was a close friend of Sir Henry Savile, Neville's kinsman and lifelong friend, so he knew the truth. Indeed, Camden even reported Sir Henry's tantalising verbal reaction to Essex's scheme: "'Tis mad, dangerous. 'Tis among the number of those things which are never praised till performed."[215] Neville even tried to keep up this pretence of innocence for most of the time he was in the Tower. But his letters from the Tower to Cecil gradually change from a tone of wronged anger to one of something almost – though not quite – approaching the contrition engendered of despair.

However, Neville's imprisonment was still in the future. Firstly, we find him changing his attitude to France completely when the Essex uprising failed. Although previously worrying all the time to be in England, he was suddenly and uncharacteristically keen to obtain permission to go and continue his duties. He had not yet been named as one of the protagonists in the revolt, so if he hurried he might just succeed in going into voluntary exile abroad. King Henri IV had known and admired the Earl of Essex, as he and Southampton had fought for his succession to the French throne. At that time, Henri was a Protestant, changing to Catholicism merely to be able to be crowned as King of France. Neville was therefore likely to obtain the French King's understanding, and a sanctuary.

Once Neville had obtained a written permission to return to France, after the Essex rebellion, he therefore left home swiftly.

His wife and children accompanied him to Dover, intending to bid him farewell. But by this time, Southampton had confessed to Cecil that Sir Henry was meant to become Secretary of State, had Essex's plans succeeded. Unsurprisingly, therefore, Cecil sent out orders for Sir Henry to be arrested by Sir Thomas Fane before he boarded the ship at Dover. Fane had Neville duly arrested, and "accompanied by some three or four men to the Court ...". But Neville was clearly conscious of his guilt, because as Fane says in a postscript, "While I sought to prevent his passage by sea, he on the sudden took horse, leaving his wife and children here with the gentlemen of his retinue." [216]

But Sir Henry did not attempt to escape again. He was brought to Court and asked to write a declaration of his involvement. That account is printed as 'Sir Henry Neville's Case' in *Winwood's Memorials of State*. [217]

His statement was clearly, though understandably, a cloaking of the facts. Neville was obviously challenged about its details (most probably by Cecil) because he wrote excuses for it in one of his later letters from the Tower. He was under house arrest at the Lord High Admiral's in Chelsea at the time he wrote his 'Case' and says that the Admiral's servant came to collect his declaration "when I had but new begun it, and signifying that he was willed to be at the Tower with it by 11 of clock;". He adds that he also "omitted both matter and circumstances which would much have justified me and cleared mine intention from consent or participation in these actions." . [218]

However, there can be little doubt that the Lord Admiral knew what he was doing: by telling his servant to set Henry a sudden deadline he was going to get his first reactions, instead of giving him time to think out any new construction of the story.

Neville's other concern in this later letter to Cecil is that neither his part in the affair nor his declaration should ever be published – a Nevillian trait we have by now come to expect. But of course he was hardly likely to have his wish fulfilled. The public must have been crying out for every detail of the affair. As things fell out, too, Neville gained quite a lot of respect from one section of the people, because Essex was a popular hero. Graffiti calling Cecil the murderer of Essex was no rare sight around London at the time. All this therefore probably went towards Neville's eventually being recognised as leader of the Popular Party in Parliament during the next monarch's reign.

When composing a letter of excuse once he was in the Tower, however, Neville shows that his chief concern is for his wife and servants (which again is what we should expect from Shakespeare, the humanist.) Again, in a letter written around 26th February, 1601, Neville encloses a note for his wife, and requests Cecil to add "some comfortable message unto her" because "I fear the apprehension of it may work some sudden and dangerous effect in her, being subject as she is to so violent a passion of the heart." [219] He also asks what he should do about his servants still in Paris.

We are gradually building up a picture of Neville's wife. On the one hand she was tough enough to have survived a great illness, the bearing of so many children, and the strife she endured while her husband was "in disgrace" – a phrase he keeps repeating in his letters and in the Shakespeare sonnets. On the other hand, Neville betrays that she is emotional. She was, however, able to write clearly-expressed letters to Sir Robert Cecil, her cousin. Her 'passion' is under the control of her pen:

> **Anne, Lady Nevill to Sir Robert Cecil.**
> My argument of writing can be nothing else but to give thanks for your goodness shewed to Mr. Nevill hitherto, and to beseech you to take pity of us both and our poor children, so that he may have a good issue of his trouble. His nature was never to be false to anybody, much less to the Queen and the State, and therefore I hope that his first fault shall not be too rigorously enforced against his service done and the whole good carriage of his former life. I hear that Cuffe, who best could tell what had passed between them, cleared him absolutely at his death. – From Lothbury, the 24th of March [1601].
> *Postscript.* – I hope you will pardon me for not attending on you at the Court, for I am so deaf that I should be very cumbersome unto you.[220]

SIR HENRY NEVILLE AND THE SONNETS IN THE TOWER

By June 1601, Anne was feeling the lack of her husband even more deeply: "If Mr. Nevill may but taste of the same favour, and be restored to me and his poor children, though we live poorly together, I shall think myself happy and have cause to pray for you."[221] She also says that her father would plead for Neville, except for the fact that he is old and sick. Even Killigrew – the strict old diplomat – therefore had sympathy for what Neville and Essex had been trying to do.

The tenor of Anne's letters reminds one of Isabella's pleas for her brother in *Measure for Measure*. But only one word reflects the vocabulary used by Shakespeare. That word is 'rigorously' which will be discussed later, in the context of some more of Neville's letters to Cecil.

Once he was in the Tower, the Queen kept pressing Neville for money to pay his fine of £5,000, which was in effect a ransom on his life. Neville kept insisting that he had no ready cash with which to pay this, and also that his lands were all in effect mortgaged, because he had been in the process of selling his Sussex lands in order to buy some of Sir Henry Unton's in Berkshire. However, as he was imprisoned, these deals were now held up. He could not even honour the contracts into which he had entered. He therefore asked Cecil to send to the Queen "... my supplication that she will be pleased ... to take my lands into her hands, and satisfy herself out of the yearly profits thereof... ."[222] He also says that he would be prepared "even to the loss of my life, to satisfy her displeasure for my offence, and to purchase her grace and favour to my children."

Was he posing, or had Neville truly become suicidal? Certainly he has stopped pleading his complete innocence, and certainly the dark lady of death is looming large. This letter was written in August, and the wording of Sonnet 97 encompasses the spring, summer and autumn which he has passed in gaol, using the imagery of his absence, his 'widow, and his 'orphans' too. It truly echoes Neville's letter, with the actual word 'burden' also being present in both[223]:

> How like a winter hath my absence been
> From thee, the pleasure of the fleeting year!
> What freezings have I felt, what dark days seen!
> What old December's bareness everywhere!
> And yet this time removed was summer's time,
> The teeming autumn big with rich increase,
> Bearing the wanton burden of the prime,

> Like widowed wombs after their lords' decease:
> Yet this abundant issue seemed to me
> But hope of orphans, and unfathered fruit,
> For summer and his pleasures wait on thee,
> And thou away, the very birds are mute.
>> Or if they sing, 'tis with so dull a cheer,
>> That leaves look pale, dreading the winter's near.

Note that the sonnet also speaks of 'abundant issue' which was certainly true of Sir Henry, who had so many children.

Sonnet 98, talks of his continuing absence from his wife during the following spring, his 'playing' with the flowers surely referring to his playing with them as images for his poem:

> From you have I been absent in the spring,
>> When proud-pied April (dressed in all his trim)
>> Hath put a spirit of youth in every thing:
>> That heavy Saturn laughed and leaped with him.
> Yet nor the lays of birds, nor the sweet smell
> Of different flowers in odour and in hue,
> Could make me any summer's story tell:
> Or from their proud lap pluck them where they grew:
> Nor did I wonder at the lily's white,
> Nor praise the deep vermilion in the rose,
> They were but sweet, but figures of delight:
> Drawn after you, you pattern of all those.
>> Yet seemed it winter still, and you away,
>> As with your shadow I with these did play.

However, one of Neville's most 'Shakespearean' letters was written the month earlier. In it, he uses the word 'clemency' which he uses only rarely in his own correspondence and is indeed used only once in the whole of Shakespeare: "But I am persuaded that if the meanness of my estate were made known to her [the Queen], she would extend her mercy further, and hold the like measure and proportion of grace and clemency towards me that she has done towards all other offenders, whom she has been pleased to chastise, but not to ruin."²²⁴ But the rare Shakespearean use of the word 'clemency' is significantly present in *Hamlet,* which Neville was almost certainly writing while in the Tower. Moreover, the frame he gives the word is appropriate for Neville's predicament, though it is remarked upon as strange in the context of the play within the play:

> Enter Prologue.
>
> **Ham.** We shall know by this fellow. The players cannot keep counsel; they'll tell all.
> **Oph.** Will he tell us what this show meant?
> **Ham.** Ay, or any show that you'll show him. Be not you asham'd to show, he'll not shame to tell you what it means.
> **Oph.** You are naught, you are naught! I'll mark the play.
>
> **Pro.** For us, and for our tragedy,
> Here stooping to your clemency,
> We beg your hearing patiently. [Exit.]
>
> **Ham.** Is this a prologue, or the posy of a ring?
> **Oph.** 'Tis brief, my lord.
> **Ham.** As woman's love.

Hamlet remarks that it is more like a verse ('posy') which is engraved inside a ring than a true Prologue. We are reminded of the story of Essex's having given just such a ring to the Countess of Nottingham (while he was in prison) with instructions to take it to the Queen. The Queen, it is said, had earlier given him a ring, instructing him to return it if ever he was in trouble or in any way repentant. Not till she was on her deathbed, however, did the Countess deliver the ring to the Queen.

Neville ends his own letter by begging for the Queen's mercy, "and I trust her Majesty, in her gracious and princely mind, will sometime think of it as a motive to her mercy. – From the Tower, 25 July 1601."

But the Queen's mercy was in short supply. Had the players 'told all' as Hamlet predicted that they would do? I don't think the players even knew the source of the plays. They would have told it, had they known it, and the secret would have been all over town. Neville did not tell them, precisely because he *knew* they would "tell all." Or had Elizabeth at last put two and two together, recalling that Neville used an enormous amount of government issue paper while he was in France? Perhaps. If so, she would have been afraid to execute such a great writer, but at the same time she would have done everything to keep him in the Tower, and therefore unable to promote works which criticised her – either openly or symbolically.

The famous 'Will' sonnets hint that either the Queen had found Neville out, or that he was ready to confess his writing to her, if she would then agree to love him just as much as she loved the works attributed to Will Shakespeare. As he says, "Make but my *name* thy love, and love that still, And then thou lov'st **me** for my name is 'Will'."

> If thy soul check thee that I come so near,
> Swear to thy blind soul that I was thy 'Will',
> And will thy soul knows is admitted there,
> Thus far for love, my love-suit sweet fulfil.
> 'Will', will fulfil the treasure of thy love,
> Ay, fill it full with wills, and my will one,
> In things of great receipt with ease we prove,
> Among a number one is reckoned none.
> Then in the number let me pass untold,
> Though in thy store's account I one must be,
> For nothing hold me, so it please thee hold,
> That nothing me, a something sweet to thee.
>   Make but my name thy love, and love that still,
>   And then thou lov'st me for my name is 'Will'."
> *Sonnet 136*

If we cast our minds back to Sonnet 121, we may recall this same obsession with negatives which we see in 136:

Among a number one is reckoned **none**. ...
For **nothing** hold me, so it please thee hold,
That **nothing** me,

The words 'not', 'none', nothing' are like the 'ne' of 'Neville', which negates the 'vile' part of his name (NE = 'NOT').[225] It therefore also negates the 'vill' or 'will' phoneme of his name, in its various spellings – NE-VVILL = NOT WILL (the letter 'w' at the time being formed in printing by two consecutive Vs - VVILL.) Neville **is** "that **nothing me**": if he is 'not will' [not ne-vvill] then he is nothing; yet his name – his pseudonym – is 'VVill.':

Make but my name thy love, and love that still,
And then thou lov'st me for my name is 'VVill'.

It is even possible to make an acrostic of Neville from the first two lines of sonnet 136:
  If thy soul check thee that I come so **n**ear,
    Swear to thy blind soul that I was thy **'VVill'**,

Unless she is both spiritually and literally blind, the Queen can see 'Ne-VVill' in his writing, yet it is only the 'Will' part which is '**admitted** there'.

Once again, Shakespeare-Neville is cleverly and mind-bogglingly word-playing on his own name. We even get a repeat of the word 'Will' (or 'wills') in sonnet 121, in which we also find an obsession about 'not' and 'ne':

'Tis better to be vile than vile esteemed,
  When not to be, receives reproach of being ...
... Or on my frailties why are frailer spies,
  Which in their **wills** count bad what I think good.

To be sure, the Queen was not his 'love', yet he (like all her courtiers and servants) was supposed to love her. He is obviously being sarcastic. Was the talk of 'wills' also hinting (among all the scurrilous overtones too) that he would be ready to leave her something in his will, if only she would love him as much as she loved his plays?

Yet for whatever reason, the Queen did her best to humiliate Neville in the eyes of his friends. This was of course a game, (even a word-playing game), that Neville could not win. On the one hand, the Queen loved his works; but on the other, there was a most important exception to that love. Will Shakespeare's play of *Richard II* appeared forever seditious in the Queen's eyes, because it had been **wilfully** performed on the eve of the Essex rebellion.

So Sir Henry had to keep trying to lure the Queen with money rather than with poetry, which was probably more an outlet for his feelings than anything else. (He would hardly have shown her these sonnets!) He repeatedly assured the Queen that he had sold his lands in Sussex and that he could not capitalise on rents from lands he was contracted to buy in Berkshire and could not complete his land sales while he was in the Tower. He says too that he had contacted his friends asking for money to help him pay his fine, in the hope he could then be released and so complete the sales. But he found they were more willing to lend him parcels of land, on whose rents he could capitalise, than they were to offer cash: "I, finding that my friends are more willing to engage their lands than their bonds, have offered of mine own and my friends' land of the yearly rent of 120 l. His Lordship made difficulty to take it for 2,000 l., so I have offered it for 1,800 l., and to put in sufficient sureties for the rest." The Queen now grabbed this land that was merely on loan to him by friends, so this was a double embarrassment for Neville. One also wonders what happened to the friends who had put up the 'sureties' for Neville – a subject which is referred to directly in the sonnets:

> So now I have confessed that he is thine,
> And I my self am mortgaged to thy will,
> My self I'll forfeit, so that other mine,
> Thou wilt restore to be my comfort still:
> But thou wilt not, nor he will not be free,
> For thou art covetous, and he is kind,
> He learned but surety-like to write for me,
> Under that bond that him as fast doth bind.
> The statute of thy beauty thou wilt take,
> Thou usurer that put'st forth all to use,
> And sue a friend, came debtor for my sake,
> So him I lose through my unkind abuse.
>   Him have I lost, thou hast both him and me,
>   He pays the whole, and yet am I not free.
> *Sonnet 134*

Neville's situation is so aptly summarised in this erstwhile difficult sonnet. The Queen has statutory laws behind what she is doing: "The statute of thy beauty thou wilt take..." She has taken his and his friend's land. If it is the 'dark lady' who has "both him [Neville's friend] and me", then Queen Elizabeth is one emanation of that dark female. But, as Shakespeare-Neville says in Sonnet 131, "In nothing art thou black save in thy deeds", which was most true, since the Queen was reputedly red-haired, with her face painted white by that stage in her life. It is also true that Neville was 'not free', even when the whole of his ransom instalments were paid, with the help of rents from his friends' lands. So the Queen is indeed dark and tyrannous:

> Thou art as tyrannous, so as thou art,
> As those whose beauties proudly make them cruel;
> For well thou know'st to my dear doting heart

SIR HENRY NEVILLE AND THE SONNETS IN THE TOWER

> Thou art the fairest and most precious jewel.
> Yet in good faith some say that thee behold,
> Thy face hath not the power to make love groan;
> To say they err, I dare not be so bold,
> Although I swear it to my self alone.
> And to be sure that is not false I swear,
> A thousand groans but thinking on thy face,
> One on another's neck do witness bear
> Thy black is fairest in my judgment's place.
>   In nothing art thou black save in thy deeds,
>   And thence this slander as I think proceeds.
> *Sonnet 131*

Sarcasm has certainly crept into Shakespeare-Neville's writing about Queen Elizabeth. He speaks of her as if he loves her. Yet it is surely only her official position which he loves. Elizabeth symbolises England for Neville, so she is the "most precious jewel" (which aptly echoes the famous lines about England from that seditious play, *Richard II.*) Yet her face "hath not the power to make love groan;" which is a fact he swears "to myself alone", in a line which extends the bitter-comic sarcasm of this poem.

Let us take the liberty of re-punctuating one playfully sarcastic line: "And to be sure that is not false: I swear A thousand groans but thinking on thy face,". Well, after what she has put him through, of course he did! Yet still "Thy black is fairest in my judgment's place." Once again, of course the way she is treating him is "fair", because the true writer – Neville – knows in his heart of hearts that her 'black' 'judgement' of him is 'fair' in the **legal** sense: it is nothing less than he deserves, after what he attempted to do.

Sonnet 132 continues this theme of sarcasm against the lack of beauty and pitiless nature of the Queen, coupled with his inner knowledge that her black judgement is the 'fairest' in his situation. He is pleading for her pity, just as he does in his letters; but when he puts it cryptically in the Sonnets, his biting sarcasm is missed, unless one knows the true story:

> Thine eyes I love, and they as pitying me,
> Knowing thy heart torment me with disdain,
> Have put on black, and loving mourners be,
> Looking with pretty ruth upon my pain.
> And truly not the morning sun of heaven

> Better becomes the grey cheeks of the east,
> Nor that full star that ushers in the even
> Doth half that glory to the sober west
> As those two mourning eyes become thy face:
> O let it then as well beseem thy heart
> To mourn for me since mourning doth thee grace,
> And suit thy pity like in every part.
>   Then will I swear beauty herself is black,
>   And all they foul that thy complexion lack.

Shakespeare-Neville cleverly overlays all these cryptic meanings with the cloak of Black Luce[226], so that the sonnet can be partially understood by some deeper-delving readers who inevitably love a scandal!

But with *Sonnet 133* he has become angry again, mentioning 'prison' quite openly:

> Beshrew that heart that makes my heart to groan
> For that deep wound it gives my friend and me;
> Is't not enough to torture me alone,
> But slave to slavery my sweet'st friend must be?
> Me from my self thy cruel eye hath taken,
> And my next self thou harder hast engrossed,
> Of him, my self, and thee I am forsaken,
> A torment thrice three-fold thus to be crossed:
> Prison my heart in thy steel bosom's ward,
> But then my friend's heart let my poor heart bail,
> Whoe'er keeps me, let my heart be his guard,
> Thou canst not then use rigour in my gaol.
>   And yet thou wilt, for I being pent in thee,
>   Perforce am thine and all that is in me.

The 'friend' from whom he had the loan of land was certainly not guilty of Neville's 'crime' yet was being punished (by having his land grabbed by the Queen) all the same. And it is in this sonnet that he uses the word 'rigour' too – the very term which he and his wife had used in their letters, pleading that the Queen should not be rigorous with Neville in his gaol.

But Neville has also repeatedly said that he would give his life as a sacrifice, if only the Queen would allow his wife and children to regain his estate and live in comfort once more. So the dark lady of the sonnets always has at least a *double* identity – the

SIR HENRY NEVILLE AND THE SONNETS IN THE TOWER

Queen and death. He is indeed 'pent' in the Queen, and "perforce [am] thine and all that is in me." She has obtained every last corner of his lands:

> **Sir Henry Nevill to Sir Robert Cecil.**
> ... This is all I can do, and shall leave scarce 50*l*. a year to maintain myself and wife and eight children, which I am sure her Majesty herself would think little enough. If I should be kept in prison, my charges would amount to above 150*l*. a year. Seeing mercy is proposed to me, let it be such as both I and mine may have cause to acknowledge with thankful mind. – From the Tower, 11 March, 1601. ...[227]

> **Sir Henry Nevill to Sir Robert Cecil.**
> ... My state is wholly decayed and my health of late much impaired. There is little left but my life, which, if it please God and her Majesty, I am willing to preserve, chiefly in hope to wipe and wear out this blemish and blot that lies now upon me in her eye; and next to approve my duty and thankfulness to you. –11 May, 1602.[228]

But Neville lets slip in his sonnets that he is truly more angry than repentant. This "precious jewel" of a monarch did not care enough for her country to ensure a peaceful succession. She castigated his friend, Essex, for being too honest to bring back pirated booty for her when he went on his mission to Cadiz. She had insisted on Neville taking up a diplomatic position which he did not want, was bad for his wife's health, and had cost him £4,000 of his own money. In the final analysis, he would never have joined the rebels, had her deeds and omissions not added up to something which endangered both the moral and physical health of the country. However much he might feign contrition, he was convinced that he occupied the moral high ground.

Finally, there is a letter to Sir Robert Cecil which might even hint at why Neville chose the strange, unknown name of 'Shylock' for his money lender in *The Merchant of Venice*. One 'Zachary

Lok' had performed accountancy duties for the Cecils over the course of many years. It was this same Lok who was behind the searching among Neville's papers, carried out at his father in law's house in Lothbury, London, shortly after his arrest:

> **Zachary Lok to Sir Robert Cecil.**
> According to your late direction, I have admitted Mr. Wynwood's man to the speech of Sir Henry Nevill; for whose better despatch in these causes I sent for a cabinet of his writings to Sir Henry Killigrew's, where he was lodged, the key whereof my lady Nevill delivered to my man. At whose return, Sir H. Nevill opened the same in my sight, and took thereout such writings as I saw were pertinent to his present business. Every till in the cabinet was full of several writings touching his employments and private estate. All are safe in the cabinet, the key whereof he delivered presently to my keeping. ... – Chelsea, the 6th of March, 1600 [1601].[229]

Neville's fear of what might become of his wife, who held the key to his writings, but which he had obviously gone through before he left for prison, is reflected in Sonnet 48:

> How careful was I when I took my way,
>   Each trifle under truest bars to thrust,
>   That to my use it might unused stay
>   From hands of falsehood, in sure wards of trust!
>   But thou, to whom my jewels trifles are,
>   Most worthy comfort, now my greatest grief,
>   Thou best of dearest, and mine only care,
>   Art left the prey of every vulgar thief.
>   Thee have I not locked up in any chest,
>   Save where thou art not, though I feel thou art,
>   Within the gentle closure of my breast,
>   From whence at pleasure thou mayst come and part,
>   And even thence thou wilt be stol'n I fear,
>   For truth proves thievish for a prize so dear.

Neville's name was in the Code contained in the Sonnets' Dedication. Because of this discovery, a hitherto unexplained number of the Sonnets themselves is finally understandable. The evidence is clearly there in the Neville Memoirs – i.e. in the writings he has left behind, both under his own name, and under that of William Shakespeare.

Addendum 1

WILLIAM SHAKESPEARE – THE SCRIBE?

> Great noble wits, be good unto yourselves
> And make a difference 'twixt poetic elves
> And poets: All that dabble in the ink
> And defile quills are not those few can think,
> Conceive, express, and steer the souls of men,
> As with a rudder, round thus, with their pen.

[from the stage prologue to *The Staple of News,* by Ben Jonson]

In his reference to a passage from *Henry VI, pt.3*, Shakespeare's contemporary, Robert Greene, implies that William Shakespeare, the actor, is *claiming* to be a writer:

> for there is an upstart Crow, beautified with our feathers, that with his *Tygers hart wrapt in a Players hyde* supposes he is as well able to bombast out a blank verse as the best of you; and being an absolute Johannes fac totum, is in his own conceit the only Shake-scene in a countery.

Greene's epithet for Shakespeare – 'Johannes fac totum' – obviously points out that Shakespeare is not an actor with a recognised patron but an odd-job man cum vagabond actor, who has serendipitously stumbled onto a great, anonymous writer's works. By way of reinforcing this message, Greene goes on to say that 'Shakespeare' is 'tarred with **our** feathers', which suggests that he uses skilled writers' 'feathers' (quills) with which to 'write'. In other words, Shakespeare does not write the works himself. Moreover, Greene chooses every word with care: tarring and feathering was a punishment for infamous behaviour, so Greene must have considered Shakespeare's pretensions as infamous. A reasonable conclusion is that Shakespeare had the works passed to him to copy out, not knowing from whence they came, but that he was therefore well aware that he was not the **author**.

Greene 'travelled extensively' between 1578 and 1583[230] which were precisely the years during which Neville toured the continent, so one cannot help wondering whether Greene knew even more than he was allowed to say. [Neville had been allowed to take one, unnamed 'man' with him on his tour; could this have been Greene, I wonder? If Greene did suspect Neville of being the writer, he would not have dared to state this: Neville was 'that noble knight' whom anyone from the lower classes approached with caution.] Thus, with what he says and what he does not say, Greene substantiates the proposition that Shakespeare was a 'vagabond actor' – a hired man – during the first half of the 1590s, *pretending* (as Greene hints) to be the writer of history plays.

Greene's comment, made in 1592, in *A Groatsworth of Wit*, attacks Shakespeare, so Halliwell (in *A Shakespeare Companion*) concludes this must mean that Shakespeare was already a successful playwright in London by that time. But how and why? Shakespeare was poor and virtually uneducated. How could he have gained the learning, leisure and financial backing to have researched and written the great and learned *Henry VI* trilogy by the time he was about 27 years old? Henslowe [the theatre manager], notes that he had obtained *Henry VI,* but Shakespeare's name was nowhere noted by him. So let's look again at what Greene means. Could he have been well aware that Shakespeare is a good copyist and formatter, rather than an author?

In their introduction to the First Folio of Shakespeare's works (1623), two actors from the Globe recall that Shakespeare gave the actors copies of their parts 'with scarce a blot'. This certainly suggests Shakespeare was more a copyist than an original writer. No *author* (or indeed anyone whose writing is intended to be read or heard by an audience wider than his private family) writes his or her first version 'with scarce a blot.' Yet an author would scarcely have the time to make *perfect* individual copies for each actor. He would surely have to hire a scribe if he wished to aim at such perfection. In *Hamlet* there is a reference to what the **real** Shakespeare knows about writing with a 'fair hand', and he certainly knows it is not the custom for those whose writing is taken seriously to spend his time forming the letters beautifully, 'with scarce a blot'. In the scene which makes this meaning clear, Hamlet has been explaining to Horatio how he discovered official letters ordering his death, and how he therefore set about forging 'official letters' to the contrary. He makes a point of saying how he had to force himself to "write fair" in order to achieve this forgery, and that this 'writing fair' is generally the task of a 'yeoman', not a professional:

HAMLET Being thus benetted round with villainies -
Ere I could make a prologue to my brains,
They had begun the play - I sat me down,
Devised a new commission, wrote it fair.
I once did hold it, as our statists do,
A baseness to write fair, and laboured much
How to forget that learning; but, sir, now
It did me yeoman's service. Wilt thou know
The effect of what I wrote?
{ACT5, SC.2}

What could be clearer? Hamlet knows the custom of the day: it is a "baseness to write fair." This being the case, it is a syllogistic argument that Shakespeare was therefore 'base' rather than a professional writer. It is as if the actors who wrote their preface to the First Folio are purposely sowing a strong hint that Shakespeare was a scribe, not the playwright. After all, if Shakespeare attended the local Stratford grammar school, then '**fair** writing' would have been a skill learned there. It would have fitted him well to becoming a scribe. Yet this is a skill he would have necessarily '**un**–learned' had he had further education, or had he written any extensive original works, such as the plays!

Moreover, the actors would not have noted this particular perfection if it had been the *usual* practice for a playwright to provide copies in such a perfect state. Perfect copies must therefore have been an unusual bonus for the actors. The actors' description of Shakespeare's copies therefore seems designed to bring to mind the work of a scribe. From his *Tower Notebook,* we even know that Neville hired a private scribe to copy out passages from the archives kept in the Tower. Hiring scribes in general, and choosing a particular scribe for his stage work, would therefore have been second nature to him.

But what might have given Shakespeare the idea to pretend authorship? Well, putting it kindly, perhaps he was so unlearned that, at first, he had not really enough vocabulary to explain the difference between physical writing and **authorship**. If he had been asked the question of whether he **wrote** the plays, he may well have answered "yes." After all, if William Shakespeare had received Neville's manuscripts (not knowing from whence they came) and then copied out the players' parts from them, he could indeed have *said* he had 'written' them, in that he had *written them out*!

The passage from *As You Like It* in which Touchstone [symbolically] accuses 'William of the Forest' of claiming more ownership of the works than he really has, may actually constitute some sort of textual hint towards William's untutored, quasi-fraudulent confusion:

> TOUCHSTONE [*Addressing William*] It is meat and drink to me to see a clown. By my troth, we that have good wits have much to answer for: we shall be flouting; we cannot hold.

('Flouting' is reminiscent of Greene's 'bombast'.) Touchstone continues, pointedly:

> TOUCHSTONE ...Art thou *wise*?

Then –

> TOUCHSTONE. Give me your hand. Art thou *learned*?

William must answer truthfully that he is not learned. The hint is that only a learned man could have written the plays. So Touchstone goes on to teach William a lesson:

> TOUCHSTONE. Then learn this of me: to have is to have; for it is a figure in rhetoric that drink, being pour'd out of cup into a glass, by filling the one doth empty the other; for all your writers do consent that ipse is he; now, you are not ipse, for I am he.

So Touchstone (Neville) is emptying himself – pouring out himself – when he pours his learned works into William (Shakespeare). Shakespeare now has a glass of water [manuscript] which was not 'filled' by him. Yet he can take it and drink it. The analogy is indeed pointed, and even more pointed when we take into account the fact that besides Shakespeare's name being William, just as in the play, Neville was a metal worker who would therefore have used a touchstone as a rough guide for discovering what was gold and what was not. Moreover, a letter written to Neville when he returned from France talked about there being a deal of touchstone (basalt) on his land in Yorkshire. The name was therefore thoroughly in his mind when this play was being finalised.

So much for some of the *textual* evidence for Shakespeare being merely a scribe – not a writer but a *writer-out* – of Neville's works. We can now turn to a series of *historical facts* pointing in the same direction. A play entitled *Locrine* was published in London in 1595. This has often been put forward as an early work by Shakespeare, and its title page bears the following inscription: "Newly set foorth, overseene and corrected, By *W. S.*" I am aware that it could be argued, from the punctuation, that the first phrase is separate from 'By W.S.', but punctuation was often used lightly at the time, and sometimes used purposely to confuse. (For instance, I demonstrated in *The Truth Will Out* how Ben Jonson's poem to Henry Neville can be re–punctuated to read that 'Neville is a *muse*' [Jonson's word for a poet.])

'Newly set foorth' could mean many things, of course, but prime among those meanings is what we would now term 'formatting', especially as this phrase is accompanied by the words 'overseene and corrected'. Altogether, then, the title page to *Locrine* carries the sense that W.S. copied out, edited the previous editions of ('corrected'), and re-formatted the author's work. (Strangely, too, the initials 'N H' are handwritten on a copy of the opening page of this play, now in the British Library.) Add to all this the fact that *Locrine* was based on a story from Virgil's *Aeneid*, and that Virgil's *Aeneid* is (almost uniquely) famed for its hendiadys – according to the Oxford English Dictionary – then we have a recipe for *Neville's* hand. (It would have been difficult for the young, penniless Shakespeare to have obtained a copy of the Virgil work, but we have proof positive of Neville's love of hendiadys,[231] the main source of this grammatical devise being Virgil.)

Next, it is remarkable how few of the plays listed by Meres in his *Palladis Tamia* in 1598 had ever been printed under Shakespeare's name. Most of them were originally printed anonymously. The plays Meres listed were: *Two Gentlemen of Verona, Comedy of Errors, Love's Labour's Lost, Love's Labour's Won, A Midsummer Night's Dream, The Merchant of Venice, Richard II, Richard III, Henry IV, King John, Titus Andronicus* and *Romeo and Juliet*.

WILLIAM SHAKESPEARE – THE SCRIBE?

The first Quarto of *Love's Labour's Lost* said "Newly augmented and Corrected by WS" (thus being reminiscent of the words used on *Locrine*). The 1599 Quarto of *Henry IV, part 1* contained a similar attribution; but this was not present on the *first* Quarto of the work, which was the only one Meres may have seen. Similarly, *The Merchant of Venice* was registered in 1598, but no author was named. Q1 did not appear until 1600, and only then contained the words "written by William Shakespeare" – no more just 'WS' and no more 'augmented by', etc., meaning that the change from a phrase suggesting 'scribe' to words suggesting 'author' must have been the result of a conscious decision, on the part of someone closely associated with the works. (As we shall see, it was uniquely Neville's circumstances which would have warranted such a change at precisely this time.)

Richard II had to wait until Q2 to have its writer named, and so did *Richard III*. (Both the 'named' editions of the two latter plays appeared in 1598 – the very year of Meres' publication, but never with a name to any edition before that time.) *Henry IV, part 2* was not published until 1600, and again appeared with the *later* version of attribution: "**Wrytten** by master Shakespeare." *The Comedy of Errors* did not appear in print until it was published in the First Folio (1623), neither did *King John*. *A Midsummer Night's Dream* was not published until 1600. *Romeo and Juliet* was not published till 1609, and then without a named author. Strangely, only *some* copies of Q4 of this play contained Shakespeare's name, and these particular copies are all undated. *Two Gentlemen of Verona* was not printed before it appeared in the First Folio. *Titus Andronicus* appeared in print in 1594, but with no authorial attribution until its copy in the First Folio. Neville became Ambassador to France in 1598 – the very year of Meres' publication. Neville would therefore have had an interest in commissioning someone to write a work naming 'Shakespeare' as the **author** of the plays. He may of course have done the commissioning by proxy, the point being that it is from this very moment that the editions of the plays first begin to be unambiguously attributed to Shakespeare's **authorship** rather than **transcription**.

Thus we are beginning to see a pattern – and it is a pattern which coincides with *Neville's* life circumstances, not with Shakespeare's. Before 1600, anything which appeared in print bearing the letters 'WS' was qualified by such terms as 'newly augmented by', etc. *After* 1600, Shakespeare's full name appears (on those works mentioned by Meres) with a fuller attribution and no remarks qualifying the authorship – until, that is, Queen Elizabeth has died, when they again sometimes return to having an unnamed author on their publications.

So what was going on? In 1600, Neville returned from France. His return (as we have seen) coincided precisely with the appearance of Shakespeare's name on the Stationer's Register for the very first time. His return also coincided with the sudden change from the naming (and qualifying) of WS into such full terms as "Wrytten by Master Shakespeare." I don't think, therefore, it's stretching a point too far to say that this may be further evidence for Neville's involvement with the burgeoning Essex plot, and therefore with his political need to have the 'WS' plays unmistakably attributed to Shakespeare, and certainly not to have the seditious, planned performances of *Richard II* even whispered about in association with Neville's own name.

Unfortunately, it is this 'fuller naming' which must have thrown doubt on what Robert Greene hinted about 'Shakespeare' merely being a formatter of the plays. Greene's words have often been twisted to mean that he resents anyone but a University man writing plays. But this is surely stretching semantics too far. He is blaming Shakespeare for being an 'upstart crow' – actor – *pretending* to be a writer. Nowhere does he attack him for lack of education. This may suggest, therefore, that Shakespeare started by being a scribe, but needed to supplement his income by becoming a vagabond actor. Perhaps becoming a scribe of Neville's plays gave him this idea. Neville was related to men and women who had contact with the Shakespeare family, so could easily have passed his manuscripts through them to Shakespeare. His uncle owned the house in which Shakespeare's mother was born, and his Worcestershire cousin's mother was Barbara Arden. Neville chose to hide some of his notebooks with his daughter on the Isle of Wight during his lifetime, so passing on his works to those far away from London was obviously a habit of his – and a safety net. But it was only Neville's dire political need that inevitably meant Shakespeare's name therefore persisted.

Which elements in the plays might have made Neville fear that his own name could be guessed at? First of all, his close friends might well have known of his authorship; and could he be sure that none of them would let his name slip out, especially if they were to be questioned after the momentous performance of

Richard II on the eve of the Essex Rebellion? Secondly, as illustrated in this book, the name, and hints within the character and deeds of, Falstaff/Oldcastle could have led a few more insiders to put two and two together. Thirdly, some people had even seen his *Sonnets* (including Meres, who mentions them as being 'among his private friends') and these too could have given away Neville's identity to some knowing readers – **unless**, that is, many of the works had already been attributed to someone else.

Moreover, it is interesting to note that the plays not mentioned by Meres, and even the later plays with a recognisably political content, did not appear with Shakespeare's name on any of the Quarto editions. For instance, the highly political *Henry VI* trilogy was not mentioned by Meres, and only Q3 of part 2 ever appeared in print with Shakespeare's name on it. Even then, however, this named edition (Q3) was not published until four years after Neville's death (i.e. 1619.) The other two parts had to wait until the First Folio edition to appear with any name on them at all.

The one exception to this rule of not naming the author of political plays was *Troilus and Cressida* which suddenly has (on the surface) a more *conformist,* pro–monarchical political outlook! And though *Hamlet* can be said to contain political elements, its ending shows the coming of a foreign monarch who represents the only hope of putting matters right. This would doubtless have rung a concordant bell with King James I, so with this play too we find an attribution to 'Shakespeare', though only in Q2 – i.e. after King James of Scotland had successfully settled on the English throne.

The listing and attribution by Meres appeared in the same year as Neville was told he must become the Ambassador to France. It would have been most apposite of him to have seen this done so as to silence any rumours of his writing whilst he was away. It would not have been 'suitable' for an Ambassador to be associated with stage plays while he was in direct contact with the court and government of a foreign country. By also referring to 'Shakespeare's' "sugred sonnets amongst his private friends" Meres was surely signalling that he had had private dealings with the 'author'. He also mentions his *Venus and Adonis* and *Lucrece,* which were prefaced by letters from Shakespeare to the Earl of Southampton. But were these 'Shakespeare–signed' letters also part of a smoke screen, done with the permission and connivance of the Earl, who was known to be Neville's friend, champion and 'dear Damon'?

Without Meres' naming of Shakespeare and this list of works Queen Elizabeth's curiosity regarding the WS canon may have been roused during Neville's absence abroad. But Meres' listing and association with William of Stratford stood a chance of damping down such curiosity.

Was there ever a hint that Elizabeth may have suspected Neville's authorship, despite the carefully-planned smokescreen? Well, in March, 1599, Sir Robert Cecil wrote to Sir Henry Neville in France, saying that the Queen had read his letters and was delighted by them. Then she added cryptically, "He is too like somebody in the World, to whom I am afraid he is a little kin, to carry coals at the hands of any Frenchman." The Queen's phrase 'to carry coals' in this very letter was cited by the Shakespearean critic, Charles Knight in 1840, as being a quotation from *Romeo and Juliet,* as it was a saying hardly known before this date. However, Charles Knight did not go on to make any further speculation which perhaps we, with hindsight, may be able to indulge in. Was "somebody in the World" perhaps meant to signify "Shakespeare in the **Globe**"? Is it possible that this very educated, linguistically-aware Queen was reminded of Shakespeare's style when she read Neville's letters? (I have indeed demonstrated in my second book how a linguistic analysis of passages from the Shakespeare plays and Neville's dispatches show great concordance.) And the 'little kin' the Queen mentioned is significant too: Shakespeare was boasting that he was descended from the Ardens of Parkhall, which would have meant that he was distantly related to the Nevilles. Shakespeare's mother was actually born in a house owned by Neville's uncle, Baron Abergavenny. Sir Henry Neville's contemporary relative, Edmund Neville, was the son of Barbara Arden, who was herself daughter of Thomas Arden of Parkhall. So it is indeed probable that the two men were (or appeared to be) 'a little kin.' Moreover, Neville had a scribe called 'William' whom he mentions in his letters now printed in *Winwood's Memorials.* Was this William Shakespeare? My research is ongoing!

But how would Queen Elizabeth have got to know all this? The answer is simple: Edmund Neville had been under constant surveillance by Francis Walsingham, Elizabeth's spymaster. Edmund belonged to the branch of the Nevilles who were

WILLIAM SHAKESPEARE – THE SCRIBE?

Catholics, and had been associated with the Parry plot. He was also suspected of being a spy for Spain, so Elizabeth would have been told all about him, and about his relationship to Sir Henry, and to the Neville Barons Abergavenny who owned extensive lands in Stratford. Indeed, the house in Stratford now called Mary Arden's house has been shown not to be the correct one. As a BBC investigator discovered, Mary was born in a house rented from the Neville Barons of Abergavenny – our Neville's first cousins, and the family to whom he lived close by when he was in Mayfield.

Elizabeth obviously chose her words carefully, however, because her phrase 'a little kin' could also have been referring to the fact that she thought the style of Sir Henry's letters resembled that of 'Shakespeare's' English! Yet who better to use as a pseudonym than a distant relative? However, it would still be possible to keep his identity hidden from William Shakespeare himself, and pass the manuscripts on through a series of hired messengers. But if Shakespeare were ever to discover the identity of his benefactor, then Neville could keep him quiet by saying that there was a family connection which he should not give away for the sake of the whole 'clan'.

The following list of anomalies should also be borne in mind:

- Shakespeare joined the Chamberlain's Company by December, 1594 But it's strange if he got patronage as an actor, if he was already getting patronage as a writer. Poems had appeared under his name by that time, and part of the *Henry VI* trilogy had appeared by then too.

- *The Comedy of Errors* was performed at Gray's Inn in 1594, but there was no publication with Shakespeare's name on it until the First Folio in 1623.

- *Love's Labour's Lost* was printed in 1598, but again only 'Newly corrected and augmented by WS'. Yet it was not known to have been performed before 1605. No original registration.

- *The Taming of the Shrew* was probably written in 1593, but with no attribution. First publication was in FF.

- *RICHARD II* was performed at Sir Edward Hoby's house, with Robert Cecil invited, on 9th December 1595. (Hoby was one of Neville's relatives.) It was not performed at the Globe until 7th February, 1601 – on the eve of the Essex rebellion. Q1 was produced in 1597, but with no attribution to Shakespeare. This was a good copy, so why did Q2 of 1598 contain errors, and why, for the first time did the words 'By William Shakespeare' appear? Isn't there a sense of 'rushing into print' here? [Henry Neville was about to go to France – perhaps already knew Essex had something brewing: there is a finger ring with roaring lion's head in Neville's portrait, painted just before he went to France. A friend of mine whose father was a Freemason tells me that this was a symbol that something was about to happen 'at the top'.] The deposition scene was omitted from Q1, and this was only added in print in 1608, Q4, i.e. after Elizabeth had died.

- *RICHARD III* – performed (possibly) under the title of 'Buckingham' in 1593. Registered 20th October 1597, Q1 1597, but not with a named author. The words 'by William Shakespeare' appear in Q2, 1598 [the year Neville knew he was going to go to France, and directly after Meres had mentioned the play as being 'by Shakespeare.']

CHRONOLOGICAL TABLE OF PLAYS, WITH DETAILS REGARDING THEIR AUTHORIAL ATTRIBUTION.

Q = Quarto
FF = First Folio
* = First appearance of Shakespeare's full name on a Quarto
† = Shakespeare's full name appears on the 1600 'rush' of authorially-attributed publications, ahead of the Essex Rebellion

Title & approx date written	Date 1st Published	Q1 names Shakespeare?	Later Q attributed to shakespeare?	Date registered, (if earlier than FF)	Noted by meres 1598?	WS name only in FF 1623
HEN VI, 2 1591	1594	no	Q3, 1619	no	no	no
HEN VI, 3 1591	1595	No, FF	no	no	no	yes
HEN VI,1 1592	1623 (FF)	No, FF	no	no	no	yes
TITUS 1592	1594	No, FF	no	1594 (registered by Danter)	yes	yes
RICHARD III 1593	1597	no	Yes, **1598,*** Q2 "By William Shakespeare"	1597	yes	no
TAMING OF THE SHREW 1593	1623 (FF)	No, FF	no	no	no	yes

UNDERSTANDING THE INVISIBLE SHAKESPEARE

Title & approx date written	Date 1st Published	Q1 names Shakespeare?	Later Q attributed to shakespeare?	Date registered, (if earlier than FF)	Noted by meres 1598?	WS name only in FF 1623
COMEDY OF ERRORS 1594	1623 (FF)	No, FF	no	no	yes	yes
ROMEO & JULIET 1595	1609	no	Yes, in *some* copies of Q4, (**no date**)	no	yes	no
RICHARD II 1595	1597	no	Yes, 1598,* Q2 (but this copy has errors!)	no	yes	no
ALL'S WELL 1595 – 1603?	1623 (FF)	No, FF	no	no	no	yes
MIDSUMMER N'S DREAM 1596	1600	yes	?	1600†	yes	no
KING JOHN 1596	1623 (FF)	no	no	no	yes	no
LOVE'S LABOUR'S L 1597	1598 *	"newly augmented and corrected by WS"	no	no	yes	no

324

CHRONOLOGICAL TABLE OF PLAYS, WITH DETAILS REGARDING THEIR AUTHORIAL ATTRIBUTION

Title & approx date written	Date 1st Published	Q1 names Shakespeare?	Later Q attributed to shakespeare?	Date registered, (if earlier than FF)	Noted by meres 1598?	WS name only in FF 1623
HENRY IV,1 1597	1598	no	Yes, 1599* "newly corrected by William Shakespeare"	1598	yes	no
MERCHANT OF VENICE 1597	1600	yes	Yes, Q2, 1619	1598	yes	no
TWO GENTLE MEN 1598	1623 (FF)	No, FF	no	no	yes	yes
HEN IV, 2 1598	1600	yes	–	1600 † "Wrytten by master Shakespeare"	no	no
MERRY WIVES 1598	1602	no	no	1602	no	yes
TROI–LUS 1598 – 1602	1609	yes	–	1603	no	no
HENRY V 1599	1600	no		1600	no	no
MUCH ADO 1599	1600	yes	–	1600 †First time Sha's name in Stat–ioner's Register	no	no

325

TITLE & approx DATE WRITTEN	Date 1st Published	Q1 NAMES SHAKE-SPEARE?	LATER Q ATTRIBUTED TO SHAKESPEARE?	DATE REGISTERED, (if earlier than FF)	NOTED BY MERES 1598?	WS NAME ONLY IN FF 1623
AS YOU LIKE IT 1599–1600	1623 (FF)	no	no	no	no	yes
JULIUS CEASAR 1599–1600	1623 (FF)	no	no	no	no	yes
TWELFTH NIGHT 1600–1601	1623 (FF)	–	–	no	no	yes
HAMLET 1600–1601	1603+	yes	No, Q2, 1604	1602	no	no
TIMON 1605–1608	1623 (FF)	no	–	–	no	yes
OTHELLO 1604	1622	yes	–	1621	no	no
MEASURE FOR MEAS. 1604	1623 (FF)	no	–	–	no	yes
MACBETH 1606	1623 (FF)	–	–	–	no	yes

CHRONOLOGICAL TABLE OF PLAYS, WITH DETAILS REGARDING THEIR AUTHORIAL ATTRIBUTION

Title & approx date written	Date 1st Published	Q1 names Shakespeare?	Later Q attributed to shakespeare?	Date registered, (if earlier than FF)	Noted by meres 1598?	WS name only in FF 1623
KING LEAR 1606	1608	yes	yes	1607 "master William Shakespeare"	no	no
AN–THONY & CLEO–PATRA 1607	1623 (FF)	no	–	1608 & 1623	no	yes
CORIO–LANUS 1607–1608	1623 (FF)	–	–	–	no	yes
PERI–CLES 1608	1609	yes	yes	1608	no	Not in FF
CYMBELINE 1609–10	1623 (FF)	–	–	1623	no	yes
WIN–TER'S T 1610 –11	1623 (FF)	–	–	–	no	yes
THE TEM–PEST 1611	1623 (FF)	–	–	–	no	yes
HENRY VIII 1612	1623 (FF)	–	–	–	no	yes

327

Finally, one must also ask why the owner of the land on which *both* Blackfriar's Playhouses were constructed dealt with 1) Sir Henry Neville's father, 2) with the actor, James Burbage; but *never* with William Shakespeare.

Our Sir Henry was born in part of the property which later became the first Blackfriar's theatre. His father leased in from Sir William More, who was closely associated with the Neville family.

Like Sir Henry Neville senior, More was a Protestant. This was, significantly, a stance they shared with Sir Thomas Carwarden, Master of the Revels. The Office of the Revels was next door to where our Sir Henry was born. More became Carwarden's executor, and was also a great supporter – and protector – of our Neville in Parliament. More worked closely with our Neville too on the cinque port defences against the Spanish in 1585. Yet despite his close association with new theatres, and with the Master of the Revels, More never mentioned Shakespeare, nor dealt with him, in any capacity whatsoever, even though he too must have known the Burbages.

Is there anything in Neville's life which might explain the absence of Shakespeare's name from the original owners and shareholders in the new Blackfriar's Theatre? Indeed there is, for the year of the contract between More and Burbage was 1597 – the year in which Neville's wife was desperately ill, and in which he was, at the same time, being bullied by the Queen to hurry up and get over to his new appointment as Ambassador in France. Neville would clearly have been too pre-occupied to oversee Shakespeare's financial arrangements at this time. Not until 1608 did Shakespeare become a shareholder in Blackfriar's Theatre. At that time, Neville was settled at the new King's Court, so would have been able both to finance and to oversee Shakespeare's contract with the Theatre. Strange how Neville had been available too at Shakespeare's sudden and unaccountable financial upturn when he gained shares in the Globe Theatre. Strange too that many others in that theatre had connections with the Iron industry! (See my article in the second edition of *The Journal of Neville Studies* 'Shakespeare and the Iron Men of the Theatre, which will also appear in my next book on Sir Henry.)

Addendum 2

IS THE CHARACTER OF MARGARET OF ANJOU in the *HENRY VI* PLAYS, BASED ON MARGUERITE DE VALOIS?

There are many unhistorical factors in Shakespeare's portrayal of Margaret of Anjou, wife of Henry VI. According to most French historians, she has been sadly maligned by the British over the ages. They have genuine reason to complain. There is no historical background or hint to think she was ever cruel or ever unfaithful to her husband. Yet both of these detrimental characteristics are portrayed in Shakespeare's plays. Perhaps one could account for some of the English misunderstandings by recalling that her husband, King Henry, went mad just before the birth of their son. This undoubtedly and necessarily demanded a strength from Margaret that she would not have needed to display, had her husband continued to be her capable protector. With his misfortune it fell to Margaret to defend her son from the two opposing sides in the Wars of the Roses. This was bound to propel her into a whirligig of changing alliances which, on the whole, and considering the circumstances, she managed very well and with as much humanity as possible.

The 'tiger's heart wrapped in a woman's hide' incident [I.iv, *Henry VI, part 3*] never really happened. Margaret simply could not have treated Richard Plantagenet so cruelly as to taunt him with a cloth soaked in his own son's blood after the battle in which he was killed: Margaret had fled and then taken sojourn in Scotland, during and after the time the battle took place.

The supposed love affair between Margaret and the Earl of Suffolk is also most unlikely: not only was he trusted by the then sane King Henry VI to look after her affairs, perform a proxy marriage with her, etc., but he was also many years older than Margaret. Indeed it was considered at Court that he was a more a surrogate father to her than anything else, her own father of course having stayed in France. Also, her strange behaviour after Suffolk's death in the plays is nowhere hinted at in any historical account, and neither is her transition from faithful wife to warring Amazon.

What, then, were Shakespeare's sources for the portrayal of Margaret? Were they all his own creation? Well, probably not. First of all, we have *Leicester's Commonwealth's* unflattering portrayal of her. Yet I am going to suggest even more additional sources which are sometimes different from, yet more substantial than, those which are usually said to have influenced the playwright.

Some critics insist that Halle portrayed Suffolk as the Queen's paramour (in his famous *Chronicles.*) However, Halle contains only the slightest hint in that direction – nothing concrete at all. As previously stated, it is only *Leicester's Commonwealth* which really spells out this alleged illicit relationship. However, it must be admitted that even the *Commonwealth's* story probably came from somewhere. Yet the strange thing is that that 'somewhere' was most likely old Yorkist tales. I say 'strange' because these plays were written and performed when a Lancastrian descendant was on the throne of England. Surely only a Yorkist playwright would have wished to perpetuate such tales. Certainly no upwardly-aspiring, poor, unknown Midland playwright would dare to have put forward the Yorkist propaganda seen in these plays generally.

This opinion is not merely my own: in 1974 Gwyn Williams wrote in the *Shakespeare Quarterly* that only the barest hints about Margaret and Suffolk are given in Halle's Chronicles, and that there "appears to be no dramatic reason" as to why Shakespeare should have extended and elaborated on this hint in such a way. Gwyn too, even without knowing about Henry Neville (the Yorkist descendant), avers that there must therefore have been a *personal* reason as to why he fabricated this 'myth'.

We have touched on some of *Neville's* personal reasons for his disparaging portrayal of Margaret and Suffolk during the course of this book, but I think there may have been yet another story and another Margaret about whom Neville knew, and whom he had personally met. The Margaret to whom I'm referring is Marguerite of Valois. Neville had most probably met Henri of Navarre – husband of Marguerite – during his visit to France when he was touring Europe with Sir Henry Savile. However, even if such a meeting did not take place, we can still be certain that Henri and Marguerite would have been talked about almost daily in

Neville's circle at the time the Henry VI plays were written. Neville's father in law had been in France at the time of Marguerite's involvement in the actual action of the St. Bartholomew day massacre, in which the Catholics suddenly and viciously slew their Protestant neighbours. As a committed Protestant, this made a terrible and lasting impression on Killigrew, and one to which he would have repeatedly referred.

Neville had married Anne Killigrew in 1584, and the couple subsequently lived for part of each year with Sir Henry Killigrew, Anne's father, in Lothbury, London. So close were Henry Killigrew and his son in law that Neville referred to him in his letters as 'my father Killigrew', so there is no doubt that Killigrew's tales of his experiences would have been heard attentively by Neville. Sir Henry Killigrew had been Sir Francis Walsingham's secretary at the time of the Bartholomew massacre in 1574, when Walsingham was Ambassador to France. Marguerite of Valois tried to help Huguenots, risking her own life. Killigrew subsequently married a Huguenot refugee from the massacre, after the death of his first wife in 1584.

At the time of the massacre, Marguerite of Valois had taken on almost the role of a double agent, for though a Catholic herself and daughter of the woman who began the slaughter of the Huguenots, she attempted to save as many of them as she could. She was a strong woman, and one who ultimately took a Huguenot lover, whose head she was said to have carried about in a bag after his execution. This is obviously a parallel story to that of Margaret of Anjou carrying around Suffolk's head after his decapitation in the play. (Interestingly, her life impinged on later English plays and French literature too, so part of her tale is doubly worth the telling here.)

Marguerite de Valois was born on 14th May 1553 and died in 1615, (four months before the death of Sir Henry Neville.) She was the daughter of Henry II of France and Catherine de Medici. She suffered for her eminent birth by being immensely 'controlled' during her early years. Her marriage to Henri of Navarre was an arranged one, while other political manoeuvring saw her imprisoned for many years. Yet she sang in her chains, for she filled her time with writing her memoirs!

Following her sympathy for the Huguenots, she actually took a Huguenot lover, Joseph Boniface de La Môle. (It was his head which she stole and carried around, after his execution.) Among her other lovers was Louis de Bussy d'Amboise, about whom Chapman was later to write an English play. Marguerite's brother, Henri III, imprisoned her for eighteen years, and she wrote continuously during this time. These memoirs included much about her husband, Henri IV – the King of France during the time that Neville was Ambassador. While Neville was in France, the King and Queen remained together, though Henri divulged to Neville that he was thinking of divorcing her and marrying Marie de Medici. In his Ambassadorial dispatches and letters to Robert Cecil, Neville betrayed much sympathy towards Marguerite, feeling sorry for her when her husband blatantly displayed his mistresses around Court, directly in front of her Her memoirs were not published until 1628, but Neville had been close enough to the Queen and to his father in law to know about some of her former life. It is even said that *Love's Labour's Lost* was based on her and the witty women of her Court, and certainly the names of the characters in that play are related to the personnel at the Court of Henri IV. (Ferdinand of Navarre is surely Henri of Navarre, for instance. Henri had initiated translations of Plato into French, so the idea of a 'Platonic' men's Court fitted in with both this influence, and with that of the French Academies of the time.)

Like Queen Margaret in the *Henry VI* plays, Marguerite [or Margot, as she was often called] had loved another at the time she was actually forced into a different alliance. In actual fact, Verdi's opera *Don Carlos* is based on her supposed love for Carlos, son of Philip II of Spain, though in real life she originally loved Henri of Guise. Her mother being the infamous and scheming Catherine de Medici meant that Margot married neither of her first two loves but became the wife of Henri of Navarre, following her mother's plan to gain a greater influence over the French succession. Marie's other children were married into powerful Catholic French families, so it seems her overall plan may have been to gain enough influence in the country to push the *succession* towards the Catholic side, no matter if the Protestant Navarre ultimately won. (Indeed, Henri IV was later forced to become a nominal Catholic in order to be crowned King.) Such a civil war situation in recent French history would surely have led Neville to make many parallels between the situation there and the Wars of the Roses, so that Marguerite's character and circumstances would have been at the forefront of his mind while he was writing the plays – and also when Paget was writing *Leicester's Commonwealth*. However, there are very few possible authorship candidates who would have experienced this French circle of influence: the Code's claim is once more upheld.

The St Bartholomew's Day Massacre took place only six days after Marguerite and Henri were married, so the image of Marguerite's intelligence and strength of character would inevitably have sprung to mind when Neville was writing the many battle scenes in the *Henry VI* plays. Not only did Marguerite have to change sides suddenly and help the Huguenots, she also had to fight against her own mother, in effect. The religious dividing lines then drawn were paralleled by very similar *factional* disputes to those involved in the Wars of the Roses, because the French 'factions' involved a major division between the House of Bourbon and the House of Guise. Even the parading of Suffolk's head before King Henry VI has its parallels with Marguerite's behaviour before her husband, because both she and Henri openly paraded their lovers in front of each other, around the French Court. Her memoirs recounted much that went on, with great candour, but they were not published until 1628, so only someone who had known of Marguerite at first or second hand (as had Neville) could have based the characterisation of Queen Margaret of England on her.

Addendum 3

THE LANGUAGE OF NEVILLE'S TREATISE

An advice [by Sir Henry Neville] touching the holding of a Parliament.[232]

1. THERE is a question grown and much debated amongst us,
2. whether the King should relieve himself in his great want
3. (whereof the world taketh knowledge both at home and abroad),[233]
4. by a Parliament, or by some projects and devices to raise
5. money, which may be set on foot to that purpose.
6. For my part, I will not examine what these projects may be, although
7. by the experience of such as have been put in use since the dissolution
8. of the last Parliament, I am induced to believe that either
9. they will fail or fall short in the practice, howsoever they may
10. appear likely in the theory; or that they will prove like some
11. medicines, which do rather take away the sense of pain for the present
12. than cure the grief for which they were applied.
13. But admit there may be other ways devised to relieve the King, yet
14. am I clearly of opinion that there is none so fit, so honourable,
15. and so necessary as by a Parliament. My reason is this: I
16. consider on what terms the King and the last Parliament parted
17. at the dissolution, full of distaste and acrimony[234] on His Majesty's
18. part, and not without some discontentment on theirs. I consider
19. also that from the Parliament, the apprehensions that are taken
20. there are spread and dispersed over the whole realm. And further
21. that the knowledge of these misunderstandings between His

22. Majesty and the Parliament is not confined within this kingdom
23. only but is flown abroad into all foreign parts that have any commerce
24. or dealing with us.

25. Now what disadvantage this opinion may breed us, and what
26. hopes it is like to raise both in our enemies abroad and our
27. discontented persons at home, may easily be gathered. For, as
28. there is nothing that more upholds the reputation of any Prince
29. than the opinion of his strength at home, which consisteth principally
30. in the love and concord between him and his people, from whence
31. there followeth naturally a sequence of all other duties on their part to
32. make him strong and able to help and hurt his neighbours, so there is
33. nothing that emboldens more an enemy, either open or secret, to
34. attempt the disturbance of the peace of any State than the
35. imagination that the Prince and people stand not in kind and
36. loving terms together.

37. And to this purpose I remember a story of
38. Antigonus, one of the immediate and mightiest successors of
39. Alexander, who, being solemnly set in great state to give
40. audience to some other prince's ambassador, as he was in that
41. solemnity, his son Demetrius came in from hunting, and being
42. arrayed in his hunting attire, with his darts in his hand, presented
43. himself so unto his father, and, after a salutation given
44. according to the manner of that people, sat down by him.

45. The audience being ended, and the ambassadors retiring themselves,
46. Antigonus called them again and willed them to report one
47. thing more to their masters, namely, in what fashion they had
48. seen his son and him converse together, intending that it would

49. be taken for a great argument of his strength and a great assurance
50. of his safety that his son and he lived in that confidence and concord.

51. If this were true in that case between the father
52. and the son, how much more is it verified between the Prince
53. and the people. And hereupon I conclude that the world
54. being possessed with a conceit that the last Parliament ended
55. with some sourness and distaste on the King's part, and not with
56. the best satisfaction on theirs, there is nothing more necessary
57. for the King's Majesty, either in regard of honour or safety,
58. than to deface that opinion, and to make it apparent to the world
59. that as he was received into the kingdom at his first entry, with
60. the greatest demonstrations of the love and joy of his people
61. that ever Prince was, so he is still rooted and established in
62. their hearts. And that whatsoever cloud or mist might seem to
63. have darkened or overshadowed the kind respects between
64. them at that time, it was no other but that which happens
65. often by some distemper between a tender father and dutiful
66. children which quickly vanish when the distemper of either side
67. is removed.

68. For the effecting of this I can think of no other way but by
69. another Parliament, for there this error grew, and there and
70. no-where else it must be repaired.
71. The harsh conclusion of the former Parliament bred that
72. ill conceit, and the sweet close of another must beget a better. And
73. by this means two notable effects will be wrought together if matters
74. be well handled: the removing of that erroneous and dangerous conceit
75. of a misunderstanding between the King and his people, and the
76. relieving of the King's present necessities in a sure, speedy and plentiful
77. manner; whereas that other cause of projects may happily

78. prove slow and fail in the most, and in very few succeed according
79. to the first design.
80. And for rectifying the misconceit between the King and his
81. people there is no hope at all that way. It is rather to be feared it will
82. do hurt, and rather aggravate than cure that malady if there be not great
83. judgement used in the choice of the projects, and much dexterity in the
84. managing of them.

85. Against this opinion there are two objections: the one
86. that the Parliament may still continue adverse and unwilling to
87. relieve the King at all, and so no hope of making
88. up the breach; the other that as long as it is conceived the
89. King cannot help himself without them, they will play upon
90. the advantage of his necessities and extort some unreasonable
91. demands from him before they yield to do anything for him.
92. Both these objections are grounded upon the same false foundation,
93. namely, that whatsoever the last Parliament did in that
94. kind, they did it out of evil affection, which I do know, and do
95. confidently avow to be otherwise, and have before in speech
96. delivered the true reasons of that averseness, as one that lived
97. and conversed inwardly with the chief of them, that were noted
98. to be most backward and know their inwardest thoughts on
99. that business, so as I dare undertake for the most of them that
100. the King's Majesty proceeding in a gracious course toward his
101. people, shall find those gentlemen exceeding willing to do him
102. service, and to give him such contentment, as may sweeten all
103. the former distastes, and leave both His Majesty and the world
104. fully satisfied of their good intentions, and of the general affection
105. of his subjects.

106. It is true (as I lately delivered unto His
107. Majesty), that some things will be desired and expected of him
108. by way of grace, which may both give some contentment to
109. them that shall pay what is given, and justify the care and
110. honest regard of them that shall give it. And without this
111. I dare promise nothing. For it is most certain that as in private
112. families and all other societies where the straitest bonds of
113. nature or election do concur to unite affections, there is almost
114. a continual necessity of mutual offices of kindness to nourish
115. and maintain that love, so in kingdoms, besides that great bond
116. of protection and allegiance between the sovereign and the subject,
117. there is a like necessary use of the frequent change of
118. mutual effects of grace and love to cherish and foster that
119. tender affection that daily is to be renewed between them. But
120. what be the things that will be demanded or expected by the
121. Parliament on behalf of the people will be hard for any one
122. man to set down. Yet what I have collected out of the desires
123. of sundry of the principal and most understanding gentlemen
124. that were of the last Parliament, (and are like to be of this) I
125. will be bold to deliver in a Memorial hereunto adjoined, whereby
126. it shall appear that they aim not at anything unjust or unreasonable,
127. or that may derogate from His Majesty in point of sovereignty
128. further than His Majesty hath already been pleased to
129. offer in writing to the last Parliament (which no doubt will be
130. remembered), nor in point of profit to any matter of certain and
131. considerable value, but only at such things as being now of
132. small moment and loss to His Majesty to depart with, because
133. they have been sifted and ransacked to tire bottom, may yet be
134. valued to the subjects, both in opinion and truth, at a high
135. rate, because they shall thereby enjoy a great repose and
136. security from vexation which any of them may otherwise be
137. subject unto.

138.These things being taken into His Majesty's consideration,
139.and receiving His gracious approbation as matters not unfit to
140.be yielded of grace unto his subjects, the next points to be
141.thought of are the time of holding the Parliament, the things
142.preceding to be done by way of preparation, and the manner
143.of proceeding with the House of Commons when the Parliament
144.is assembled. For the first, I see no cause why it should
145.be deferred longer than Michaelmas, for after the session there
146.must be a time proportionable for the Commissioners to sit, and
147.for the money to be levied and brought into the Exchequer,
148.which the sooner it is done, the sooner will the King be eased of
149.his debts for which he payeth interest, and the sooner will his
150.reputation be recovered and settled, which is the thing that
151.most deserves to be respected. If the Parliament begin at
152.Michaelmas, the Term may be adjourned to Hallowtide or, if
153.not, yet till that time there is little business done, so as the
154.lawyers may well attend the Parliament, whose absence will
155.otherwise breed delay. And I do not see but in a month or
156.five weeks this point of supplying the King, and of his retribution,
157.will be easily determined if it be proposed betimes and
158.followed close afterwards.

159.For the second, which concerns
160.matter of preparation, these be the things that I would
161.humbly offer to His Majesty's gracious consideration: to forbear
162.to use any speech to the Parliament that may irritate, and to seem
163.rather confident than diffident of their affections, casting the
164.fault of any former error upon evil offices done on both sides, and
165.want of true understanding rather than want of good affection.
166.To speak graciously and benignly to the people that shall f lock to
167.see His Majesty this progress. And especially to take notice
168.of the principal gentlemen, and let them kiss his hand, and do
169.them some other grace. To give order to the Archbishop to

170. prohibit all books and invective sermons against the Parliament,
171. so as notice may be taken of His Majesty's commandment
172. before the meeting. To peruse the grievances exhibited
173. the last Parliament, and if His Majesty would please to be
174. gracious in any of them, to do it of himself before he be pressed,
175. for a small thing in that manner will give more contentment
176. than much more obtained with importunity. And especially to
177. call to mind if His Majesty promised anything to the last Parliament
178. which is not yet performed; for upon the performance
179. of that men will be like to ground their trust and hopes in
180. those things which shall be offered now. For the last point
181. concerning the manner of proceeding, I wish that His Majesty
182. will be pleased to make his propositions unto the Commons
183. by himself or by his ministers and servants that are of their own body,
184. and not by mediation of the Lords. For the Commons will be rather willing
185. to make oblation of their affections themselves unto His
186. Majesty than that any others should do it, and intercept both
187. the merit and thanks from them.

188. I wish also that the King
189. should forbear to nominate any particular men to be sent unto
190. him from the Commons to treat upon any point or occasion,
191. but after His Majesty hath declared his own desires and made
192. likewise known his gracious inclination to gratify his subjects
193. with any favours and graces that with reason and moderation
194. they can desire for them, His Majesty may be pleased to
195. require the House to nominate a competent number of thirty
196. or forty or fewer which may repair unto him with their
197. demands, and be authorized both to ask and answer such questions
198. as the debate about them shall beget, without concluding
199. or binding the House in any point but only to clear things and
200. report all back to the House. This course, I conceive, will
201. much expedite the business, avoid jealousies, and give good
202. satisfaction to the most, when they shall see that the King
203. shall understand their desire immediately from themselves
204. without any interposition, or danger of misinterpretation, and

205. that upon any point of doubt they shall be admitted to clear
206. their own intentions and not to be subject to the construction
207. of others. Matters being thus prepared beforehand, and thus
208. managed at the time, and His Majesty being pleased to be
209. gracious to his people in the points proposed or any other of
210. the like nature which may be thought of by the House, when
211. they meet (for beforehand no man can precisely say these
212. things will be demanded and no other) I have no doubt, but am
213. very confident, that His Majesty shall receive as much contentment
214. of this next Parliament as he received distaste of the
215. former, and that all things will end in that sweet accord that
216. will be both honourable and comfortable for His Majesty and
217. happy for the whole realm. And when His Majesty hath made
218. use of his people's affection to put him out of want, any fit
219. projects that shall be offered may be the boldlier entertained to
220. fill his coffers. For whatsoever shall be done in that kind will
221. be the less subject to offence when there is a perfect renewing
222. and reunion of affections gone before; whereas otherwise whiles dislikes continue *seu bene, se male facta premunt.*

Endorsed:
"Sir H[enry] Neville of Billingbar his opinion which he presented to His Majesty between the end of the last session of the first Parliament, in the eight year of King James, and for the calling of the Parliament following, in the twelfth year of his Majesty's reign, in anno 1614"

ANALYSIS OF THE LANGUAGE USED IN SIR HENRY NEVILLE'S TREATISE

LINE NO. (in Treatise)	WORD OR PHRASE	NUMBER OF TIMES USED IN TREATISE	NUMBER OF INSTANCES IN SHAKESPEARE
2	on foot	1	14, e.g. '...this instant action - a cause on foot' (*Henry IV, 1*), and twice in the late play, *Coriolanus*.
4, 6, 77, 83, 217	project(s)	5	12 (only once in plural, in *Coriolanus*, a late play.)
4	device(s)	1	52 (six in plural)
6	For my part	1	26
8	induced/ induce/ induces 'induced to believe'	1	6 (all in late plays) '...I do believe, Induced by potent circumstances, ' *Henry VIII*
9	in the practice	1	36 (ie. roughly once in each play)
9	howsoever	1	9
12	the grief (meaning 'illness' or 'injury')	1	'Or take away the grief of a wound?' *Henry IV, 1* [11 instances of 'the grief' in all]

13	But admit there may be other ways...		In *Measure for Measure* - written during James' reign - there is a sentence which begins in the same way: ANGELO. 'Admit no other way to save his life,' *ACT2. SC.4*
13	devised	1	77 instances of 'devise, devised'
14, 214	honourable	2	115 (one of Shakespeare's favourite words.)
17, 55, 103, 212	distaste	4	4 (in late plays only)
17	acrimony	1	0
19	'apprehens–ions' (meaning 'comprehen–sion')	1	17
20	dispersed/ diperse/ disperses	1	14
28	uphold/ upholds	1	10
30, 51	concord	2	9
31	sequence	1	4
33	embolden[s	1	3 (in *Timon of Athens, Pericles,* and *The Merry Wives of Windsor* – all late plays)
38, 46	Antigonus		(A character in *The Winter's Tale*. c. 1610)

39	Alexander (the Great)		mentioned **18** times in the plays.	
41	Demetrius		Name of characters in 3 plays - *Titus A.*, *A MND*, and *Anthony and Cleopatra*	
41	solemnity	1	11	
42	arrayed/ arrays/array	1	14	
42	attire	1	14	
41,42	hunting	2	18	
42	darts/dart	1	19	
43	salutation	1	7	
46 - 47	'one thing more'(Shakespeare never uses the more common phrase 'one more thing')	1	5	
47	'in what fashion'	1	4 "what fashion" is used 4 times by Shakespeare, and 'in what fashion' once - in *Coriolanus* - a late play, written around the time Neville was sending his advice to King James.	
49	'great argument'	1	4	
50	confidence	1	16	

52	verified/verify	1	8
54, 72, 74. 80	conceit (meaning 'concept')	4	48
55	sourness	1	'sourness' is not used, but 'sour' appears 38 times
56, 200	satisfaction	2	33
25 & 155	breed	2	57 {also 'breed' followed by an object pronoun, which would today be dependent on a preposition - "might, through their amity, **Breed him** some prejudice, ..." [*Henry VIII*] and can **breed me** quiet? [*Pericles*]}
58	deface/defaced	1	7
60	Demonstration(s)	1	2
61	rooted	1	9
61	established	1	4
62, 218	whatsoever	3	15
63	overshadowed/overshadow/overshadows	1	0
	darkened/darkens/darken	1	6
65, 66	distemper	2	27

65	dutiful	1	3
68	effecting	1	2
4, 8, 15, 69, 7, 86, 93, 121, 124, etc.	parliament [the subject of this treatise]	23 [the subject of the Treatise]	26
72, 196,	beget	2	23
74,	erroneous	1	2
75	misunderstanding	2	0
76	speedy	1	21
76	plentiful	1	4
77	happily ('as it [may] happen[s]')	1	29
78	in the most		4 (all in late plays)
80	rectify[ing]	1	2 in two late plays, *Henry VIII* and *The Tempest* (written 1614-15)
83	dexterity	1	6
76 & 90	necessities [in the plural]	2	13
89	play upon		8 (Used in exactly this metaphorical way by 'Shakespeare'.)
90	extort/ extorted	1	7
96	averseness, averse, aversion	1	0

THE LANGUAGE OF NEVILLE'S TREATISE

97	inwardly	1	3
99	undertake	1	46
	[undertaker]*		2
112	strait[est]	1	15
113	election (meaning 'choice')	1	22
113	concur	1	1 (in *Troilus and Cressida*)
114 & 118	mutual	2	17
123	sundry	1	5
125	hereunto	1	0
125	whereby	1	13
127	derogate	1	3
133	sifted	1	1 (3 uses of 'sift')
133	ransacked/ ransack	1	2
136	vexation	1	11
139	approbation	1	14
146	proportionable	1	1
152	adjourn[ed]	1	1
156	retribution	1	0
157	betimes	1	24
163	diffident/ diffidence	1	No 'diffident', but 2 instances of 'diffidence'.

347

163	'rather confident than diffident'		The separation of 'rather' from 'than' is poetic and occurs in Henry V - 'And rather choose to hide them in a net /Than amply to embar their crooked titles' Henry VI, 1 – 'rather with their teeth/... than forsake the siege. ....' + another instance.Similarly in Henry VI, 2, (twice) Henry VI, 3, Julius Caesar, (5 times) King John, King Lear (3 times) The Winter's Tale (3) Love's Labour's Lost (2), etc.
166	benign[ly]	1	1
170	invective	1	1 (in the Argument to Lucrece, which has political implications)
172	peruse	1	15
176	importunity	1	3
185	oblation	1	1
186	intercept	1	4
187	merit	1	52
151 & 189	forbear	2	60
189 &195	nominate	2	3

THE LANGUAGE OF NEVILLE'S TREATISE

7 ins–tances in this short paper, last one on l. 209	gracious	7	200
192	gracious inclination		(used in adjacent lines in Coriolanus)
192	likewise	1	27
192	gratify	1	9
193	favours and graces		'grace and favour' used twice
193	graces (plural)	1	50
193	favours (plural)	1	40
197	authorized [exact spelling]	1	2
199	binding	1	1 (Measure for Measure)
88 & 200	conceive	2	27
201	expedite	1	0
201	jealousies (plural)	1	12
202	to the most	1	2
204	interposition	1	0
204	[interpose]		3 (all in later plays)
204	misinterpretation	1	0
	[misinterpret]		1

349

104 & 206	intention[s]	2	2 (in late plays only)
206	construction	1	9 (mainly in later plays)
206 & 221	subject to	2	21
95, 163, 213	confident	3	19
72, 102, 215	sweet	3	Over 700 instances - one of Shakespeare's favourite adjectives
216	comfortable	1	13
20 & 217	whole realm	2	1 (in Henry VIII)
	realm		55
219	boldlier	1	no instances of this particular word, but about 30 instances of the comparative ending – 'lier', including unusual usage, e.g. quicklier, goodlier, timelier, freelier. proudlier, statelier, earthlier, etc.
220	fill [his] coffers	1	'...did the general coffers fill' (Julius Caesar, 3.2)
220	in that kind	1	4 (in later plays only)
222	reunion	1	0
220	whiles	1	81

ENDNOTES

ABBREVIATIONS
WMS = *Winwood's Memorials of State,* 1724
ODNB = Dictionary of National Biography (Oxford)
HMC = Historical Manuscripts Commission

1. Kenneth Muir, *Shakespeare and Lewkenor,* Review of English Studies, Apr. 7 (26): 182-83, 1956. When referring to Lewkenor's translation of *De magistratibus et republica venetorum,* Muir says: "Taken in conjunction with the parallels offered by Malone and Hart, this new evidence seems to provide good grounds for believing that Shakespeare knew the book."
2. Maria Stella Florio, *So flourishing a Commonwealth: Some Aspects of Lewkenor's Translation (1599) of Contarini's 'La Republica e i magistrati di Vinegia'* (1544), [Doctoral Thesis]
3. Thomas Coryate, *Coryate's Crudities,* 1611
4. This opinion was expressed by Lewkenor in his *A Discours of the Usage of the English Fugitives by the Spaniard* (1588) and is explained on p.260, Michael C. Questier, *Catholicism and Community in Early Modern England: Politics, Aristocratic Patronage and Religion, c.1550–1640* Cambridge Studies in Early Modern British History, April 2006
5. See ODNB notes for Francis Langley (1548–1602), by William Ingram.
6. John Chamberlaine to Sir Ralph Winwood, p.407, WMS, vol. 3
7. Chamberlaine, ibid
8. p.453 WMS, vol. III, John Chamberlaine to Sir Ralph Winwood, 6th May 1613: King James I asks Sir Henry Neville to "confer with some of the Council..."
9. See Frank Kermode, *Shakespeare's Language,* Penguin 2000
10. The text of the Neville Treatise is taken from appendix. v in *History of England from the Accession of James I to the Outbreak of Civil War, 1603–1642,* by Samuel Rawson Gardiner (1884)
11. Line 3 - Foreign countries were always seeking whom best to ally with. If economic problems were perceived in England, it was unlikely that they would place England high on the list of those with whom to make treaties.
12. **acrimony** is never used in Shakespeare

13. Frank Kermode, *Shakespeare's Language*, op.cit
14. George Puttenham, *The Arte of English Poesie*, III xvi (1589)
15. For further examples of hendiadys and other Shakespeare and Neville linguistic constructions, see Chapter 12 "The Language of Shakespeare and Neville" in Brenda James, *Henry Neville and the Shakespeare Code*, Sussex, 2008.
16. This point will be illustrated and expanded upon in subsequent chapters.
17. Henry Neville *Plato Redivivus, or A Dialogue concerning Government* (1681), available at www.constitution.org/neville.pla_red.htm
18. See p. 346 *Proceedings in Parliament 1614*, ed. By Maija Jansson, American Philosophical Society (Aug. 1988) entry dated 25th May, 1614: Sir Henry Neville is seated next to John Donne on a select committee to "consider of the words, the grounds thereof, and the fittest course to take by search of precedents..." Dudley Digges was also on this committee.
19. House of Commons Journal, Vol.1 : 14, May, 1614
20. *Proceedings in Parliament, 1614* (House of Commons), ed. by Maija Jansson, op.cit.
21. HMC MONTAGU HOUSE PAPERS, op.cit. 1612 Sep 6 Windsor Sir Henry Neville to Ralph Winwood "...*But for the time he prays you to have patience, and to refer it to the King's own humour, which must be followed, and against which there is no striving, without hazard of doing hurt.*"
22. e.g. Harl. 4289, ff231-33, S.P. 14/74;45(1),
23. **super-serviceable** is used in *King Lear*
24. See Jonson's reference (in *Conversations at Hawthornden*) to Shakespeare not always *intending* his double entendres.
25. (National Archives, PROB 11/126).
26. Used 25 times in Shakespeare's work
27. **compass** is used 69 times in Shakespeare, and 'within the compass of...' 10 times
28. A phrase used by Shakespeare: ...With rounds of waxen tapers on their heads,/ And rattles in their hands. Upon a sudden, As Falstaff, she, and I, are newly met, ... *Merry wives of Windsor*
29. **abundantly** is used once, in *Coriolanus*
30. *Report on the Manuscripts of the Duke of Buccleuch and Queensberry, preserved at Montagu House, Whitehall, vol. 1* [Eyre and Spottiswoode, under HM Staionery Office, 1899.] p.118, referring to 'Henry Neville to Winwood,' 6th September, 1612
31. WMS, p.45, Vol.1, Winwood's Memorials of State, (a collection of transcriptions of diplomatic and other correspondence, referring to the years 1598 – 1613) published in three volumes in 1725 [For further details of this collection, together with extracts from the letters of Sir Henry Neville, see *The Journal of Neville Studies,* ed. Brenda James, April 2007, available from www.musicforstrings.com

ENDNOTES

32. P. 140, Dudley Carleton to John Chamberlain, 1603 – 1624, Jacobean Letters, ed. Maurice Lee, Jr., Rutgers University Press, 1972
33. Neville left money to the poor of Berkshire – see notes for Sir Henry Neville by M. Greengrass – Oxford Dictionary of National Biography (ODNB online)
34. For an exposition of this, see Zachary Lesser, *Mixed Government and Mixed Marriage in 'A King and No King': Sir Henry Neville reads Beaumont and Fletcher* ELH 69 (2002)
35. Chapter 1, *The French Academies of the Sixteenth Century* by Frances Yates, 1947
36. See F.E. Halliday, *A Shakespeare Companion*, Duckworth, 1955, and Brenda James, *Henry Neville and the Shakespeare Code*, 2008
37. p.10, Frances Yates, op.cit.
38. Ascham, Roger, 1515-1568. The Scholemaster / Roger Ascham Electronic Text Center, University of Virginia Library
39. See the analysis of sonnet 121 in Brenda James, op.cit., and further analysis in Chapter 5 of this book
40. Katherine Duncan Jones, *Ungentle Shakespeare*, The Arden Shakespeare, 2001.
41. Andrew Hadfield, *Shakespeare and Republicanism*, Cambridge University Press, (2005)
42. For a discussion of the play and its dating see Brenda James, *Henry Neville and the Shakespeare Code*, chapter 11
43. "I would be glad of some small amenities to my younger sons, whereby I might be able to give them good education at the least, being eased of that charge, to do the more for my daughters." Henry Neville, 'my copy of a Letter to a noble Lord', Berkshire R.O.
44. p.245, Maija Jansson, op. cit.
45. p.217, WMS, Vol.2
46. Brenda James, *Henry Neville and the Shakespeare Code*, chapter chapter 11, op.cit., which contains pointers to his probable (technical) illegitimacy, as his father was previously affianced [possibly even married] to someone other than Neville's mother. Also, Henry Neville senior and Elizabeth Gresham were married 'in settlement' in 1568, i.e. five years after Henry's birth
47. See Dr Janette Rutterford, Professor of Financial Management at the OU Business School: article on Married Women's Property http://www.open2.net/money/briefs_20060127women.html
48. From TH/VOL/LXXVIII (documents held at Longleat House) it seems Elizabeth Gresham was affianced to one Thomas Masoun in 1557; yet her mother signed a document alongside Sir Henry Neville in the 1560s, suggesting that she was by then treating him – not Masoun – as her son in law.
49. TH/VOL/I 1549-1580, Longleat House

50   Even his portrait, now hanging in Audley End house, contains an inscription which is half in plain Greek and half encrypted. The plain Greek reads "everywhere without" followed by the encrypted words "visible signs."
51   Thucydides, Book 2, paragraph 65
52   p. 140, *Dudley Carleton to John Chamberlain, 1603 – 1624, Jacobean Letters,* ed. Maurice Lee, Jr., Rutgers University Press, 1972
53   WMS Vol.3, p.410, footnote
54   Arthur Conan-Doyle, *The Adventure of the Noble Batchelor.*
55   See Ben Jonson's *epigram on Sir Henry Neville*; also, notes 81 and 215
56   p.396 *The Politics of Shakespeare's History Plays* (1874) by Richard Simpson [New Shakespeare Society trans.]
57   Andrew Hadfield *Shakespeare and Republicanism,* Cambridge, 2005
58   ODNB notes for Geoffrey Chaucer
59   Sir Edward Bulwer-Lytton, p. ix, Dedicatory Epistle to *The Last of the Barons,* London, 1854
60   See *Notes and Queries,* Letter to that journal, written by S.W. Singer, August 17, 1850 (which I quoted also in the endnotes of *The Truth Will Out,* Longman, 2005.) Apparently, "The late Mr. Yarnold" had a manuscript copy of a work entitled, *In Praise of Richard III,* which was prefixed to the following dedication:
TO THE HONOURABLE SIR HENRY NEVILL, KNIGHTE, and contained a work attempting to put right what he thought were the wrong reports given to the world concerning that king. "...*Kinge Richard the Third, who albeit I shold guilde with farre better termes of eloquence then I have don, and freate myself to deathe in pursuite of his commendations, yet his disgrace being so publicke, and the worlde so opinionate of his misdoings, as I shold not be able so farre to justifie him as they to condemne him.*" It is signed, "Your honours most affecionat servant, HEN W
61   p.123 *A Companion to Chaucer* by Peter Brown, Blackwell Publishing, 2002
62   Mitchell, J. Allan. *The Fall of Princes:* The Literary Encyclopaedia. 7th March, 2007.
63   Mitchell, ibid.
64   Lydgate studied at Oxford University [see his notes in the ODNB]
65   Line 1683,Vol 3, *The Complete Works of Geoffrey Chaucer,* edited from numerous manuscripts by the Rev. Walter W. Skeat (2nd ed.) (Oxford: Clarendon Press, 1899). 7 vols.
66   Lincolnshire Archives, Worsley Papers: *'Extracts Copyed and collected of the Recordes in the Tower Ann:1602'*
67   Terry Jones, et al *Who Murdered Chaucer? A Medieval Mystery* Methuen, 2003
68   ODNB notes for John Stubbe

ENDNOTES

69   "**Philip against Monsieur**" is written on the Northumberland MS. See my Chapter II in *The Truth Will Out*, op.cit.

70   Chapter II, *The Truth Will Out*, ibid.

71   Chapter II, *The Truth Will Out*, ibid.

72   See, for example, *A Notable and Comfortable Exposition upon Matthew IV, Concerning the Temptations of Christ in the Wilderness* by John Knox 1556, which ends with the words: 'The God of all comfort and consolation confirm and strengthen you in his virtue [power] unto the end. Amen.'

73   WMS, Vol.1, p. 120. Letter from Sir Henry Neville to Sir Robert Cecil, 11th October, 1599 "The King himself, at my Audience at Orleans, used these Speeches unto me, talking of the Warre of Ireland: *The Queen your Mistress thought I dealt too basely in making Composition with my Subjects, and buying my Peace; we shall see which shall speed better, she with her Gloriousness, or I with that she calls Baseness.*"

74   Maija Jansson, op.cit.

75   The transcriptions from *Leicester's Commonwealth* are my own - from the copies in the Lincolnshire Archives. However, I shall point to page numbers for Dr. Dwight Peck's ed. of *Leicester's Commonwealth*, which is available at http:www.dpeck.info The above passage appears at p. 65 of the pdf version.

76   For a fuller description of further evidence that these documents were owned by Henry Neville, see my Chapter II, *The Truth Will Out*, op.cit.

77   Ibid.

78   Lincolnshire Archives, Worsley 47, p. 62 (left)

79   Lincolnshire Archives, Worsley 47

80   Peck, op. cit. p. 58

81   p91, ibid.

82   Hatfield House, Cecil Papers, 101.16

83   Quoted by Jean Overton Fuller in *Sir Francis Bacon, A Biography*, Maidstone, 1981, p.146

84   Bodl. Oxf., MS Rawl. B.223, fols. 1–16

85   Notes for Tobie Matthew, by A.J. Loomie, in ODNB

86   p. 558, Irwin Smith, *Shakespeare's Blackfriars Playhouse*, New York University Press, 1964

87   WMS, Vol. 3, p. 467 "Sir Henry Nevill arrived here [Brussels] to see these Princes and this Court in its Glory, by the Confluence of many Noblemen and Strangers hither to see the Procession of the Sacrament of Miracles. He departed from hence ... well satysfied ..." Mr. Trumbull to Sir Ralph Winwood, Brussels, 6th July 1613

88   Dudley Carleton to John Chamberlain, p. 121, and footnote 1, p. 124, Lee (ed.) op.cit.

89   *Sixteen Plays of Shakespeare*, ed. G.L. Kittredge, Boston, 1946

90 WMS, p.235, Vol.III *Letter from John More to Sir Ralph Winwood, 1st Dec. 1610* "...*when Sir Francis Verulam Bacon had began to Answer in a more extravagent Stile then*[than] *his Majesty delighted to hear, he* [King James I] *pick'd out Sir Henry Neville, commanding him to Answer according to his Conscience...*"

91 Notes for Sir Francis Bacon, by G.V. Benson & rev. J.M. Blatchly, in ODNB

92 WMS,vol. 1, p.229 Winwood to Neville, Paris, July 17th, 1600

93 See pp. 243–244 *The Truth Will Out*, op.cit.

94 Ref. D/EN/L4, *The Neville Papers,* Berkshire Record Office, (Case relating to Peter Gandon, a Frenchman who brought it into Star Chamber, accusing Henry Neville (junior) of piracy. See discussion of this in *Henry Neville and the Shakespeare Code*, pp.195 – 6

95 p.115 Winwood's Memorials, Vol. 1

96 Violet A Wilson *Queen Elizabeth's Maids of Honour* , London, 1922

97 Ben Jonson, *Bartholomew Fair,* Act 1, Sc.1"*A pox to these pretenders to wit! your Three Cranes, Mitre and Mermaid men! not a corn of true salt, not a grain of right mustard amongst them all. They may stand for places, or so, again the next wit–fall, and pay two pence in a quart more for their canary than other men...*"

98 HMC, Montagu House, op.cit. p.112

99 Historical MSS Commission, ibid

100 WM, vol. 1, p.231, Letter from Sir Henry Neville to Mr. Winwood, 'Bulloigne', 23rd July, 1600

101 WM, vol. 1, p.250

102 *The Original Letters of John Colville,* produced by the Bannatyne Club

103 ibid

104 See chapter 10, *Henry Neville and the Shakespeare Code,* Brenda James, 2008

105 See chapters 1 and 2 of this present book

106 For a discussion of this phrase, etc., as used in *2, Henry IV,* see previous chapter

107 WMS Vol. 1, p.20, (Sir Henry Neville to Robert Cecil, 15 May, 1599) "I found the King in the Gallery, who uppon my approche unto him, advanced himselfe to embrace me; and told me I was very welcome, and that he had advanced himself to embrace me, but to the Spanish Ambassador he had not styrred one foote ..." Obviously, the King recognised Neville, and felt comfortable about him. He would hardly have risked the embrace if he had never seen him before. Moreover, as a close friend of the Earls of Southampton and Essex, he would certainly have been known to the King of France – by name at least – because those two Earls fought in battles promoting Henri of Navarre to become King of France.

108 p.165, Adam Nicholson, *Power and Glory*, Harper Collins, 2003

ENDNOTES

109 See Frances Yates, *A Study of Love's Labour's Lost,* 1936
110 I am indebted to the notes on Sir Henry Killigrew, by Luke MacMahon, in theOxford Dictionary of National Biography for the information on Killigrew's presence in France, and to F.E. Halliday's *A Shakespeare Companion* for his notes on Henri of Navarre.
111 *The Second Part of King Henry IV, Introduction,* p.xiii, Arden edition, 1987, ed. A.R. Humphreys
112 Terry Jones, et al *Who Murdered Chaucer? A Medieval Mystery* Methuen, 2003
113 See *The Last of the Barons* by Edward Bulwer Lytton, 1854
114 See notes for Thomas, Duke of Gloucester, by Anthony Tuck, in ODNB
115 See Brenda James, SHAKESPEARE-NEVILLE, CERVANTES, AND THE TREATY OF BOULOGNE, in *The Journal of Neville Studies,* Vol.2, issue 1, available through www.musicforstrings.com
116 p. 153, *The History of Chivalry; Or, Knighthood and Its Times* By Charles Mills, 1844
117 p. 68, *A History of Education: During the Middle Ages and the Transition to Modern Times*
by Frank Pierrepont Graves; Macmillan, 1914.
118 Frank Pierrepont Graves, op.cit.
119 William Camden (a contemporary historian who knew Neville and Savile personally) rarely speaks of Sir Henry without calling him 'noble': *"He appeached also Sir Henry Nevill, **a most Noble Knight**, as being not ignorant of the conspiracy, who was now ready to returne Embassador Legier into France about the ratifying of the treaty of Bloys and restrayning of depredations on both sides, whereupon he was called backe from his journey and committed to the Lord Admirals custody."* and, reporting Cuffe's speech from the scaffold following the Essex rebellion, *"...But whereas I have brought **that Noble Knight** Sir Henry Nevill into danger, I am hartily sory for it, and I earnestly intreat him to forgive mee."* (from Camden's *Annales,* Book IV, published posthumously in Latin at Leiden in 1625, appearing in London in 1627 – available at http://www.philological.bham.ac.uk/camden/1601e.html
120 p.164 Charles Mills, op.cit., Philadelphia: 1844.
121 Winston Graham, *The Spanish Armadas,* 1972
122 See details of the Wessex Archaeology Project exploring the shipwreck in the Thames, at http://www.wessexarch.co.uk/projects/marine/thameswreck/gresham.html
123 p. 165, Adam Nicholson, op.cit.
124 Thomas Digges, *Strategicos,* 1579
125 Neville notes the corruption of Dudley, then Earl of Warwick, and his deputy, Pistor, saying the former *referred me for the despatching of it*

[i.e. his request to obtain a licence to export more cannons] *to one Pistor that then was his deputy, Mr Pistor plainly told me that I should have no licence unless I would give (my Lord as he said) forty shillings upon every ton, which I then refused, and I hope may do still.* (Footnote: Lansdowne MSS 65 no 22, f 82).

126 See Brenda James, *The Tangled World of Elizabethan Espionage: Sir Henry Neville and Charles Paget, Double Agent,* Journal of Neville Studies, Vol.1.2 (available as an e–journal. The revised text of this paper will also appear in my next book on Sir Henry.)

127 p.715, Calendar of State Papers – Foreign (1584 – 5) HMSO 1916

128 The French scholar Emmanuel Rey discovered the historical references to the Abbey of Our Lady of Mount Zion and published his findings in 1888. Mémoires de la Société nationale des antiquaires de France, tome XLVIII. The File Reference Number to this article in the French National Library in Paris is 8-O2F-762.

129 See chapter 11

130 Queen Elizabeth refused to believe a word against her 'Robin' Dudley, even though her chief minister and adviser - William Cecil, Lord Burghley - always suspected the Earl's behaviour, motives and adverse influence on the Queen. This fact alone may give rise to the suspicion that old Lord Burghley would not have minded Henry Neville's involvement with *Leicester's Commonwealth* had he ever discovered this to be the case. Political matters are rarely so clear-cut as outsiders are led to believe. *Leicester's Commonwealth* looks very much as if it could have been 'commissioned' by Walsingham and William Cecil in order to discredit the Earl of Leicester in the Queen's eyes.

131 p.717, Calendar of State Papers – Foreign (1584 – 5), op.cit

132 p. 717, ibid

133 See p.102, Leslie Hotson, *I, William Shakespeare,* where Dr. Hotson implies he has actually seen a document confirming our Henry Neville as the one knighted by Essex at Cadiz.

134 p.53 *Tudor Knight* by Christopher Gravett, Graham Turner Osprey Publishing, 2006

135 W.R. Stretberger Court Revels 1485 – 1559. University of Toronto Press, 1994.

136 Robert Lomas, *The Invisible College,* Corgi, (2003)

137 p. 314 Christopher Tyerman *England and the Crusades,* University of Chicago Press, 1988

138 See records of this case among the 'Neville Papers' in the Berkshire Record Office

139 pp. 229–30, Charlotte Carmichael Stopes, *The Third Earl of Southampton,* Cambridge, 1922. Stopes has copied out 'The Confession of the Earl of Southampton' from the Salisbury Papers, vol. 11, p.72

ENDNOTES

140 Camden, op. cit.

141 WMS, p.467, Vol.3, *"Sir Henry Nevill arrived here* [Brussels] *to see these Princes and this Court in its Glory, by the Confluence of many Noblemen and Strangers hither to see the Procession of the Sacrament of Miracles. He departed from hence ... well satysfied ..."* Mr. Trumbull to Sir Ralph Winwood, Brussels, 6th July, 1613

142 See frontispiece illustrations, headed 'Royal Emblems' in John Julius Norwich, *Shakespeare's Kings,* Simon and Schuster, 1999

143 p.102 *Oxford Guide to Heraldry* by Thomas Wood cock and John Martin Robinson, Oxford, 1988

144 See my notes on this and other poems in 'Appendix 1' in *The Truth Will Out,* op.cit.

145 Mr. George Sayn provided me with these facts.

146 See my theory regarding Davenant's origins in *Henry Neville and the Shakespeare Code,* op.cit.

147 See some of my arguments for this on p.131. *The Truth Will Out,* op. cit.

148 For examples of Maier's esotericism, see, for instance, the notes for Robert Fludd, the alchemist, in ODNB, "[Michael Maier] *was not the Rosicrucian doctor* [to whom Fludd dedicated one of his works] *as had previously been thought..."* Also, Maier was the first person to publish the alchemist Thomas Norton's *Ordinals* (see ODNB notes for Thomas Norton.)

149 See ODNB notes for Robert Fludd

150 See Frances Yates, *The Rosicrucian Enlightenment,* 1972 and *The Occult Philosophy in the Elizabethan Age,* 1979

151 Brenda James, *Henry Neville and the Shakespeare Code, op. cit.* p.27, row 9 on the matrix of the fourth transformation of the Dedication Code, (and explanations leading up to this result.)

152 Brenda James, ibid.

153 P.165, Adam Nicholson, op.cit.

154 p.2, Frances Yates, *Giordano Bruno and the Hermetic Tradition,* Routledge and Kegan Paul, 1964

155 Michael Baigent, *Ancient Egypt and Freemasonry* 'Freemasonry Today' Winter 1998/99 - Issue 07

156 p. 407 *Dictionary of Deities and Demons* K. van der Toorn, et.al.

157 ibid

158 John Warrington, *Classical Dictionary,* J.M. Dent, 1970

159 See http://en.wikipedia.org/wiki/List_of_17th_century_BCE_lunar_eclipses

160 Lomas *The Invisible College,* op.cit.

161 Frances Yates, p.274, *Giordano Bruno,* op.cit.

[162] p.257 *Restoring the Temple of Vision: Cabalistic Freemasonry and Stuart Culture* (Brill's Studies in Intellectual History) by Marsha Keith Schuchard, 2002

[163] P.176, Frances Yates, op.cit.

[164] See entry for Hermes in *Everyman's Classical Dictionary,* by John Warrington, J.M. Dent & Sons Ltd. London, Third Edition, 1978

[165] Warrington, ibid.

[166] Brenda James, op.cit.

[167] See *The Greatest Story Never Told,* by Leon Davin, The Trafford Press, Canada, (2003)

[168] p.30, WMS, Vol.1. Sir Henry Neville and King Henri IV were talking about the Pope's assertion to King Henri that "...*no violence could force Mens Consciences and Beliefs, but they must be wonne by teaching and good Example.*" However, Neville suggested that he knew this was Henri's opinion (which Neville shared) rather than the Pope's, because he said directly to King Henri that the Pope would say anything to a monarch that he found politic, and that he knew he (the Pope) had said exactly the opposite to the King of Spain!

[169] p.552 *Kenning's Masonic Encyclopaedia and Handbook of Masonic Archeology, History and Biography* (1878) By George Kenning, A. F. A. Woodford , Published by Kessinger Publishing, 2003. See also Robert Lomas, op.cit.

[170] p. 178, ibid

[171] p. 661, F.E. Halliday, *A Shakespeare Companion,* London, 1955, where the whole of the Epistle to the second edition of *Troilus and Cressida* is given.

[172] Leon Davin, *The Ritual –The Greatest Story Never Told,* op.cit.

[173] p. 63, Leon Davin, ibid

[174] Canon Richard Tydeman, *Who Was Hiram Abif?* 'Freemasonry Today' autumn 2008, issue 46

[175] John Leslie, *Origine...Scotorum,* 1578, quoted in the New Cambridge Shakespeare edition of *Macbeth,* ed. A. R. Braunmuller, CUP 1997

[176] p. 105, Carleton to John Chamberlain, Lee (ed.) op.cit.

[177] WMS, vol.II, p.54, Samuel Calvert to Mr. Winwood, 28th March, 1605, "The Plays do not forbear to present upon their Stage the whole Course of this present Time, not sparing either King, State or Religion, in so great Absurdity, and with such Liberty, that any would be afraid to hear them."

[178] See notes for George Neville, third baron Bergavenny in ODNB

[179] See Brenda James, *Journal of Neville Studies* article on Charles Paget, op.cit. (see note 83)

[180] e.g. HMC, Montagu House papers, op. cit. 1613? [no other date] Winwood to Neville Has received his letter of the 10th enjoining secresy. ends"*There is great reason you should again and again recommend this*

ENDNOTES

cause to my secresy; for if there come forth but the least vent of it, I know actum est de me."

[181] WMS, Vol. III, p.78: Henry Neville to Ralph Winwood, 21st June, 1605
[182] p.112 *The History of Chivalry*, Mills, op.cit.
[183] G.A. Holmes, *Cardinal Beaufort and the Crusade against the Hussites* English Historical Review 88(1973),
[184] ODNB notes for Earl of Suffolk
[185] See Roger Ascham's remarks on the poor state of village grammar schools during the Shakespeare era, quoted in Chapter 2.
[186] Killigrew's letter to Sir Henry Neville, ref. D/EN F6 2/1, Berkshire Record Office
[187] Terry Jones, op.cit.
[188] An entry in Henslowe's diary, 3 March, 1592, records a performance of 'Harey vj' at the Rose Theatre by Lord Strange's Men, with the letters 'ne' written after it.
[189] See also Frances Yates' analysis of *Henry VIII*, in *Shakespeare's Last Plays*
[190] See Frances Yates, *The French Academies of the Sixteenth Century* op.cit.
[191] Richard Eedes, *Iter Boreale*, 1583. Available at http://www.philological.bham.ac.uk/eedes/ translated by Dana F. Sutton, The University of California, Irvine.
[192] WMS, Vol.1, p.128
[193] p. 270, John Julius Norwich, op.cit.
[194] p.1, (introductory notes) 'New Cambridge Shakespeare' edition of *Henry VIII*, edited by John Margeson, 1990, where a letter concerning a performance of the play, (from Sir Henry Wotton to Edmund Bacon, 2nd July, 1613), is quoted: The stage, it seems, was peopled by "...*the Knights of the Order..., the guards with their embroidered coats and the like: sufficient in truth within a while to make greatness very familiar, if not ridiculous.*"
[195] See ODNB notes for Richard Neville.
[196] See Brenda James, *Shakespeare–Neville: Forests, Islands and Folklore* Journal Of Neville Studies, Vol.1.2, April, 2007, op.cit.
[197] Stopes, op.cit.
[198] See the background to my discovery of Sir Henry Neville's Tower Notebook in James and Rubinstein, *The Truth Will Out*, Longman, 2005, and Brenda James *Henry Neville and the Shakespeare Code*, 2008
[199] See the Stationer's Note, prefacing Beaumont and Fletcher's *A King and No King*, in which the Stationer says he is *returning* the play to Sir Henry Neville's hands, and that the writers are most grateful for the encouragement they have received from Sir Henry.
[200] See James and Rubinstein, op.cit.

201 'Henry VIII: January 1512', Letters and Papers, Foreign and Domestic, Henry VIII, Volume 1: 1509-1514 (1920), pp. 502-510.
202 ibid
203 ibid
204 LP [J. S. Brewer, J. Gardiner, and R. H. Brodie, eds., Letters and papers, foreign and domestic, of the reign of Henry VIII, 23 vols. in 38 (1862–1932); repr. (1965)] Henry VIII, 13/2, no. 804
205 p. 144 *The Rise and Fall of Anne Boleyn: Family Politics at the Court of Henry VIII* by Retha M. Warnicke, Cambridge University Press, 1991
206 See Chapter 4, footnote 25, James and Rubinstein, *The Truth Will Out*, op.cit.
207 Richard Marius, *Thomas More: A Biography*, 1999, Harvard University Press
208 John Margerson, editor, *King Henry VIII* 'New Cambridge Shakespeare', 1989
209 p.185, vol. 1, WMS, Letter from Sir Robert Cecil to Sir Henry Neville: *"... but now attend what will be the first Prologue to that Comedy; being of the opinion that Monsieur Villeroy would have us fall out at the Meeting, because we should never agree at the end...."*
See also a description of this meeting: Brenda James, Journal of Neville Studies, Vol.2, issue 3, February, 2008, SHAKESPEARE-NEVILLE, CERVANTES, AND THE TREATY OF BOULOGNE
210 Henry Nevill to Sir Robert Cecil, Lothbury, the 6 of May, 1598. Cecil Papers, Hatfield House, Ref. 60.14. [IHR]
211 See my work on the Tower Notebook (now located in the Lincolnshire Archives) in *The Truth Will Out*, James and Rubinstein, Longman, 2005
212 Sir Henry Nevill to Sir Robert Cecil, Cecil Papers, op.cit. (81. 19.)
213 Sir Thomas Fane to Lord Cobham from Dover Castle 2nd August,1600
214 Cecil Papers, ibid (87. 46.)
215 William Camden, *Annales* published posthumously in Leiden, 1625, and in London in 1627, available at http://www.philological.bham.ac.uk/camden/1601e.html
216 1601, Feb. 22., Sir Thomas Fane to Sir Robert Cecil, Cecil Papers, ibid (76. 100.)
217 WMS Vol.1, pp.302 – 304
218 Cecil Papers, op.cit. (86. 1.)
219 Cecil Papers, ibid, . (77. 15.)
220 Cecil Papers, ibid, (77. 90.)
221 Cecil Papers, ibid, (77. 90.)
222 Henry Neville to Sir Robert Cecil, 4 August 1601, Cecil Papers, ibid, (87. 61.)
223 Cecil Papers, ibid, (87. 61.)
224 Cecil Papers, ibid., (87. 20.)

ENDNOTES

[225] See Chapter 4
[226] See Brenda James, *Henry Neville and the Shakespeare Code,* op.cit.
[227] Cecil Papers, op.cit. (85. 76.)
[228] Cecil Papers, ibid (93. 44.)
[229] Cecil Papers, ibid . (7. 32.)
[230] Halliday *A Shakespeare Companion* p. 247, op.cit.
[231] See Chapter 2
[232] The text of the Neville Treatise is taken from appendix. v in *History of England from the Accession of James I to the Outbreak of Civil War, 1603–1642,* by Samuel Rawson Gardiner (1884)
[233] Line 3 - Foreign countries were always seeking whom best to ally with. If economic problems were perceived in England, it was unlikely that they would place England high on the list of those with whom to make treaties.
[234] **acrimony** is never used in Shakespeare

INDEX

A Midsummer Night's Dream, 223, 237, 277, 296, 317
Abergavenny
 Baron, 157, 209, 320, 321
Aeneid, 316
Aesop, 239, 261
Alexander
 classical character mentioned in Neville's political treatise, 24, 32, 34, 38, 335
Anne Boleyn, 286, 289
Anne of Denmark
 Queen
 wife of King James I, 227
Antigonus, 24, 34, 335
Arden
 Mary, 321
 Thomas, of Parkhall, 320
Aristotle, 239
As You Like It, 142, 188, 211, 238, 315
Ascham
 Roger (1515-68) scholar and author
 referenced the paucity of the teaching and learning at village grammar schools, 54
 Roger (1515-68), scholar and author, 54, 55
Astrology
 16th and 17th century belief in, 252
Audley End House, 16, 187
Bacon
 Anthony, brother of Sir Francis, 138, 99
 Edmund, 140
 Elizabeth, Neville's step mother, 138
 Sir Francis, 57, 98, 99, 117, 118, 119, 123, 124, 125, 127, 128, 129, 130, 131, 132, 133, 134, 135, 136, 137, 138, 139, 140, 141, 142, 143, 144, 145, 208
Bartholowmew Fair, 147
BBC, 79, 152, 321
Beauchamps, 176, 210, 211, 243, 268
Beaumont
 Francis, playwright, 52, 228, 285, 292
Beaumont and Fletcher, 52, 285, 292
Biron
 Duc de, 173
Bisham Abbey, 118, 208
Bishop
 Martin, actor, 117, 244
Black Death, 180
Blackfriar's, 328
Boccaccio, 89, 90
Bolingbroke
 Henry, later King of England, 76, 93, 94, 95, 174
Brandon
 Charles, Duke of Suffolk, 281, 282
Brooke
 Christopher, writer, friend of John Donne, Henry Neville and Inigo Jones, 36
 Richard, Neville's son-in-law, 80
 Sir Richard, Neville's son in law, 118
Buckingham
 Duke of, 76, 283, 284, 291, 322
Bulmer
 Sir William, 283
Burbage
 family of actors and theatre owners, 119, 328
Burghley
 William Cecil, Lord, 72, 97, 145, 226, 266

Index

Cade's rebellion, 50, 71, 90
Camden
  William, 97, 298
  William,(1551–1623) historian, 209
Carleton
  Dudley, 118, 120, 122, 227
  Dudley, diplomat and letter writer, 49
Carlos
  son of Phillip II of Spain, 332
Carwarden
  Sir Thomas, master of the revels, 328
Catherine de' Medici, 331
Catherine of Aragon, 100, 204, 287, 288, 289, 292
Cavendish
  George (1494 - 1562), author, 292
Cecil
  Sir Robert, Secretary of State and cousin to Neville's wife, 21, 49, 61, 66, 72, 75, 100, 103, 145, 146, 148, 150, 153, 154, 155, 176, 191, 195, 196, 197, 208, 211, 222, 264, 295, 296, 297, 298, 299, 300, 301, 309, 310, 320, 322, 332
Chamberlain
  John, Court gossip and letter writer, 49, 321
Chapman
  George (1559-1634), dramatist, 332
Chivalry
  and chivalric knights, 182, 183, 184, 194, 198, 202
Christ Church
  College, Oxford, 117, 118
Christianity, 33, 192, 207, 212, 224, 240, 241, 242, 243, 245, 246, 252, 255, 257, 258, 260, 262, 272
Chrysostom
  St. John, 32, 167, 220
Cicero, 223
Cinque Ports, 191, 297
Clarence
  Duke of, 269, 270, 291

Cobham
  Lord, warden of the Cinque Ports, 297
Code, 33, 57, 77, 80, 101, 140, 158, 163, 167, 195, 212, 214, 220, 222, 225, 236, 262, 310, 333
Colville
  John, Scottish spy, 150, 153, 154, 155
Comedy of Errors, 143, 237, 316, 317, 321
Conan-Doyle
  Sir Arthur, 77
Cooke
  Sir Anthony, 171
Cooke Manuscript, 214
Cornwall, 118, 285
Coverdale
  Miles (1488-1569) translator of the Bible, 81, 226
Crusades, 184, 191, 192, 194, 199, 207
Cymbeline, 217, 237
d'Amboise
  Bussy, 331
dark lady
  of the Sonnets, 301, 306, 308
Davenant
  William, playwright, 36, 211
Davin
  Leon, Freemason and author, 224, 225
DECLARATION TO PARLIAMENT
  substance and analysis of Sir Henry Neville's
  see chapters 1 and 2, *21*
Dedication
  to the Sonnets, 57, 77, 78, 83, 101, 140, 158, 162, 163, 212, 213, 214, 217, 220, 221, 225, 236, 262, 310
Dedication code
  preceding Shakespeare's Sonnets, 158, 162
Demetrius
  mentioned in Neville's treatise, *24, 335*
Demetrius,, 32, 34
Dering
  Sir Anthony, 297

365

Digges
  Dudley, 37
  Sir Dudley, brother of Leonard (who contributed a Commendatory Verse in the First Folio of Shakespeare's Works), 35
Donne
  John, poet
    as M.P. for Taunton, 36
Downes
  Andrew, Secretary to Sir Henry Savile and one of the compilers of the King James Bible, 81
Doyly
  Lady Elizabeth (nee Bacon), Neville's stepmother, 67
Ede
  Richard, writer, Latin poet, 117
Edmondes
  Thomas, 121, 264, 285
Edward IV
  King, 87
Essex
  Robert Devereux (1566-1601)
    Earl of, 21, 32, 37, 45, 58, 63, 68, 77, 93, 110, 117, 119, 130, 131, 141, 142, 144, 145, 146, 147, 153, 156, 164, 172, 173, 174, 175, 176, 178, 184, 185, 187, 189, 196, 199, 202, 208, 220, 248, 278, 285, 290, 298, 299, 301, 303, 305, 309, 318, 319, 322, 323
Euripides, 238, 239
Falstaff, 76, 116, 117, 119, 120, 121, 122, 123, 125, 126, 127, 128, 135, 136, 138, 139, 140, 141, 143, 144, 145, 146, 147, 148, 149, 150, 151, 152, 154, 155, 156, 157, 162, 167, 171, 210, 223, 296, 319
Fane Sir Thomas, 297, 299
Flavius
  Josephus, Jewish Roman historian who wrote in Greek, 239
Fletcher
  John, playwright, 228, 292

Fludd
  Robert, esotericist, 211
Francis scene in 'Henry IV, part 1' ff, 124
Freemasonry, 207, 208, 213, 217, 220, 222, 223, 224, 225
  and Gresham College, 206
Galileo, 223
Gentilis
  Albericus, 117, 118
Ghetto
  Jewish Ghetto in Venice, 190
Globe
  Theatre, 119, 156, 287, 313, 320, 322, 328
Gloucester
  Humphrey, Duke of, 90, 112, 181, 235, 244, 247, 248, 253, 254, 255, 266, 267, 268, 269, 275
Gnostic, 192, 215
Godfroi de Bouillon, 211
Gower
  John, poet (1330-1408), 88, 89, 94, 95
Gowrie
  Earl of, 227, 228
Grammar Schools
  in Tudor times
    contemporary accounts tell how poor they were as places of learning, 55
Greek, 16, 19, 32, 33, 36, 41, 68, 69, 70, 72, 117, 212, 224, 237, 238, 239, 240, 243, 246, 249, 260, 261, 262, 264, 265
  Theatre, 237
Greene
  Robert (1560-92), dramatist and prose writer, 79, 312, 313, 315, 318
Gresham
  Elizabeth, Neville's mother, 67
  Sir John, Neville's grandfather, 67
  Sir Thomas, 138, 190, 223
    early Grand Master of Freemasonry, 224
Gresham College, 148, 206, 223
Greville
  Fulke, Earl of Warwick, 211

Hakewill
 William, 36
Hall
 Joseph, (1574-1656) Bishop of Norwich, writer and satirist, 79, 127, 128, 129, 130, 131, 132, 133, 134, 135, 136, 137, 138, 139, 140, 141
Halle's Chronicles, 85, 102, 110, 113, 283, 291, 330
Hamlet, 83, 159, 220, 227, 240, 250, 302, 303, 319
hendiadys, 22, 23, 29, 30, 32, 316
Hendiadys, 32
Henri II
 King of France, 173
Henri IV
 King of France, 100, 148, 172, 173, 186, 221, 222, 298, 332
Henry II of France, 331
Henry IV, 94, 96, 116, 120, 122, 123, 127, 128, 132, 133, 135, 137, 142, 143, 147, 148, 150, 151, 152, 153, 162, 174, 175, 176, 178, 242, 297, 316, 317
 King, 210
Henry IV, part 1, 116, 120, 123, 127, 128, 132, 133, 135, 137, 142, 147, 152, 297, 317
Henry IV, part 2, 122, 127, 148, 150, 151, 153, 162, 174, 175, 317
Henry V, 38, 39, 41, 122, 189, 210, 232, 235, 242, 243, 245, 253, 254, 255, 257
Henry VI, 50, 53, 60, 71, 85, 86, 90, 91, 107, 108, 109, 110, 112, 179, 189, 191, 192, 195, 197, 198, 201, 202, 209, 212, 228, 229, 232, 233, 234, 235, 239, 240, 241, 242, 243, 244, 245, 246, 248, 249, 250, 252, 253, 254, 257, 260, 263, 265, 267, 268, 269, 271, 272, 276, 281, 284, 312, 313, 319, 321, 329, 331, 332, 333
Henry VII, 106, 203, 283
Henry VII, King, 279
Henry VIII, 63, 76, 100, 181, 182, 187, 197, 203, 265, 279, 280, 281, 282, 283, 284, 285, 286, 287, 288, 289, 291, 292, 293, 296
 King, 280
Herbert
 Philip, brother of William Herbert and, with him, patron of the First Folio, 119
 Sir John
  secretary to Robert Cecil, 297
Hermes
 and Hermetic philosophy, 213, 214, 215, 217, 223
Hermetic rituals, 217
Herodotus
 Greek historian, 212, 239, 261
Hiram Abiff, 224, 225
Hoby
 Sir Edward, 322
 Thomas Posthumous, cousin of Neville's wife, 118
Holbrooke
 Richard, American diplomat, 78
Holinshed
 Raphael, 1525-80, chronicler, 34, 85, 86, 113
Homer, 239
Horace
 Roman writer, 215, 232
Hoskins
 John, politician, 121, 122
 John, rebel Parliamentarian and writer, 36
Hospitallers, 184, 198, 201, 229, 230, 234
Huguenots, 221, 331, 333
illegitimacy
 the likelihood of Sir Henry Neville's 'technical' illegitimacy, 66
IMAGERY, 252
 in the 'Henry VI' plays chapter 8, 252
James I
 association with Freemasonry, 207
 King, 21, 33, 35, 36, 49, 50, 60, 69, 70, 75, 97, 99, 131, 162, 207, 217, 220, 224, 225, 227, 232, 265, 266,

270, 271, 290, 293, 319, 351
Joan of Arc, 228, 243, 244, 254, 257, 258, 259, 260, 261, 262, 263, 272
John of Gaunt, 85, 94, 242, 287
Jonson
    Ben, playwright, 30, 36, 97, 121, 122, 130, 141, 147, 148, 157, 210, 211, 237, 238, 316
Journal of Neville Studies, 328
Keen
    Alan, author of 'The Annotator', 110
    Alan, writer of 'The Annotator', 102
Killigrew
    Anne
        her letters, 301
    Anne, wife of Henry Neville, 210, 211
    Henry, Neville's father in law, 86, 118, 171, 172, 331
Killigrews
    seal of, 224
King
    Mark Barty (publisher), 193
King John, 60, 188, 208, 265, 316, 317
King Lear, 141, 237, 277
King of Jerusalem, 192, 197, 211, 231, 232, 233, 234
Knights
    and knighthood, 59, 80, 102, 167, 180, 181, 183, 184, 185, 186, 187, 188, 189, 192, 196, 197, 198, 200, 202, 203, 204, 205, 206, 207, 208, 211, 231, 232, 233, 242, 243, 245, 268, 276
Knox
    John, Scottish Calvinist, 171, 172
Labeo
    Roman lawyer, 130, 131, 132, 133, 134, 136
LANGUAGE
    analysis, and tables of language used in Neville's treatise...ff, 342

Leicester
    Robert Dudley, Earl of, 46, 72, 80, 99, 101, 102, 103, 104, 105, 106, 107, 108, 109, 110, 111, 113, 195, 196, 228, 236, 330
Leicester's Commonwealth, 46, 72, 80, 99, 101, 103, 104, 106, 107, 108, 109, 110, 111, 113, 195, 228, 236, 330
Leslie
    John, Bishop of Ross, 226, 227
Lewkenor, 17, 18, 19, 33, 351
Lincolnshire Archives, 80, 102, 104, 195, 236
Livery companies, 205
Lok
    Zachary, 310
Longleat House, 67
Longueville
    Duc de, 171, 173
Love's Labour's Lost, 140, 169, 171, 173, 172, 174, 316, 317, 321, 332
Love's Labour's Won, 316
Lucrece, 46, 84, 85, 88, 90, 91, 93, 98, 104, 319
Lydgate
    John, poet, (1370-1450), 89, 90, 91, 92
Lytton
    Sir Edward Bulwer
        politician and writer, 85
Macbeth, 226, 228
Machiavelli, 197
Mackey
    Albert G., masonic historian, 213, 222
magic
    in the Shakespeare plays, 276
Margaret
    Queen, wife of Henry VI, 329
Margaret of Anjou, 85, 195, 209, 244, 260, 329, 331
Marguerite de Valois, 173, 330, 331, 329
marriage 'in settlement.'
    definition, 66
Marston
    John (1575-1634) writer, 132, 134, 135
Mary of Guise, 171, 172, 173

Mary Queen of Scots, 171, 226
Masques
   at the Court of King James I
      their relationship to Hermetic rituals, 217
Massacre
   St. Bartholomew's Day, 333
Matthew
   Tobie (son), 117, 141
   Tobie, friend of Sir Francis Bacon (father and son of the same name), 117, 118, 119, 120, 121, 123, 124, 135, 139, 142, 144, 149
   Tobie, senior, 117
Mayenne
   Duc de, 173
Mayfield
   town in East Sussex where Neville ran his iron works, 190, 292, 321
Merchant of Venice, 140, 238, 309, 316, 317
Meres
   Francis, 316, 317, 318, 319, 320, 322
Mitre
   Club frequented by Neville, Ben Jonson, John Donne and others, 36, 80, 83, 121, 122, 147, 208, 210, 224, 228, 285
Môle
   Joseph Boniface de La, 331
Moore
   Francis, 36
More
   Sir Thomas, 291
Mornay
   Phillipe Du Plesis, French Protestant writer, 221
Much Ado About Nothing., 140
Nashe
   Thomas, writer, 99
Naunton
   Sir Robert, 149
Neoplatonist
   ideas and symbols, 212, 216
Neville
   Anne, daughter of Richard Neville, 87

   Anne, nee Killigrew
      her deafness, 296
   Edmund, 320
   Edward, Henry Neville's grandfather, 278
      evidence that only a Neville would have written the 'Henry VI' plays, 273
   George
      third Baron Bergavenny, 279
   Hugh de, 207
   Richard
      a family secret, 85
   Richard, Earl of Warwick, 87, 118, 199, 209, 249
      compared with Robert Dudley, Earl of Leicester, 105
   Richard, why he chose the white rose of York, 200
   Sir Edward, Henry Neville's grandfather, 187, 197, 279, 286
   Sir Henry
      and 'Macbeth', 226
      and the portrayal of strong women in the plays, 228
      as owner of Keen's copy of Halle's Chronicles, 110
      evidence of membership of secret societies, ff, 208
      hidden clues to his authorship, 16
      his cleverly-engineered Parliamentary presentation, 49
      his fine following the Essex rebellion, 301
      his grandfather's experiences reflected in the Shakespeare plays, 278
      his ideas of Kingship explicit in the Shakespeare plays, 270, 271
      his knowledge of mathematics, 220
      his Protestant yet tolerant outlook on religion, 222
      his return from Boulogne, 295

his voiced excuse for not owning up to his writing, 36
in France and Italy, 53
knighted at Cadiz, 184, 196
political views, 50
proposed changes to some laws, ff, 44
under house arrest, 299
Sir Henry, and republicanism, 82
Sir Henry, his knowledge of diplomatic codes, 220
Sir Henry, his political criticisms reflected in the Shakespeare plays, 76
Sir Thomas
  Speaker of the House of Commons, 279
Neville and anonymity, 52
Neville,
  George
    second Baron Bergavenny, 279
  Richard, Earl of Warwick
    father in law of Duke of Clarence, 291
NEVILLE'S GRANDFATHER
  Chapter 10, 278
Nevilles
  Their general relationship with the Tudors, 197
New River
  project to bring water to North London, 69
Northumberland
  Earl of
    suspicious death of, 196
Northumberland Manuscript, 97, 98, 99, 104, 109, 194, 195
Norwich
  John Julius, Viscount, 90, 129
Nottingham
  Countess of, 303
Order of Sion, 193, 194, 195, 226, 233, 234
Othello, 17, 18, 51, 237
Owen
  Sir Roger, 36
Oxford
  Earl of, 32, 57, 63, 64, 92, 117, 141, 143, 166, 167, 186,
190, 191, 211, 220, 252, 316
Oxford University
  and occultism, 211
Packer
  John, Sir Henry Neville's scribe, 80
Paget
  Charles, spy and writer, 78, 103, 111, 194, 195, 196, 226, 229
Painter
  William, 290
Parliament, 20, 21, 22, 23, 24, 25, 26, 27, 28, 29, 33, 34, 35, 36, 37, 38, 41, 44, 47, 48, 49, 52, 58, 60, 61, 64, 66, 70, 74, 131, 137, 162, 164, 166, 241, 242, 251, 270, 271, 273, 276, 299, 328, 334, 335, 336, 337, 338, 339, 340, 341
  at the time of Sir Henry Neville's treatise, 21
  situation between King James I and, 22
Parliamentary responses
  to Sir Henry Neville's treatise, ff, 35
Parsons
  or 'Persons', Robert, English Jesuit, 118, 195
Pembroke
  William Herbert, Earl of , friend of Neville and patron of the First Folio, 63, 224, 285
Pericles, 34, 68, 69, 70, 71, 217, 237
Pericles, Prince of Tyre, 70
Phillips
  James Emerson, literary critic, 238
Plantagenet, 52, 162, 199, 200, 201, 244, 274, 275, 285, 329
Plato, 72, 172, 215, 332
Plato Redivivus, 72
Platt
  Neal, Special Professor of Law, 158, 159, 161, 162, 167
Plays, 19, 20, 38, 59, 63, 65, 68, 77, 82, 90, 157, 179, 238, 239, 265, 284

370

Plutarch, 34
  c.46-120, Greek biographer and essayist, 34
Pole
  Sir Geoffrey, 291
political context
  of the Shakespeare works, 62
political persuasion
  in Neville's treatise is the same as that used in the Shakespeare plays, 38
political treatise
  by Sir Henry Neville, 29, 30, 52, 70, 72, 75, 166, 202, 254, 256, 263, 270
portrait
  inscription on Sir Henry Neville's at Audley End, 16, 68, 69, 70, 71, 187, 208, 322
Puttenham
  George (1529-90) courtier, poet and critic, 32
reform
  of governmental structures under the Tudors, 63
religion
  anti-Catholic stance evidenced by the writer of the plays, 198
René
  d'Anjou (also called Regnier), 192, 197, 198, 231, 232, 233, 243
rhetoric
  The art of, in the Shakespeare plays, 17, 32, 53, 54, 133, 136, 178, 237, 238, 242, 249, 256, 257, 315
Rich
  Penelope, 145
Richard II, 76, 77, 88, 93, 95, 98, 108, 113, 155, 157, 174, 179, 181, 183, 199, 232, 242, 245, 305, 307, 316, 317, 318, 319
Richard III, 87, 98, 203, 273, 291, 316, 317
  A 'restricted' source for the play, 291
  reasons for Henry Neville's animosity towards, 87

Roe
  Sir Thomas, diplomat, 36
Rogers
  Thomas, spy, 193, 194, 195, 196, 226
Roman Empire, 105, 112, 181, 216, 260
Romeo and Juliet, 40, 61, 316, 317, 320
Ronsard
  Pierre de (1524-85) French poet, 53
Rosicrucian
  secret society, 208, 277
Rosslyn chapel, 225
Royal Society, 206, 223, 224
Sandys
  Sir Edwin, 36, 37
  Neville's political discussion with him, 47
Savile
  Sir Henry (1549-1622), scholar, Warden of Merton College, Oxford, and friend of Sir Henry Neville, 32, 69, 81, 97, 117, 167, 172, 176, 190, 220, 224, 226, 237, 263, 285, 298, 330
Schaw
  Willie, Steward to James VI of Scotland, and Masonic Grand Master, 225
secret societies, 205, 207, 212, 214, 277
Shakespeare
  plays' anti-Catholic stance, 235
  William, released by the Queen after being questioned about 'Richard II', 199
SHAKESPEARE
  William
    was he a scribe?, 312
Shakespeare plays
  political nature of, 50
Shakespeare Quarterly, 330
Shylock, 240, 309
Sidney
  Henry, father of Sir Philip, 184
  Sir Philip, poet and courtier, 98
Simpson
  Richard (1820-1876) literary critic, 83

Sonnet 1, 225
Sonnet 105, 185
Sonnet 106, 185
Sonnet 107, 214
sonnet 121, 57, 81, 158, 164, 167, 168, 171, 304, 305
Sonnet 131, 306
Sonnet 132, 307
Sonnet 133, 308
Sonnet 134, 164, 306
sonnet 136, 304, 305
sonnet 44, 169
Sonnet 48, 310
sonnet 50, 168
Sonnet 97, 301
Sonnet 98, 302
Southampton
  Countess
    dating her letter re 'Falstaff', 145
  Countess of, 116, 117, 120, 141, 144, 297
  Earl of, 142, 174
  Henry Wriothesley, Earl of, 21, 63, 68, 88, 98, 173, 202, 222, 298
    his **Protestant** stance, 290
    kinship with Sir Henry Neville, 282
  motto of the Earl of, 276
Stafford
  Edward, 291
  Edward, Duke of Buckingham, 283
Stubbe
  John, secretary to William Cecil, 67, 97, 98
Suffolk
  Earl of, 105, 106, 107, 108, 109, 112, 197, 198, 201, 235, 236, 243, 244, 249, 265, 266, 275, 281, 288, 329, 330, 331, 333
swan
  as a symbol, 209, 210, 211
syncretic, 221
syncretism, 19, 61, 216
  in Sir Henry's Works and Philosophy, 19
tables
  of language usage, etc., 23, 30, 31, 231, 295

Templars, 184, 192, 193, 194, 195, 198, 199, 201, 206, 207, 228, 229, 233
Temple Garden
  scene in 'Henry VI, part 1', 274
The Tempest, 217, 277
The Winter's Tale, 217, 222, 223, 237, 265, 277
Thoreau
  David Henry (1817-62) American philosopher, 77
Thoth, 213, 214, 216, 222, 262
  Egyptian god of writing, etc., 212, 214, 221, 225
Throckmorton
  Arthur, 196
  Nicholas, Ambassador to France, 172
Thucydides, 68, 69, 70, 71, 239
Timon of Athens, 237, 278, 279, 290
Titus Andronicus, 60, 63, 85, 189, 191, 316, 317
TOUCHSTONE, 315
Tower Notebook
  Notebook owned by Sir Henry Neville, 80, 86, 93, 102, 286, 314
trade guilds, 212
Troilus and Cressida, 65, 90, 237, 319
Twelfth Night, 35
Two Gentlemen of Verona, 316, 317
Undertaker
  term used for Parliamentarians seeking to manage (secretly) the relationship between King and Commons, 35
Unton
  Sir Henry, 296, 301
Venus and Adonis, 46, 91, 134, 319
VINTNER
  character in 'Henry IV, part 1', 126, 141
Walsingham
  Sir Francis, head of Queen Elizabeth's spy service, 36, 97, 98, 103, 108, 113, 117, 150, 153, 172, 187, 193,

194, 195, 196, 226, 320, 331
warfare
  Neville's attitude to, 191
Wars of the Roses, 63, 80, 103, 110, 111, 180, 182, 192, 198, 199, 202, 203, 244, 260, 270, 272, 288, 289, 329, 332, 333
Warwick
  Earl of, 85, 86, 87, 104, 105, 106, 110, 112, 175, 177, 178, 180, 186, 198, 199, 200, 201, 208, 209, 210, 211, 234, 243, 247, 248, 249, 250, 251, 268, 269, 270, 271, 273, 274, 281, 291
Wentworth
  Thomas, lawyer, 36
Westmoreland
  Earl of
    character in the History Plays, and also ancestor of Sir Henry Neville, 151, 152, 157
Whitelock
  James, judge, 36

Williams
  Gwyn, writer, 330
Winchester
  Bishop of, Cardinal Beaufort, 235, 241, 243, 244, 246, 247, 248, 255, 258, 263, 265, 266, 267, 268
Winwood
  Sir Ralph, Neville's friend and secretary, 49, 75, 131, 138, 149, 153, 154, 202, 227, 232, 264, 270, 285, 299, 351
Wolsey, Thomas
  Cardinal, 76, 203, 279, 280, 281, 283, 284, 292
Woodstock
  Thomas of, Duke of Gloucester, 181
Worsley, 61, 79, 80, 81, 97, 102, 104, 106, 107, 108, 110, 195
Worsley Collection, 79, 80, 195
Yates
  Frances, 212, 217, 221, 222, 224, 245, 265, 276, 277
  The French Academies, *53*

373

www.ingramcontent.com/pod-product-compliance
Ingram Content Group UK Ltd.
Pitfield, Milton Keynes, MK11 3LW, UK
UKHW041432180426
11947UKWH00007B/400